"Fleming Rutledge has done it again! Her new collection of sermons, *Not Ashamed of the Gospel,* is elegant, literary, and theologically rich. She manages to write sermons that are timeless yet very much rooted in contemporary challenges and opportunities. Her fellow preachers will find this volume invaluable."

— JOHN E. PHELAN JR.
North Park Theological Seminary

"Preaching on Pauline texts is a tough assignment for any minister. It is always easier to work through a Gospel narrative. Fleming Rutledge has not only tackled Paul; she has tackled Romans! Her book of sermons on Romans faces the theological issues of the letter head-on and provides a marvelous model for ministers who have heretofore shied away from the Apostle. Rutledge writes with clarity and grace and highlights the contemporary relevance of the letter. Her book should be on the shelf of every minister who seeks to interpret Paul for today."

— CHARLES B. COUSAR
Columbia Theological Seminary

"At once both a sensitive plumbing of human existence and a bold confession of the Christian faith, Fleming Rutledge's sermons are as winsome as they are penetrating, as timeless as they are timely. This volume will quickly earn a place on every preacher's bookshelf beside the commentaries of Luther and Barth on Paul's letter to the Romans."

— DAVID J. LOSE
Luther Seminary

Not Ashamed of the Gospel

SERMONS FROM

PAUL'S LETTER TO THE ROMANS

to Jon Widing
from his friend Judith — and with the very best wishes
of the author —

Fleming Rutledge

Fleming Rutledge

Christmastide 2007

WILLIAM B. EERDMANS PUBLISHING COMPANY
GRAND RAPIDS, MICHIGAN / CAMBRIDGE, U.K.

© 2007 Fleming Rutledge

Published 2007 by
Wm. B. Eerdmans Publishing Co.
2140 Oak Industrial Drive N.E., Grand Rapids, Michigan 49505 /
P.O. Box 163, Cambridge CB3 9PU U.K.

Printed in the United States of America

12 11 10 09 08 07   7 6 5 4 3 2 1

Library of Congress Cataloging-in-Publication Data

Rutledge, Fleming.
Not ashamed of the gospel: sermons from Paul's letter to the Romans /
Fleming Rutledge.
p.   cm.
ISBN 978-0-8028-2737-1 (pbk.: alk. paper)
1. Bible. N.T. Romans — Sermons.   I. Title.

BS2665.54.R88   2007
252 — dc22

2007018535

www.eerdmans.com

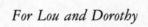

For Lou and Dorothy

Contents

Contents

Contents

Contents

Author's Introduction

Why Romans?

The unique importance of the apostle Paul's letter to the Christians in Rome can readily be seen in the history of its interpretation. Romans has provided the impetus for the major theological revolutions of the Christian era, a claim that cannot be made for any other single biblical book.

The Epistle is theological dynamite, as the Western world discovered when Martin Luther's reading of it (together with Galatians) resulted in the explosion of faith that started the Reformation. John Calvin gratefully mined Augustine's still-radical reading of Romans. This letter was the source of John Wesley's consequential conversion at Aldersgate in 1738. Karl Barth's commentary on Romans, published in 1922, "fell like a bombshell on the playground of the theologians,"[1] and the repercussions have never died away. Romans sent these interpreters out onto the theological frontiers as God sent Abraham forth from his home at the dawn of the Story, and the Church lives still by the galvanizing power of those movements. As for myself, I was fifteen years old when the message of St. Paul to the Romans first began to dawn on me, and my life has never been the same since.

1. As Karl Adam, a Roman Catholic theologian and historian, famously said.

[1]

In many of our mainline congregations today, however, sermons are largely based on passages from the Gospels, less frequently from the Old Testament, and rarely from Paul's Epistles.[2] The old suspicion that Paul took the simple teachings of Jesus and complicated them with doctrinaire intellectualizing is still with us. This misunderstanding should be corrected. It may be obvious to seminary-trained clergy, but most people in our congregations need to be reminded over and over that Paul's genuine Epistles are by far the earliest of the New Testament writings, and that there is not the slightest hint in the canonical Scriptures that there is any conflict between the Gospels and Paul's letters.[3]

In preaching from Romans I have repeatedly sought to show how Paul, in his letters, is commenting upon, interpreting, expanding, extending, and drawing out the implications of Jesus' parables, teachings, and deeds. Several of the sermons are therefore based on two passages, one from the Gospels and one from Romans. Quite a few others bring in references from the Gospels to make this same point. A principal goal of this volume of sermons is to demonstrate that without Paul to make explicit what is implicit in the Gospel narratives, the true radicality of Jesus' ministry would not be manifest to us.

Paul the Apostle

It is distressing that so many faithful churchgoers of today disdain Paul.[4] This distaste is a largely a result of ignorance, since he is in-

---

2. A few verses from Paul, such as Galatians 3:16, 1 Corinthians 13, and the ending of chapter 8 in Romans are selectively used, but the popularity of these passages serves to highlight the neglect of the great body of Paul's writing.

3. Paul's authorship of Romans, 1 and 2 Corinthians, Galatians, Philippians, 1 Thessalonians and Philemon is undisputed. Conservative commentators still include 2 Thessalonians and the Pastoral Epistles. There are some leading scholars who continue to argue strongly for Pauline authorship of Colossians and, especially, Ephesians.

4. This is less true among Lutherans, many of whom still retain some of the freshness of their founder's discoveries about Paul's letters.

sufficiently preached and taught in the mainline congregations. If this book inspires anyone to focus on Paul's letters with a new ear and eye, it will have served its purpose.

There are several reasons for Paul's unpopularity in addition to the dearth of preaching and teaching. He is polemical, and ours is an age that recoils at polemic. In legislative bodies working at their best, heated debate can take place without personal rancor, but this is not the daily atmosphere in our seminaries and congregations. Theological debate, we think, should always be amiable.[5] Admittedly there are times (especially in Galatians) when Paul's ferocity seems to become personal, but this is in the heat of battle when he genuinely fears for "the freedom we have in Christ Jesus." There are places in the letters where we need to think of Paul as a commander on a battlefield, receiving dispatches from the front where the gospel is in danger of being swept off the field. This explains his urgency and, occasionally, his intemperance.

Some have found Paul's military imagery off-putting. Yet there is none of us who cannot understand the language of "fighting" against cancer, for instance, or waging a "war" against drunk driving. When we understand that Paul envisions the entire cosmos as a battlefield where the principalities and powers assail the human race and, indeed, the creation itself, we learn to interpret Paul's metaphors as readily as we understand a legislator who proposes a war on child pornography.

There is a persistent belief that Paul did not like women. It is true that his understanding of sexual relations was underdeveloped (we look to other parts of the Bible to fill out the picture), but no one reading the passages in his letters where he gives exceptional prominence to women can continue to hold the view that he was a misogynist. On the contrary, his references, particularly in Romans 16, are warmly personal. In Philippians 4:2-3, an especially impor-

---

5. That is, unless boundaries are crossed with regard to ideological correctness, in which case rudeness is permitted. A professor in a leading divinity school mused that he was permitted anything and everything in his classroom with one exception — he could not get by with "exclusive" gender-related language.

tant but frequently overlooked passage, he cites Euodia and Syntyche, two women in the congregation who have "contended shoulder to shoulder with me for the gospel." Note the word "contended," with its hint of battle; these are women warriors!

In spite of Paul's reputation for being intellectual, abstract, and dogmatic, his concerns are overwhelmingly pastoral and evangelistic. His description of his own ministry in 1 Thessalonians 2 could not have been written by a man who was cold and distant. Moreover it is clear, taking the witness of the letters as a whole, that Paul himself was greatly loved. To this day, many who have really lived with Paul for a period of time, reading and rereading the letters as one reads a cherished letter from a beloved friend, will come to love him. His words have been for me an incomparable source of faith in times of radical doubt. Hearing the conviction in his voice as he declares the truth of the Resurrection in 1 Corinthians 15 has brought me back from the brink of unbelief many a time. Knowing of his sufferings, recounted in 2 Corinthians especially, has helped me to make light of my own lesser ones. The very existence of world Christianity is the result of God's call to a fire-breathing Saul of Tarsus, and the radical nature of this converted man's mission to embrace the far corners of the earth has never been superseded or equaled. God did a mighty work through his servant Paul. Without him we would never have known the full dimensions of God's project to reclaim the cosmos and everything in it for himself.

Major Themes in Romans

It may be helpful, since these sermons are not concerned with point-by-point exposition, to summarize some of the main ideas and motifs in the letter. Particularly important are these:

- The righteousness *(dikaiosunē)* of God is a dynamic outgoing *activity* of God, not just a static characteristic or quality possessed by God.
- Sin and Death are independent demonic Powers, having seized

the Law of God to use as a weapon against the captive human being ("all human beings are under the power of Sin" — 3:9).

- Christ is the new Adam who, by taking on human nature, has recapitulated in his person all of human history since the Fall, reversing its downward direction toward destruction.

- The Cross and Resurrection of Christ is the first event of the Age to Come and the fulfillment of the promises of God to Abraham.

- Faith is the human response ignited by the fire of the Word and the Holy Spirit.

- Jesus Christ is *kosmokratōr* (ruler of the universe). Paul's most frequent title for him is Lord *(kurios)*.

- The work of God in Christ is expressed by the Greek word *dikaiosunē* (righteousness), which presents a problem in English translation. The righteousness of God in Paul, as in the Old Testament, has the force of a verb. Therefore the noun "righteousness" in English does not do the trick, nor does the verb "justification," since they need to be the same word. The closest English equivalent is "rectification" and "rectify," because — and this is crucial — God not only *declares* righteous but actually *makes* righteous.

- The righteousness of God is both 1) revealed *(apokaluptetai)* — meaning put into action; and 2) imputed *(logizomai)* — meaning spoken into existence. Hence imputation is not a "legal fiction" as some have charged, but a reality.

- Baptism into Christ is the recapitulation in each human life of 1) the victory of the new Adam over the old, and 2) deliverance from the Powers of Sin and Death.

- Christ died for the ungodly, not the godly. Salvation therefore will extend beyond what we can now imagine.

- Conformation into Christ, the rectifying work of God, is the sign of the new community (12:1-2) until the Lord comes again (13:11-14). Paul also calls this "the obedience of faith."

Omissions and Commissions

Anyone looking at the Table of Contents will notice that there are more sermons on some texts from Romans than there are on others. I make no apology for this. For instance, "God has consigned all men to disobedience, that he may have mercy upon all" (11:32) is worth a thousand times ten thousand sermons, yet in all my years of churchgoing I have never heard one, so in a sense I suppose I am trying to make up for a deficit. Similarly, the story of Adam and Christ in Romans 5 is our fundamental story, yet it is virtually unknown to many of our people; a hundred variations on it could be preached without superfluity, for it is the universal explanation of human history. Romans 8:18-25 is the gospel for the entire *kosmos,* yet even in this age of cosmic and environmental concern, Christians do not know this passage and continue to cling to a sentimental view of nature. In my opinion, such texts cannot be preached too often.

At the same time I am painfully aware that many key texts are not represented here. Had I been able to preach every Sunday from the same pulpit over a period of years, I would have been able to preach from every verse. I particularly miss 15:7-13 and the wonderful chapter 16, which reveals the richly personal humanity of the apostle and the attention he pays to women. I would like to have done much more with the opening salutation and thanksgiving, and with the theme of election in Romans 9. I hope that some of the preachers reading this collection will be inspired to fill the gaps.

Conspicuously missing are the verses about homosexual activity in 1:26-28. There is a reason for this. By the time the issue had become so central and so vexed in the churches, I was no longer attached to a particular congregation. It is hard to imagine preaching on these verses when one is merely a visiting preacher for, at most, a weekend; the context is all wrong. The right context would be the pulpit or podium in a congregation where Paul's central message is already well understood and where the preacher/teacher is well known and trusted. I once spoke publicly at some length on the issues surrounding homosexuality in a congregation where I was well known, but I spoke only in a provisional kind of way, since I do not believe that at present we are able to know the mind of Christ on this matter.

Too Much Sin and Death?

The critic who wants to complain that too many of the sermons are about Sin will find evidence that this is so; but again, I make no apology. Sin is one of the main subjects of the Old and New Testaments. It is also one of the main subjects in the daily news. What these sermons seek to demonstrate is that God has the power to overcome Sin, and in Jesus Christ has done so. The news about Sin and judgment is therefore not only followed but also preceded by the gospel of God's grace and mercy.

Readers may be puzzled by the way I sometimes capitalize Sin, Death, Law, and Power(s). I do this to indicate their status as autonomous entities deriving their strength from a source of energy separate from the human individual and outside the human race collectively. This is one of the most important things to grasp about Paul's thought. He does not think of Sin as a collection of sins, and he rarely uses the word in the plural. For Paul, Sin and Death are cosmic Powers at war with the purposes of God. They have made the Law their weapon (as Paul describes in Romans 7). Further reflections on this crucial subject appear throughout the sermons. Understanding Sin as a Power is essential to grasping the heart of the gospel of Christ victorious. People need to understand that they are in the grip of an Enemy that has the capacity to defeat them.[6] They need to hear the news of their deliverance from this Enemy through the victory of the One who submitted to the utmost that Sin could do.

As for Death, I have long since learned that if a congregation's

---

6. All of this is symbolized in the New Testament in the figure of Satan, the great Antagonist. Paul uses the name of Satan infrequently; he is chiefly concerned to identify the Powers holding humanity in thrall as Sin and Death. This will become clearer as the sermons unfold.

attention is wandering, all you have to do is utter the word Death. People snap to attention instantly. Paul was right to call it "the last enemy" (1 Corinthians 15:26). Death is the chief Enemy still standing on the battlefield. As the lay theologian William Stringfellow has powerfully shown, Death is the object of our worship and the goal of our striving. If you look at the racks of sympathy cards in the shops, you will never find the word Death on them. It has been banished. That is a sign of its fearsome power. We must utter the forbidden word in our churches; to utter it is to bring it into the realm of the Word of God where it cannot conquer. Sin and Death have no dominion in the preaching of the Word.

Preaching Styles in Various Contexts

It is always tempting, when publishing one's early work, to revise it according to one's present angle of vision. I have resisted this temptation and in almost all cases have published the sermons essentially as they were delivered.

My homiletical style has changed over the thirty years represented here. There is a lot of biblical and theological teaching in almost all the sermons, but the exposition in the post-1995 sermons is much less detailed, because after that date I was usually preaching in contexts where I could not assume that people would tolerate a teaching style. If I was preaching to theological students, of course I could assume more, and I have indicated those examples.

Generally speaking, I have identified the place where the sermon was preached if that seems relevant. If the sermon seemed to me to be more generally applicable to any location, I have omitted such identification.[7] In every case, however, the date has been included.

---

7. In a couple of recent cases the congregation asked to be identified in this volume and I am happy to honor their wish.

The Grace Church Sermons

The sermons preached at Grace Church in New York City have some special characteristics, because the congregation during those years was distinctive. In the late 70s and early 80s there was a powerful renewal there, so that in addition to a solid core of old-line Episcopalians there were large numbers of young single people who made up a majority. Many, though not all, of these were from conservative evangelical backgrounds who had come to the Episcopal Church because they sought liturgical worship and free-wheeling, intellectually challenging sermons. Moreover, they were very bright and, typically, had come to New York City because they were adventurous and somewhat unconventional. (A significant number of these young people later went on to seminary.) Therefore the clergy (there were five of us during much of that period) had the luxury of preaching to a congregation accustomed to longer, more expository sermons than in the typical Episcopal church today. The congregation came to hear the gospel and expected to be changed by it, week by week.

How to Use This Book

In compiling this volume I have had two groups of people in mind:

1. Preachers, teachers, and other church professionals who seek specific insights into Romans
2. Inquiring readers who are not professionals but who seek a deeper knowledge of the gospel

Because sermons are designed largely for congregations of lay people, they have several advantages for the general reader which more scholarly presentations do not,. Readers can take this book up, put it down, and take it up again in a week or a month with no loss of continuity. However, because I hope that other preachers will find help here, *the sermons are arranged in the order of the verses they treat,* beginning with the first chapter of Romans and going on from there. If a preacher is looking for help with a particular passage, the Table of Contents will direct him or her to the right place. It would make the whole enterprise worthwhile if the Spirit uses these offerings to encourage other preachers.

This arrangement, however, has certain disadvantages. Because Romans 1:18–3:20 deal with the wrath of God, and because chapters 5 and 7 treat significantly with the presence and power of Sin, the first third of this book is necessarily weighted in that direction. The unwary reader who begins at the beginning and starts to read through the sermons in order may very well get discouraged. Even though there is no sermon in this book that does not proclaim the victory of God's grace, nevertheless there is a certain amount of heavy going in the first hundred pages and also in the sermons that treat Romans 5.

The reader who is seeking an introduction to Romans, therefore, is urged to begin in the middle. I especially recommend reading these sermons first:

- The sequence of three sermons on chapters 9–11 called "The Israelite Connection" ("The Clue on the Beach," "The Better Bet," and "God's Cosmic Inclusion Plan"). In our day, more and more interpreters are beginning to recognize that this section is the inmost core of the letter.
- I also recommend "The Enemy Lines Are Hard to Find" and "Whose Way of Life?" to start with, and perhaps going on from there to the sermons on Romans 8, 12, and 14 before tackling the earlier texts.

Preaching from Romans

Preaching from the Epistles is more difficult than from the Gospels, because their narrative structure, though it exists, is concealed.[8]

8. The underlying narrative structure of Paul's theology has recently received attention in *Narrative Dynamics in Paul: A Critical Assessment,* ed. Bruce Longenecker (Louisville: Westminster John Knox, 2002).

Unlike the Gospels which are specifically designed to be preached in units, Romans requires line-by-line, if not indeed phrase-by-phrase, exposition, so that it is hardly possible to preach a sermon from Romans that is complete in itself. A series is better than a single sermon, and best of all is preaching with concurrent weekday teaching at Bible classes and in study groups. I can testify that this sort of total immersion in Scripture will have powerful effects in a congregation.

There are many commentaries on Romans, and it is remarkable how many of them have stood the test of time. I was in seminary at precisely the period (early 1970s) when the historical-critical method was just beginning to yield to the canonical, literary interpretations that have returned to favor today, and I remember discovering some of the older commentaries and noting how helpful most of them were for preaching.

When I was first learning to preach, one of the most helpful practices was reading the sermons of contemporary preachers, and I did a lot of that. I have worn out two copies of Theodore P. Ferris's little sermon collection *What Jesus Did.* Even more important was my discovery that Calvin's multi-volume biblical commentaries and Barth's biblical commentaries in the *Church Dogmatics* were incomparably helpful. William H. Willimon's *Conversations with Barth about Preaching,* to my mind the most exciting book about preaching in years, has a distinctly Pauline ring to it. In recent years I have been reading more of the acknowledged masters of the past — Spurgeon, McLaren, Simeon, Krummacher — and wishing that I could preach in the all-stops-out manner that they did (not to mention the gorgeous language). John Donne is probably the greatest of them all and I am dumb in his presence. But each of us is called to his or her own place and time, and the Word of God will not return to God empty, but will accomplish that which God purposes, and prosper in the thing for which God sends it (Isaiah 55:11).

I no longer worry about being quoted without attribution. I used to be indignant about it, but I don't feel that way anymore. Obviously, if a preacher is lifting portions of the sermons of others week by week and word by word, it will call his/her whole ministry into question; but if someone wants to borrow from this or that sermon in this book, I would be glad. I feel a little bit like Paul writing to the Philippians; he acknowledges that there are some who preach Christ with less than perfect integrity, but concludes:

> What then? Only that in every way, whether in pretense or in truth, Christ is proclaimed; and in that I rejoice. (Philippians 1:15-18)

What I have sought to do more than anything else is to offer as full an exposition of the Epistle to the Romans as I can. I recognize that the sermons collected here are not all of equal quality, but they help to fill in the theological picture. I do believe that all of the sermons taken together amount to a coherent whole — a contemporary homiletical presentation of the radical gospel of Paul.

I prayerfully hope, therefore, that a perusal of the collection will yield, over time, a more expansive perspective on the first preaching of the gospel of Jesus Christ to the Gentiles than we have been accustomed to hearing. The message of Romans is truly universal. In it we are permitted a vision of the goal of history. God's plan of salvation transcends the individual and even the Christian community, because God goes before us to prepare the way for the redemption of the entire created order.

Acknowledgment

There is one person above all who has made this book possible. The Rev. Lucia Lloyd spent countless hours scrutinizing these sermons, getting them in order, and helping me to decide which ones to include and which to leave out. Lucia is not only a fine preacher and a theologian herself, but also a master of the English language, fully at home with every sort of text, from the Bible to Strunk & White to *A Manual of Style.* There are not many people whose opinion and judgment I would have trusted for this project. She is a lover of literature as I am, and I trust her instincts. I have taken most of her suggestions with gladness, and on the two or three occasions where I decided to resist them, I did so with trepidation, knowing the excellence of her discernment.

Lucia has a ministry of her own, so it is with the deepest gratitude that I acknowledge her superb skills as an editor and her generosity in giving of her best. And because she worked unstintingly into the night on numerous occasions as we traded dozens of emails, I thank her husband Michael and her children also for their partnership in the gospel. It has all been a most gracious gift of the Lord to this project. May it redound to the greater glory of God.

Not Ashamed of the Gospel

BAYSIDE PRESBYTERIAN CHURCH, VIRGINIA BEACH

NOTE TO THE READER: This was not a Sunday morning
sermon but a "teaching" sermon of greater length.

For I am not ashamed of the gospel. . . .

ROMANS 1:16

Why would the apostle Paul say right off the bat at the beginning
of his letter to the Christians in Rome that he is not ashamed of the
gospel? Why would he be ashamed of the gospel?

Are you ashamed of being a Christian? Some people are, you
know; it is a fact that the Christian Church has been involved in
some terrible things over the centuries, things of which we should
rightly be ashamed. We don't have to look far to find an example.
When the authorities in Prince Edward County, Virginia, shut
down the public schools rather than integrate them, my Episcopal
Church, right here in the Diocese of Southern Virginia, said nothing and did nothing. Segregation academies were formed in order to
accommodate the white children, but the black children in that de-
voutly Christian population did not go to school for five years. If I
were to meet any of those black children now grown up today, I
would like to apologize to them.

That was fifty years ago, but I am also ashamed today. For instance, I am ashamed of something that happened recently in Nigeria. *The New York Times* reported that groups of Christians were at-
tacked in the streets by Muslims who were enraged by those Danish

cartoons. Christian groups then overreacted, actually killing Muslims with machetes. While this was going on, a mosque was burned by a mob of so-called Christians, and someone wrote on the scorched wall, "Jesus is Lord." This should make us profoundly ashamed.

But that kind of shame is not the same thing as being ashamed of *the gospel itself*. Why would Paul begin his message by declaring that he is not ashamed of the gospel? The Church hadn't done anything terrible yet; it was too young and too small. So why would he be ashamed? I have been thinking about this for many years.

One possibility among several is that the new faith had no snob appeal, no status whatsoever. It had arisen out of a circle of largely poor and uneducated Galileans, the low end of a backwater of the mighty Roman Empire. Paul himself was the opposite of that; he was not only highly educated but also a Roman citizen, a distinction of which he had been proud, and he was moreover an aristocrat among the Jews, a Pharisee — and we know what contempt the Pharisees had for the disciples of Jesus. So we can see how the new gospel might be an embarrassment to a person like Paul. Whenever I read the local paper in my home town of Franklin, I am astonished by the dozens and dozens of little tiny rural churches who run big ads every week. The members of the local mainline churches sometimes say snooty things about these little congregations. Paul, as a man of the top echelons, might well have been similarly embarrassed by the working-class origins of his faith, but not so. When he was called to be an apostle of Jesus Christ he left such distinctions behind for ever.

Another possible reason to be ashamed of the gospel, or at the very least to keep quiet about it, is that it was just plain dangerous. Paul's message was a direct assault on the stability of the Roman Empire.[1] The first Christian creed was *Kurios Iēsous,* "Jesus is Lord."

---

1. This may explain why, in Romans 13, Paul feels it is necessary to insert a passage about the God-ordained function of government. The gospel was so revolutionary that Christians may have felt that they could not and should not honor or respect the laws of the Empire. For more on this subject, see the sermon on Romans 13 and Revelation 13, "Between the Two Thirteens."

I'm not sure that we can adequately imagine how subversive this was. In those early days it was emphatically *not* the slogan of the winning team. It is hard for us in America, with our cathedrals and megachurches, to understand what it was like for Christians in the city of Rome in those days. We don't have anything to compare it to. We haven't had the experience of being a subject population under a world-dominating empire — we *are* the world-dominating empire (for the moment). We have to try to imagine Rome: the Colosseum, the Appian Way, the Forum, the palaces, the tread of the Roman legions on the Roman roads, the chariots and the horses, the aqueducts and viaducts stretching across three continents. We have to remember that the emperor was more than a king; he was a kind of god, requiring worship, sacrifice, and absolute loyalty. The Roman creed was *Kurios Kaisar,* "Caesar is Lord." Since we've all seen a zillion Nazi movies, maybe the closest analogy is "Heil Hitler." Anyone who said "Heil Jesus" would soon hear the midnight knock at the door.

It is in the nature of empires to keep seditious elements under control at all costs. We need to imagine what it is like today to be a Christian in, for example, the underground churches in provincial China where at this very hour Christians continue to be imprisoned, tortured, and killed by agents of the state. An image occurs to me: the famous films of that young man, whose fate is unknown to us, who danced in front of the tank in Tienanmen Square. One man in front of a line of huge tanks. That was the Christian Church in Rome.

So there are at least two reasons for backing away from the gospel:

1. the gospel seems to appeal to people that we are embarrassed by, or feel superior to
2. the gospel can get you into very big trouble.

Beyond these two factors, however, lies another — a fundamental and decisive one.

In the Epistle to the Hebrews there is a telling verse: "[We look] to Jesus the pioneer and perfecter of our faith, who . . . endured the cross, despising the shame" (Hebrews 12:2). This verse makes explicit what is implied elsewhere: crucifixion was *shameful.* It was specifically designed by the Romans to be degrading and dehumanizing to an extreme degree. It was considered an offense against polite society even to mention it. To a Jew it would be indescribably *shameful* as well, for several reasons. It may be hard for us to grasp today when models and actors take off their clothes every five minutes, but for Jews of biblical times as for Arabs today, public nakedness was extraordinarily shameful, and the condition of a publicly crucified victim was shocking to a degree we can scarcely imagine.[2]

So it must have been incredibly challenging for the early Christians to explain why their Messiah and Lord had been condemned by both Romans and Jews, state and church, to a hideous, degrading, public death. By either Roman or Jewish standards, you would have to be deluded or crazy to worship a crucified man. Paul surely had this in mind when he quoted Isaiah. "The scripture says, 'No one who believes in him will be put to shame.'" And again in the next chapter he quotes from the prophet, "[Thus says the Lord], behold, I am laying in Zion a stone that will make men stumble . . . and he who believes in him will not be put to shame" (Romans 9:33; Romans 10:11). Summing up, therefore: the "shame" of the gospel is the Cross itself. "[Jesus] endured the cross, despising the shame."

Listen now to what Paul writes to the church in Corinth about God's use of shame: "God chose what is foolish in the world to shame the wise, God chose what is weak in the world to shame the strong, God chose what is low and despised in the world, even things that do not exist, to bring to nothing things that are." When Paul preaches, he connects the words *shame* and *foolishness* with the word *gospel.* In our text today, from his introduction to

2. Today's Arabs would understand it; nakedness is shameful to them, a fact that Americans in Iraq have exploited — to our shame. The Americans at Abu Ghraib knew about Arabs' attitudes when they photographed their naked captives. Even in our own culture most people have disturbing dreams about being shamefully naked in public.

Romans, "I am under obligation both to [educated] Greeks and to barbarians, both to the wise and to the *foolish:* so I am eager to preach the *gospel* to you also who are in Rome. For I am *not ashamed* of the gospel. . . ."

God chose what is foolish, weak, low, and despised in the world precisely to *shame* those who consider themselves wise, strong, and powerful. This is what we call counterintuitive, to say the least. It would have been easy for God to show his power through the *powerful.* That wouldn't have been a challenge for God at all. Arrangements would have just stayed the same as they already were. In fact, you would hardly need God for that; God could just add something on to what had already been achieved. Indeed, the American creed is that God helps those who help themselves. "Self-help," a term that would have been unthinkable for Paul, is part of American religion.

So now we come tonight to ourselves here in this church, this congregation. I have been thinking about this theme for a long time. There is a particularly American type of being ashamed of the gospel. I think that for affluent, mainline white Protestant Americans it is difficult for us to admit that we need salvation. A little *help,* maybe, just enough to touch us up a little, enough to improve on what we have already accomplished, but mostly we want to do it ourselves so we can congratulate ourselves for being successful people — nice, quiet, discreet congratulations, of course, but congratulations nonetheless. I think that's why we tend to be disdainful about those who say they are "born again." Like Nicodemus, we don't really think we need to be born again. And if we think this, brothers and sisters, then we are ashamed of the gospel.

On NPR as I was driving to the Beach, I heard a discussion of the terrible murders in the Amish schoolhouse.[3] Various factors were mentioned — guns, copycat crime, the Internet, the stress of modern life, and so forth. Finally a wise person said, "It isn't any of those things. It's human nature." He told how the story of the Pied Piper originated in Germany in the Middle Ages when a man lured

---

3. The nation was horrified by the shooting of eight Amish girls inside their one-room Pennsylvania schoolhouse.

a bunch of children and then killed them.[4] There is something in human nature that has been with us from time immemorial. According to the gospel, human beings are trapped in human nature.

In Romans, Paul the apostle explains what is wrong with human nature. His name for this is "Adam." The figure of Adam stands at the head of a distorted line of human development, the story of us all. The biblical narrative of Adam and Eve tells us that something went terribly wrong with what God intended for us, and it was our rebellion that made it happen. We are to blame. That's what the story means and I wish we had time to read Paul's explanation of it right now. It's in the second half of Romans 5.[5] We are trapped in "Adam."

Let's look what's going on right now in the United States Congress, supposedly made up of the wise, strong, and powerful. How many times have we heard it said that the cover-up is worse than the crime?[6] Wouldn't you think that we would have learned that by now? The examples are so many that they go on forever. If only Nixon hadn't tried to cover up Watergate. If only Bill Clinton had not lied on camera. If only the Roman Catholic bishops hadn't tried to cover up for the clergy that molested children. And now we have the powers in Washington covering up for Congressman Mark Foley. A man who specializes in crisis management said on NPR yesterday that the basic rules were: tell it all, tell it early, tell it yourself. He said that the Speaker of the House of Representatives had broken all three rules.[7] Why haven't we learned anything?

Because of human nature.

According to what I heard on NPR, Representative Foley was

4. This is not the only explanation of the origin of the Pied Piper story, but it is one of the oldest.

5. Sermons on this subject will be found in the section on chapter 5.

6. Congressman Foley had just resigned after it became public knowledge that he had been sending sexually explicit messages to young male Congressional pages.

7. He said further that the three things not to do were (1) deny, (2) change the subject, and (3) go on the attack, all of which, according to him, the Speaker had done. This is not a partisan observation because Democrats have also failed in these ways. Alas, it is human nature.

approached three years ago about inappropriate behavior and he promised to stop. This reminds me of a thousand and one stories I have heard in my ministry about people who promised to stop drinking, promised to stop abusing their spouses, promised to lose weight, promised to end an extramarital affair, promised to . . . you fill in the blank. Why do we go on believing such promises? Perhaps it is because we have an unrealistically optimistic view of human nature.

That's what the Christian faith teaches us. Have you noticed how often people say, when someone like the BTK killer is discovered, "But he was so nice! He shoveled my snow! He changed my tire! He took his children to school every day!" Optimism serves quite well as a strategy for getting through the everyday setbacks of life, but the only view that fits the data is a tragic one. Optimism about human nature should not have survived the terrible 20th century. Human beings, we have learned, can very quickly become murderous under certain conditions. It was not so very long ago that white people in the American South knew that if you wanted to kill a black person, you could do so, because you would be protected by the system.

So what we need is a new humanity. The Adam story in Romans 5 teaches us that Sin and Death were unleashed into the world by human disobedience. It isn't important to think of Adam as a literal person; the important thing is to understand Genesis 2–3 and Romans 5:12-21 as true descriptions of the human condition. Paul sums it up: Sin came into the world through the disobedience of Adam, and Death came through Sin, and so Death spread to all human beings because all human beings had fallen into the grip of Sin. "Adam" is a dead man. He cannot deliver himself. He cannot save himself. Eve can no longer help herself. She can promise to become a new woman but she cannot keep her promise. Just ask a recovering alcoholic.

The first thing that a recovering human being does on the way to becoming a new human being is to stop worrying about being ashamed. One of the wonderful things about adult baptism is that the adult has to shed a certain amount of embarrassment about taking this step. The language of baptism is the language of new birth.[8] The problem is that we don't want to embrace this new birth for ourselves because it implies helplessness on our part. It doesn't fit the American image of the self-made man or woman. We don't want to be "foolish, weak, low and despised in the world" and utterly dependent upon God. So it seems to me that we do not fully embrace the gospel because we don't want to admit that we need to be remade. It suggests a sort of weakness on our part.

Don't you agree that it's a little *embarrassing?* To talk about helplessness and need for salvation? It just isn't the way that achievers talk. Paul understood this. He was on his way to Rome, the center of the world's achievers. He writes his letter to a tiny little group of Christians there; they do not even have a building to meet in. He is on his way to visit them. He will not leave Rome alive. We know that he was put to death by the Emperor Nero.[9] Quite possibly Paul foresaw this. He had already narrowly escaped death many times. With supernatural courage he is preparing to bring the living gospel of the living God to the capital of the Empire. Caesar is *not Lord*. Jesus is Lord. Paul was not ashamed of the gospel, though all the empires of the earth be arrayed against him. As the old joke goes, two thousand years after the death of the apostle, people name their sons Paul and their dogs Nero.

Human nature. It needs a Savior.

We have one. The Holy Spirit of our Lord Jesus Christ is powerful to change us into something we ourselves cannot become.

Yesterday in the Norfolk *Virginian-Pilot* I read that one of the little Amish girls who survived the massacre told of something that happened inside the schoolhouse. She said that Marian Fisher, the oldest of the captive girls, spoke up and said, "Shoot me. Shoot just me, and leave the others go." She was thirteen years old.[10]

---

8. It is a pity that we mainline Protestants tend to use the phrase "born again" negatively, because it comes from Jesus himself, and all baptized Christians are "born again," or, better, "born from above" (John 1:13, 3:3-5).

9. Ironically, he did not die in the Colosseum or at the stake, since Roman citizens were executed in a more dignified fashion by a professional stroke of the sword.

10. There is a somewhat fuller account of this girl in the sermon on Romans

Was she a saint? Was she some sort of perfect human being far beyond the reach of most of us?

The Christian gospel says no. She was made of the same human nature as the rest of us. What shone forth from her in the moment of her death was not human nature. It was the divine nature. It was Christ in us, the hope of glory. It was the righteousness of God which is by faith in Jesus Christ. This gift is not for special saintly Amish children. It is for all who are born again in the Spirit. It is for you, and you, and you, and me. It is "not I, but Christ in me." The next time you let someone else go first, or back off from a fight, or forgive someone, or stand up for someone weaker than you are, that's not you doing it.

That's Christ in you.

May we all remember this power beyond all earthly power whenever we are tempted to be ashamed of the gospel.

AMEN.

1:6, "The Power of Obedience." The quaint phrasing seems to reflect her Amish way of speaking.

Sermons on Romans 1–8

October 2006

The Power of Obedience

Paul, a servant of Jesus Christ, called to be an apostle, set apart for the gospel of God which {God} promised beforehand through his prophets in the holy scriptures, the gospel concerning his Son, who was descended from David according to the flesh and designated Son of God in power according to the Spirit of holiness by his resurrection from the dead, Jesus Christ our Lord, through whom we have received grace and apostleship to bring about the obedience of faith for the sake of his name among all the nations, including yourselves who are called to belong to Jesus Christ. . . .

ROMANS 1:1-6

When Paul wrote his letter to the Christians in Rome he introduced himself as "an apostle set apart for the gospel." It seems to me that when we think today of people who are set apart, we mean they have set themselves apart, like monks, or nuns, or Amish people; or they are set apart because they have special skills or training, like Special Ops troops, or Olympic teams. But this isn't at all what Paul meant when he said he had been set apart as an apostle for the gospel. He hadn't chosen this role; he was commandeered by the risen Christ on the road to Damascus. He didn't suit the role; on the contrary, as he himself wrote,

I am the least of the apostles, unfit to be called an apostle, because I persecuted the church of God. But by the grace of God I am what I am, and his grace toward me was not in vain. (1 Corinthians 15:9-10)

Let's remember: Saul of Tarsus, as he was then called, was an arrogant, self-righteous pharisaical type — indeed, he was the very thing itself, a Pharisee — who was fanatically committed to exterminating the new Christian faith. He was literally on the road, "breathing threats and murder against the disciples of the Lord" as the book of Acts says (Acts 9:1), aiming to do whatever was necessary to get rid of this heretical sect when the Lord Jesus Christ knocked him off his horse and blinded him for three days That was the moment of his calling, his set-apart-ness, to be an apostle with credentials just as good as Peter's and John's even though he had never known Jesus personally. An apostle (Greek *apostolos*) was a disciple who had been promoted; a disciple is a follower, but an apostle is a fully commissioned ambassador. That is what God did with Paul. He took him from the camp of the enemy and sent him out to carry the gospel precisely to the people that Saul the Pharisee would have considered beneath him — namely, the ungodly Gentiles. It is a wonder that the other disciples did not resent him more than they did. It is comforting, actually, to know that there was tension between Paul and Peter (Galatians); they were not stained glass saints, but remained fully human beings struggling with their faults just as we do.

So this man, this apostle Paul risked life and limb a hundred times over as he traveled around the Mediterranean world in conditions so rugged that people today who try to trace his steps are amazed that he could do it. Add to that the fact that he was persecuted, imprisoned, and threatened with death almost everywhere he went, and you get some idea of how much we who sit in this place owe to the Lord's calling and commissioning of this apostle to the Gentiles — that is, to us. Without Paul, there would have been no worldwide Christian faith. Most important to remember, it was not Paul by himself. It was, as he said repeatedly, "not I, but Christ in me."

Paul wrote wonderful things about his apostolic ministry. He wrote to his troublesome Corinthian church that he knew there were a lot of things about him to criticize, but, he insisted, "We [apostles] have this treasure [the gospel] in earthen vessels [lowly clay pots, not fine china] to show that the transcendent power belongs to God and not to us" (2 Corinthians 4:7). That's Paul's theme throughout; the transcendent power belongs to God. If there is anything of value that comes to you through the preaching of the gospel today, it is from God, not this earthen vessel.

In this same passage Paul reflects on the dangerous, difficult life of an apostle, knowing that he will most probably be killed eventually. He knows that his martyrdom would be life-giving for the Church. Listen to what he says about that, remembering that the suffering he speaks about is not the kind that comes to every one sooner or later but the suffering that is specific to the Christian messenger:

> We [apostles] are afflicted in every way, but not crushed; perplexed, but not driven to despair; persecuted, but not forsaken; struck down, but not destroyed; always carrying in the body the *death* of Jesus, so that the *life* of Jesus may also be manifested in our bodies. For while we [apostles] live we are always being given up to death for Jesus' sake, so that the life of Jesus may be manifested in our mortal flesh. So death is at work in us [apostles], but life in you [who receive the apostolic message in faith]. (2 Corinthians 4:8-12)

Hold this in your minds as we go on: "Death is at work in us, but life in you." Now to go back to the beginning of Romans, let's recall that Paul is preparing for his biggest trip so far. He is coming to imperial Rome. We need to imagine the might of the Roman Empire compared to the infinitesimally small band of Christians there — the Colosseum looming over a handful of ants. Paul is determined to come in spite of the very real possibility that he will lose his life — as indeed he did. His letter is written to prepare the little congregation for his coming; many of them are personally named and greeted by Paul in the wonderful chapter 16. The central focus of this message tonight is a phrase that Paul uses in his greeting to them. Here it is again:

> Paul, a servant of Jesus Christ . . . through whom we [apostles] have received grace and apostleship to bring about *the obedience of faith* for the sake of his name. . . .

The obedience of faith. What exactly does that mean?

"Obedience" is not in favor today. American culture prizes everything that is rebellious, "edgy," and — a favorite word of the cultural elite — "transgressive." Staying within boundaries is nerdy; pushing the edge of the envelope is hip. Baaaaad is good. It is *dis*obedience that's in fashion, not obedience. It takes some effort to reappropriate obedience in the way that Paul means it. He, of course, means obedience to God. He returns to this theme at the end of his letter:

> I have written to you very boldly . . . because of the grace given me by God to be a minister . . . of the gospel of God, so that the offering of the Gentiles may be sanctified by the Holy Spirit. . . . I will not venture to speak of anything except what Christ has wrought through me to win *obedience* from the Gentiles . . . by the power of the Holy Spirit. (Romans 15:15-19)

To win obedience from the Gentiles — that's you and me. Obedience by the power of the Holy Spirit. *The obedience of faith.*

I have one goal today and that is to offer this message: True freedom is not found in rebellion against God. Rebellion against God leads to the death of the soul and the spirit. Obedience to God may mean the death of the body, but it means life for the world. "We [apostles] are always carrying in the body the *death* of Jesus, so that the *life* of Jesus may also be manifested in our bodies." Paul speaks specifically here of his own apostleship, but by extension the apostleship of the apostolic Church (that's us). How do we carry around in our bodies the death of Jesus?

That 13-year-old Amish girl, Marian Fisher, has lodged in my mind.[1] She stepped forward and said, "Shoot just me, and leave the others go." This is as striking an example of *the obedience of faith* that could be imagined. This young girl's words carry with them the distinct, unmistakable, unique character of the death of Jesus Christ. She offered herself in the place of others who were younger, smaller, and weaker. It is an almost exact parallel to the death of Christ in our place, we who in our human nature were in every way smaller, and weaker, indeed sinful, polluted, distorted, and perfectly capable of hounding him to death.

And here's more: the Amish community was prepared to extend that sacrifice immediately to embrace the father, wife, and children of the man who shot and killed their children before killing himself. This is nothing short of miraculous. This is God at work. This is an extension of our Lord's words as he was dying in agony, "Father, forgive them, for they know not what they do."

It would be a great mistake to romanticize or idealize the Amish people. They have their strengths and weaknesses just as we all do, and I am sure that they and we would have theological disagreements. But there is this to be said for them. In this terrible trial they have proven themselves to be a people prepared. The strength of their ties to one another, to their biblical faith, and to their way of life has, so to speak, rooted "the obedience of faith" in their communal DNA. During this terrible episode they have "carried in their bodies the death of Jesus."

You see, when Paul speaks of the obedience of faith, it is not generic religion of which he speaks. He speaks of being "in Christ" (Romans 8:1, 12:5, 16:9, etc.). He speaks of having "the mind of Christ" (1 Corinthians 2:16; Philippians 2:5), "formation" in Christ (Galatians 4:19), being "in accord with Christ" (Romans 15:5), "dying and rising" with Christ (Romans 6:4-8, etc.). He speaks of "putting on the Lord Jesus Christ" (Romans 13:14). He says we are

---

1. The week that this sermon was preached, the country was horrified by the premeditated shooting of eight Amish girls (five died) in their one-room schoolhouse in rural Pennsylvania.

letters from Christ to the world, "written not with ink but with the Spirit of the living God, not on tablets of stone but on tablets of human hearts" (2 Corinthians 3:3). He even says that we are the fragrant aroma of Christ being spread by God throughout the world (2 Corinthians 2:15). He says all these things so that we, those who are "baptized into Christ" (Romans 6:3), would be a people prepared. This is the obedience of faith.

The obedience of faith in Jesus Christ does not mean restriction or claustrophobia or imprisonment. It means freedom. It means liberty. It means power. Karl Barth uses a phrase that caught my attention: "the power of obedience." Aligning oneself with the power of God in obedience to the Spirit: this is the power that overcomes the world.

Who said that? Another apostle. Listen to this from the first letter of John:

> For whatever is born of God overcomes the world; and this is the victory that overcomes the world, our faith. Who is it that overcomes the world but he who believes that Jesus is the Son of God?

I am not an apostle. The age of the apostles ended before the close of the first century. But as the Nicene Creed declares, the church is still apostolic. That means that earthly vessels, clay pots like Christians of today, can still be agents of the transcendent power of God as the Spirit sees fit. I long to impart to you these thoughts. It is not very likely that any of us will be called upon to lay down our lives in the name of Christ (although you never know). For the great majority of us, the obedience of faith is lived day to day in the humdrum details. The purpose and meaning of regular worship with fellow believers is to be a people prepared for the daily decisions:

- Shall I reach out to that person who is unloved?
- Shall I protest against unfair treatment of my fellow worker?
- Shall I speak out against racial prejudice?

[32]

- Shall I write a letter about Darfur, or torture, or the death penalty?
- Shall I take time to teach my children the ways of the Lord as well as taking them to soccer practice?
- Shall I forego financial reward in order to serve God better?

In such mundane decisions as these, the mind of Christ takes shape within the Christian community. As we share the Lord's supper together, we rejoice to remember whose Spirit it is that bears us up and links us together in the power of the obedience of faith — the faith that overcomes the world.

AMEN.

Not Ashamed of Jesus

For I am not ashamed of the gospel.

ROMANS 1:16

*For whoever is ashamed of me and of my words in this adulter-
ous and sinful generation, of him will the Son of man also be
ashamed, when he comes in the glory of his Father with the holy
angels.*

MARK 8:38

Something has been happening in the Church that seems different
to me, both in quantity and in quality; it is happening more often
and it has a sharper edge. A number of scholars with attractive per-
sonalities and considerable media skills have been steadily building a case against the Church's two-thousand-year-old confession
of Jesus as Lord, and some of them have been doing it from within
the Church. The "Jesus Seminar," as one project calls itself, generally times its pronouncements for Christmas and Easter so it will
have the biggest impact. This is only one group, however, and perhaps the least influential in a sense; the more insidious develop-
ments are occurring without our noticing because they have affected the thinking of all the clergy and lay people in a time when

theological precision is suspect in the mainline denominations. So the gospel of Jesus Christ the Son of God has subtly shifted into a style of story-telling about Jesus the admirable human being and spiritual exemplar.

St. Paul had something to say about this sort of thing in his second letter to the Corinthians, a church that gave him no end of trouble. In this letter he refers to the earliest Christian creed, "Jesus is Lord" *(kurios Iesous).* He writes that "no one speaking by the Spirit of God ever says 'Jesus be cursed!' and no one can say 'Jesus is Lord' except by the Holy Spirit" (1 Corinthians 12:3). So we would be wrong to think that there is any thing new going on among us; apparently there were people in the Corinthian church who were denying Jesus as Lord two thousand years ago.[1] Still, the current level of antagonism to the Church's traditional affirmation seems new to me. Many of us have simply ignored these attacks, figuring that they would go away — and eventually they will — but in the meantime we are beginning to see significant erosion. Even the most faithful churches are going to feel the effects of these persistent assaults. Throughout the mainline denominations, many clergy are dodging and backtracking, causing congregations to be confused and drained of energy. The words of Jesus in today's gospel, therefore, seem especially pertinent for our time: "Whoever is ashamed of me and of my words in this adulterous and sinful generation, of him will the Son of man also be ashamed, when he comes in the glory of his Father with the holy angels."

Now the iconoclasts will say that Jesus never said those words at all. I'll be the first to admit that we can no longer read ancient texts as innocently as our forebears did. We know more now about

---

1. It should be noted that biblical theologian Larry Hurtado, in his important works *Lord Jesus Christ* and *How on Earth Did Jesus Become a God?* (both published Grand Rapids: Eerdmans, 2005), has rigorously argued that the confession of Jesus as the Christ goes back to the very beginning of the New Testament church, contrary to those who argue that it was a much later development. Unfortunately there is a good deal of irresponsible speculation about this, producing the sort of credibility that makes possible the uncritical acceptance of blockbuster books such as *The Da Vinci Code.*

how such texts are formed. It would be foolish to deny that the Gospel narratives were shaped and reshaped by the early church, as the story of Jesus was preached to new believers. Nowadays, however, there is so much emphasis on the refashioning of the text that Jesus, himself, becomes either a purely literary presence, or else a greatly reduced historical figure standing at a great remove from the New Testament accounts. Here are a couple of examples. There have been a number of print ads for Thomas Cahill's new book about Jesus.[2] One of the blurbs featured in the ads praises the book for making Jesus "once again a vital literary presence." Similarly, another ad in my files recommends a book about Jesus by a NYU professor, saying that it "may even bring the Sage of Nazareth back to life." In other words, he lives in the text — whether ancient or modern — but nowhere else. We could compare him to a literary character like Ebenezer Scrooge, who never really lived, but who is made real to successive generations every Christmas as the story is read and acted out.[3] Or we could say that Jesus is like a long-dead historical figure who "comes alive" when a new biography appears.

That's a simplified explanation of how Jesus might be understood as a "literary presence." That's not the only angle on him these days, however. Another angle is to chip away at the New Testament narratives, discarding all the portions that don't sound "historical" according to various criteria, until there is almost nothing left. The Gospel of John, for example, is said by these scholars to have no authentic words of Jesus at all. There are various criticisms that can be made of this procedure. It has often been pointed out that there is a kind of naiveté at work here, because the Seminar members are sim-

2. Thomas Cahill, *Desire of the Everlasting Hills: The World Before and After Jesus* (New York: Nan A. Talese, 1999). Cahill is a prodigiously talented writer for general readers and there is much here to admire, but this particular book in his "Hinges of History" series is seriously flawed by his limited research. Protestant biblical theology and biblical scholarship is terra incognita for him.

3. Sherlock Holmes is probably the most potent "literary presence" of all. Hundreds of letters still pour in to 221-B Baker Street, London. Thousands of people (I am one of them) have reverently gone to Baker Street to visit this imaginary person at an imaginary address.

ply substituting their own Jesus for the Jesus they are rejecting, with no real foundation to build on except the one that they build themselves. There have been "quests for the historical Jesus" before, and they have not gotten us very far.[4] The truth is that we know nothing about Jesus whatsoever except what we read in the New Testament. There is no contemporary testimony to him anywhere else.[5] It can't be said too often: if the story of Jesus of Nazareth had ended with the Crucifixion, we would never have heard of him. That fact is part of what keeps me going as I expound the New Testament year in and year out. In spite of the very serious doubts that frequently assail me, the unique character of the early witnesses brings me back again and again.

Built into the apostolic testimony is a clear-sighted awareness that generations of believers are going to be tempted to retreat from Jesus in embarrassment, fearing to seem outmoded, outclassed, lacking in intellectual or moral courage. No one knew this temptation better than St. Paul himself. He begins his Epistle to the Romans with these ringing words, "I am not ashamed of the gospel" (Romans 1:16). He closes the Epistle to the Galatians on the same defiant note: "Henceforth let no man trouble me; for I bear on my body the marks of Jesus" (Galatians 6:17). Clearly, Paul was being "troubled" by all sorts of alternative interpretations. His letters to the Galatian and Corinthian churches, in particular, show him engaged in a tumultuous struggle for the hearts and minds of his congregations. And right at the center of it all he placed the Cross. He rebukes the Galatians for losing hold of the Cross, saying, "O foolish Galatians! Who has bewitched you, before whose eyes Jesus Christ was publicly portrayed as crucified?" (Galatians 2:1). And to the Corinthians he says, "I decided to know nothing among you except Jesus Christ and him crucified" (1 Corinthians 2:2). Both the Galatian churches and the Corinthian church were acting as if they

4. Highly recommended is Luke Timothy Johnson's readable little book, *The Real Jesus* (San Francisco: HarperSanFrancisco, 1996), which addresses these issues in a lucid, lively way.

5. There are contemporaneous references to John the Baptist in non-biblical sources, but not to Jesus.

were ashamed of Christ crucified, each in their own way and for somewhat different reasons. The Corinthians thought the Cross was unspiritual. They were right about that. As for the Galatians, they wanted to drift back into forms of religious legalism, undercutting the utter radicality of Christ's death for the ungodly. That's what Paul says in Romans 5: "Christ died for the ungodly." He died an ungodly death for ungodly people. That was the scandal of the Cross.

It is not at all clear on Sunday morning in the mainline churches of our land that Christ died for the ungodly. We all look pretty fixed up to me. I don't know if any of you think of yourselves as ungodly or not. After all, the point of coming to church is to be godly, isn't it? — or to be religious, or to be spiritual. But Paul means to say that Christ died an unspiritual death for unspiritual people. It is not possible to emphasize too strongly the offensive nature of the Cross; it was a shameful, irreligious death. That's why people have always been tempted to be ashamed of Jesus. That's why Paul introduced his letter to the Romans by saying, "I am not ashamed of the gospel." And that is why Jesus says in today's gospel, "whoever is ashamed of me and of my words in this adulterous and sinful [this *ungodly*] generation, of him will the Son of man also be ashamed, when he comes in the glory of his Father with the holy angels."[6]

Ashamed of Jesus? Let's look back at those verses from Mark again. "And he began to teach them that the Son of man must suffer many things, and be rejected . . . and be killed . . . and he said this plainly. And Peter took him, and began to rebuke him." Here is the first indication that something shameful is going to happen to the Master. Peter can't stand it. He steps out of his place as a follower; he comes up to Jesus and grabs hold of him as though he and Jesus were equals. Jesus says, "Get back in your place, Peter" — only Jesus doesn't call him Peter, he calls him Satan. When the Cross of Christ is rejected, it is the work of evil. If this story is read carefully, it gives us a whole new perspective on what it means to follow Je-

6. The parallels are Matthew 10:38 and 16:24 and, especially, Luke 9:23.

sus. Listen again to Jesus' words: "If any one would come after me, let him deny himself and take up his cross and follow me." In their gospel context, it becomes clear that these famous words do not mean what we thought they meant. "Whoever would save his life will lose it; and whoever loses his life for my sake and the gospel's will save it. . . . For whoever is ashamed of me and of my words . . . of him will the Son of man also be ashamed, when he comes in the glory of his Father with the holy angels." Do you see how the saying about taking up the Cross is linked with the saying about being ashamed of Jesus? "Taking up the cross" has been trivialized all too often. We talk about "the cross I have to bear," meaning almost anything, from a long commute to a difficult mother-in-law. But the ordinary sufferings of life, even the most serious and challenging ones, are not in view here. When Jesus speaks of taking up the cross, he means, quite specifically, taking up the shame that comes upon his disciples because they belong to him. As we read in the Epistle to the Hebrews, he "endured the cross, despising the shame" (12:2).

It is fashionable today to be skeptical about Jesus. In elevated scholarly conversation, not only in secular circles but also in departments of religion, the most stylish intellectual move you can make is to speak of Jesus as a *literary presence.* He is in very good company, if so; Hamlet and Captain Ahab and Jane Eyre continue to serve us powerfully. But is that the way Jesus lives among us? and how do we find the answer to that question? Jesus himself put it to the disciples: "Who do you say that I am?"

Let us look back at the lesson from the Epistle to the Romans. Paul is asking a similar question when he writes, "What then shall we say . . . ? If God is for us, who is against us? He who did not spare his own Son but gave him up for us all, will he not also give us all things with him? It is Christ Jesus, who died, yes, who was raised from the dead, who is at the right hand of God, who indeed intercedes for us" (Romans 8:31-34). This is Paul's answer to the question, "Who do you say that I am." You can see how this is set against the Old Testament lesson, the story of Abraham and Isaac; Paul clearly intends a reference to this story when he says, "He who did not spare his own Son but gave him up for us all."[7] The Cross is at the center of the story.

The final portion of today's reading from Romans is one of the most well-known passages from the New Testament. Everyone loves to hear about how nothing shall separate us from the love of God. But it is not always recognized that this is not a generic religious sentiment. It is too specific in reference and too elevated in tone to be slapped on an all-purpose greeting card. "For I am sure that neither death, nor life, nor angels, nor principalities, nor things present, nor things to come, nor powers, nor height, nor depth, nor anything else in all creation, will be able to separate us from the love of God in Christ Jesus our Lord." Does Paul speak of a purely literary presence? Or is he simply referring to a religious personage who was, to be sure, interesting and significant on some levels, whom Paul then inflated to suit his own purposes?

Some would say so . . . some would say so.

But "who do *you* say that I am?"

I know a couple whose son has for many years been a very high risk for suicide. Many doctors have been involved and many avenues explored. He has been in and out of hospitals, on and off of medication, back and forth on ECT (shock) treatments. Everything is being done for him, but the struggle to treat his depression continues. The mother and father know that their son, now in his late twenties, may at any time decide to end his life. They will never be free of this terrible fear. In their search for strength, this passage from Romans has been a constant resource. But not on general principles. The passage is not an expression of religious optimism about things working out for the best, though it has often been used that way. The passage depends for its truth on who Jesus is. Who can separate us from the love of God? Can death? can the principalities and powers? can "things present, or things to come"? It all depends on

---

7. It is important to understand that this does not mean that the Father gave Jesus up without Jesus' willing consent and active participation. The Father and the Son are doing this together, as is clear from other passages (e.g., 2 Corinthians 5:18-19; John 10:17-18; Philippians 2:5-8).

whether Paul is telling the truth when he says that Jesus is "raised from the dead, who is at the right hand of God, who indeed intercedes for us." If that is not true then it is not true that nothing can separate us from the love of God. If Paul is not telling the truth, then there *is* something that can separate us from the love of God and that is ourselves. We can separate *ourselves* from the love of God if we choose to. If it is not true that Jesus sits at the right hand of God, if he is a literary or historical presence only, then this hope that lies beyond human hope is just wishful thinking.

Are you embarrassed by Jesus? If so, you have a lot of company. There are many in the mainline churches at this very moment who want you to turn away from the church's ancient confession to some other Jesus. But being ashamed of Jesus means being robbed of the everlasting arm of God in your darkest hour. Being ashamed of Jesus means that the Son of God will fade from your view. Being ashamed of Jesus means that you will have substituted a generic religious figure for the unique Messiah who died to save the *ungodly.*

"No one can say 'Jesus is Lord' except by the Holy Spirit." With all my heart I pray that you today will find the Spirit moving in your spirit, saying "I believe in God the Father almighty, maker of heaven and earth, and in Jesus Christ, his only Son, our Lord."

AMEN.

Witness for the Defense

ALL SAINTS EPISCOPAL CHURCH,
LINVILLE NORTH CAROLINA

For I am not ashamed of the gospel: it is the power of God for salvation to every one who has faith. . . .

ROMANS 1:16

There is therefore now no condemnation for those who are in Christ Jesus. For the law of the Spirit of life in Christ Jesus has set me free from the law of sin and death. For God has done what the law, weakened by the flesh, could not do: sending his own Son in the likeness of sinful flesh and for sin, he condemned sin in the flesh, in order that the just requirement of the law might be fulfilled in us, who walk not according to the flesh but according to the Spirit.

ROMANS 8:1-4

Now there was a man of the Pharisees, named Nicodemus, a ruler of the Jews. This man came to Jesus by night. . . . Jesus {said to him}, "Truly, truly, I say to you, unless one is born of water and the Spirit, he cannot enter the kingdom of God. That which is born of the flesh is flesh, and that which is born of the Spirit is spirit. Do not marvel that I said to you, 'You must be born anew.' The wind blows where it wills. . . . So it is with every one who is born of the Spirit."

JOHN 3:1-8

There was a little article in the *Charlotte Observer* on Friday which reported that the Pew Research Group had ascertained that the happiest people in America are (1) rich, (2) Republican, and (3) religious.[1]

Here is some news about people who are not so happy. *Larry King Live* has been visiting the infamous San Quentin prison. On Thursday night, the hour-long broadcast consisted of an interview with six men. Four of them were prisoners, one was a former prisoner now on the outside, and one was a prison warden who has worked at San Quentin for thirty years. Among the five prisoners one was Hispanic, two were black, and two were white. All of them were convicted murderers and all of them admitted their guilt.

Now these particular convicts had obviously been carefully chosen. None of them were serial killers. All of them were articulate, all had educated themselves in prison, all of them expressed remorse. It was made clear to the TV audience that there were plenty of men at San Quentin who had not chosen this better way, who were still rebellious and dangerous. But these five, the four still inside and the one on the outside, had committed themselves to rebuilding their lives on a different foundation.

I don't want you to think that this sermon is soft on murder. It's important to note that the TV program was not a sentimental whitewash. The next night Larry King devoted a whole hour to interviews with the families of the victims. One family member said, "I am not a proponent of restorative justice." Though he did not explicitly say so, he was contrasting *restorative* justice with *retributive* justice, which he supports.

Larry King gave the five convicted murderers plenty of air time to talk about their determination to atone for their crimes, but there was one feature of the discussion that he didn't want to give a

---

1. *Charlotte Observer,* June 9, 2006.

lot of time to, and that was the fact that every single one of the five men had, as they put it, turned their lives over to Jesus Christ. They kept bringing this up and Larry kept changing the subject. The more he changed the subject the more they kept bringing it up. They bore their witness. It was the strength they had found in Christ, they said, that had made the difference for them. They were sorry that more of their fellow inmates had not taken the same path. The African-American man who had been released spoke about how his church had made it possible for him to make it on the outside. Without the support of his congregation, he said, it would have been so much more difficult. He credited the church members for his success in rejoining society.

Now I have been noticing, over the years, that every time a convicted felon is converted to Christ, indignant voices are raised. People say scornfully, "They always find Jesus *after they get locked up.*" Karla Faye Tucker, for instance: she was on *Larry King Live* too, and she gave her powerful testimony. The Governor of Texas at the time was George W. Bush. He refused to commute her sentence to life in prison, and she was put to death. People said sarcastically about her, "She didn't 'find Jesus' until she was in prison for an axe murder."

St. Paul had attitudes like this in mind when he wrote to the Christians in Rome, "I am not ashamed of the gospel." I don't mean that he was thinking specifically of murderers in prisons, but he was certainly thinking of the way that becoming a Christian opens a person to ridicule. Paul himself was a man of towering intellectual stature and considerable privilege. He was not only a Pharisee of the highest class, he was also a Roman citizen — and that was no mean thing in those days. Paul could have remained rich, republican, and religious all his life and died peacefully in bed. But something happened to him. On the road to Damascus where he was headed with the intention of persecuting and even killing members of the new Christian faith, he was knocked from his horse with the force of a blow by the living Jesus Christ, and his entire world outlook was revolutionized.

We should remember that when Stephen, the first Christian

martyr, was stoned to death, Paul (then called Saul) consented to the deed and even held the cloaks of those who threw the stones (Acts 7:58–8:3). Thus, 20-25 years later, Paul writes to the Corinthians, "I am the least of the apostles, unfit to be called an apostle, because I persecuted the church of God." But, he continues, "by the grace of God I am what I am, and his grace toward me was not in vain" (1 Corinthians 15:9). After undergoing indescribable trials and hardships on three missionary journeys that took him through some of the most dangerous and inhospitable terrain in the Mediterranean world, Paul finally made it to Rome where the Emperor Nero had him executed by beheading with a sword.

All during these missionary years Paul knew exactly what the elites thought of him and the new faith. Jews called it scandalous (Greek *skandalon,* stumbling-block) and Gentiles called it foolishness (1 Corinthians 1:23). The "wise men," the great orators and philosophers, the religion professors all ridiculed the gospel of Christ crucified, "but God has chosen what is foolish in the world to shame the wise" (1 Corinthians 1:20-24). So when Paul preaches the gospel, you see, he connects the two words *foolishness* and *gospel.* He writes in his introduction to Romans, "I am under obligation both to Greeks and to barbarians, both to the wise and to the *foolish:* so I am eager to preach the *gospel* to you also who are in Rome. For I am not ashamed of the gospel. . . ."

Now to all those who are affluent churchgoers, like all of us here in Linville — the preacher included — the unvarnished gospel of Christ crucified still presents itself under the heading of *foolishness.* The gospel that Paul preached, the gospel that set the Mediterranean world afire, the gospel preached to the Gentiles by this unworthy but God-sent apostle — this gospel, when preached in its undiluted form, has never fit into any of the world's molds. It does not bring "happiness" as the world understands happiness. It does not bring riches or status or guarantees of worldly security. It brings accusations: "Why are you hanging around with those born-again people?" "You brought my dinner party to a dead halt with your embarrassing testimony." "You ought to be ashamed of reading the Bible — in this day and age! — as if it were the Lord's truth. You're acting like a Baptist." To which Paul replies, for all days and all ages, "I am not ashamed of the gospel. It is the power of God for salvation."

People — especially the kinds of comfortable people that you and I are — are embarrassed by converts. We are ashamed of converted murderers. We want murderers to be shamed for ever, with retributive justice. We worry that our dignified religion will be brought down if we admit that the power of God for salvation reaches into the prisons and the ghettos and the gangs. Perhaps even more, we are embarrassed by people like Paul, people whose lives have been radically transformed. St. Francis was one of those, but we are embarrassed by him, so we have put him in a little slot where all he does is bless animals. There is another leisure community just like this one, I won't name it, but it has a very large statue of St. Francis blessing birds, and everyone in that community just adores this statue. If St. Francis came down off that pedestal and started preaching — as he did in real life — about giving away everything to the poor, he would be disinvited so fast the man at the gate would hardly have time to let him through on the way out.

Last Sunday was Pentecost and this Sunday is Trinity Sunday, so this is the right time to bring the neglected third person of the Blessed Trinity to the forefront. St. Paul writes:

> There is therefore now no condemnation for those who are in Christ Jesus. For the law of the Spirit of life in Christ Jesus has set me free from the law of sin and death. For God has done what the law, weakened by the flesh, could not do: sending his own Son in the likeness of sinful flesh and for sin, he condemned sin in the flesh, in order that the just requirement of the law might be fulfilled in us, who walk not according to the flesh but according to the Spirit.

Paul's language is often dense and difficult to understand, but once you catch on to it, it blasts you with joyful good news. In this passage Paul is contrasting two kinds of law. The *first* is the law that condemns people and imprisons them without hope — he calls that the law of the flesh, or the law of sin and death. The *second* kind of law is the law of the Spirit that creates new life. Our Lord Jesus Christ, Paul says, was born into the realm of the flesh, that is, the realm of the first kind of law — the law that judges, condemns, and executes. That's why he was crucified, you see. He took upon himself the condemnation of the law that hands human beings over to trial and judgment and execution. He suffered and died under this law, the law that says it's all right to torture people to death if it's in a good cause.

But there is another kind of law, the law that connects the good commandments of God the Father with the new life of God the Holy Spirit. Paul declares that when our Lord died under the law of sin, he was fulfilling in his own body — his own flesh — the just requirement of God's law. I know this is hard to understand at first, but once you get it you will never forget it. In the Cross of Christ, *retributive justice* — the law that condemns — is put to death and is replaced by *restorative justice* — the law that gives life. You and I disobey the Ten Commandments every day of the week, but in him, because he was perfectly righteous, the just requirement of the law is fulfilled *for us* and, Paul writes, *in us* — so that we are enabled, by his grace, to move into and live the new life of the Spirit.[2]

The action of the Holy Spirit in all this is to make Christ's saving death present and powerful in the lives of sinners. By the agency of the Spirit, there is a new creation. The role of the Spirit is elaborated in the Gospel of John. The Spirit is called the Paraclete, a Greek word meaning *advocate,* or — get this — lawyer for the defense. At God's bar of judgment, the Holy Spirit is your defense counsel.

C. S. Lewis gave a wonderful title to a chapter in one of his

---

2. This paradox remains true of us all of our lives in this world. We must still struggle with sin, but because we are a new creation in Christ we are being enabled even now to live according to the Spirit. In classic theology we are "saints and sinners simultaneously" *(simul peccator et iustus).*

books: "Nice People, or New Men?"[3] As I remember it, his point was that the gospel does not confer blessings upon nice people. The gospel radically challenges "nice" people to become *new* people, new creations, people who by the power of the Spirit are being changed into the likeness of Christ.

We are the elite, this morning — the nice people. We are like Nicodemus in this morning's gospel. He was one of the privileged people among the Jews, the kind of person who is mortified by anyone who claims to be "born again." It was a great shock to him to hear our Lord say, "you must be born anew" — yes, Nicodemus, even you. Nicodemus came to Jesus by night because he was ashamed to be seen. But it is far better to come to Jesus by night than not to come at all. The Spirit blows where it wills. It might even blow on you this very hour.

Think now of yourself. Somebody, somewhere does not want you to be a new person in Jesus Christ, let alone "born again." It would embarrass them. Or maybe they would even like to see you in trouble. The useful German word *Schadenfreude* identifies this universal human trait — taking pleasure in the troubles of others. Somewhere out there, someone is feeling that way about you. Maybe it's a person you blackballed, or a person you fired, or a person you wronged. Maybe that person is your rival in business, or your first wife, or even one of your children. Somewhere there is someone who does not want you to be a new person.

But life in the Holy Spirit means not being ashamed of the gospel of the new birth. It means dying to the standards of this world. It means not caring if Larry King is embarrassed by you, or if your fellow sinners are embarrassed by you, or even if your friends and family are embarrassed by you, because you have an Advocate with the Father. "The law of the Spirit of life in Christ Jesus has set me free from the law of sin and death." The just requirement of the law has been fulfilled in us by the death of Jesus Christ. That, truly, is restorative justice. We no longer live "according to the flesh but according to the Spirit." There is a whole new world open to us, a

3. *Mere Christianity* (New York: Macmillan, 1953), p. 161.

world in which God does not weigh our merits, but pardons our offenses[4] — and then rebuilds our lives according to "the law of the Spirit of life in Christ Jesus."

> For I am not ashamed of the gospel. . . . There is therefore now no condemnation for those who are in Christ Jesus.

AMEN.

---

4. *Book of Common Prayer,* Eucharistic Rite I.

There Is No Distinction

TEXT: ROMANS 1:18–3:31

This is the first sermon of a series on Romans, since the lectionary assigns it to be read all this summer. I played around with a title based on the first two-and-a-half chapters. I thought about calling it "The Wrath of God," but we don't do that in the Episcopal Church, and besides, I want to keep my job. So I chose another verse from the early part of the Epistle: "There Is No Distinction." Martin Luther selected "this staccato negation as the very center and kernel of all scripture."[1] The whole verse goes like this: "There is no distinction, since all have sinned and fall short of the glory of God" (Romans 3:22-23).

Luther has a very good point here about "there is no distinction." I wish we could take the time to go through the first chapters verse by verse and see how cleverly Paul draws the readers into thinking someone else is being described, not themselves. This is human nature; if something unflattering is being said, we would like it to be about some *other* person or group. That's why Paul's sentence, "There is no distinction; all have sinned," is so startling. It levels the playing field beyond recognition; there is no advanced placement here, no inner circle, no honor roll. "There is no distinction."

It's important to note that this declaration of universal human sinfulness is not the first thing in Paul's letter. It is the summation

1. Paul Minear, *The Obedience of Faith* (Naperville, IL: SCM Press, 1971), p. 96.

of his long section on the Wrath of God (Romans 1:18-3:21), but he does not begin with the Wrath of God. He begins his letter with the grace and peace of God (Romans 1:5-7). After his salutation and the customary thanksgiving, he introduces his theme: "I am not ashamed of the gospel; it is the power of God for salvation to everyone who has faith, to the Jews first and also to the Gentiles" (1:16). Paul constructs his letter to illustrate that the righteous anger of God is entirely enclosed in his love and mercy. The Wrath of God is very real, but it is not an emotion of God's that comes and goes. It is his steady, unwavering, purposeful opposition to Sin.

Sin is a very unpopular subject these days. Worse even than being unpopular, it is unfashionable. Most of us would probably risk unpopularity sooner than we would risk being thought *passé*. But let us give Paul the benefit of the doubt here. After all, Jesus himself talked of sin a great deal, without apology. Indeed, the whole letter to the church in Rome could be called a commentary on the saying of Jesus, "I came not to call the righteous, but sinners" (Matthew 9:13). So let us listen to Paul's discussion.

After the gracious salutation and the first statement of his theme, Paul launches into his first main section with these startling words:

> The wrath of God is revealed from heaven against all ungodliness and wickedness of human beings. (1:18)

I wonder how many of you have the idea that the Old Testament presents us with a picture of a God of wrath and judgment whereas the New Testament depicts a loving and merciful God. This is such a serious distortion that one wonders how it ever got started. Just a couple of weeks ago my sermon text was from the Old Testament prophet Hosea, who taught unforgettably about God's tender love and amazing grace. Today we see that the Wrath of God plays a central part in the *New* Testament message. Nor should we be sentimental about Jesus himself; he spoke far more often of Hell than Paul does.[2]

2. Indeed, Paul never speaks about Hell at all, and his references to condemna-

What we need to understand is that for virtually all the biblical writers, and perhaps especially for Paul, the Wrath of God is part of the good news, part of the gospel itself. This is difficult for modern people, but those of us who call ourselves Christians will gain greatly in depth of faith and strength of hope if we can grasp this matter. It will help us on our way to the finest possible understanding of who we are and who God is.

In the first three chapters of Romans, Paul, in an elaborate argument, addresses the Christians in Rome on the subject of ungodliness and wickedness (1:18). (We should keep that word *ungodly* in our minds because it will make a dramatic reappearance in chapters 4 and 5.) First, using the pronoun "they," Paul describes the condition of sinful humankind.

> They did not honor him as God or give thanks to him. . . . they exchanged the truth about God for a lie and worshipped and served the creature rather than the Creator. (1:25)

> They are gossips, slanderers, haters of God, insolent, haughty, boastful, inventors of evil . . . faithless, heartless, ruthless. . . . Those who do such things deserve to die. (1:29-32)

Up to this point, Paul's readers will have been nodding their heads in agreement. Yes indeed, those people over there are intolerant, narrow-minded, vindictive, bad-mannered, lazy, dishonest, pushy, hypocritical, and un-Christian. We can certainly understand that God would be very displeased with *them.*

But Paul turns the argument around. Instead of saying *they,* he suddenly starts saying *you.* Now he is addressing the moral people, the religious people:

> Therefore, you have no excuse, O man, whoever you are, when you judge another. . . . Do you suppose, O man, that when you

---

tion have been construed by many interpreters (I am one of them) as penultimate rather than final — including even the difficult 1 Thessalonians 2:16.

judge those who do such things and yet do them yourself, you will escape the judgment of God? (2:1-3)

Just because God has been good to you, Paul suggests, do you believe yourself to be out of the reach of his Wrath? On the contrary,

In passing judgment upon another, you condemn yourself. . . . You are storing up wrath for yourself on the day of wrath when God's righteous judgment will be revealed. (2:1, 5)

Paul's argument is based on a distinction between Jews and Gentiles. The Gentiles are the foreigners, the strangers, the people who are "not our kind." The Jews are the in-group, the religious aristocracy, the Episcopalians, if you will. First he shows that Gentiles stand under the judgment of God because of their godlessness; then he turns to the Jewish Christians, who are proud of their special standing with God, and demonstrates that they, too, are deserving of God's Wrath. In condemning others, they have presumed to set themselves on a level above condemnation — this is the true meaning of Paul's saying, "In passing judgment upon another, you condemn yourself." He concludes his argument in this way:

All human beings, both Jews and Gentiles, are under the power of sin. . . . None is righteous, no, not one. (3:9-10)

There is no distinction. . . . All have sinned and fall short of the glory of God. (3:22-23)

In order to understand what this is all about, we have to empty our minds of all the ideas that we were raised with concerning sin. Almost all of us were brought up to believe that sin has to do with specific forbidden acts, mostly sexual. In this modern era, we have managed to convince ourselves (perhaps wrongly, though this is not the time for that particular discussion) that those things are not sins, that all we need to do is get rid of our Victorian hang-ups and we will be able to live free, abundant lives. But that is not what the

Bible means by sin at all. There is a big difference between sins (plural) and Sin (singular). Once we get this, it will help us to understand what comes next.

Sins (with an "s") are individual transgressions — fibs, shoplifting, speeding, cheating the government, things like that. We've all managed to convince ourselves that these things aren't too bad, that everybody has a few secret sins, and so what? Over against this we have the predominant biblical view that Sin is a condition. It is a disease, an infection, that the whole human race has got. Paul explains in chapter 5:

> Sin came into the world through one man [Adam] and Death through Sin, and so Death spread to all men because all men sinned. (5:12)

Notice the connection between Death and Sin. Paul declares that "the wages of Sin is Death" (6:23). Death, the ultimate separation from God and from all whom we love, is the punishment that has come upon the human race because of the original sin, the disobedience of Adam.[3] Do not make the mistake of thinking that individual persons are stricken for individual sins in sudden catastrophic ways, as though a child who is hit by a truck were being punished for stealing a pack of gum. That would be mixing up sins with Sin again. God's righteous sentence of death lies upon us all, Jew and Greek alike, religious and irreligious, moral and immoral, godly and ungodly — "There is no distinction. . . . All have sinned, all fall short of the glory of God. . . . There is no one righteous, no, not one."

All of this is summed up in what is often referred to as the doctrine of original sin. Reinhold Niebuhr has spoken of "the good news of original sin," and that's profoundly true. That's why Paul

---

3. It is not necessary to believe that there was a literal person named Adam in order to affirm the underlying content of Paul's message, namely, that human rebellion against God spoiled the design of creation and unleashed Sin and Death. The story of Adam and Eve is true in the grand mythological sense; it explains us to ourselves.

begins his letter with 17 verses of good news before he gets to the bad. It is a great mistake, however, to skip the bad news altogether, as most people do in the churches today. God's grace is absolutely *free,* but it is not *cheap.*[4] To be a Christian is primarily to know God's grace, but it is also to know the enormity of human resistance to that grace and the price that God paid to overcome that resistance. We need to know the facts of our condition, and the facts as Paul outlines them are these:

- "All human beings are under the power of Sin" (3:9).
- God hates sin; "the Wrath of God is revealed from heaven against all ungodliness and wickedness of men" (1:18).

Now perhaps you do not feel that you are a sinner. If you do not, then you can join the great majority of 20th-century people. Dr. Karl Menninger, the famous psychiatrist, published a book five years ago (1973) called *Whatever Became of Sin?* One of his chapters is entitled "The Disappearance of Sin: An Eyewitness Account." To-day (he says) we have crime, we have neurosis, we have symptoms, we have errors in judgment and self-destructive behavior and anti-social tendencies but we do not have sin. His book, written from his point of view as a practicing psychiatrist, is an impassioned plea for the return of the word "sin" to the vocabulary of doctors and clergy-men alike.

It is very important to notice what Dr. Menninger has in mind when he speaks of sin. A theologian he is not, but he comes very close to the mark when he says that "sin traditionally implies guilt, answerability, and . . . responsibility." "My proposal," he says, "is for the revival or reassertion of personal responsibility in all human acts. . . ."[5]

4. This distinction was famously made by Dietrich Bonhoeffer in his book *The Cost of Discipleship.*

5. Karl Menninger, *Whatever Became of Sin?* (New York: Hawthorne Press, 1973), pp. 20, 178. When preparing this collection for publication, I went back and looked at Menninger again, thinking that his book would be dated. On the contrary, it remains a powerful statement by a justifiably revered psychiatrist. He makes some

This is what St. Paul says too:

The whole world is held accountable to God. (3:19)

Do you suppose, O man, that you will escape the judgment of God? (2:2)

You can see for yourself that Paul is right; we are in a terrible mess. We are in bondage to the Power of Sin. Notice Paul's conception of this Power (3:9). We are not talking about a combination of little individual sins added up together to make one big sin. We are talking about an actual Power, an alien and hostile force that deals death to the human race and acts in implacable enmity to God and his purposes.

> Sin works death in me. . . . I am the purchased slave of sin. . . . I do not do what I want, but I do the very thing I hate. . . . it is no longer I that do it, but sin which dwells within me. . . . I can will what is right, but I cannot do it. . . . the evil I do not want is what I do. . . . I am captive to the law of sin which dwells in my members. Wretched man that I am! Who will deliver me from this body of death? (7:13-24)

In William Golding's classic novel *Lord of the Flies,* a group of English boys marooned on a desert island make an attempt to govern themselves in a civilized fashion, but it is not long before their

---

theological mistakes, but on the whole it contains invaluable insights. For instance, he writes, "Confession must include a recognition of the aggression of the sins committed" (p. 195). Moreover, he uses good illustrations: for example, in arguing against the prevailing tendency to refer to sin as illness, he cites the widespread practice of pilfering from employers (he cites several shocking articles from the *Wall Street Journal*). Then he writes indignantly, "No one would faintly suggest that 72 percent of store employees or 83 percent of bank employees are 'sick' because they pilfer. Almost no one is charged; no one is convicted. Obviously these are not 'criminals.' What is this, then, I would ask, other than clear, typical, unadulterated *sin?* What else can you call it?" (emphasis original).

efforts are overtaken by savage instincts. As their island life reaches a climax of murderous depravity, the adult world comes to the rescue in the form of a British Naval officer, dispatched ashore by a passing cruiser. Golding himself, commenting on his own book, says,

> The theme is an attempt to trace the defects of society back to the *defects of human nature*. . . . The whole book is symbolic in nature except the rescue in the end where adult life appears, dignified and capable, but in reality enmeshed in the same evil as the symbolic life of the children on the island. The officer, having interrupted a manhunt, prepares to take the children off the island in a cruiser which will presently be hunting its enemy in the same implacable way. *And who will rescue the adult and his cruiser?*[6]

Wretched human beings that we are! Who will deliver us from this body of death? (7:24)

Let us be quite clear about what Sin is. Let us not trivialize it or domesticate it. Sin is not a matter of a few sins here and a few sins there. What is Sin? Sin is the basic condition of man, the condition of rebellion against God, in his place. Sin is "mankind's essential illness,"[7] it is a condition we are all heir to, it is a demonic Power that enslaves us and binds us and prevents us from being either free or good. We are responsible before God for Sin, and yet we are unable to liberate ourselves from its grip. We are in a desperate situation, deserving of God's Wrath and marked out for his judgment, each of us individually and all of us collectively.

This sermon is going to come to an end in a minute. We are not going to turn the corner today. It is good for us to sit with Paul's words for a while: "There is no distinction. . . . All have sinned. . . . The wrath of God is revealed from heaven against all un-

6. William Golding, *Lord of the Flies* (New York: Capricorn Books, 1959), p. 189; emphasis added.
7. *Lord of the Flies*, p. 82.

godliness and wickedness of men." It is good for us to meditate on the knowledge of the reality of sin and the reality of God's anger against Sin. It is good for us to know that God's forgiveness is not simply automatic, as though we could take it for granted.

Perhaps you know the cynical remark of Catherine the Great: *Dieu pardonnera; c'est son métier,* which loosely translated says, God forgives you — it's his thing. Today we are trying to avoid the easy assumptions that Catherine was mocking. Beware of a glib belief that forgiveness is God's thing! We are endeavoring to look Sin straight in the face. "Sentimental evasions are long-range cruelties . . . an experience of the worst of the problem (is) the opportunity to know the best of the solution."[8]

Let us not evade. Let us not flinch from the truth about ourselves. Let us submit to the word of the apostle, as sisters and brothers in the same sinking lifeboat; "There is no distinction. . . . All have sinned. . . . There is none righteous, no, not one." There is not one of us here that is not guilty — guilty of hurting our spouses and children and friends, guilty of self-indulgence and self-hatred, guilty of jealousy and dishonesty and laziness and selfishness, guilty of seeking power for ourselves at someone else's expense, guilty of not behaving like Christians, guilty of not caring, guilty above all of worshipping gods other than the one true God. And the point of this sermon is to summon every one of us here to realize and to confess that the words of St. Paul, "All have sinned," refer to us personally, and not to somebody else. For it is one of the great works of the Holy Spirit to convict us of sin. Thus we know that the conviction itself is a working of the grace of God.

Let us therefore say together the words of our General Confession:

> Almighty and most merciful Father, we have erred and strayed from thy ways like lost sheep. We have followed too much the devices and desires of our own hearts. We have offended against thy holy laws. We have left undone those things which we ought to

8. FitzSimons Allison in the Grace Church (NYC) bulletin, October 1977.

have done, and we have done those things which we ought not to have done; and there is no health in us. But thou, O Lord, have mercy upon us, miserable offenders. Spare thou those who confess their faults. Restore those who are penitent; according to thy promises declared unto mankind in Christ Jesus our Lord. And grant, O most merciful Father, for his sake, that we may hereafter live a godly, righteous and sober life, to the glory of thy holy Name. Amen.[9]

9. This is the original version of Thomas Cranmer's great Confession for Morning and Evening Prayer. Christ's Church, Rye, where this sermon was preached, was still using this version in 1978.

The Line between Good and Evil

LENAPE VALLEY PRESBYTERIAN CHURCH

All human beings are under the power of sin.

ROMANS 3:9

It is significant that you included a prayer for our enemies in the intercessions this morning. In my travels around the country I have noticed that very few churches are praying for our enemies, even though our Lord specifically taught that we should do so. It is not good for our Christian health to fail him in this regard. Ever since September 11, 2001, the rhetoric of good vs. evil has dominated our public discourse. The battle against terrorism has been framed as a battle of good against evil, which has encouraged us Americans to think of ourselves as entirely benevolent. President Bush often refers to us as "good and compassionate." But this is not the way that most of the rest of the world thinks about us. Indeed, our self-confidence puts us in some degree of spiritual danger. The book of Proverbs has some wisdom on this subject: "All the ways of a man are pure in his own eyes, but the Lord weighs the spirit. . . . Pride goes before destruction, and a haughty spirit before a fall. It is better to be of a lowly spirit with the poor than to divide the spoil with the proud" (Proverbs 16:2, 18-19). Another proverb, stated more strongly, asserts, "There are those who are pure in their own eyes but are not cleansed of their filth" (Proverbs 30:12). So the really important question is, Are we deceived about ourselves? How do we stand before *God?*

Our two greatest Presidents understood something about the need for collective repentance before the divine judgment. George Washington and Abraham Lincoln both called America to repentance. It is hard to imagine any President doing that today. Lincoln, who was greatly influenced by the Presbyterian preaching that he heard, was a theologian profound enough to stand alongside the giants of Christian history. I am quite serious about that. Southerners have never liked Lincoln. My understanding is that the Lincoln automobile never sold well in the South. It has taken us Southerners a long time to recognize that Lincoln, had he lived, would have been the best friend the South could ever have had.

It is well known that Lincoln changed his mind about slavery. This has often been negatively construed by Southerners as an insincere political shift, but his writings do not support that conclusion. Lincoln wrestled long and hard with theological questions raised in his mind by slavery and the Civil War. In a private letter to a newspaper editor in Kentucky, a slave-holding state, he wrote that both the South *and the North* would be judged for complicity in the sin of slavery, and that such judgment would ultimately cause men "to attest and revere the justice and goodness of God." Judgment as good news! — a message well suited to this season just before Advent.

In his essay "Meditation on the Divine Will," Lincoln mused, "In great contests each party claims to act in accordance with the will of God. Both *may* be, and one *must* be wrong. God can not be *for,* and *against* the same thing at the same time. In the present civil war it is quite possible that God's purpose is something different from the purpose of either party. . . ."[1]

These amazing reflections are very different from what we hear coming from the White House today. Lincoln never spoke of "evildoers" or "the evil ones" as President Bush does. Slavery was a great

---

1. "Meditation on the Divine Will," September 1862. Both quotations are taken from Ronald White, *Lincoln's Greatest Speech* (New York: Simon & Schuster, 2002).

wrong, he came gradually to understand, but he did not cut up the nation neatly into good and evil with the Union on the good side and the Confederacy on the evil side. In this respect he was profoundly biblical in his understanding. He had read and pondered the Psalms and prophets, where God's most severe judgments are directed against his own people. When the Lord spoke to the prophet Isaiah saying, "Destruction is decreed" (Isaiah 10:22), he did not mean that he was going to destroy the bad guys. He meant that he was going to *chasten his own people,* the people of Israel, for their idolatry.

In any polarized situation, the overriding human tendency is to draw a line with oneself and one's allies on the good side and the opposing party on the wicked side, with very little attempt made by either side to understand the other. As these positions harden it becomes almost impossible to achieve the insight necessary for a breakthrough. For some years now I have kept a file that I call "The Line Runs Through." This title is from Václav Havel, former President of the Czech Republic and one of the very few profound public thinkers of our time. You will remember that Havel was one of those who resisted the Communists and was put in prison for his activities. When he came to power after the Velvet Revolution, Havel was conspicuously forgiving toward his former enemies and other collaborators. Some blamed him for this, but he maintained his position. In the Central European regimes of the seventies and eighties, Havel said, "The line [between good and evil] did not run clearly between 'them' and 'us,' but through each person."[2]

---

2. The full quotation reads: "No one was simply a victim; everyone was in some measure co-responsible. . . . *Many people were on both sides.* Society was kept down by millions of tiny Lilliputian threads of *everyday mendacity, conformity, and compromise.* . . . If that is true," he continued, "it is much less clear who . . . should be put on trial." Quoted in Timothy Garton Ash, "The Truth about Dictatorship," *The New York Review of Books,* February 19, 1998, pp. 36-37; emphasis added. The resistance leader and former Solidarity spokesman Adam Michnik, in Poland, has taken much the same position since 1989. Moreover, Aleksandr Solzhenitsyn made the same observation in almost the same terms in his famous book *The Gulag Archipelago.*

I have often remembered the rather passionate outburst of a friend of mine, who was congratulated effusively for having won a Silver Star in World War II. He reacted strongly to this, saying with some vehemence that it meant little because, as he put it, "nobody knows who deserves what." He felt that his "deserving" was almost a fluke and that many others who had not won anything might be more deserving than he.[3]

The line between good and evil runs through each person. Listen to St. Paul: "Sin came into the world through one man and death through sin, and so death spread to all men because all men sinned" (Romans 5:12). "There is none righteous, no, not one; no one understands, no one seeks for God. All have turned aside, together they have gone wrong; no one does good, not even one. . . . There is no distinction; all have sinned and fall short of the glory of God" (Romans 3:10-12, 22-23). The line between good and evil runs through each person. In Shakespeare's play, *All's Well That Ends Well,* two young noblemen are discussing the mixed motives of the characters around them. One says to the other, "The web of our life is of *a mingled yarn, good and ill together."*

A couple of years ago, there was a major exposé of the McWain company of Birmingham, one of the most dangerous companies to work for in America. The evidence of brutal conditions for workers and callous neglect of their injuries in pursuit of profit was simply overwhelming.[4] Yet the McWains are church members and philanthropists. The line runs through each company. Here is another illustration from my files, a bulletin from the entertainment industry: a headline reads, "Violence in Media Aimed at Young, FTC

---

3. This incident is recounted more fully in my book *The Bible and "The New York Times"* (Grand Rapids: Eerdmans, 1999). An important aspect of my friend's outburst is that he had a deep sense of the infinite variety of inner handicaps, drives, and propensities that characterize human beings over which they have little control. One person may be more brave than another in a given situation owing to factors that were present without that person's deserving, such as a brave father's example (on the positive side) or a neurotic need to perform heroics (on the more negative side).

4. *The New York Times* ran front-page articles on McWain for four consecutive days in early 2002, with photos of severely injured men. (Several died.)

Study Says. Denial from Hollywood."[5] Reading on, we see that various entertainment officials deny that their companies deliberately direct their advertising towards children, but "studio executives acknowledged privately that the reports had some validity. 'Everyone's hands are dirty,'" said one executive who chose to remain unidentified.

Also in my file is a famous photograph, often reproduced. It shows a group of beautiful girls, about sixteen or seventeen, dressed impeccably in the fashion of the early sixties, with gleaming hair, flawless makeup, and fresh, pretty dresses. They look like debutantes. They look like daughters we would be proud to have. But something is wrong with the picture. The faces of the girls are contorted. They are screaming something. They look as though they are consumed with anger and hate. The caption on the photograph is "Montgomery, Alabama, 1963." It is the time of the Montgomery Bus Boycott, and the young women are screaming at black people.

Were these girls evil? or were they just young people who didn't know any better? These young women would be ten years younger than I am now. I wonder what they think of that picture of themselves today. Forty years ago one of them might have been me, or you, captured in sin by the camera for life. There is a saying that you have all heard: "There but for the grace of God go I."[6] It isn't in the Bible, but it is a profoundly biblical idea; think for instance of Psalm 130:3, "If thou, O Lord, shouldst mark iniquities, Lord, who could stand?" In other words, if God were to count up our sins, we would all be condemned.

"Everyone's hands are dirty." "There is none righteous, no, not one."

So this morning we are placing the emphasis on the predicament that you and I share, every single one of us here today. "Evil lies

---

5. *The New York Times,* February 2002.

6. As recounted elsewhere in this volume, the quotation is attributed to a seventeenth-century English Puritan, John Bradford. He was watching some convicts led through the streets of London to be executed, and he said, "There but for the grace of God goes John Bradford." Obviously this has important implications for the death penalty issue.

close at hand." Who said that? Well, actually, it was St. Paul. "I find it to be a law that when I want to do right, evil lies close at hand." And he continues: "I do not understand my own actions. For I do not do what I want, but I do the very thing I hate. . . . I can will what is right, but I cannot do it. For I do not do the good I want, but the evil I do not want is what I do. Now if I do what I do not want, it is no longer I that do it, but sin which dwells within me" (Romans 7:15-20). Is there anyone here today who does not recognize this?

The human being is in the grip of impulses that are more powerful than our wish to do good. A poignant story was told me just recently by one who had participated in it. It concerned a much beloved and very distinguished man, the head of a prominent institution and a deeply committed Christian. After his wife died it became obvious that he was sinking into the morass of alcoholism. (No doubt he had been drinking all along but his wife had covered up for him. This was in the 60s, before we knew what we know now about alcoholic intervention.) Three colleagues of equal stature made a formal call on their friend. They told him in some detail what his drinking was doing to him, his work, his relationships, and his legacy. They poured out their souls into this difficult confrontation and it left them emotionally exhausted. At the end of the call, the man who was the object of their concern thanked them for their godly visit and solemnly promised them that he would stop drinking. They went away grateful, feeling that their mission had been accomplished, because, as one of them told me, "we knew John to be a man of his word." It seems incredibly naive now, doesn't it? Great was their disillusionment when it became clear that he was not going to stop, could not stop, and in fact, in the end, drank himself to death. The three friends had disastrously underestimated the power of the forces holding him in thrall.

Our Lord wants us to know of the power of these forces. In the words of Jesus in the Gospels, in the writings of St. Paul, we are told over and over in various ways that the powers we face are untiring, malevolent, and extremely clever. These powers seek nothing less than our destruction. But we are not defenseless. The apostle counsels us:

Put on the whole armor of God, that you may be able to stand against the wiles of the devil. For we are not contending against flesh and blood, but against the principalities, against the powers, against the world rulers of this present darkness, against the spiritual hosts of wickedness in the heavenly places. (Ephesians 6:10-17)

The forces that we face are overwhelming, and the suffering that they cause is incalculable. The Christian should not be deceived about this. Our Lord warned his disciples of the terrors they faced (this is the text for the last Sunday before Advent):

When you hear of wars and rumors of wars, do not be alarmed; this must take place, but the end is not yet. For nation will rise against nation, and kingdom against kingdom; there will be earthquakes in various places, there will be famines; this is but the beginning of the birth-pangs. . . . you will be hated by all for my name's sake. But he who endures to the end will be saved. . . . (Mark 13:7-13)

And then the Lord says, "I have told you all things beforehand" (Mark 13:23). Jesus wants us to know ahead of time that the Christian life is going to be a long struggle against evil, sin, and death — most of all, the evil, sin, and death that threatens our own being.

It is important that we use the word "we" when we say the Confession in the worship service. That "we" points toward our solidarity in the sin of Adam. The clearest exposition of this solidarity is found in Romans 5:12-21. Paul gives all humankind the name of Adam. The fraternity of Adam is the most comprehensive community of all, for it is universal. "Sin came into the world through one person and death through sin, and so death spread to all humanity because all humans sinned" (5:12). This is repeated in 1 Corinthians 15:22: "In Adam all die." Human solidarity in bondage to the power of sin is one of the most important of all concepts for Christians to grasp.

At the same time, though, saying the words of the Confession communally in church does not always cause us to appropriate its truth deep in our being. All of us need to say also (in the words of Thomas Cranmer's General Confession) "*I* have erred and strayed from God's ways like a lost sheep. *I* have followed too much the devices and desires of *my own* heart." This is not so easy for us. All of us, to one degree or another, participate in that psychological phenomenon famously called *denial.* Denial, or avoidance, is a way of keeping consciousness of sin at bay. We think we can make sin go away by pretending it is not there; we are like the little girl who says, "I've got my eyes closed so nobody can see me." Many parish clergy will tell of the frustration they feel when attempting to counsel parishioners with stubborn problems when there is no willingness to acknowledge any fault, accept any blame, or acknowledge any need for change. I think of one churchgoing couple in particular. The wife was dying inside because the husband would not accept his part of the struggle to hold the marriage together. He did not think there was any problem. He did not see that there was anything he needed to do differently. He said, "If Janet would just let go of all these complaints, everything would be fine."

The line between good and evil runs through each person. The tragedy, the true tragedy, is not to see it in oneself. The truly tragic person is not the one who commits a crime or causes harm to others; the truly tragic person is the one who causes harm and never repents of it, never admits it even to himself. That person is blocked from receiving the promise of the gospel that God's grace is retroactive. If it weren't, the promise it holds out to us would be empty. God's power is able to make right all that has happened in the past. Paul seldom uses the word "forgiveness." His stronger word is "justification." Justification means that we sinners will not only be *forgiven,* we will be *justified,* which means that we will be set right by the power of God, and all who have suffered as a result of our faults will have perfect restitution.

How can this be?

The sacrifice of Jesus our Lord is this: he has gone into the Day of Judgment utterly alone, separated from the Father, taking the sentence of condemnation upon himself, bearing it away from us.

This is the gospel. This is the good news of the Christian faith. There has been an invasion from on high. The landing troops have arrived. Neutrality is no longer possible. Satan is slashing and burning, but he is in retreat. His time will come. There is no longer any room for self-deception, excuses, denial or evasion, for as C. S. Lewis puts it, "Fallen man is not simply an imperfect creature who needs improvement; he is a rebel who must lay down his arms."[7] It is the Lord Jesus Christ who disarms us.

But listen: we are not *disarmed* in order to be *disempowered.* There is *"power* in the blood of the Lamb." It is the power of the Word of God which spoke, *and it was so.* It is the power that overcame Satan in the wilderness. It is the power that lifted the paralyzed man to his feet. It is the power that spoke through the voice of the Son of God when he said, "Peace! Be still!" and the wind and waves obeyed their Creator. It is the power that sustains every Christian in the struggles of this life. This power is able to do things that we can only dream about. For this is the might of the God in whom Abraham believed, the God whose power "raises the dead and calls into existence the things that do not exist" (Romans 4:17). The God who reckoned Abraham righteous is the God who justifies sinners. For the righteousness reckoned to Abraham was *not for his sake alone, but for ours also.* The promise of God to sinners today is that "it will be reckoned to us who believe in him that raised from the dead Jesus our Lord" (Romans 4:24).

AMEN.

7. C. S. Lewis, *Mere Christianity* (New York: Macmillan, 1953), p. 59.

But Now . . .

But now the righteousness of God has been manifested apart from law . . . the righteousness of God through faith in Jesus Christ for all who believe.

ROMANS 3:21-22

When Paul the apostle sat down (or rather, stood up, for we believe he dictated his letters) to write to his churches, he always began with the good news, not the bad. Even in the case of the Galatian church, which was provoking him almost to apoplexy, he begins with a short but particularly powerful statement of the gospel (Galatians 1:1-5). So we can say as a theological principle of the first order that the proclamation of the Christian faith never begins with sin, but with grace and mercy. The story of God and his world begins and comes to its consummation in his inexhaustible love.

However, in a time such as ours when one hardly hears anything about sin at all, it is an enormous challenge for preachers to know what to do with the pervasive and overwhelming testimony of the Bible about sin. Throughout the entire Old and New Testaments, sin is a huge presence. If we are not prepared to talk about sin, we really cannot read the Bible at all.

The subject of sin in the context of Romans leads us right away into the subject of the relation of the apostle Paul to the teaching of Jesus. People are confused about this. It has often been said that Paul, with his rigorous and complex intellect, took the simple story of Jesus and spoiled it with complex doctrine. It is true that Paul virtually never refers to the teaching of Jesus, nor to the story of his life — with the all-important exception of the Crucifixion and Resurrection. But this set of priorities is precisely what we all need to understand in order to be Christians. It is Paul who turns our attention to the central core of our faith and orients us fully to appropriate it. All of us need to make a decision: will we read the letters of Paul as secondary to the four Gospels, or will we read them as an indispensable — indeed *the* indispensable — commentary on them? Certainly the early Church was clear about this, for if they had not been, they would not have placed Paul's letters so reverently at the center of the New Testament, so that they make up the largest portion of it by any one writer.

Equally if not more important is the fact that Paul's letters were written much earlier than the versions of the Gospels that we have today. The "Jesus tradition" circulated orally for a long time before it was put down in the form of Matthew, Mark, Luke, and John. The earliest letter of Paul (1 Thessalonians) dates from no more than twenty to twenty-five years after the Resurrection, whereas most scholars date the Gospels from after the Roman destruction of the Temple in AD 70. When the average person dismisses Paul as secondary to the Gospels, he or she is generally unaware of this dating.[1]

If we did not have Paul's teaching about sin, we would not really know what it is. The Apostle proclaims that when Jesus of Nazareth appeared among us as the incarnate Christ, was "crucified, dead and buried" (to use the words of the Creed), and on the third day raised, it changed everything. As Paul puts it in 1 Corinthians:

---

1. For the general reader interested in tracking down dates and other issues related to the writing and collection of Paul's Epistles, Raymond E. Brown's *Introduction to the New Testament* (New York: Doubleday, 1997) can't be bettered. Theologically, Brown is better on the Gospels than on Paul, but for meticulous thoroughness and clarity of expression he is in a class by himself.

From now on, therefore, we regard no one from a human point of view; even though we once regarded Christ from a human point of view, we regard him thus no longer. Therefore, if any one is in Christ, he is a new creation; the old has passed away, behold, the new has come. (1 Corinthians 5:16-17)

It is Paul who hammers home the fact that in Christ something utterly unprecedented has occurred, something that makes us look at everything in a new light. This was foretold by the prophet Isaiah ("Behold, I am doing a new thing . . ." 43:19) but shown by Paul to have actually happened in Jesus Christ. The story in Luke 4 about Jesus' inaugural sermon in the synagogue at Capernaum makes this same point, but not with the same clarity and thrust as Paul; we do not know the Old Testament background so we do not readily get the point of Luke's story, which is that the very presence of Jesus is the sign that the Messianic age has arrived.

Similarly, we can read the Gospels from year to year and not understand what sin is unless we have Paul to explain it to us. In the Gospels, it is easy to think of sin as cheating taxpayers, adultery, stealing, abandoning one's sheep, withholding money from God, being hypocritical, and various other discrete acts which can be defined as "sins." We read that Jesus eats with sinners, and we assume that this means people who have been condemned by society for their specific sinful actions. When the Lord says "I did not come to call the righteous, but sinners" (Matthew 9:13), we naturally assume that he divides up the world into two categories that way, so we do the same. It comes as a surprise to us therefore, in Romans 3, when we hear Paul say,

> All human beings, both Jews and Gentiles, are under the power of sin . . . None is righteous, no, not one . . . There is no distinction . . . All have sinned and fall short of the glory of God . . .

"Under the power of sin." That is the clue. Sin (with a capital letter) is not the same thing as sin*s*. Sin*s* are individual misdeeds that you can tot up at the end of the day, or that God will add up at the end of your life. You can make a list of sins and then congratulate yourself because you haven't committed very many of them. If we think of Sin in this way we will never understand what the Son of God came to do.

Sin is not the sum total of a bunch of individual transgressions. Sin is the fundamental condition of man, the disease that we have all got, "a deep interior dislocation in the very center of human personality."[2] The human race is enmeshed in the consequences of a vast primordial catastrophe, as John Cardinal Newman put it. The world has been thrown violently off course by an alien power hostile to God, and paradoxically, each of us is responsible for his own part in the resulting mess. According to Paul, Sin is both "an enslaving power" external to man, and "man's own culpable act" for which each human being singly and all human beings collectively deserve the judgment of God.[3] This is true whether we know it or not, whether we feel it or not. Paul does not begin his discussion of Sin with subjective feelings of guilt, which his hearers may or may not have; he begins with our objective situation before God as fallen creatures in bondage to a Power far greater than we are. The tragedies and follies and depredations that we see all around us in our world are signs that "the wrath of God is revealed from heaven against all ungodliness and wickedness of human beings" (Romans 1:18).

So, to recap what we've said, the prologue to Paul's story (and it *is* a story, even though it might not look like one) is his declaration of God's mighty acts of redemption: "I am not ashamed of the gospel, for it is the power of God for salvation" (Romans 1:16). Only when he has made this clear does he embark upon his long passage about the Wrath of God against Sin, which goes on for two chapters and a half. In the course of this passage he is counting on us to understand that God's wrath is against *Sin,* not against *us.* We *experience* the Wrath of God in the form of all the terrible things that happen, but if we listen carefully to Paul's story, we learn that this Wrath is not God's bad temper, as if he were an irritable parent prone to rages, but

2. Dorothy L. Sayers, in *Creed or Chaos.*
3. Günther Bornkamm, *Paul* (New York: Harper & Row, 1971), pp. 124, 126.

his implacable opposition to the evil Power than holds his creatures in bondage. God's enmity toward Sin is not capricious or malign. It is the face of God turned steadily and with unshakable purpose toward the Enemy of his creation. Thus it is possible for us to acknowledge our own identity as sinful creatures and yet, at the same time, rejoice to know that God is on our side against our common Foe. When we recognize ourselves in Paul's description, "All human beings are under the power of Sin," we are already safely placed where that Power can no longer do us ultimate harm.

But how people do resist the power of Sin! G. K. Chesterton once said that "Original Sin is the only Christian doctrine that is empirically verifiable," but still we stubbornly refuse to see it. We cling to the myth of our own innocence. Many times I have listened to people protesting that there could not possibly be such a thing as Original Sin when I knew, even as they spoke, that they and their parents and their children and their children's children were locked into a pattern of family pathology that was being handed down from generation to generation.

"I have a sense of everything closing in on me," said a woman to me not long ago. That is the power of Sin that she feels, and she is both responsible and not responsible for it. I pray for a way to tell her that her feeling is already a sign that God's grace is at work in her life. People who have a sense of the tragedy and the futility of life are living closer to the truth than those who are perpetually trying to "live on the sunny side." You cannot know that you are lost until deliverance has begun to dawn on you. The darkness of Sin is revealed by the rising Sun of oncoming salvation. This is the clue, the paradox that only the Christian understands: the knowledge of Sin is given only to those who have begun to know the mercy of God.

In the year 1515, a German monk named Martin Luther sat in his study poring over the words of Paul to the Romans.[4] During the months and years preceding, Luther had been on the brink of an

---

4. This is not entirely accurate because I have not mentioned Galatians, which was even more important to Luther as an initial catalyst for theological transformation, but the basic outline of the great conversion stands, I think.

abyss of despair. In all human history we know of few who have suffered as acutely on account of their own sinfulness as did Luther. He tried everything: confession, penance, mysticism, the sacraments, self-mortification, spiritual counsel of every kind. Nothing worked. He felt himself utterly condemned before God, with no hope of escape. His biographer describes it: "He had arrived at a valid impasse. Sins, to be forgiven, must be confessed. If they are not recognized and remembered, they cannot be confessed. If they are not confessed, they cannot be forgiven."[5] Try as he might, Brother Martin could not remember them all or call them all by name. He believed himself lost, pronounced guilty before the divine tribunal.

Again and again Luther read to himself the words of Paul in Romans 1:16-17, where Paul sets out his theme: "In [the gospel], the righteousness of God is revealed through faith for faith." The word "gospel" (*evangel* in Greek) means "good news." *The good news is that God's righteousness is revealed.* How could this be good news? Wouldn't the revelation of God's righteousness be bad news? The very thought of God's righteousness made Luther tremble. After all, it was the contrast between God's righteousness and his own unrighteousness that made him tremble. What did Paul mean? Luther continued to struggle with the text:

> I am not ashamed of the gospel: it is the power of God for salvation to everyone who has faith . . . for in it [the gospel] the righteousness of God is revealed through faith for faith. As it is written, he who through faith is righteous will live. (Romans 1:16-17)

And he read this:

> Sin came into the world through one man [Adam] and Death through Sin, and so death spread to all men because all men sinned. . . .

5. Roland H. Bainton, *Here I Stand: A Life of Martin Luther* (New York: Mentor Books, 1950), p. 42.

[But] if many died through one man's trespass, much more have the grace of God and the free gift in the grace of that one man Jesus Christ abounded for many. . . . For the judgment following one trespass [of Adam] brought condemnation, but the free gift following many trespasses [of all humanity] brings justification. . . .

Then as one man's [Adam's] trespass led to condemnation for all men, so one man's [Jesus Christ's] act of righteousness leads to acquittal and life for all men. For as by one man's disobedience many were made sinners, so by one man's obedience many will be made righteous. . . . where sin increased, grace abounded all the more, so that, as sin reigned in death, grace also might reign through righteousness to eternal life through Jesus Christ our Lord. (Romans 5:12-21)

And Martin Luther, wrestling with the Greek text, began to see something that you and I, reading the English text, cannot see: he saw that the word meaning *righteousness,* as in "the righteousness of God," and the word meaning *justification* or *acquittal,* as in "Christ's act of righteousness leads to acquittal and life for all men" (5:18), were in fact the same word. *The same word!* Luther began to realize that God had acted in Jesus Christ powerfully to impute[6] his righteousness to us, even though we had done nothing to deserve it. Luther saw that God had *justified* (*made righteous,* same word) sinful man, thereby enabling him to stand with robes washed clean before the heavenly throne. In the Cross of Christ, Luther suddenly saw, the wrath and mercy of God were fused. The heavy door slammed in the face of humanity began to move on its great hinges as Paul says, "But now . . ."

6. The classic word for this is "impute," to be distinguished from "infuse." This distinction continues at the center of Lutheran-Catholic disagreements. The dispute can be moved several steps forward if we translate the word "justification" (*dikaiosunē*) as "rectification," thus preserving the word both as a noun (justification/rectification) and as a verb (justify/rectify). Thus God does not simply pronounce the sinner to be justified; he is powerfully acting in the life of the Christian (and of the cosmos) to rectify all that is wrong.

Listen as Paul says *But now!* It is the "world-transforming *now*," the passage from the old condemned life to the free justified life, the act of God in Christ to transform "the old lost man" into "the new one set free by God,"[7] the pivot between the evil aeon of Sin and Death and the new one of righteousness and life. The great "but now" is the fulcrum on which the ages turn, the hinge of salvation.

> But now the righteousness of God has been manifested apart from law . . . the righteousness of God through faith in Jesus Christ for all who believe. For there is no distinction; since all have sinned and fall short of the glory of God, they are justified by his grace as a gift, through the redemption which is in Christ Jesus, whom God put forward as an expiation by his blood, to be received by faith. This was to show God's righteousness . . . it was to prove at the present time that he himself is *righteous* and that he *justifies* [same word!] the one who has faith in Jesus.

And for Luther, and for every other Christian who has been grasped by this great good news, it seemed as though the righteous Judge himself had gotten up off the bench and come down into the dock to stand alongside the guilty prisoner and pronounce him free. The terrifying righteousness of God had become God's power reaching out for the world, recapturing the world and the individual human being for himself.[8] In Luther's own words, "The whole of Scripture took on a new meaning, and whereas before 'the righteousness of God' had filled me with hate, now it became to me inexpressibly sweet in greater love. This passage of Paul became to me a gate to heaven. . . ."[9]

Thus Paul expounds and emphasizes what the four Gospels illustrate. Our gracious Lord does not wait for us to perfect ourselves. He sees us entangled in Sin and Death, and he comes to

---

7. Bornkamm, *Paul,* pp. 118, 121.

8. Ernst Käsemann, "The Righteousness of God in Paul," in *New Testament Questions of Today* (Philadelphia: Fortress Press, 1969), p. 182.

9. Quoted in Bainton, *Here I Stand,* p. 50.

meet us and liberate us from the grip of this terrible Enemy. He comes to meet us when we are at our very worst, for when he was crucified there we were, the human race at its utmost worst. If we think we are above and beyond the judgment of God, then we will remain ignorant of his righteousness. Robert M. Cooper has said: "The Christian doctrine of sin leads us to believe that for the most part people will do what they want to if they can, and that if necessary they will find some justification for doing so and continuing to do so." But if we know ourselves for what we really are, rebellious creatures caught in a web of our own making but unable to extricate ourselves, then we will hear and receive with joy the great good news from the apostle:

So:

- if you are troubled by anything you have ever done
- or if you are troubled by something you are afraid you might do
- or if you are troubled by the damage you have done to your children
- or if you are plagued by some secret darkness that you hardly dare admit even to yourself
- or if you are sickened by the cruelty and the senselessness in the world
- or if you acknowledge your own participation in systems that cause prejudice and pollution and poverty and war
- or indeed if you are in any sense aware that before God all our lives are poor, distorted, and miserable

then rejoice! For to you the power of God for salvation is revealed today. "While we were still sinners," Paul says, "Christ died for us . . . While we were still helpless, Christ died for the ungodly" (Romans 5:6, 8).

"Behold, now is the acceptable time; behold, now is the day of salvation" (2 Corinthians 6:2). Now, today. Now is the time to recognize that world-transforming event occurring in your own life. Now is the time to see that Sin and Death no longer have dominion over you (Romans 6:9-11). We were "tied and bound by the chain of our sins," but Christ our Lord "was put to death for our trespasses and raised for our justification" (Romans 4:25).

For in fact, the righteousness of God is Jesus our Lord himself.

AMEN.

Guilt and Innocence

TEXT: ROMANS 3:9-10, 21-25

Palm Sunday is the Trojan horse of the church year. You remember the story from Greek mythology: a huge, splendid wooden horse was accepted by the Trojans as a present from the Greeks (so it really ought to be called the Greek horse, but never mind). The horse was wheeled in through the walls of the city of Troy. In the night, Greek soldiers hidden in the horse slipped out and admitted the Greek army, who proceeded to sack the city.

Palm Sunday is a little bit like that. My grandchildren say its their favorite Sunday of the year, but when pressed to say why, they say they like the palms and especially the palm crosses that their father makes for them. It's really a set-up. What we do is, we lure you in here with palm-waving and festivity, but we have smuggled in the Passion narrative and you have found yourselves shouting "Crucify him!" On this day, the ancient liturgy of the Church brings us to Jerusalem to participate in an atrocity. Thus the proper name for this day is not Palm Sunday, but Passion Sunday. Today in Jerusalem a crime is committed, and we are the perpetrators.

It is my impression that since September 11, 2001, two English words have become much more frequently used than they were before, in my lifetime anyway — one is "hero" — and the other is "innocent." It is the word "innocent" that is especially relevant on this Palm Sunday, the Sunday of the Passion.

Innocence can mean two rather different things, depending on how it's used. When we say that the people who died in the World Trade Center were *innocent,* what we mean is that they, as individuals, had done absolutely nothing to provoke the murderous rage of the men who flew the planes into the towers. To give another example, we use the word "innocent" to describe a person who is shot in a crossfire by a bullet intended for someone else. The words "innocent bystander" go together. When we say "innocent" in this context, there can't be much argument about its suitability.

But there is another way of using the word "innocent" that is more problematic. Take for instance the so-called myth of American innocence. All of us grew up with this myth. It was enacted in the movies by iconic stars like John Wayne and Jimmy Stewart, who could do no wrong to save their lives. The French, the Germans, the Japanese, the Russians: *they* were cynical or villainous or cruel or devious, but *Americans* were wholesome and upstanding. The distribution of the photographs from Abu Ghraib two years ago was widely described as "the end of American innocence."[1] We protested against this for many months, saying, "But these were just a few out-of-control rogues, a handful of rotten apples!" After two years of testimony from numerous Army and Marine personnel and the disclosure of many details from American prisons and from Guantánamo, it is no longer possible to hold that view.

Yes, Palm Sunday — the Sunday of the Passion — is the Trojan horse. We are besieged not from without, but *from within.*

Sweeping declarations of innocence contradict a fundamental truth of the Christian faith. In his letter to the Christians in Rome, St. Paul teaches at length about guilt and innocence. Sin is not a mistake here and a misjudgment there. Sin is a Power that has seized control of the human race. The story of Adam and Eve was

---

1. This phrase has been used before, for instance in regard to the massacre at My Lai. It was also used at the time of the Oklahoma City bombing, and again at 9/11, but in those cases it was used to mean that America could no longer consider itself immune to terrorism. My Lai is a good example, but there were no globally distributed photographs (or, indeed, any photographs at all). This factor among others meant that the worldwide reaction to Abu Ghraib and the consequent soiling of the American image has been hugely greater than that of My Lai.

not meant to be taken literally; it is a story that explains to us how things got to be the way they are. Since Adam, Paul writes:

> All human beings, both Jews and Greeks, are under the power of sin, as it is written: "None is righteous, no, not one."

Paul is quoting one of the Psalms when he says "there is no one righteous." The oldest parts of the Old Testament teach the same thing about sin using a different set of concepts. The position of humanity before God is that of gross impurity confronted by perfect holiness. Sin defined this way is a *condition,* a *contagion* which infects us all, with no more respect for our moral credentials than a germ or virus has.

Take for instance the current case of the lacrosse team at Duke University.[2] We do not know what happened there, but we do know that since the alleged assault no one so far has come forward to break the wall of silence, and we know that a truly vile email was sent by a team member within two hours of the episode. Now as it happens, five members of the team are graduates of an exclusive boys' prep school, the Delbarton School in Morristown, New Jersey. It is a Catholic school, run by an order of Benedictine monks whose purpose states that they intentionally seek to teach Christian values. You can imagine how proud they were to have five students at highly selective Duke. When the news of the alleged attack by the lacrosse team broke, as you can imagine, the school was besieged by calls from the media. *The New York Times* spoke with the Catholic priest who is the headmaster. He said, "These are wonderful boys from wonderful families; we're all worried for them."[3]

---

2. At the time of this sermon the media were consumed by this case of possible rape.

3. "Scrutiny of Duke Players Builds," *The New York Times,* March 30, 2006. Subsequent to the preaching of this sermon the prosecution's case was undermined by a number of factors, including changing testimonies by witnesses and by the supposed victim, as well as a strong alibi for one of the young men accused (the case was later dismissed for lack of evidence). This does not at all affect the point made here, which revolves largely around the email. There was never any doubt about the authenticity or the vileness of the email.

The headmaster now regrets that he made such a sweeping statement. How do I know that? Because I called him on the phone. I asked him if he wanted to rethink what he had said. I could feel his distress as I spoke with him, and my heart went out to him. It was obvious that he loved his school and his students and that this episode has shaken him to the core. The revelation of the email that one of his boys had sent was the factor that pulled the rug out from under him. He said he had called the schoolboys together and talked to them in impassioned terms about the sinfulness of violent, misogynist, racially motivated hate speech.

"These are wonderful boys from wonderful families." Perhaps we should be more careful about the way we romanticize each other. The headmaster wants very much to believe in the innocence of his boys, as all of us want to believe in the innocence of our children. But perhaps this is naïve. In a very important sense there are no wonderful children from wonderful families. Every family — *every* family has its dysfunctional aspects. Every human being no matter how "wonderful" is capable of certain things under certain conditions, especially when acting as part of a group. Many of you will remember the novel *Lord of the Flies.* After the climax in which terrible deeds are done by the "innocent" marooned schoolboys, the novel ends on the explicit note of "the loss of innocence" and "the darkness of man's heart." "Sin came into the world through one man and death through sin, and so death spread to all men" (Romans 5:12) Yet we still resist this truth, don't we?

At the end of this service we will sing one of our greatest hymns, "Ah, holy Jesus." This hymn is sung during Holy Week. Pay special attention to the second verse:

Who was the guilty? Who brought this upon thee?
Alas, my treason, Jesus, hath undone thee.
'Twas I, Lord Jesus, I it was denied thee,
I crucified thee.[4]

4. By Johann Heermann (1585-1647).

"I crucified thee." This is what we confess when, on Palm Sunday, we play the part of the people in the crowd who shout, "Crucify him!" This is in many ways the most profound moment of the church year. Even if we do not understand exactly what is going on, we sense that the dramatic reading of the Passion means that somehow we are *not innocent bystanders.* We are *implicated* in the event. I remember a woman in my first parish who took great pride in not participating in the shout of "Crucify him!" "I just couldn't say it!" she announced at coffee hour afterward. "I couldn't possibly say those words!" I knew this woman well. Her whole life was organized around the myth of her own innocence. I felt sad for her; her self-righteousness cut her off from the truth — the truth about herself and the truth about our Lord Jesus Christ.

Very few Episcopal parishes today still use Thomas Cranmer's great General Confession. I hope some of you, at least, remember it: "We have followed too much the devices and desires of our own hearts. . . . We have left undone those things which we ought to have done, and we have done those things which we ought not to have done, and there is no health in us." We are imprisoned in Sin, and "the wages of sin is death" (Romans 6:23).

Today is the day that we begin to prepare to see our Lord as he really is, not handsome and haloed, but marred, broken, bloodied — submitting himself fully to the power of Sin, Evil, and Death. I particularly commend to you the service of Maundy Thursday. On Thursday of Holy Week we re-enact the agony of our Lord in the Garden of Gethsemane as he prepares to meet his destiny. As long as the Lord allows me to retain my wits I will never forget the impression the Maundy Thursday service had on me as a young person. I urge you to bring children to this service, anyone seven or eight and older. It is an unforgettable moment in the church year. On this night we see our Lord Jesus abandoned, betrayed, given up to the powers of darkness.

Why did he do this? Why did the Son of God do this?

Listen: He is the only innocent One. He is the only innocent One who has ever lived. The innocent One placed himself squarely in the path of the annihilating Powers. He interposed himself between Sin and us.

We are hearing a great deal these days about how early Christianity was a mixed bag, how there were all these Gnostic gospels, how there was a wicked orthodox conspiracy to suppress alternative truth. We hear a lot about how we are all on a spiritual journey, how all religions are basically the same. These religious ideas have always been popular with the self-defined righteous, the spiritual elite. That's what the Pharisees were — the righteous. That's what the Gnostics were — the spiritual elite. There is a certain titillating quality to *The Da Vinci Code* and *The Gospel of Judas*. It is always tempting to cast oneself in the role of the virtuous knight-errant exposing sinister conspiracies by powerful, oppressive forces.[5]

But there is one basic problem with all of this. These other gospels are fine — for the innocent. But there is only one gospel that has good news for the perps. Good news for the spiritual, good news for the righteous, good news for the innocent — that's easy. "God helps those who help themselves."[6] But the Christian gospel, dear friends, is good news for sinners. "While we were still helpless," Paul writes, "Christ died for the ungodly" (Romans 5:6).

Listen now once again to these great words from the Word of God:

> All human beings, both Jews and Greeks, are under the power of sin, as it is written:
> "None is righteous, no, not one. . . ."
> But now the righteousness of God has been manifested . . . through faith in Jesus Christ for all who believe. For there is no distinction; since all have sinned and fall short of the glory of God, they are justified by his grace as a gift, through the redemption which is in Christ Jesus, whom God put forward as an expiation by his blood, to be received by faith.

> AMEN.

5. When this sermon was preached, a cascade of mega-hype was flooding the media concerning the meretricious *Da Vinci Code* movie and the dramatically timed announcement by *National Geographic* that the Gospel of Judas had been "discovered." (Irenaeus knew it was nonsense in the third century.)

6. Contrary to popular opinion, there is nothing like this in the Bible.

Why Did He Do It?

Tonight I invite you to reflect on two passages from the letters of St. Paul. The first is the one you have just heard read, from Philippians (a different translation):

> Christ Jesus, though he was in the form *(morphē)* of God, did not count equality with God a thing to be clutched at [or held on to], but emptied himself, taking the form *(morphē)* of a slave, being born in the likeness of men. And being found in human form *(morphē)* he humbled himself and became obedient unto death, even death on a cross. (Philippians 2:7-8)

And from Romans, this passage:

> All human beings, both Jews and Greeks, are under the power of sin, as it is written:
> "None is righteous, no, not one. . . ."
> But now the righteousness of God has been manifested . . . through faith in Jesus Christ for all who believe. For there is no distinction; since all have sinned and fall short of the glory of God, they are justified by his grace as a gift, through the redemption which is in Christ Jesus, whom God put forward as an expiation by his blood, to be received by faith. (Romans 3:9-10, 21-24)

About the first passage, we're going to ask "Why?" Then we will look at the second passage to find the answer.

Why did our Lord empty himself of his divinity? That's what Paul tells us he did. He was in the form of God, but he did not regard equality with God something to be grasped, clutched, held on to. One of the most characteristic things that we see children doing is clutching things. If a child thinks that someone else is going to take away his favorite toy, he clutches it and says, "Mine!" When the child grows up, he knows better than to say "mine!" in such an obvious way, but he (or she) *acts* the same way. If we think someone is going to spoil our neighborhood and drive down our property values, we say "mine!" and circle the wagons. If we are Republicans and we think the Democrats are going to take our Congressional seats (or *vice versa*), we will say things we might not otherwise say in order to hold on to power. Our Lord Jesus Christ is exactly the opposite. He was in the form of God, but he did not clutch at his divinity, but emptied himself, poured himself out, entered into the realm of sin and death.

Why would God do that? It is hard for us to imagine this exchange. If you lived in paradise, would you voluntarily leave where you are and come down into the mud, blood, and refuse of a world full of wickedness? C. S. Lewis says it's as if God had exchanged his divine form to become a slug. Why would God do that?

First let's notice something very basic but often not understood. This passage has what we call in the profession a very high Christology. Don't be alarmed by the fancy terminology; it means something very simple: Jesus of Nazareth, the human being, was God incarnate, God become man. He was God before he became a man. Well, actually it's not so simple, because he was the Second Person of the Blessed Trinity, but we won't get into that tonight. He was in the form of God. He was not what Karen Armstrong calls "an axial sage" along with various other religious geniuses. He was not, as so many people assume, a rarely gifted spiritual leader with a special program leading to illumination. He was not, as many are now teaching even from within the church, a highly evolved human being who gave us a uniquely admirable example. Paul was writing no more than thirty years after the Resurrection when he declared that *Christ Jesus was in the form of God* before he was a man. St. John teaches that he was in the form of God before the creation (John 1:1-3). So this is what you call a high Christology. This is important, because many of the religious teachers that you hear about today have a low Christology. They are for the most part very respectful of the man Jesus, the sage, the healer, the religious genius, but they certainly don't believe that he was God.

In the Nicene Creed we say, "I believe in Jesus Christ our Lord, begotten of his Father before all worlds, God of God, Light of Light, Very God of Very God." That's the church's confession and if we don't believe this foundational truth we might as well turn this building into a museum of the history of religion.

But again our question: Why did God do this? Why did he empty himself in a way that no one else ever has, in a way that no other religion ever conceived? To be sure, the ancient Mediterranean world was full of dying and rising gods. There were plenty of gods in human form, too, a dime a dozen. The differences between these gods and the Trinity of Christian faith are much greater than the resemblances. Unlike all the other mythical figures from that time, Jesus Christ was a historical figure who really lived and really died. That in itself would not mean anything earth-shaking. Paul, however, makes literally earth-shaking claims: "Christ Jesus, though he was in the form of God, did not count equality with God a thing to be grasped, but emptied himself, taking the form of a slave, being born in the likeness of men. And being found in human form he humbled himself and became obedient unto death, even death on a cross. Therefore God has highly exalted him and bestowed on him the name which is above every name, that at the name of Jesus every knee should bow, in heaven and on earth and under the earth."

This human being who was condemned to a slave's death by all the best people of church and state is the Name above every name, enthroned as the Lord of heaven and earth, the Savior of the entire cosmos and everything in it.

But for the third time, why? Why the human form? Above all, why the slave's death on the Cross?

Here are Paul's words in Romans 3:

> Since all have sinned and fall short of the glory of God, they are justified by his grace as a gift, through the redemption which is in Christ Jesus, whom God put forward as an expiation by his blood, to be received by faith.

The blood of Christ, Paul declares, has accomplished something that has changed the course of history and the direction of the universe. God did this. God in Jesus Christ put himself forward as a sacrifice for sin, *as a gift.* Today we are so accustomed to having banks and cosmetic companies offer us a "free gift!" that we tend to forget that of course a gift is free; that is its nature. If it isn't free, it isn't a gift. The death of Christ was the gift of God to us when we were utterly helpless and unable to do anything for ourselves. Why were we helpless? Because we were in bondage to the power of sin. Thus Paul writes: *All human beings, both Jews and Greeks, are under the power of sin. . . . "None is righteous, no, not one. . . ."*

Maybe you don't think this is true for you. If you don't think so, and a great many people don't, then you are refusing the greatest thing ever accomplished, the gift of the grace of God. Everybody sings "Amazing Grace" but a great many people who sing it haven't a clue what it means. The true sign of the grace of God at work is the confession of a redeemed sinner. If you think that you don't need anyone to die for your sins, then you don't need Christianity — or rather, you *think* you don't, which is another matter. If tonight, however, you know that you need a Savior, then you are blessed indeed. You can go home joyful and renewed. Christ emptied himself out, poured himself out, for you. He himself, God the Son, voluntarily offered himself up to die the death of one who was enslaved by sin and death, because that is exactly what *we* were — enslaved by sin and death. He took our place, he paid the price, he exchanged our destiny for his, so that we would be released from that dreadful bondage forever.

As our response to this incomparable message let us sing the next hymn prayerfully, with special emphasis on the last two, very personal verses:

For me, kind Jesus, was thy incarnation,
Thy mortal sorrow, and thy life's oblation;
Thy death of anguish and thy bitter passion,
For my salvation.

Therefore, kind Jesus, since I cannot pay thee,
I do adore thee, and will ever pray thee,
Think on thy pity, and thy love unswerving,
Not my deserving.

AMEN.

Wrath Redeemed

CHURCH OF ST. MICHAEL AND ST. GEORGE, ST. LOUIS
TEXT: ROMANS 3:9-25

This week's *Time* magazine features a remarkable essay by a retired three-star Marine Corps general, Gregory Newbold, who was the top operations officer for the military before the invasion of Iraq. He writes for two reasons: (1) to express regret that he was not more outspoken about his doubts before the invasion happened, and (2) to urge active-duty officers who have been silent about their concerns to speak out. He has very harsh words for the war planners in the Pentagon but takes blame for not opposing them more forcefully in the beginning. He acknowledges the reluctance of officers still in uniform to speak for attribution. Many Army and Marine officers in Iraq express unhappiness about the conduct of the war to their families back home, but they do not speak publicly.[1] It is traditional in American military life to respect civilian control of the armed forces, required by the Constitution, but there is another factor too. As one combat veteran said to a reporter, "The officer corps is willing to sacrifice their *lives* for their country, but not their *careers.*"[2] The point is illustrated by the well-known case of General Shinseki, whose distinguished career came to an ignoble end as he was shunted aside by the Defense Department for insisting that we

---

1. I know this through personal contacts as well as from the newspapers.
2. Thom Shanker, "Third Retired General Wants Rumsfeld Out," *The New York Times,* April 10, 2006.

[90]

needed many more boots on the ground in Iraq. This essay by General Newbold is depressing. It is *not good news.*

The letter to the Romans begins with the gospel, that is, *good news.* That is of first importance. It does not begin with bad news. It begins with a ringing introduction in which Paul sets out his theme, saying "I am not ashamed of the gospel, for it is the power of God for salvation to everyone who has faith, to the Jew first and also to the Greek" (Romans 1:16).

But then, startlingly, Paul shifts into the *bad news,* a long section on the Wrath of God that goes on for two and a half chapters. This section rewards careful study. The cumulative effect of this Wrath of God section is quite overwhelming. You think that you are off the hook at first, because Paul is going after *people other than you* (in this case, the Gentile heathen) but then he turns the charges around to indict the good religious people too, the ones who thought God approved of them (in this case, the Jews).[3] And so the section comes to a climax with a resounding summary of his case, pronouncing every single human being unrighteous before God and judged by God's law. Paul has assembled a number of passages from the Psalms and the prophet Isaiah to clinch his argument:

- none is righteous, no, not one
- all have turned aside, together they have gone wrong
- no one does good, not even one
- their throat is an open grave
- they use their tongues to deceive
- their feet are swift to shed blood
- in their paths are ruin and misery
- the way of peace they do not know
- there is no fear of God before their eyes

3. It's important to transpose Paul's terms "Jews" and "Greeks/Gentiles" into modern terms, to avoid implications of anti-Semitism that Paul did not intend. Karl Barth has taught us to think of "Jews," in today's terms, as religious people (church members, and/or generically "spiritual" people) and "Gentiles" as secular people.

Harsh condemnations, you will agree. This is not the sort of text that I would choose for a typical Sunday morning, but this is Holy Week, and you are a special collection of people because you are willing to come out to this service on a weeknight. So I am paying you the compliment of assuming that you are ready for some challenges.

We need always to remember something about the Wrath of God. The Wrath of God does not mean that God is enraged, or cruel, or wicked. Wrath is not an emotion of God. Wrath is the face of Holiness when it is turned toward Sin.[4] We said yesterday in the Palm Sunday sermon that the position of humanity before God is that of gross impurity confronted by perfect holiness. We need to deepen our understanding of the vast distance between ourselves and a righteous God. Habitual readers of Scripture would understand this, and would understand that "the fear of the Lord is the beginning of wisdom" as the Psalms and Proverbs repeatedly say, but unfortunately we are no longer habitual readers of Scripture, so we don't understand these things. If we are to take account of righteousness, our standing before God is less than nothing. It takes courage and honesty to see that — the courage and honesty that go along with true faith. By faith we see that *"All* are under the power of sin" (3:9), and *all* are condemned by God's law in one way or another — not only those who know the law, but also those who are *a law unto themselves* (that's where that expression comes from, by the way — Romans 2:14). Sin is a Power in partnership with the Law (Romans 7), and "Law brings wrath" because of our utter failure to keep it (Romans 4:15). Paul concludes that in the end, the Law declares "the whole world held accountable to God," and "every mouth silenced."

Now back to the retired generals. The problems of the military officers still in uniform who can't, or don't, make themselves heard illustrates how the power of Sin takes over people and organizations. The military-industrial complex that Eisenhower warned of has become unstoppable. Even the American Constitution, one of

4. Paul Ricoeur, *The Symbolism of Evil* (New York: Harper & Row, 1967), p. 63.

the greatest documents ever to be penned on this earth, causes problems for generals who want to speak out, because they are constrained by their respect for the chain of command and do not want to become politicized. War is indeed a law unto itself, creating its own conditions and sucking armies, governments, infrastructure, civilians and children into its maw. The Second World War is called "the good war," and I subscribe to that (more or less), but that war also had its evils. The firebombings of Dresden and Tokyo would not be countenanced by international standards today. The willed ignorance of the Holocaust, or ignoring of the Holocaust, by Roosevelt and others is now well documented. It is not enough for Christians to say with General Sherman that "war is hell" as if that excuses anything done in the cause of war. Before a righteous God we should all be on our knees.

I wonder if any of you have ever seen the famous ballet, *The Green Table*. It is widely revered, but not often produced. It depicts diplomats gathered around a long table covered with a green cloth. They are debating the fate of nations. Individually some of these diplomats may be men of good will, but we cannot know, because they are faceless. They wear masks, to indicate their status as undifferentiated pawns in the grip of War. At the conclusion the grim figure of Death appears and asserts domination over the entire scene and all its would-be players. Its victory is complete. It is a depiction of the Wrath of God and the power of Sin. Earlier in Romans 3, Paul describes Sin three times with the words "God gave them up." The idea is that God gave us over to the kind of life we wanted, a life without his commandments:

> Since they [Paul here is leading up to the revelation that *they* really means *we*, or all humanity] did not see fit to acknowledge God, God gave them up to a base mind. . . . They were filled with all manner of wickedness, evil, covetousness, malice. Full of envy, murder, strife, deceit, malignity. . . . (Romans 1:28-29)

The purpose of the Lenten season is to give us all an opportunity to mourn our captivity under Sin. Paul's cosmic indictment means that we understand ourselves not just as people who commit a little error here and a minor mistake there. We are implicated in a global network of ungodliness. In a just world, the names of the civilians killed in Iraq as a result of the occupation would be listed alongside the names of the American dead, but this is not a just world. Thomas Jefferson wrote that he trembled for his country when he reflected that God is just; if a Unitarian like Jefferson could say that, how much more those who have been shaped by the story of Jesus Christ. It is that story that Paul tells in Romans.

On this night in Holy Week, let us reflect on the lesson of Palm Sunday — the Sunday of the Passion. We are not innocent bystanders to the march of Sin throughout the world. As affluent Americans we are deeply implicated in the problems of our planet. I for one believe that something truly terrible lies ahead of us — bioterrorism, environmental catastrophe, dirty bombs, or some horror as undreamed of today as 9/11 was five years ago. Paul could not have known of these 21st century nightmares, but he would not have been surprised, because the gospel that he proclaimed was not only global but cosmic in its sweep. "Every mouth is stopped, and the whole world is accountable to God."

But now. Whenever you hear the words "but now" in Scripture, lift up your heads! The words "but now" are the signal for the arrival of the gospel. In order to grasp this, remember that Paul has shown that we are all condemned under God's law. Here is the place for the turning point:

> But now the righteousness of God has been manifested apart from law . . . the righteousness of God through faith in Jesus Christ for all who believe. For there is no distinction; since all have sinned and fall short of the glory of God, they are justified by his grace as a gift, through the redemption which is in Christ Jesus. . . .

The redemption which is in Christ Jesus. What does it mean to *redeem* something? It means to pay a price to buy it back. That's what God has done. He has paid the ultimate price to buy back his world. Whatever cataclysm occurs it will be no match for God's divine universal purpose. The unrighteousness of all humanity is no match for the righteousness of God.

Think now about yourself. You may not be thinking about global issues right now. You are thinking about the problem you have with your children, or your elderly parents. You are concerned about some of your relationships. Or you are asking yourself if you are really making it in your job. Maybe you have a problem with drinking, or eating, or bad stuff on the Internet. Maybe your bills are too high and your credit is not what it was. You may wonder if you are just a cog in a machine, or if you can really make a difference. If you are reflective, you sometimes ask yourself what your life adds up to.

Yesterday the choir treated us to a beautiful arrangement of the spiritual, "Steal away to Jesus."

> The trumpet sounds within my soul,
> I han't got long to stay here . . .
> The sinner stands a'trembling,
> The trumpet sounds within my soul,
> I han't got long to stay here.[6]

That's it exactly. "The day is coming," Paul writes, "when God will judge men's secrets through Jesus Christ as [the] gospel declares" (2:16) "The sinner stands a-trembling," and those of us who are a certain age know we haven't got long to stay here. What then does our life mean? And what is our defense against the Wrath of God?

The good news of God in Jesus Christ is not just a declaration of innocence for the guilty. That would involve God in a cheat. It would be overlooking evil and denying the horrific suffering of many millions. The letter to the Romans declares a gospel far more

---

6. I am aware that this spiritual may have had a double meaning for the slave community. "Steal away" might mean steal away to the Underground Railroad, out of slavery. But its application is universal nonetheless.

comprehensive than that. The righteousness of God, which is really
the theme of Romans, does not mean that God sits off in heaven being righteous and expressing anger from time to time because *we*
are *not* righteous. You get that idea from preachers sometimes, but
it isn't the gospel. The righteousness of God means that God calls
servants for himself *who he then makes righteous,* who risk their careers
and tell the truth. The righteousness of God means that God has
given a new law written on the heart, a law that does not condemn
but saves.

The righteousness of God means that God takes action. It
means that the Red Sea parts and the sun stands still over Gibeon
(Joshua 10:12) and the Spirit breathes on the dry bones and the
trumpet sounds and the dead are raised. It means that God will call
into existence the things that do not exist (Romans 4:17) — which
means that there will be peace where there was war, and love where
there was hate, and truth where there were lies, and righteousness
where there was only unrighteousness, for God did not come to congratulate the worthy but to save sinners, meaning you and me and
all the generals and all the politicians. And that means that there is
nothing in the universe, and especially not the Wrath of God, that
can condemn us, because in the Cross of Christ, God himself — the
Father and the Son acting together — God himself has found the
way to absorb, neutralize, and satisfy[7] his own wrath, for now "the
righteousness of God has been manifested apart from the law. . . ."

> For there is no distinction; since all have sinned and fall short of
> the glory of God, [we] are justified by his grace as a gift, through
> the redemption which is in Christ Jesus, whom God put forward
> as an expiation by his blood, to be received by faith.

AMEN.

7. This word from Anselm of Canterbury has been called into question for
many good reasons. However, just as Thomas Cranmer saw fit to use it in his
Eucharistic Prayer ("a full, perfect, and sufficient sacrifice, oblation, and *satisfaction*
for the sins of the whole world"), I think it has a rightness in the context of Romans 3.

A Sermon in Celebration of Full Communion

The Episcopal Church in the USA
The Evangelical Lutheran Church in America

TRINITY CATHEDRAL, COLUMBIA, SOUTH CAROLINA

Dedicated to the memory of the Rev. Professor Edmund Steimle

But now the righteousness of God has been manifested apart from law, although the law and the prophets bear witness to it, the righteousness of God through faith in Jesus Christ for all who believe. For there is no distinction; since all have sinned and fall short of the glory of God, they are justified by his grace as a gift, through the redemption which is in Christ Jesus. . . .

ROMANS 3:21-24

In the context of this service in which we have just renewed our baptismal covenant, I greet you with these words of Martin Luther about what he calls "the glory of baptism":

Baptism is the prime sacrament, the foundation of them all. . . . There are two things which baptism signifies, namely, death and resurrection. . . . We call this death and resurrection a new creation, a regeneration, a spiritual birth. . . . The sacrament of baptism, even as a sign, is not a momentary action, but something permanent. While the rite itself is quite transitory, yet the purpose which it signifies lasts until death; indeed, till the Resurrec-

tion at the last day. Baptism means something by which ever-
more you die and live. . . . All our experience of life should be
baptismal in character . . . to die and live by our faith in Christ.[1]

To lay hold of our baptismal promises together, Lutherans and
Episcopalians — what a glorious day and what a glorious service!
What care and planning it has taken, what years of prayer and labor
lie behind it, what grace our Lord has shown to us in its coming to
fruition. Symbolically, what could be more fitting than the location
of this service within Lent? Today, with the Feast of the Incarnation
nine months hence, the blessed Virgin Mary receives the implanted
Word. She must live by promise; she must wait a long time; the
purpose of God is only partially revealed; the way is dark; the consummation is not yet. It is an image of the Church; but just as Mary
sang "He has put down the mighty from their seats and has exalted
the humble and meek" as if it had already happened, so we also sing
by faith, "Christ is made the sure foundation, Christ the head and
cornerstone . . . binding all the Church in one."[2] I must say that the
proximity of Anglicanism's own Henry Purcell to the Lutheran ti-
tan Johann Sebastian Bach during this service reminds me of
Flannery O'Connor's comparison of herself to William Faulkner as a
donkey cart trying to get out of the way of the Dixie Limited roar-
ing down the track. But surely someone made a most generous and
happy decision to let us have Purcell's *Westminster Abbey* this afternoon instead of Luther's *Ein feste Burg.*

This is a moment of gratitude and awe for me as I think of my
professor of homiletics, the great Lutheran preacher Edmund
Steimle, rejoicing with us today in the communion of saints. May
God bless the words of my mouth and the meditations of all our
hearts.

The second lesson appointed for the Annunciation of the birth

1. Martin Luther, "The Pagan Servitude of the Church," *Martin Luther: Selec-
tions from His Writings,* ed. John Dillenberger (Garden City, NY: Anchor Books
[Doubleday], 1961), on the principalities and powers, pp. 294ff.

2. This hymn is sung to the tune *Westminster Abbey,* by Anglican composer
Henry Purcell.

of our Lord Jesus Christ (Hebrews 10:5-10) is a breathtaking example of the imaginative leaps characteristic of the Epistle to the Hebrews. God the Father and God the Son are seen working together
from the beginning. The Son is speaking to the Father in words
from the Old Testament — from Psalm 40. Christ speaks first (it
seems) in his earthly form, then in his pre-incarnate form, then in
his earthly form again. He seems to speak from *above,* face to face
with the Father, saying "Thou hast neither desired nor taken pleasure in sacrifices and offerings"; and he seems to speak from *below,* at
the time when he comes into the world: "A body thou hast prepared
for me." It's a brilliant passage and a brilliant choice for this Feast,
as the Son offers himself up from before his earthly conception to be
the perfect offering for our sanctification. Thus Christ speaks to the
Father: "Lo, I have come to do thy will, O God," and the apostolic
writer continues, "By that will we have been sanctified through the
offering of the body of Jesus Christ once for all."

By that will. Let us ponder this. Our sanctification is accomplished by the will of God. Yet we live in a culture, today in America, in which we are famously certain that we are *self*-determined,
self-created, *self*-invented. We routinely speak of reinventing our-
selves. We speak of *self*-care, *self*-motivation, *self*-chosen values without stopping to think about it. Indeed, it could be argued that self-
determination is the great American gospel. All of us Lutherans and
Episcopalians are affected by this. It is in the air we breathe and the
water we drink. It has deeply affected the theology of every denomination. Yet it is not biblical. Jesus is our prototype: "Not my will,
but thine, be done." "By that will we have been sanctified."

When I was sixteen years old, I saw a movie about Martin Luther (this was in the early fifties). It made an impression on me that
has lasted my entire life. That movie would probably seem very
dated to us now, but its depiction of Luther perusing the Scriptures
and finding there the revelation of God's justification of sinful humanity by grace through faith was in some ways the most crucial
event in my life. I have loved blessed Martin ever since and have re-
joiced to read his writings over the years. When I went back to
them in preparation for this sermon, however, I was very surprised

to discover that much of his work sounds different now that the cultural context has changed. All the great qualities are still there: the vitality and exuberance, the bold defense of the faith, the robust Protestant conscience, the single-minded passion for the person of Christ. But we do not live in a time like Luther's. Polemic is out of fashion. Episcopal ecumenical officer Philip Whitehead of Columbia, a leading figure in planning today's service, is quoted in yesterday's paper: "We've come back to the center, to Jesus Christ. We're really tired of the intricate differences that cause people to argue." That gracious statement captures the mood of today's America. Luther's vehemence, his sarcasm, his bite, and what one might call his "exclusiveness" do not sit well with the needs of today's church as we seek to come to terms with multiculturalism. But every theologian must be reinterpreted in each new generation. Let us see what a new reading of Luther might have to say to our present situation. I shall be following the lead of the great Lutheran New Testament theologian Ernst Käsemann whose re-reading of justification — especially in Romans — is the most radical.

The watchword of the mainline churches today is "inclusivity." I venture to say that no other culture has ever made such a strenuous attempt to treat all kinds of people fairly and their religious beliefs respectfully as we are doing in America today. The point of mentioning this is that the move toward inclusion has arisen out of Christianity itself. Biblical prophecy, the teachings of our Lord and the example of countless Christians who have exemplified forbearance, charity, forgiveness, and solidarity with the oppressed have pushed us further toward inclusiveness than any other society has ever gone. This is not to deny the Church's lamentable guilt with regard to such horrors as the Crusades, the Inquisition, and Christian anti-Semitism. There is need for continual vigilance, but at the same time there is good reason to argue that the Judeo-Christian tradition has been (at the very least) a hospitable environment and (at the most) a driving force for human freedom.[3] Pressed

---

3. I have in mind the Enlightenment, land reform, universal literacy and health care, the abolitionist movement, the human rights movement, the Civil Rights

to its logical conclusion, Christian faith does point toward radical inclusion. But this leads to a question. *What is the basis* for this unprecedented approach to human arrangements?

The question of inclusion and exclusion arises sharply in the New Testament. The most obvious example is Jesus' table fellowship with sinners and tax collectors. In honor of Martin Luther, however, let us go directly to the Epistle to the Galatians, where we find the two greatest figures in the New Testament church, Peter and Paul, at a church dinner having a public fight about inclusion and exclusion. We all know and love Peter for his all-too-obvious flawed humanity; true to character, he has gotten up from the non-kosher table and moved over to the kosher one. Why has he done that? For the same reason that, when I go to the Episcopal General Convention, I don't want to be seen hanging around the booths of the ultra-conservatives. For the same reason that George W. Bush doesn't want to be seen with Yasir Arafat right now. For the same reason that you might take your unattractive friend to lunch at an unfashionable restaurant where the in-crowd won't see you. Peter doesn't want the hotshots from Jerusalem to catch him eating with the unrighteous, so he scoots over to the other end of the room where the tables are filled with the politically correct. Paul recounts the story: "I opposed [Peter] to his face [that's Paul, for sure], because he stood condemned." Condemned for what? Condemned for being exclusionary, of course. But on what basis? Paul goes on: "We ourselves, who are [moral aristocrats] by birth and not [benighted] Gentile sinners, yet . . . *even we* have believed in Christ Jesus, in order to be justified by faith in Christ, and not by works of the law, because by works of the law shall no one be justified" (Galatians 2:15-17). Those are not the reasons for inclusion usually given in the mainline churches today, at least not in my hearing. The reason usually given is, "Jesus loves everybody." But is that a sufficient account of what Jesus does?

A remarkable column appeared just yesterday in the South

---

movement, the women's movement, freedom of speech, freedom of religion, democracy, and perhaps most interestingly, secularization itself.

Carolina *State* newspaper. It concerns the controversy about a proposed statue to honor Denmark Vesey, the free black man who was hanged in Charleston in 1822 along with thirty-five others when it was discovered that he was about to lead a massive slave rebellion which may or may not have resulted in the massacre of the white women and children of Charleston.[4] The column also refers to the recent appearance in Charleston of black writer Jamaica Kincaid who spoke unkindly of John C. Calhoun at a garden club event in Charleston.[5] There were some who said that she had "unforgivably" offended against local hospitality. (This charge was also brought against Jesus as he dined in the homes of Pharisees.) The columnist describes the various viewpoints being expressed in South Carolina as "parallel universes," which exist without touching one another. To large numbers of white Southerners, John C. Calhoun is worthy of a statue and Denmark Vesey is not. To African-Americans, Denmark Vesey is a freedom fighter and Calhoun is an oppressor. Can we communicate at all about this? asks the columnist. Is there any common ground? Is Jesus' love for each of these people enough to smooth over these drastic differences?

The rector of a large Episcopal parish recently told me the story of what happened when, in obedience to Jesus' teaching that we should pray for our enemies, he put Saddam Hussein on the prayer list at a Sunday service at the onset of the Gulf War. Three people stormed out of the church, the senior warden was apoplectic, and the congregation was in an uproar. The rector said it was the most genuinely frightening time of his life. The only thing that saved us, he said, was the brevity of the Gulf War.

Does Jesus love Saddam Hussein? Does he love fundamentalists? (I hope so, since I've been called one.) Does he love racists and homophobes and child molesters? Some of you may remember the vision of fellow Southerner Will Campbell, probably the only person in America who could get away with this: musing about uncon-

4. Claudia Smith Brinson, "State's Past on Collision with Future," *The State,* March 24, 2001.

5. This is recounted by Kincaid in *The New Yorker,* January 22, 2001.

ditional grace, he imagines "Golda Meir chasing Hitler around the pinnacles of heaven, and after a thousand years he stops and lets her pin a Star of David on his chest."[6]

Is that enough? Can we really say that God loves Hitler? Don't we have to say something more than that? What does God's sanctification of the human race mean and how is it to be accomplished?

Our mutual friend Ernst Käsemann has helped us to see that the much-debated connection between justification and sanctification is in the biblical phrase that rings through Romans: *the righteousness of God.* Käsemann's reading of Romans led him to realize that justification is not simply a declaration of acquittal. Justification also means that God is actively and powerfully at work *making right what is wrong.*[7] Forgiveness in and of itself does not encompass the entire will of God. In order to grasp what God's future means for the world, we need to see that the action of God in Jesus Christ means not only the forgiveness of sins but also the rectification of all wrong. It is this insight that enables Paul to say, in Romans 8, "In all things God is working together for good." It enables him to say "I consider that the sufferings of this present time are not worth comparing with the glory that is to be revealed to us." When Paul says that "the whole creation waits with eager longing . . . to obtain the glorious liberty of the children of God," he means that the righteousness of God *is being* made and *will be* made real in human beings and in human society, not because we will it so but because God wills it so. Jesus *does* love everybody, but that is not a sufficient theological basis to motivate us to include the Saddam Husseins and the child molesters of the world. We must say more. We must speak of the power of God working through the Cross, Resurrection, and Second Coming of his Son Jesus Christ to make all people righteous and all things right as they are meant to be.

It may be that some of you are feeling lost in all this theologi-

---

6. Will D. Campbell, *And Also with You: Duncan Gray and the American Dilemma* (Franklin, TN: Providence House Publishers, 1997).

7. This is developed in the new Anchor Bible commentary on Galatians by one of Käsemann's post-doctoral students, J. Louis Martyn.

cal talk. What does all this mean for you personally? What does it mean for your *self?* And what does it mean for church life today?

It means freedom. It means what Paul calls in Galatians "the freedom we have in Christ Jesus" (Galatians 2:4). It means joy in who you are and what you are without worrying so much about how you're doing. It means confidence; if you know that *God* is at work making right what is wrong, you can step along with what he is already doing without spending so much time being frustrated with other people. There was an amazing anecdote in *The New York Times* last year about the march from Charleston to Columbia to protest the display of the Confederate battle flag at the Capitol across the street here. As the marchers were assembling at the starting point, a white man identified as Carter Sabo of Charleston stood alone on the sidelines holding the battle flag. "He stood briefly by Sandra and Tommie Gordon, an African-American couple from Maldin, and [as the marchers started out for Columbia] Ms. Gordon gave Mr. Sabo a hug."[8]

Where does that kind of redemptive action come from? It comes from the certainty that the righteousness of God is not going to leave us as we are, but is actively working for us and in us by the power of the Spirit, not only to forgive us, but to *rectify* us — to bring justification and sanctification together in us for our great good and for his great glory. *God's* work, dear brothers and sisters, not ours. As Robert Farrar Capon has written, God did not come to love the loveable and improve the improveable, but to raise the dead.[9] And so let us come with joyful hearts to the table of the Lord who in his own body made the sacrifice for us all. Let us close as we began with the words of Martin Luther, who knew as well as any man that he needed some fixing up:

When a person has lost Christ, he must fall into the confidence of his own works. . . . Take great care that no one goes to mass trust-

8. "Protest March Against Flag Attracts 600 in South Carolina," *The New York Times,* April 3, 2000.

9. Robert Farrar Capon, *The Foolishness of Preaching* (Grand Rapids: Eerdmans, 2000).

ing in confession, or prayer, or self-preparation; but lacking confidence in all these things let him rather go in high confidence in the Christ who gives the promise.[10]

To the same Jesus Christ our Lord, and to the Father, and to the Holy Spirit be all might, majesty, dominion, and glory, now and for ever.

AMEN.

---

10. Martin Luther, "The Bondage of the Will."

Father and Mother of the Ungodly

TRINITY CHURCH, COPLEY SQUARE, BOSTON

Now the Lord said to Abram, "Go from your country and your kindred and your father's house to the land that I will show you. And I will make of you a great nation . . . and by you all the families of the earth shall bless themselves."

GENESIS 12:1-3

What then shall we say about Abraham, our forefather according to the flesh? For if Abraham was justified by works, he has something to boast about, but not before God. For what does the scripture say? "Abraham believed God, and it was reckoned to him as righteousness." . . . Now to one who does not work but trusts him who justifies the ungodly, his faith is reckoned as righteousness. . . . For {Abraham} is the father of us all, as it is written {in Genesis 12}, "I {the Lord} have made you the father of many nations" — in the presence of the God in whom {Abraham} believed, who gives life to the dead and calls into existence the things that do not exist.

ROMANS 4:1-5, 16-17

As the first lesson was being read from Genesis this morning, how many of you, I wonder, realized that you were listening to the most momentous personal address in the history of the created world? Yes, we really could say exactly that. At the opening of the twelfth chapter, we read, "The Lord spoke to Abraham."[1] The word spoken by God to his chosen servant in Mesopotamia some four thousand years ago is the opening event in the story of salvation for the entire race of humanity.[2]

1. *Ab{i}ram* meant something like "my father [the god] is exalted." *Sarai,* the name of Abram's wife, meant "princess." There is nothing remarkable about these conventional near-Eastern names. Abram's name is later changed to mean something much more portentous: *Abraham,* "father of a multitude." (Sarai will become "Sarah," but the first name is simply a more archaic form of the second, both meaning the same thing; the change is made without any explanation.) Some of Abraham's family's names seem to reflect worship of a moon god back in Ur and in Haran (*they served other gods* in those days — Joshua 24:2).

2. In doing some background work for this sermon I was reminded of the extraordinary archaeological finds in Nuzi and Mari, near Abraham's Haran in what is now northern Iraq. Tens of thousands of clay tablets with ancient writing were excavated from these sites in the 1930s, extending our knowledge of the patriarchal period with "a degree of detail that is truly astonishing" (Nahum M. Sarna, *Understanding Genesis* [New York: Schocken Books, 1972]). *Caveat:* since Sarna wrote his superb commentary, it has become apparent that interpreting the Nuzi and Mari texts is not as straightforward as was first thought. See William A. Dever, *Where Did the Early Israelites Come From?* (Grand Rapids: Eerdmans, 2003).

The immediate present significance of this is tied to the situation in occupied Iraq. It is extremely distressing for lovers of the Bible to reflect upon the chaotic state of archaeology there today. For example, an article in *The New York Times* just four months ago quotes Zainab Bahrani, archaeology professor at Columbia: "Tens of thousands of objects have just gone completely missing [from archeological sites] in the past two years. It's a cultural disaster of massive proportions." She stated further that looting at the sites has increased almost uncontrollably since the American occupation began in 2003. Much has been made of the fact that the looting of the Iraqi Museum two days after the fall of Baghdad was exaggerated, but it is now generally accepted that 10,000 to 15,000 objects are missing. As for looting at the digs, a professor at the Massachusetts College of Art who was a senior art advisor in Iraq estimated that as many as 400,000 significant artifacts may have been stolen. One smuggler alone was caught with 3,000 cuneiform tablets, and he said that he had been making such shipments two or three times a week. In recent months the Iraqis have made some progress in restraining the looters, but they need exponentially more money, trucks, and guards than they have at present in order to stop it altogether. David Johnston, "Picking Up the Stolen Pieces of Iraq's Cultural Heritage," *The New York Times,* February 14, 2005.

Jews, Gentiles, and Muslims all claim descent from Abraham one way or another; we have all grown accustomed to hearing about "the Abrahamic faiths." It is not within the scope of this sermon to describe the role of Abraham for Muslims, but for us of the Judeo-Christian heritage who are here today, the message of the Lord God to this man who would otherwise have been of no significance is of first, present, and final importance. It is of *first* importance because it shows us where we are rooted and grounded. It is of *present* importance because it shows us how to live as the people of God. And it is of *final* importance because it points ahead to the only future that can be trusted absolutely in this world of earthquakes and tsunamis, not only in the soil and the seas, but also in the cultural, ecological, and geopolitical fabric of our increasingly endangered planet. The covenant that God made with Abraham is the only force for the future that can be trusted.[3]

God spoke to Abraham. There was a television series about Abraham a few years back. The director made a deliberate decision to have the actor playing Abraham speak God's lines also. In other words, the voice of God, in the film, is a projection out of the depths of Abraham's inner being. That is what a great many people believe about the Hebrew Bible in general — that it was produced out of the religious consciousness of a highly advanced people. This has become the received opinion in many academically elite circles, so that many people in the churches take it for granted. But if we read the Bible the way it is meant to be read, we discover that it is a story about how *God* spoke and acted to reveal God's own self and God's own purposes. Reading the Bible that way is not even remotely the same thing as fundamentalism — let's get that bugaboo out of the way from the start. Many postmodern interpreters who are skeptical about religious faith are nevertheless very helpful in

3. One of the central theological features of the Bible is the parallel development of two different types of covenant: the Abrahamic (and Davidic) covenant which is *unconditional,* and the *conditional* Mosaic covenant. These two strands can be traced throughout the Old Testament, but the superiority of the Abrahamic covenant is foreshadowed in the Old Testament (e.g., Jeremiah 31:31ff.) prior to its triumph in the New (e.g., Romans 4, 9–11).

showing how a text should be read on its own terms, not terms that we invent for it.[4] We don't have to accept the biblical premise lock, stock, and barrel in order to give it a try. The point is to get started.

The Lord spoke to Abraham. What did he say? First of all he told him to do something unthinkable for a man of that era. *The Lord said, "Go from your country and your kindred and your father's house to the land that I will show you."* We need to remember that people of that time and place had no concept of themselves as individuals in the modern American sense. A person uprooted from his ancestral land and tradition was hardly a person at all. His whole identity, indeed his entire existence, was invested in his extended family. This command of God, therefore, is truly scary. It is very difficult for us moderns to understand this in a day of jet travel and second homes, but if we want to understand the story of how salvation began with Abraham we have to imagine Abraham's venture as literally impossible, except for one thing: the *power* of the *promise* of God.

The promise of God had three main features:

1. Abraham and his descendants would possess a land.
2. They would become a great nation with more descendants than anyone could count.[5]
3. Abraham's descendants would be a blessing to all the families of the earth.[6]

4. I am thinking, for instance, of Jacques Derrida and Susan Sontag ("Against Interpretation"), as well as figures more or less friendly to Christian faith like Northrop Frye, Stanley Fish, and Paul Ricoeur.

5. As many as the grains of dust in the earth or the stars in the heavens, we learn soon after (Genesis 13:16; 15:5).

6. I have an older Bible with notes that say the promise to Abraham had two components, the land and the descendants. But a more recent commentary notes that the promise of God has *three* main points with special emphasis on the stipulation that Abraham's descendants would be a blessing to all the families of the earth. This is a good example of how circumstances can shape interpretation. In our present global context it is much more noticeable to us that the promise includes all the families (and/or nations) of the earth. St. Paul seized upon this, but this part of Paul's teaching has not always been emphasized. Reading the Bible is often a matter of emphasis more than it is actual interpretation. The part about the blessing to all the families of

Now I wonder if we can agree upon something, at least temporarily for the space of this sermon we are putting together, you and I in the power of the Holy Spirit. *First, God spoke to Abraham.* Not an inner voice of Abraham's consciousness, not the promptings of Abraham's religious aspirations, not the powerful wishes of Abraham's unconscious as Freud would say (and Freud is the best of all the naysayers) — no, the word spoken to Abraham did not come from any of these humanly produced voices, but from the one and only living and true God.

Second, God inaugurates a cosmic plan of salvation through this one man and his wife Sarah. Abraham will become, as the Scripture says, the father of multitudes (that is what his new name Abraham means) and Sarah will become "mother of nations [listen to this] and kings of the peoples will come to her" (Genesis 17:16). All the rulers of all the peoples whatsoever will bow the knee before this otherwise unremarkable woman. Forget Cleopatra, forget Catherine the Great, forget Margaret Thatcher — this woman will be *the mother of all earthly power whatsoever.* Did I really say that? When I was sitting at my laptop writing this sermon I could hardly believe what had just appeared on the screen. In chapter 17, the promise about Sarah is phrased even more emphatically and inclusively than that about Abraham. "Kings of the peoples will come to her [and bow before her]." Remember, though, this is not so much about Sarah the person or Abraham the person; it is more about their descendants and the role that God has destined for them. They represent, first, their own family, then the emerging people of the covenant, and finally, *all of humanity* — all the families of the earth.[7]

---

the earth was always *there,* but it was not always *noticed.* Today, we need to notice it. *By you {by Abraham and his descendants} all the peoples of the earth will be blessed.* (To be sure, I am oversimplifying somewhat to make a point. It would not be true to say that none of the older commentators noticed that the blessing would extend to the whole world.)

7. And yet, and this is very important, the children of Abraham and Sarah will not simply blend into the rest. They will be a *blessing* to all the rest, but they *will remain distinct* and will have *a distinct vocation.* No one can teach Christians better about this than the Jews.

So Abraham is a name representing a multitude, but at the same time he and Sarah are individuals as well. Because they appear in Scripture as human beings with specific traits, we learn something more about the promise God has made to them. These two are not always paragons of virtue. Sarah, we learn, is so beautiful in her middle age that during the time they spend in Egypt, Abraham passes her off as his sister so he can enrich himself by dangling her in front of Pharaoh. Later, when it becomes obvious that she isn't going to have any children of her own, Sarah gives her servant girl Hagar to her husband, with the presumably unselfish thought that at least Abraham would have an heir in that way, but then she becomes insanely jealous of Hagar and demands that Abraham cast her and her child out into the desert to die. Abraham comes out of this like a typical man caught between two powerful women, in other words, not very well. So you can see that this raises some questions about how we are to think of Mother Sarah and Father Abraham.[8]

A few years ago at Kanuga, the Episcopal conference center in North Carolina, our 4-year-old grandson and his age group performed a little song, with hand and foot motions to match. It went like this (perhaps some of your children have heard it).

> Father Abraham
> Had many sons;
> Many sons had Father Abraham;
> And I am one of them,
> And so are you,
> So let's all praise the Lord.

To tell the truth, in these politically correct days I was surprised that they let the children sing this, but if you can get past the "father" and "sons" part, it's very good theology. We are all chil-

8. Referring to the misdeeds of Abraham and Sarah, a great Old Testament theologian wrote, "If Yahweh did not go astray in his work of sacred history because of the failure and guilt of the recipient of promise, then his word was [all the more] truly to be believed." Gerhard von Rad, *Genesis: A Commentary* (Philadelphia: Westminster, 1972), p. 170.

dren of Abraham and Sarah, and it is entirely the doing of the Lord, so let's praise God and give him the glory.

But is that right? Are we all children of Abraham? And is it entirely the doing of the Lord? To what extent should we praise Abraham and Sarah themselves? Here's where St. Paul comes in.

Romans 4 together with Galatians 3 are the places where Paul puts Abraham at the very center of his argument. The debate in the Galatian church revolved around the question of who the real children of Abraham were. Were they descendants according to the flesh, so that Gentiles could never be first-class heirs of Abraham? Or were they descendants according to some other criterion, and if so, what criterion was that? And what difference does this make? The question is as contemporary today as it ever was. Just think for a moment about the words that stand at the center of debate in the mainline churches today: *inclusion* and *exclusion.* Who is included and who is excluded? And on what basis? Abraham is at the dead center of that question, or rather, we should say the *live* center.

Let me just say a little bit about my history, such as it is, with Trinity Church. By invitation of my good friend Sam Lloyd, I have had the great privilege of preaching from this Phillips Brooks pulpit several times over the past few years. I have mailed out numerous postcards of the statue of Phillips Brooks with our Lord standing behind him, and as a preacher I take great comfort and strength from that image. Moreover, I had the opportunity of hearing Dr. Ferris preach. He was rector here for thirty years. I only heard him once, but it was the Good Friday Three Hour service and I was never the same again. About once a week, I walk past Dr. Ferris's grave in the beautiful wooded cemetery in Rye, New York, where he is buried with his parents and grandparents. For me that cemetery is a place not of death, but of life. I have dedicated one of my books to the memory of Dr. Ferris.[9] To this day I still meet people whose faith was quickened by his preaching. So I am with you, in this incomparable building, in this extraordinary location at the heart of the great city of Boston, as one who owes something

9. *The Seven Last Words from the Cross* (Grand Rapids: Eerdmans, 2005).

to your ministries past even as you look forward together to ministries future.

Ministries past, present, and future have something in common: all of them stand under the judgment of God. Let me try to explain. My ministry for the past ten years has consisted of traveling all over this country and visiting churches of all sizes in the various mainline denominations. I have noticed that there is a common theme in many of these congregations. On the covers of their newsletters or service leaflets there will be a description of themselves which typically says, we are an open, friendly, inclusive, welcoming congregation. I have seen this so often in one form or another that I think we can agree it is a real trend of our time. And yet I have *personal knowledge* of quite a few people who were either *not befriended* or were *outright rejected* by those same congregations, for various reasons — not because they were black or gay or Latino or poor, but because they were mentally ill, or had politically incorrect views, or were terribly disfigured, or were poorly socialized, or for that matter because they still loved the 1928 Prayer Book. It is not possible for any congregation to be "inclusive" of everyone. Someone is always going to be alone at the coffee hour. That is because of a thing called Sin. Because of Sin, it is not possible, humanly speaking, for any congregation to "unconditionally accept" everyone that comes through the door, and we should be wary of boasting about such a thing.[10] We can strive for it, but we are not capable of it.[11] Only our Lord Jesus Christ was capable of it and he was capable of it because he was God incarnate.

---

10. "Let him who boasts, boast of the Lord" (1 Corinthians 19:17); "I will all the more gladly boast of my *weaknesses,* that the power of Christ may rest upon me" (1 Corinthians 12:9; emphasis added).

11. Jon Levenson of Harvard, in a well-known essay (*Christian Century,* February 5-12, 1992) called "Theological Liberalism Aborting Itself," recalled an occasion in which a professor from a prominent liberal seminary explained proudly that his institution had renounced its former affiliations and no longer required any beliefs or practices from its faculty. Not any? inquired a person present. "No," responded the professor firmly — but then "as an afterthought and in an undertone, he added, 'except the requirement to use inclusive language.'"

Does that mean we should give up the idea? Does that mean we should not pray and work and aim every day to be more "inclusive"? Of course not. Let's be clear about that. No Episcopal Church can survive as a bastion of old-line WASPS and Boston Brahmins.[12] Besides, it isn't just a matter of survival. Far more important, it is the purpose of God that the Church should be the image of his embracing and unconditional love for the world. But in order to move out into a more radical understanding of inclusion, we need a better theological grounding for it. Here's where Abraham comes in. In Romans 4, Paul writes that Abraham, the original chosen person, the original "included" person, the father of us all, *had no ground for boasting* (4:2). Why does Paul say that?

Abraham can be interpreted two ways. The most obvious way, the most familiar way, is as a model of righteousness for us to emulate. That's the way the Galatian church started understanding Abraham after Paul left. Paul writes back in considerable alarm to show the congregation that if they continue in that direction, they will lose "the freedom [they] have in Christ Jesus" (Galatians 2:4). They will be drawn back into a realm where there is competition between who is more righteous than whom, who is more inclusive than whom, who is more Christian than whom. That sort of rivalry about who is worthy and who isn't has been wired into our DNA since Cain and Abel, and there is nothing that we can do to change it. Only God can change it, the God who brought the heathen Gentiles into his family before we could do a thing to deserve it. Paul quotes from Genesis, saying that "the scripture, foreseeing that God would justify the Gentiles by faith, preached the gospel beforehand to Abraham, saying, 'In you shall all the nations be blessed.'" But here's the key thought. At no point has Abraham done anything to earn this honor. He *has no ground for boasting*. Paul's exact words are,

12. I am enthusiastically in favor of programs that attract and seek to integrate people of all kinds, especially the unchurched. I am only seeking to show that we need a more *theological* grounding for inclusive congregational goals. If we aren't aware of the degree that Sin can undo even the most noble of our efforts, we will find ourselves in a morass of self-righteousness and will not even notice that we continue to fail people and must continually maintain a posture of repentance.

if Abraham was justified by works, he has something to boast about, but not before God. For what does the scripture say? "Abraham believed God, and it was reckoned to him as righteousness." . . . to one who does not work but *trusts him who justifies the ungodly, his faith is reckoned as righteousness.* (Romans 4:2-5)

So here is the most truly radical thing of all. Abraham, far from being a model of righteousness, is first and foremost the original justified sinner, the original "ungodly" person who is reshaped by God into godliness, not because of his own deeds but because of the God who does the unimaginable thing — the God who justifies, rectifies, redeems, and remakes the *least* acceptable, most *ungodly* person.

The usual way of talking about Abraham and Sarah is to emphasize their courage in venturing into the unknown. The stress is upon their journey, their faith, their perseverance. But this is not the way that the Bible sees it. The first verses of the 12th chapter of Genesis are the opening announcement of a completely new religious arrangement. People will not be assessed by their journeys of faith or habits of prayer or their works of inclusiveness or indeed any other works. They will not be "assessed" at all, but rather will be "justified," that is to say, made right, made whole, made human in the image of Jesus Christ who is *the pioneer and perfecter of our faith* (Hebrews 12:2). This is a qualitatively and quantitatively different outcome from anything that we human beings can do for ourselves.

No human group is going to be able to include everybody. Sin will see to that. Besides, no congregation can come up with a plan that will appeal to absolutely everyone. In order to appeal to *absolutely everyone,* God chose *one man to begin with.* In order to bring *all the rulers of the earth* under his one reign, *God chose one mother of nations to begin with.* In order to include *everyone,* Jesus chose *twelve to begin with.* Thus the smaller group becomes a sign of God's purpose for the greater world. That's what a congregation of Christians is, an outpost of God's kingdom planted in the territory of the enemy. But mark this: for any person or congregation or group that is powerfully used by God, the greatest temptation is that of boasting, of being self-righteous, of calling attention to ourselves and our achievements. The temptation is to forget that we owe it all to the irresistible grace of God.

The last time I was here, your rector Sam Lloyd and I talked a lot about the incomparable Southern activist, folklorist, and theologian Will Campbell. Will's extraordinary New Testament radicality enabled him to maintain relationships with black victims of the KKK and *at the same time* with the KKK murderers. Literally.[13] Brothers and sisters, that's not "inclusion." That's the resurrection of the dead. Indeed that is exactly what Paul says toward the end of Romans 11:

> For if [God's temporary judgment upon unbelievers] means the reconciliation of the world, what will their acceptance mean but life from the dead? . . . So do not become proud, but stand in awe.

All his life, Will Campbell has said, over and over, that it is God's intention, not just to "accept" the ungodly, but to *unmake* the ungodly, that is you and me, in a way that we could never do ourselves, by *giving life to the dead and calling into existence the things that do not exist* (Romans 4:17). What are these things that do not exist? They are people who are righteous as he is righteous. That is the promised future of God.

And so the story of Abraham and Sarah brings us within the circle of those who *bear witness* continually, in daily repentance and humility, not to our own human programs of inclusion or of anything else, but to the *truly radical power of the promise of God.* For there has never been anything even remotely as inclusive as the plan of God *to justify the ungodly.*

---

13. At the 1998 trial of KKK Grand Imperial Wizard Sam Bowers, Will Campbell went back and forth between Bowers and the family of a man he killed, civil rights activist Vernon Dahmer. When asked by reporters how he could do this, Will growled, "Because I'm a God-damned Christian" (See "God-damned Christian" in my sermon collection, *Help My Unbelief* [Grand Rapids: Eerdmans, 2000]).

Father Abraham
Had many sons;
Many sons had Father Abraham;
And I am one of them,
And so are you,
So let's all praise the Lord.

AMEN.

The Great Reckoning

GRACE CHURCH IN NEW YORK

The words, "It was reckoned to {Abraham}," were written not for his sake alone, but for ours also.

ROMANS 4:23

This winter we had our basement waterproofed. The man whom we hired to do this job was proud of the fact that he had done similar work in some of the local churches. He and I struck up a friendship and he was continually asking me to pray for him. In fact, though I always protested, he kept remarking that I was "close to God." The implication was that I was closer to God than he was, and that my prayers were more efficacious than his.

Clergy run into this kind of thing frequently, and I think it makes most of us very uncomfortable. We know it's not true, and yet we also know that we play a special role in life, standing as embodiments of God's work in the world. People always have and always will invest the clergy with hopes and wishes, yearnings to believe in a world where there is goodness and where God draws near to us.

Lay people sometimes find themselves in this position also. We have a beloved member of our Wednesday morning women's Bible study (not a member of this parish, but very much a part of our group) whose manifest holiness of life leads many to speak of her as being "close to God." Another way of describing such a person that is not necessarily so friendly would be to call her "very religious." Sometimes such descriptions are complimentary and sometimes not, but in any case the general effect of these varying ways of understanding another person's faith and life is to separate us from them, to divide us from them, to make a distinction between us and them.

In the Hebrew tradition inherited by Jesus and Paul, the patriarch Abraham was considered to be the model of a man who was close to God. He was the archetypal righteous man. He was the example of the religious life lived at its best. This inherited conception had several results. Abraham was idealized; his flesh-and-blood descendants came to regard themselves as distinct from others, possessing special righteousness. At the same time Abraham's qualities of faith and holiness came to be regarded as human attainments, possible for some, impossible for many others.

It seems to me that we do this same number on our religious leaders today. We idealize them and are scandalized when their faults are revealed; we attach ourselves to them and draw a sense of self-regard from our proximity; and we invest them with special spiritual powers. Sometimes we seek to imitate their lives, but at other times when we want to get off the hook, we think of them as being too far above us to aspire to.[1]

All of these attitudes are dead wrong, the apostle Paul is telling us — and I use the term "dead wrong" advisedly. When we think of Abraham or Father Ritter or Mother Teresa or our own clergy or anyone else as models of righteousness and godliness, it leads to death, because it is a form of idolatry.[2] Against this type of

---

1. The great Dorothy Day said, "Don't call me a saint! I don't want to be dismissed so easily."

2. Bruce Ritter, a much-honored social worker and priest in New York City, was soon to resign from the leadership of the ministry he founded as a result of allegations that he had engaged in sexual misconduct with underage boys. Nothing of the sort has ever been alleged about Mother Teresa, of course, but the sanctity that has gathered around her image has had the unfortunate result of making her seem too good to be true.

thinking St. Paul writes: "There is no distinction" (Romans 3:22), "There is no difference" (14:13). And in Romans 4, Paul picks the man who is called "the father of us all" (4:11) to illustrate his point. He selects the truly heroic figure of Abraham to demonstrate the unrighteousness and ungodliness of all mankind.

On the face of it, this seems like an egregious offense on Paul's part, and in a way it is, because Abraham really is an authentic hero of faith if ever there was one — he heads the list of such heroes in Hebrews 11. But Paul has drawn his interpretation of Abraham from the Hebrew scriptures. He has meditated long and hard on the passages from Genesis that describe God's dealings with Abraham. In Jesus Christ, Paul is convinced, the true nature of the patriarch's great calling is revealed.

In Genesis 12, we are told that the Lord spoke to Abraham. This is what he said:

> Go from your country and your kindred and your father's house to the land that I will show you. And I will make of you a great nation, and I will bless you and make your name great, so that you will be a blessing . . . and by you all the nations of the earth will be blessed.

This passage is usually identified as "Abraham's call." But did any of you notice, when Romans 4 was read just now, the thing that Paul noticed about that speech of the Lord's? Paul was struck by the fact that it was not only a *call,* but also a *promise,* and that the promise was *unconditional.* There are no "ifs" in it. God didn't say to Abraham, *if* you're righteous I will bless you, or *if* you believe I will bless you, or *if* you repent I will bless you. He just said, "I will bless you." Period. And then he said that Abraham's descendants would be a blessing to all the peoples of the earth — *all* of them. This passage from Genesis strikes one of the first universalist notes in the Scriptures.

You can see from this that it came to be considered quite a privilege to be a child of Abraham. The New Testament is full of discussion about who is and who is not a child of Abraham. By the time of St. Paul, being a child of Abraham had become a real status symbol, and a lot of conditions had been put on it. It was being taken for granted by many that children of Abraham were righteous and godly; they were "very religious" and they were "close to God," and this separated them from the common herd.

The first person in the New Testament to challenge this was John the Baptist, who shouted at the "religious" people who came to him, "Do not presume to say to yourselves, 'We are children of Abraham,' for I tell you, God is able to raise up children to Abraham from these stones" (Matthew 3:9). Paul takes up this theme in his own characteristic way in chapter 4 of Romans (as well as chapter 3 of Galatians). Paul wants to show us, from the Old Testament, what the true foundation of righteousness and godliness is. Paul's message was shocking in his own time, and it is still shocking today, but for those who hear it and receive it, it is nothing less than life out of death.

Paul found a word in Genesis 15:6, and again in Psalm 32:2, that he made the centerpiece of his discussion of Abraham in Romans 4. The word is "reckon."

We Southerners tend to say "reckon" more than other English-speaking peoples. "I reckon so," we say, or "I reckon it is," or "I reckon I will." Other than that, the word seems not to be used much nowadays. Paul doesn't use it the way Southerners use it. He uses it the way an accountant would use it if he were going to "reckon" up a column of figures, or if he were going to do a "reckoning," or if he were going to "reckon" a sum to someone's credit. Paul uses the Old Testament word in order to show how Abraham became righteous. Quoting Genesis 15:6 from his Greek translation, Paul says that Abraham was righteous, not because he was faithful or obedient or godly, but because God "reckoned" him as righteous. It really is another way of saying that Abraham was not righteous, was not godly, indeed that he was one of the *un*godly until God reckoned him righteous. It is all very startling. It is no longer possible to say that Abraham has anything to his credit. Credit comes to him as a pure, unearned gift from God. This is called grace.

one sided

This unilateral "reckoning" of God is *God's* action. Abraham did not get close to God; God came close to him. Abraham was not spiritually prepared for this; he was not possessed of any special religious consciousness. He was just an ordinary man who became extraordinary because God grabbed hold of him. Paul identifies this action of God in a remarkable phrase: "the justification of the ungodly" (Romans 4:5).

Now what this means for us is that everything that separates us from each other is swept away. The heroic figures that seem so distant from us are sinners just like us; whereas we sinners are justified and reckoned righteous just as they are. God is just as close to my basement waterproofing man as he is to me. He is just as close to you, and just as able to work righteousness in your life, as he is in the life of whomever it is that you most respect and admire. This righteousness of God will take different forms in different lives, depending upon the dispensation of gifts as God chooses to bestow them, but, since it is his distribution, we are freed from anxiety about it. And it means that your prayers are just as good as mine or John Stott's or the Pope's.

It is always a very special joy to bring this message once again at Grace Church. Our community as we know it today has been built on the Epistle to the Romans, on its message of the "justification of the ungodly." Whatever grace you have found here, whatever freedom, whatever fellowship, whatever blessing, is all a product of the discovery that we are a people who have been reckoned righteous by God through faith in Jesus. There is not one of us who can claim any sort of special merit for who we are or what we do. Rather, we are a community of sinners who are daily rediscovering our utter dependence on the faithfulness and mercy of God.

When Fitz Allison, our former rector, left Grace Church to become Bishop of South Carolina, this community expressed its gratitude to him for the message of grace that he so faithfully and unfailingly proclaimed to us by presenting him with a gold cross and chain. On the back of the cross there was one word, engraved, in Greek — *logizomai,* the word for "reckon." I have referred to this many times, but as I tell it over and over it never fails to renew my faith. In this word — *logizomai* — lies my deliverance, and yours. Karl Barth, who understood the meaning of this word as well as any one ever has, called it "this unromantic word 'reckon.'" In this unromantic word *logizomai* lies my salvation, and yours. God, looking upon our sin and our need, has had mercy upon us. He has unilaterally reckoned us righteous. We stand on the same ground as our great father Abraham. Our ground for boasting is the same as his — not our own righteousness, but the "righteousness of God" (3:21).

Even as this wonderful news, this gospel, enters into our hearts, however, the cry invariably goes up, "But does this mean we don't have to *do* anything?" As Paul puts it in 6:1, "Are we then to continue in sin in order that grace may abound?" His answer to this is, "God forbid!" For those who have really felt the force of the divine *logizomai,* the divine reckoning, the new life in Christ can only take shape as an intense longing to do good instead of evil, to love mercy, to do battle against injustice, to serve God in the least of these his brethren. The world does not need to see any more badness. The world needs to see goodness. The world needs to see the righteousness of God being enacted in the community that calls upon the name of the Lord Jesus Christ. There is power in this name, power to make godliness out of ungodliness. Actually to make it, that is, not just to pretend that it is there when it isn't.

In 1981, we gave our departing rector a bishop's cross with *logizomai* engraved on the back. Now it is 1990. We have experienced many things together in the intervening nine years. The Lord only knows how many sins have been forgiven since then in this fellowship, how many people have been reckoned righteous through faith in the Lord Jesus. Now it is time for us to think about what we want to engrave *logizomai* on in the 1990s.

We have embarked upon a capital fund drive to restore our Federal Buildings for future use. What will we inscribe upon these buildings? Will we think of them as meritorious works whereby we seek to reckon ourselves as righteous before God? Will we put conditions on them, attempting to control and shape them to our own purposes as a means of self-justification? Or will we offer them humbly to God for his use, asking him how we can best serve his covenant of unconditional promise for all the peoples of this city and this world?

I would like to read you a few words written by a vestryman of this parish. This is taken from a description of our last building project, fifteen years ago when the new space, now called Tuttle Hall, was created out of an old space. At that time it was not at all clear what the future of Grace Church would be, for membership in the late 60s and early 70s had dropped alarmingly. The growth that we have seen since Tuttle Hall was finished was directly related to the Epistle to the Romans and to the proclamation of the justification of the ungodly, which has been heard here by so many as gospel truth. This is what Tom Hall wrote about the Tuttle Hall project:

> Although the only consideration when planning the construction (in 1974) was the narrow needs of the Grace community, it is hard to imagine how we could carry on outreach ministries and evangelical activities such as New Life, the Grace Opportunity Project, FOCUS, and our many prayer groups without the new hall. *Our modest aspirations in the planning were overtaken and surpassed by God's providence for his ministry.* (emphasis added)

Those are wonderful words. They describe God's activity of reckoning righteousness to his unrighteous people. He creates righteousness where there was none before. He "overtakes and surpasses" our narrow capabilities. There is no limit to what he is able to do with us and through us.

Dear people of God, we have all come together this morning to worship and call upon the name of our redeemer, Jesus Christ. May we all offer our prayers as one prayer; may we pray all together that God will continue to pour out his grace upon us, enabling us to be like Abraham, who "trusted the one who justifies the ungodly and reckons [their] faith to them as righteousness." May we pray that our parish and our renovation program and our future as the people of God will be "overtaken and surpassed by God's providence for his ministry." And may we above all receive into our hearts the astonishing news that the Father on his throne of judgment in heaven has turned his face to us and, beholding us ungodly offenders through the eyes of his beloved Son, has said to us, "Your faith is reckoned to you as righteousness."

AMEN.

Beyond the Imagination of Man

In the presence of the God in whom {Abraham} believed, who gives life to the dead and calls into existence the things that do not exist.

ROMANS 4:17

He {God} who raised the Lord Jesus will raise us also with Jesus and bring us with you into his presence.

2 CORINTHIANS 4:14

There may be some people here today who think that Easter is over. That is not the case, however. The Easter season is not even half over. It is called the Great Fifty Days because it lasts from Easter Day to Pentecost.

But does that really matter? Is Eastertide just a custom, or is there more to it than that? The newspapers dutifully inform their readers every year that this is the season in which Christians celebrate the Resurrection of Christ. They also tell us that Muslims believe the Dome of the Rock to be the place where the prophet Mohammed ascended into heaven. Not to leave anyone out, they also print pictures of Hindus bathing in the Ganges and explain that Hindus believe this ritual will wash away impurities. It all sounds like more or less the same thing — this religion believes this, that religion believes that, varieties of religious belief pop up all around the globe. You can take a National Geographic tour of world religion, finding this belief here and that belief there, none of it particularly true or distinctive.

I wonder. I wonder how many of you here this morning really believe in the Resurrection. Do you believe that two thousand years ago, in the land formerly called Palestine and now called Israel, a man who was crucified, dead and buried, not just comatose but certifiably dead, burst through his wrappings and the rock of the tomb he was buried in and appeared to his friends not only alive but restored to full health and strength?

Count yourselves profoundly blessed if you answer "yes" to that. None of us, however, can be completely immune to the skeptical voices that surround us.[1] I spend a good deal of time with people not only outside but inside the Church who say that belief in the Resurrection of Christ needs to be altered to fit our twenty-first-century sensibilities. What really happened — we are being told — is that the disciples came to realize that even though Jesus had died, what he had meant to them had not died, and they were able to sense his presence with them when they gathered together to remember him. Another way of looking at it would be to say that all of us are immortal in some way, or that love is stronger than death. When the disciples realized these things, it changed their lives.

I am the member of a group that gets together once a month for dinner and raises a glass to toast a departed member whom we all loved. We pause to tell a story about him or reminisce about him. Then we go on to other subjects. It remains to be seen how long this custom will continue. After all, the rest of us are going to

---

1. These voices, which have received widespread publicity in recent years, come from the "Jesus Seminar" in part, but only in part. Many who are saying these things are not members of the Jesus Seminar. Bishop Spong's books have sold over half a million copies. The mainline churches have been deeply affected by these ideas, as can be seen in the weakness of many Easter sermons. One recent sermon reported to me consisted entirely of the preacher's discussion of the wonders of nature he discovered on a recent trip to Kiawah Island.

start dropping off one by one ourselves, and we can't go on toasting each other forever.[2] On the other hand, there is the hallowed custom of the British Navy; once a year the British naval officers gather for a banquet and a toast to Admiral Lord Nelson, who was killed in the midst of his glorious victory over Napoleon at Trafalgar. The presiding officer raises his glass and says, "Gentlemen, the immortal memory!" This splendid custom has been going on for some two hundred years. Lord Nelson is indeed an excellent candidate for immortality of a sort among the English-speaking peoples, but the French would not be interested. We could not start a worldwide movement based on the "immortal memory" of either Nelson or Napoleon. One might think of other candidates. In Charlottesville, Virginia, where I spent much of my youth, it was said that people talked about "Mr. Jefferson" as though he might enter the room at any moment. And then there's always Elvis, who is reported alive about once a week.[3]

Well, you get the point. Is Jesus like that? Is belief in the Resurrection just one of many religious options? Did anything really happen in the darkness of the tomb that night two thousand years ago? And in the end, does it really matter? Does it matter to *you?*

About twenty years after the alleged Resurrection of Jesus, St. Paul wrote to the Christians in Corinth. He was distressed because they had drifted away from the gospel message of the Cross and Resurrection. They were more into generic spirituality. Some of them did not believe that the Resurrection really mattered, because they thought they were immortal anyway, through mystical union.[4] They would have been right at home with Oprah, who was described recently in a magazine article as a "post-modern priestess, an icon of church-free spirituality."[5] That's the Corinthians, right

2. As this book is prepared for publication, the custom is already dying out as new members join the table.

3. Four years later, this phenomenon, too, is beginning to wane as the Elvis fans age.

4. They seem to have believed that the Eucharist conferred a "medicine of immortality."

5. *Columbus Ledger-Enquirer,* March 30, 2002, quoting from *Christianity Today.*

there. Church-free spirituality, free-floating religion, no need to bother with doctrine, automatic immortality for everyone.

My sermon texts this morning come from the letters of the apostle Paul to the congregations of Rome and Corinth. To the Corinthians he writes, *"{God} who raised the Lord Jesus {from the dead} will raise us also with Jesus and bring us with you into his presence"* (2 Corinthians 4:14).

The earliest and firmest testimony to the Resurrection that we have is in Paul's letters. Paul is widely disliked and misunderstood by people who don't know anything about him. This is unfortunate verging on calamitous for the Church, because whatever his faults may have been, Paul was a man to be reckoned with, and we have enough of his letters to get a clear sense of a distinct human individual with a very specific and identifiable point of view. So when Paul declares that God raised Jesus from the dead it is not so easy to explain it away as though it were just some vague form of religious wishing. When Paul founded his churches and wrote his letters, most of the people who had known Jesus during his earthly life — those who had seen him alive again after the Resurrection — were still living. We do not have the slightest hint that anyone in authority in those earliest years was in disagreement with Paul's proclamation. They disagreed with him about other things, like circumcision and dietary laws, but not about this. The New Testament church came into being as a result of this announcement: "He [God] who raised the Lord Jesus will raise us also with Jesus and bring us with you into his presence."

One of the interesting things about the naysayers who don't believe in the Resurrection is that they don't generally focus on God one way or the other. Their point is that the disciples had this or that experience of the presence of Jesus after he died. Paul says something quite different. He says that *God raised Jesus from the dead.* The early Jewish Christians had no trouble understanding this. It was analogous to what they had known all along about God — that he had brought them "out of the land of Egypt, out of the house of bondage, with a mighty hand and with an outstretched arm" (Deuteronomy 26:8). The God they had always known was the

God who made a way out of no way at the Red Sea. God is the purposeful mover of the whole thing. It is *God* who has brought his people out of slavery into freedom. And it is *God* who raised Jesus from the dead. And it is *God* who, the apostle says, will raise *us also* with Jesus. So, in a sense, the question about the Resurrection depends on whether you believe in God or not, and if you do, what kind of God you believe in.

In Romans, Paul writes with exceptional emphasis of a God "who raises the dead and calls into existence the things that do not exist" (Romans 4:17). Can God bring peace into existence where peace does not exist? A few days ago I heard an interview on CNN with former Secretary of State Eagleburger. He was asked about the prospects of ending the violence between the Israelis and the Palestinians. He thought the outlook was not good. He said the situation was far worse that it had been in his day and that he did not know where the solution could be found. He said (this is an exact quote) "It goes beyond the imagination of man." As of yesterday, the latest bombing had brought Colin Powell's mission to Israel to a standstill. Sharon has declared yet again that "the Israeli military mission will continue until it destroys the Palestinian 'terrorist infrastructure.'"[6]

Now listen to this. A column in *The New York Times* featured an article by Yossi Beilin, Israeli minister of justice under Ehud Barak, gloomily analyzing the present situation. He wrote something remarkable: "The Israeli war against the terrorist infrastructure will give birth to more terrorists *because the terrorist infrastructure lies within people's hearts.*"[7] This is an amazing statement. If you were alive and listening during Lent and Holy Week, you know that there is a terrorist infrastructure called Sin and Death within the human heart and there is no human antidote to it. *It is beyond the imagination of the human being.* Something new has to come into the world from somewhere else. That is what happened in the Resurrection. Jesus is not an "immortal memory." Jesus is the living Son of God, present in all his risen power. *God raised Jesus from the dead.*

6. Front page, *The New York Times,* April 6, 2002.

7. *The New York Times* op-ed page, March 30, 2002; emphasis added.

Everyone agrees that something happened in the year AD 33, more or less, that created a worldwide, wildfire movement out of an utterly defeated, discredited group of disciples. The question is, what was it? The debunkers want us to give up the New Testament proclamation and accept something that anyone could have dreamed up about anybody. But the New Testament says that what happened on Easter Day *is beyond the imagination of man.* God raised Jesus from the dead. The terrorist infrastructure of the human heart lay in pieces around him.

And what's more, dear people of God this glorious Eastertide, the God who has done this mighty and unlooked-for thing that we sinners had no right to expect, the God who has raised the Lord Jesus "will raise us also with Jesus and bring us with you into his presence." This news of a crucified man raised from the dead and able to bring his beloved brothers and sisters along with him is entirely beyond human imagination. This is not the very common human vision of everyone being wafted up to heaven by his or her own personal angel.

Don't get me wrong; I believe in angels — but not the angels of popular imagination. According to the New Testament, not even angels could have imagined the Resurrection (1 Peter 1:12). The Resurrection was something completely new in the world. In order to grasp even a tiny bit of its newness we have to imagine letting go of everything else, because God is *the one who calls into existence the things that do not exist.* And truly, the God who can do that can do anything. He can create faith where there is no faith. He can bring peace where there is no peace. He can cause reconciliation where there is no reconciliation. There is no ethical content to a generic belief in life after death, but belief in the Resurrection is something else again. Faith in the Resurrection can break down barriers that were unbreakable. Belief in the Resurrection takes shape in the world as the faith of those in the Southern black churches who believed that segregation could be overcome, those in small Christian groups in Eastern Europe who believed that the Berlin Wall would come down, those in the Dutch Reformed Church and the Anglican Church of South Africa who believed that apartheid would be ended, those who — right here in this parish — spoke to me just yesterday of their hope for this community as one where classes of people can freely intermingle and respect each other. That is what Resurrection looks like when it is lived in the world. God raises the dead and calls into existence the things that do not yet exist. He who raised the Lord Jesus will raise us also with Jesus and bring those who once were enemies reconciled into his presence. God will do this. He has promised it.

There will always be those who prefer free-floating spirituality. There will always be those who will choose to hang on to a generic religious belief in life beyond death. There will always be those who would rather think that human beings can do these things on our own. But these beliefs do not have teeth in them. They cannot overcome the terrorist infrastructure in the human heart that causes not just violence in the Middle East but trouble in families and communities right here in the USA. Generic religiosity cannot compare to the promise of a transformed future in the presence of Jesus Christ our Lord, a very real human person who is at the same time God, who enfolded friend and enemy alike into his transforming embrace, who stared down Pontius Pilate with a sovereign self-command that still speaks, who gave himself up to the depths of the terrorist infrastructure in the human heart yet emerged victorious on the other side of the grave. Rejoice today. For this is the God who raises the dead and calls into existence the things that do not exist. He who raised the Lord Jesus will raise us also with Jesus and bring us with you into his presence.

Christ is risen! The Lord is risen indeed! Alleluia!

AMEN.

The Things That Do Not Exist

SARDIS PRESBYTERIAN CHURCH, CHARLOTTE, NORTH CAROLINA

NOTE TO THE READER: The occasion for this sermon was a very large gathering of clergy and lay people from the Church of Scotland, which is experiencing steep decline, and members of the four largest Presbyterian congregations in Charlotte.

> *. . . in the presence of the God in whom he believed, who gives life to the dead and calls into existence the things that do not yet exist.*
>
> ROMANS 4:17

Last week my husband and I went to a screening of *Sophie Scholl: The Last Days,* a film of unforgettable power. Its subject is The White Rose, a small group of German university students, ardent Christians, who resisted the Nazis. Every one of them was captured and executed. This riveting movie was nominated for an Oscar this past April and a lot of us were very sorry it did not win. It is essentially a reenactment of the transcripts of Sophie Scholl's trial, conducted by the man who was called "Hitler's Hanging Judge."[1] After the movie

---

1. His name was Roland Freisler. Some who saw the movie complained that the actor playing this role was too demonic to be convincing. Yet the script adheres strictly to the transcript, and moreover there is ample contemporary testimony to Freisler's extreme behavior in the courtroom. (Helmut James von Moltke wrote that he "banged on the table, turned as red as his robe, and roared . . . ," adding many other details.) It was also said by some that the movie's Sophie is too good to be true;

there was a discussion. A man in an imposing suit, obviously a person of some means accustomed to having his way, got up and said very angrily, "What good did those students do? What is the point of throwing your life away like that? Did it shorten the war one day? Did it save one life?" There was a shocked silence as the man stalked out.

> Abraham is the father of us all, as it is written, "I will make you the father of many nations" — in the presence of the God in whom he believed, who gives life to the dead and calls into existence the things that do not exist. (Romans 4:17)

What are some things that do not exist? Peace does not exist where there is war. Growth does not exist where there is decay. Faith does not exist where there is disbelief. Love does not exist where there is hate. But most of all, life does not exist where there is death. Death is the great nothing, the ultimate negation.

Try as we may, we cannot bring life out of death. When the legendary American baseball player Ted Williams died, the nation celebrated his career and mourned his death — until we found out that his head had been frozen in a can and his body suspended in a tank at the Alcor Life Extension Foundation. Biostasis, they call it. At that point Ted Williams became a joke; but which of us can come any closer to preserving life when death comes to pay its call? As Shakespeare's Hamlet says, "This fell sergeant, death, is strict in his arrest."

Death is the great stalker of us all — in more ways than one. The recent fifth anniversary of the terror attacks on the eleventh of September called forth a concentrated focus on death that we rarely see in America. This might have been healthy were it not for the fact that we seized the death inflicted on us and directed it outward toward a huge and growing number of civilians in Iraq who had absolutely nothing to do with 9/11. Death begets death. That is the

---

yet again, the script scrupulously records her own transcribed words. The transcript was discovered in East Germany after the fall of the Berlin Wall in 1989.

human story. Life out of death is not the human story. Life out of death is the *divine* story. It is *God* who gives life to the dead and calls into being the things that do not exist.

We're confused about this. We use analogies to suggest life out of death, like that of the brown tulip bulb that emerges in the spring as a brilliant flower, or the green shoot that pokes out of the apparently dead tree stump. These natural processes are wonders, of course, that bring genuine refreshment to our hearts; but they only *point to* life out of death; they are not the thing itself. In the natural world, there is no resurrection of the dead. The bulb, the tree, the butterfly — all will some day die.

Now in our text this morning, the apostle Paul is talking about Abraham. Why Abraham? If you follow Paul's train of thought in chapter 4 of Romans, you'll remember that he wants us to understand that Abraham is the father of us all, the "father of all who believe," or, if you prefer, the ancestor of all who believe. The reason for this *stands against* reason: Abraham is called the progenitor of all people not because of his strength but because of his *impotence*. Abraham's place in the story of salvation depends not upon Abraham's sufficiency, but upon his *lack*. He is renowned not because he was righteous, but because he *had no* righteousness. As theologian Douglas Harink has recently pointed out, in an age when talk about "human potential" is everywhere, we who are biblical people need to remind ourselves of Abraham's distinguishing feature: *he had no human potential.*[2] His human potential *did not exist.*

Remember God's promise to Abraham. In the book of Genesis God promises on at least four different occasions that Abraham's descendants would be innumerable. Yet, as Paul emphasizes in Romans 4, Abraham's body "was as good as dead because he was about a hundred years old" and he had a wife who was almost as old and had never conceived any children. In the passage from Genesis that especially impressed Paul, God brings Abraham outside his tent at night time. We need to imagine the night sky as it must

2. Douglas Harink, professor of systematic theology at Kings University College in Edmonton, in a recent sermon.

have been four or five thousand years ago — no city lights, no pollution. If you've ever been out in the desert at night you'll have some idea of what Abraham saw:

> God brought [Abraham] outside and said, "Look toward heaven, and number the stars, if you are able to number them." Then he said to him, "So shall your descendants be." And [Abraham] believed the Lord, and [the Lord] reckoned it to him as righteousness.

Fasten onto that word *reckon,* as Paul did. *Logizomai.* What a universe of meaning is there in this "unromantic word"![3] The root is *logos,* word. Abraham was not righteous in himself. God reckoned, "worded," spoke him into righteousness. *Logos,* the Word of God. Go back further: Genesis, chapter one: "And God said, 'Let there be light.'" As Will Willimon so rightly declares, the entire Christian enterprise depends on the three words, *". . . and God said."*[4] "And God said, 'Let there be light'; *and there was light."* Creation by the Word! God spoke; *and it was so.*

Move forward to the New Testament, the stupendous prologue of the Gospel of John:

> In the beginning was the Word, and the Word was with God, and the Word was God. He [the Word is a "he," not an "it"!] was in the beginning with God; all things were made through him, and without him was not anything made that was made [nothing was made without the Word!]. . . . And the Word was made flesh and dwelt among us, full of grace and truth.

This towering passage links the creation of the world by the Word ("all things were made through" the Word) with the coming of Christ into the world that was made through him. It boggles the

3. Karl Barth in *Romans.*

4. William H. Willimon, *Conversations with Barth about Preaching* (Nashville: Abingdon, 2006). Dr. Willimon had preached to the same gathering the night before.

mind, doesn't it? There is no other story like this story of the creation by the Word of God — the Word that comes into the world incarnate as Jesus Christ. This is the Word that "gives life to the dead and calls into existence the things that do not exist" — creation *ex nihilo,* creation out of nothing.

So this is the Word that "reckons" life where there is no potential for life, and righteousness where there is no human capacity for it. This is the Word that calls forth faith in God's promise when there is no earthly indicator that it will come true.

It is rare to hear this passage from Romans preached. I don't think we want to believe that God can create something out of nothing. We want to reserve some of the credit for ourselves. I love the writings of St. Augustine; he is still so modern! When he was arguing with Pelagius, he made fun of what Pelagius had written. Pelagius wrote that we need God in order to help us "more easily to resist the evil spirit." Augustine says (I'm paraphrasing): What's with this "more easily"? Why not just say simply, we need the help of God to overcome evil? What does that "more easily" add? It adds human potential. We can beat evil on our own, Pelagius would have us think, but we appreciate God's help so we can do it "more easily."[5]

The letters of Paul and the prophecies of Isaiah are saying something radically different. Why Isaiah? Because the portion of that book written during the Exile (40–55) is a sustained outpouring of promises from the God who is going to do a completely new thing, something out of nothing:

> Behold . . . new things I now declare; before they spring forth I tell you of them. (42:9)

> From this time forth I make you hear new things, hidden things which you have not known . . . before today you have never heard of them. (48:6-7)

5. Augustine, *A Treatise on the Grace of Christ, and On Original Sin,* Book I, ch. 28, xxvii.

See how the prophet emphasizes that God's new thing is completely out of our power. We cannot even imagine it, let alone create it. It is declared, spoken, announced by God alone without our cooperation.

Paul links this creation out of nothing with the promise made to Abraham. What does he promise? What is the essence of the nonexistent thing that God will call into existence? It is a new creation, with a new humanity as its crown and glory.

A new humanity. The old humanity is named Adam and it is imprisoned by Sin and Death. We are locked into this cycle of destruction. Last week there was a rumor that Osama bin Laden had died. If he had, would that make any difference? Not really. Terror is abroad in the world. We need a God who can create peace where peace does not exist.

There was a time when people believed *we* could make a new humanity happen. Some people still seem to believe that. Americans are known to be incurably optimistic about human nature and about our own nature in particular. President Bush reminds us regularly that Americans are good, compassionate people. Christian faith says not so. The Christian view of humanity is tragic. The Christian view of humanity means that we are horrified but not surprised that nice American boys do terrible things to Iraqi civilians, and who can say that you and I would not do the same thing under certain circumstances? I have just finished reading *Ordinary Men,* a book about a World War II battalion of reserve police who were deployed to Poland from their home town of Hamburg, Germany. They could have been from Charlotte, or Glasgow. They were just regular guys, laborers, teachers, shop owners; hardly any of them had ever seen military service. They were set to work in Poland rounding up Jewish men, women, and children and shooting them at close range, leaving the bodies in the woods or in hastily dug mass graves. When they weren't doing that, they were loading Jews onto death trains, packing them in so tightly that there was no room for them to move. By the time their tour was over this one battalion of fewer than five hundred men had murdered more than seventy thousand people. Ordinary men.

A striking article appeared last week in *The New York Times*. A Cambodian man named Youk Chhang somehow managed to survive the Khmer Rouge genocide, which killed two million Cambodians, many of them intellectuals, professionals, and educators. Youk Chhang has committed his life to collecting testimonies from Khmer Rouge killers. The article describes his interview of one of them, who was a boy of 14 at the time and became a killer for fear of his own life. Youk Chhang (the interviewer) concluded that he and the man he interviewed could quite easily have changed places. "They are us, and we are them. [The killers] are the evil side of us. Crimes are committed by human beings, by people just like us."[6] In other words, only circumstances separate you and me from the white people who lynched black people in the American South and had their pictures taken on the spot, for souvenirs.[7]

We need a new humanity. But where is it to come from? The message of the Bible is that it is to come from God.

Let us now return to Sophie Scholl, the White Rose, and the question, "What is the point of throwing away your life like that? What good did it do?" This question deserves a response. After all, the new humanity, the new creation of God exists at present only in the form of promise. Signs of it in this life are only signs; they are not the thing itself. Yet signs are what you and I are here to give. Our lives as Christians are signs, pointers to the promise, purpose, and power of God. Today, when young Germans are asked which Germans in history they most admire, Sophie Scholl and her brother Hans are consistently in the top five.

There was another young German Christian resister, Helmut James von Moltke. He also was executed by the Nazis, condemned by the same judge. His letters to his wife, suffused with his Christian faith, have been published; the book is called simply *Letters to Freya.* You probably know the name of George Kennan, perhaps the

6. Seth Mydans, "Survivor Gently Adds Voices to Cambodia's Dark Tale," *The New York Times*, September 16, 2006.

7. These photos of hanged black bodies and grinning white spectators were made into postcards. Many of them survived and can be seen in museums today.

most revered diplomat of the twentieth century. Kennan knew Moltke, from their prewar days in the diplomatic service. Many years after Moltke's execution, Kennan wrote these words:

> [Moltke was] the greatest person morally . . . that I met on either side of the battle-lines in the Second World War. . . . The image of this lonely, struggling man, one of the few genuine Protestant-Christian martyrs of our time, has remained for me over the years a pillar of moral conscience and an unfailing source of political and intellectual inspiration.

I wish I had had those words with me to read to the angry man in the movie audience. Well, the angry man was right about one thing: courageous deeds do not in themselves bring in the new creation. Only God can do that. Nor do people who perform such deeds usher in the new humanity. Not yet. However, such deeds and such people are signs; and because they are signs of what the Word of God has promised, their deeds are "reckoned" by God as "the power that raises the dead and calls into existence the things that do not exist."

A few days ago I read a story in the paper about a man in the small town of Stonewall, Mississippi, who has done quite well in business. He has decided to use a significant amount of his company's money to rebuild the municipal swimming pool. The pool, which had always been for whites only, was filled in with dirt many years ago rather than let blacks into it. More than forty years later, it is about to be opened again to all the citizens.[8] Now what does this mean? What good will the new pool do for a whole generation of children who never learned to swim? What good will it do in a community where racial tensions remain? Maybe there will be fights. Maybe the whites won't want to swim in it. Maybe. But it is a sign.

Full reconciliation, lasting peace, universal liberation: at the

---

8. Adam Nossiter, "Unearthing a Town Pool, and Not for Whites Only," *The New York Times,* September 18, 2006.

present time these things are present to us only in the mode of promise. The Resurrection of the dead does not yet exist. If the human race were capable of restoring life by "biostasis" or any other means, it would just be the same old life — more Sin, more Death. We cannot create the things that do not exist. But we are not speaking humanly. We are speaking of the God who created us without our cooperation and spoke to us before we could imagine him. We are speaking of the God who is able to raise the dead, and who promises to raise the dead, and who makes this promise powerful in us even now through the accomplished Resurrection of Jesus Christ, our hope of glory.

I have not come from New York to Charlotte to preach human potential. I have not come as an American to suggest human methods to the Church of Scotland. I have come by the grace of God with the apostolic message entrusted to me, to declare to you the presence and power of "the God who raises the dead and calls into existence the things that do not exist."

AMEN.

To Die For

TEXTS: ROMANS 5:6-11; LUKE 18:11-14

On Saturday, when I had just arrived here and took a walk around the neighborhood, the spring bloom was so beautiful that I thought to myself, using the current colloquial expression, this is "to die for." Then I started wondering how that expression got started and what it really meant to die for something.

These thoughts came back to me when I began to reread to-day's text from Romans.

> While we were still weak, at the right time Christ died for the ungodly. Why, one will hardly die for a righteous man — though perhaps for a good man one will dare even to die. But God shows his love for us in that while we were yet sinners Christ died for us.

Paul is dictating to a secretary, which is the way most of his letters were written, and you can often see how his thoughts tumble over each other. For instance, in this passage, Paul begins by declaring that "Christ died for the ungodly." Then he starts thinking, "What did I just say? Died for the ungodly? Who would die for an ungodly person? Most people wouldn't even die for a righteous person. Well . . . maybe a person might conceivably dare to die for a *righteous* person" ("although I doubt it," you can almost hear him thinking). If you look at those two verses, 6 and 7, you can see how he's thinking out loud. Verse 7 has parentheses around it, so to speak. The question is, who would die for what? What is "to die for"? *Who* is to die for? That is the theme of the sermon tonight.

It is safe to say that there is no sentient human being in the entire world who cannot grasp the extraordinary significance of someone dying for someone else. This week the movie called *United {Flight}* 93 will open around the country. By now the story is well known, but it will never grow stale for those of us who remember September 11. It is an immortal story for all Americans, because we know that in a very real sense those heroic passengers of Flight 93 died for us all. If the plane had succeeded in striking the Capitol or the White House — well, the thought is simply too dreadful to entertain.

Dying for others, dying for one's country, dying so that others may live: this is a routine description of what soldiers do. Many military memorials contain Jesus' words from the Gospel of John, "Greater love hath no man than this, that a man lay down his life for his friends" (John 15:13). It is universally acknowledged that such ultimate sacrifices are worthy of remembrance and reverence.

But in this particular instance, Paul is more radical than John. In order to understand this passage from Romans in all its revolutionary power, we have to put aside the idea of dying for one's friends, for one's family, for one's countrymen, for one's comrades in arms. Paul does not say that Christ died for his friends. He says that Christ died *for the ungodly.* He says that Christ died for us *while we were his enemies.* He says that *while we were still* [or *yet*] *sinners* Christ died for us.

Notice that little word *yet,* or *still.* While we were *still sinners* he died for us. That word carries a lot of freight. It means that we hadn't made any progress toward being sinless. Have you got that? A lot of religion is based on the idea that people can make progress toward being sinless. The Old Testament shows us that it's not true; the people of Israel flunked the Covenant, over and over and over. As the Prayer Book says somewhere, "We are tied and bound with the chain of our sins." We can indeed make progress against our drinking or smoking or road rage or racism — and the Holy Spirit works in us to do that — but we remain sinners. In this life, there never comes a time when we can stop saying, "Lord, have mercy on me, a sinner." In fact, that is the prayer that we should have on our lips and in our hearts at all times. If our Lord were to walk into this church right this minute those are the words that we should immediately utter.[1]

Jesus told us a parable about that prayer. St. Luke tells us that he told it to "some people who trusted in themselves that they were righteous and looked down on others." Here's the story:

> Two men went up into the temple to pray, one a Pharisee and the other a tax collector. [In order to get the point of the story, remember that the tax collectors were despised on two counts — they were collaborators, and they took profits for themselves.] The Pharisee stood and prayed thus with himself, "God, I thank thee that I am not like other men, extortioners, unjust, adulterers, or even like this tax collector. I fast twice a week, I give tithes of all that I get." But the tax collector, standing far off, would not even lift up his eyes to heaven, but beat his breast, saying, "God, be merciful to me a sinner!" [Jesus, looking straight at the self-righteous people who were listening, said,] I tell you, this man went down to his house justified rather than the other. (Luke 18:11-14)

Jesus got killed for telling stories like that.

Only the converted think of themselves as sinners. The unconverted won't have anything to do with the idea. That's why we reject Paul's gospel; we don't like thinking of ourselves as sinners. Let's get rid of all that gloomy talk about sin, people say. Nobody wants to come to church to hear about sin. (We enjoy reading in the gossip columns about *other* people's sins, but that's *their* problem.) We're all Pharisees of one sort or another, you see. That's why we resist the gospel which tells us that "While we were still helpless, at

---

1. And indeed, since his living presence is here in Word and Sacrament, we always say a confession of sin.

the right time Christ died for [us]." We don't like that part about being helpless, so we substitute another gospel, the American gospel: "God helps those who help themselves." As many polls have shown, vast numbers of Americans think that comes from the Bible. It can't be said too many times: it does not come from the Bible. The Bible tells us exactly the opposite: When we could not help ourselves, Christ died for us [paraphrase of 5:6].

"God shows his love for us in that while we were yet sinners Christ died for us . . . therefore, we are now justified by his blood." This word *justified* is the same word that Jesus uses in the parable of the Pharisee and the tax collector. "I tell you, this man [the unrighteous one, the ungodly one] went down to his house justified rather than the other." This word *justified* is central to understanding the Christian gospel. Think of a person who is suggesting a certain action, a questionable action. He consults another person, who says, "How are you going to justify that?" It means to make something right, or at least to make it *seem* right. How does Jeffrey Skilling justify what he did as CEO of Enron?[2] He's trying to *justify himself* in court right now.

There has always been debate about the word *justification,* so central to St. Paul's teaching. Does it mean to make things *look* right, or to *really make* things right? Some have said that Paul's concept of justification is a legal fiction, a declaration of "not guilty" even though the accused person really is guilty. But that doesn't get at the core of what Paul means. Paul means that the righteousness of God (which is the theme of the letter) is actively transforming, that it actually *makes right what is wrong,* and that that was what Christ was doing when he died for us all.

Paul's gospel is more radical than Luke's. The parable of the Pharisee and the tax collector is wonderful. It has comforted me many a time, and it teaches us how to pray. But taken by itself it might tempt us to divide up sinners into two camps. You have the

2. The 2001 collapse of the multi-billion dollar company in Houston roiled the whole capitalist world. Innocent stockholders lost mega-millions when it was revealed that the company's finances were smoke and mirrors.

good sinners, like the repentant tax collector, who beat their breasts and can't even look up to heaven, so great is their remorse. But then you have the bad sinners, who do not repent and show no remorse. What about them?

Here's where Paul's word *ungodly* comes to the fore. Remember we said earlier that Paul doesn't say Christ died for his friends? Paul says Christ died for his enemies. "While we were enemies we were reconciled to God by the death of his Son." Nothing is said about repentance, nothing is said about remorse. Repentance is not the condition for our restoration. Remorse and breast-beating are not the conditions for our restoration. There are no conditions for our restoration. Here is the gospel: "While we were still sinners Christ died for the ungodly. While we were enemies we were reconciled to God by the death of his Son . . . saved by him from the wrath of God." Remorse and breast-beating are not the conditions. They are consequences. They are *our response* to this good news.

Remember the question we asked at the beginning? Who would die for an ungodly person? Who is the ungodliest person you can think of right now? Saddam Hussein, maybe, or Osama bin Laden. Can you imagine asking American troops to go and give their lives for Osama? It is too crazy even to consider. Yet that, Paul says, is exactly what Jesus did. He died precisely for the sort of person that would crucify the Son of God and mock him while they were doing it.

You see, Christianity at its deepest center is not religious. The Cross is too offensive to be religious. Paul was the first person to put that into written words. He referred to the Cross as a *scandal* (1 Corinthians 1:23).[3] If you look up "religion" in the dictionary you will notice that all the definitions are about us — human beings. We are the doers. Systems of belief, worship, prayer, rituals — these are things that *we do* in seeking after God. But the story of the Bible is not the story of our seeking after God. It is the story of God seeking after us. "Adam, where are you?" Those are the first words Adam

---

3. The Greek word *skandalon* is more offensive than our word "scandal," which has a slightly titillating sound.

heard after he rebelled and plunged the entire creation into Sin and Death. The work of redemption is God's and God's alone. That is our great confidence and our great hope. God has done a work which is so comprehensive that it is able to rectify the greatest wrongs. In the ultimate courtroom, we are justified by the blood of Christ which not only acquits us but sets us on the path to God's righteousness.

This means that our standing before God is completely changed. It is no longer what it was. It is no longer that of his enemies. Imagine that you have had your life saved by a person that you once persecuted or despised. It would radically change your attitude to that person. Now imagine that that person not only saved your life but actually stepped into a lethal situation — between you and your certain death — and died instead of you, taking your place. Can it be doubted that your life would be changed?

That's what has happened to us as a result of the Cross of Christ. Listen to Isaiah:

> He was despised, he was rejected by men — but upon him was the chastisement that made us whole, and with his wounds we are healed.

Listen to Paul:

> While we were enemies [enemies of God, enemies of one another] we were reconciled to God by the death of his Son. How much more, now that we are reconciled, shall we be saved by his life!

By his death, by his life. That is what the Triduum teaches us. What's the Triduum? It is the three sacred services of this week: Maundy Thursday, Good Friday, and the service of the Resurrection. They go together. If you aren't here for all three, you will miss the sequence of salvation. Enemies seated around the same table, fed by the same bread, sharing the same cup, falling asleep, abandoning him, running away to hide, denying him three times — yet reconciled by his death, saved by his life. There is nothing in the world's religions that is remotely like this story of the self-giving of the Son of God to effect *the salvation of the ungodly.*

What is "to die for"? We are.

You are.

AMEN.

The Third Sunday in Lent, 1999

Living Water for the Ungodly

EMMANUEL EPISCOPAL CHURCH, FRANKLIN, VIRGINIA

NOTE TO THE READER: This sermon shows how the Epistle to the Romans illuminates a story from the Gospels.

> *While we were still weak, at the right time Christ died for the* ✓
> *ungodly. . . . God shows his love for us in that while we were yet*
> *sinners Christ died for us.*
>
> ROMANS 5:6, 8

> *There came a woman of Samaria to draw water. . . . Jesus said*
> *to her, "Whoever drinks of the water that I shall give him will* ✓
> *never thirst; the water that I shall give him will become in him*
> *a spring of water welling up to eternal life."*   *Sam. Woman* (handwritten)
>
> JOHN 4:7, 13

When I was a little girl here in Franklin, my grandmother, Emily Norfleet Parker, used to read to me out of the Bible. There is no question in my mind that her devoted love for me created the context for my lifelong love for the Bible. I was only eight when she died, but her gift abides. One of my most vivid memories is of her reading Psalm 24. She read from the King James Version, by the way, and it never occurred to me to complain that I couldn't understand it. Part of Psalm 24 goes like this:

Who shall ascend into the hill of the Lord?
 or who shall stand in his holy place?
He that hath clean hands, and a pure heart. . . .

When I listened to her reading this Psalm it was clear to me that nothing was more important in all the world than ascending to the hill of the Lord and standing in his holy place. But how was I going to do that? Who was worthy to stand in the holy place of the Lord? "He that hath clean hands and a pure heart." I remember as if it were last week how I looked down at my child's hands and inspected them. The pure heart I wasn't so sure about, but I knew I could achieve clean hands. (The last thing I was worried about was that "he." I knew it meant me.) For the next few days I was extra careful about washing my hands. I figured that if I could manage to live up to fifty percent of the Psalm's requirements right away, maybe I could postpone having a pure heart until later. Well, after a while my grandmother read me Psalm 24 a second time. "Who shall ascend into the hill of the Lord? or who shall stand in his holy place? He that hath clean hands, and a pure heart." I looked smugly down at my freshly scrubbed hands. My grandmother read my mind, apparently, because she said, gently, "You know, it doesn't mean that you should keep your hands washed. It means that you should never use your hands to do anything wrong."

Uh-oh. There went my fifty percent. I was back at square one. It was my first introduction to biblical images. I quit looking at my hands and started looking into my heart and I knew I was in Big Trouble.

Later I learned that we are all in Big Trouble, and it starts early in life. When my children were little I drove a lot of car pools. It was always very illuminating because the children would forget that I was there and they would talk about other children. "Matthew is a jerk." "Mary's clothes are stupid." "Jimmy wet his pants." It was a perfect demonstration of original sin, an ailment that afflicts every human being on this earth. Last Wednesday night, Monica Lewinsky made a big point of distancing herself from Linda Tripp. "I would hate to be her," she said. "I'm not like her." However much trouble Monica might be in, she isn't ugly and middle-aged and hated by the world like Linda Tripp. We all play this game. We can always find someone worse that we feel superior to. We all divide up people into classes and groups, in order to believe that we are in the best group and somebody else is in the worst. Insecure as we are, this is a universal phenomenon. We're *not like them; we would hate to be them.*

When Jesus was on this earth, he did not obey this universal human rule of behavior. Instead, he acted in a way that got him into trouble everywhere he went. What was it? What did Jesus do that made everybody, and especially the religious people, so mad? Let's take a look at the Gospel story that we just read this morning.

Jesus went into a village of Samaria. Now you need to know that Samaria was not a good neighborhood. As we all know, one of the ways we divide people into groups is by neighborhood. Real estate prices are driven by this idea of good and not-so-good location. In Jesus' time, Judea was good, Galilee was not so good, and Samaria was, as we say, the pits. Jews like Jesus did not go to Samaria if they could help it. Samaritans were not a good element. Parents wouldn't want their children to go to Samaritan schools.

Jesus, however, has deliberately gone into this bad neighborhood. According to the story in John's Gospel, he was tired from his long walk, so he sat down by the village well. Jesus got tired, just as we do. He understands just what it is like to be human. He isn't above us looking down on us and saying, "John is a loser. Sally is a failure. Michael is a weakling." He came among us in our weaknesses and failures and losses. He got tired and he sat down to rest. At the same time, as we shall see, he is not thinking primarily of his own needs, but the needs of others.

Now as you know, nobody in Jesus' time had running water except the Roman aristocracy. Every town in those days had a well and you had to come to the well to get your water. This was not a man's job; it was a woman's job. So already Jesus was lowering himself three notches. First of all, he was in Samaria. That was bad enough. Then, second, he wasn't visiting the best people in town, the ones who had their own water. Third, he was sitting in the place where the women gathered; that's three notches down. Men didn't want to hang around where the women were; that would undermine their masculine status. However, when Jesus arrived there was nobody there, male or female, because it was the middle of the day, hot and dusty. The women did not come for their water until the cool of the early evening, when they could have a little visit with each other and exchange their news before getting back to the kitchen. But look! Here comes somebody! Here comes a woman all alone, with her big water jug balanced on her shoulder. Why is she coming in the middle of the day? We soon find out. Jesus looks up at this Samaritan woman and he says, "Give me a drink."

We have to give our Lord another demerit here. He couldn't even draw his own water, because he had no container to put it in. He is dependent on the woman to help him. This was not the way a dignified Jewish man was supposed to act. Jesus, however, is not ashamed to place himself in the company of those who are needy. Notice, however, that he does not ask for water in a tentative or obsequious way. He calls for it as though from a great height, signifying to us his human frailty, yes, but at the same time his Messianic authority: Give me a drink.

Now remember, this is a despised Samaritan, and a woman at that. Jewish men of that day were not supposed to address women in public, even Jewish women, let alone Samaritan women. How many demerits do we have against Jesus so far? *One:* he had stopped in a bad neighborhood. *Two:* he had run out of steam, physically speaking. *Three:* he had sat down, all by himself, in the women's gathering place — not macho, to say the least. *Four:* he showed weakness by asking a mere woman to help him. *Five:* the woman was a despised Samaritan.

Now. The story turns at this point. We learn that this woman is not only a Samaritan, not only a woman. That's bad enough. Worse still, she is an outcast in a community of outcasts. That's the climactic point *six* against Jesus. Even among Samaritans this woman is beyond the pale. That's why she comes alone to the well at noon, instead of coming with the other women in the evening.

Jesus said to the Samaritan woman, Go, bring your husband to the well. The woman said, I have no husband. Now listen to what Jesus replies. "You are right in saying 'I have no husband,' for you have had five husbands, and he whom you now have is not your husband; this you said truly." That is the reason for the woman coming to the well in the middle of the day; she did not want to face the other women of the town. She had had too many men in her life. She was not a good wife and mother like the other women. They looked down on her. "We're not like her," they would say. "We would hate to be her."

So this woman that Jesus is paying special attention to was an undesirable. She was not a proper person at all. We learn from the story that even the woman herself was amazed by Jesus' behavior: she said to him, "How is it that you, a Jew, ask a drink of me, a woman of Samaria? For Jews have no dealings with Samaritans." So you see, one of the most important things to remember about Jesus is that he made a special point of reaching out to the people that no one else wanted to be with.

Virginia Durr of Birmingham, Alabama, died last week. I wonder how many of you know who she was. As *The New York Times* obituary noted, she was brought up in the traditions of the Old South.[1] She made her debut and was active in the Junior League. She was blue blood and old money and upper class, a genuine representative of the storied "Southern Way of Life."[2] But she and her husband Clifford Durr, also a native of Alabama, became pariahs because they went over to the Samaritans. When Rosa Parks was jailed in Montgomery because she would not give up her seat on the bus, Mr. and Mrs. Durr were there to help bail her out.[3] Their support of the Montgomery bus boycott and other civil rights activities cost them in ways that you and I can scarcely imagine. Clifford Durr lost most of his law practice. Almost all their friends abandoned them.

1. *The New York Times,* February 25, 1999.

2. This famous phrase, "the Southern Way of Life," was in widespread usage during the 1950s and 1960s among Southern whites who were unconditionally committed to racial segregation.

3. Virginia Foster Durr, *Outside the Magic Circle,* ed. Hollinger F. Barnard (University of Alabama Press, 1985).

They were shunned on the street. In those violent days in Alabama, their very lives, and the lives of their children, were at risk.[4]

More than forty years have passed since the bus boycott. Every schoolchild knows the name of Rosa Parks. But what of Virginia Durr? In her obituary last week, we learn that Mrs. Parks wrote a letter to the Durr family, the President issued a testimonial — but to this day she is regarded by large numbers of white Alabamians as a traitor. What is the truth here? Who is a traitor and who is a hero? Who is behaving in a Christlike manner? Who are the "Samaritans" and who are the "Jews"?

During the civil-rights movement, the most courageous and heroic of all the people who put their lives on the line were the black sharecroppers, many of them illiterate or semi-literate, who labored for months and years in the highly dangerous voter-registration movement in Mississippi. These sharecroppers were the lowest of the low in the movement; they were regarded with a degree of disdain by the middle-class members of their own race in the movement.[5] The white college students and other volunteers — the dread "outside agitators" — who risked their lives by coming to Mississippi to help were housed among these dirt-poor local people. They lived in their shacks and ate their food. One of the sharecroppers later testified about the young volunteers, "We had wondered if there was anybody human enough to see us as human beings instead of animals. These young people were so Christlike."[6] Not only had they come to live and work among the "Sa-

---

4. Actually, this extraordinary couple had already started losing clients and friends ten years before, when they refused to cooperate with the shameful red-baiting (Communist hunting) that swept the nation during the McCarthy era. See *Freedom Writer* (New York: Routledge, 2003), a collection of Virginia Durr's letters.

5. This is described in a number of books including *Pillar of Fire,* the second volume of Taylor Branch's history of the civil rights movement (New York: Simon & Schuster, 1998). At the Democratic Convention of 1964, Hubert Humphrey referred to the powerful sharecropper leader Fannie Lou Hamer as "that illiterate woman" (*Pillar of Fire,* 470).

6. Fannie Lou Hamer, quoted in *God's Long Summer* by Charles Marsh (Princeton: Princeton University Press, 1997).

maritans," they seemed to the lowly sharecroppers like another kind of Samaritan, the Good Samaritan of Jesus' parable.

Jesus made a most wonderful promise to the Samaritan woman in the story: "Whoever drinks of the water that I shall give him will never thirst; the water that I shall give will become in him a spring of water welling up to eternal life." The woman was so thrilled that she left her water jar behind at the well and rushed off to tell everyone that she could find — and St. John tells us that, as a result, "Many Samaritans from that place believed in [Jesus] because of the woman's testimony." So you see, Jesus caused that outcast woman to become a missionary, an evangelist. In the event of meeting Jesus, the unholy Samaritan woman became the equal of any upstanding Jewish man.

That is what Jesus does. He reaches out especially to those who are outcast and downtrodden, and he transforms them. He gives them water for eternal life. The water, like those clean hands, stands for something else. The water that Jesus gives is his own self, his own divine life. In receiving Jesus, we become new people. We begin a new journey. We won't want to set ourselves up against others. We won't want to divide up the world into good neighborhoods and bad neighborhoods. We will understand that even those who live in nice neighborhoods don't have clean hands and a pure heart. For instance, you may well ask what I, the preacher, was doing to help the civil rights movement. I wasn't doing a thing. I was living in Richmond in a white neighborhood and going to a white church and paying our housekeeper some appallingly subhuman wage. I can't congratulate myself on anything. The preacher of the gospel is a weak human vessel with no claims to superior righteousness. In the deathless words of the aforementioned Linda Tripp, "I'm just like you."

So the miracle of today's story is that the Lord's wonderful message today is for every one of us. St. Paul makes it clear in the second lesson for today:

While we were still helpless, Christ died for the ungodly. . . .
God shows his love for us in that while we were still sinners
Christ died for us. (Romans 5:6, 8)

[155]

He didn't wait until we had clean hands and a pure heart. He didn't say "God helps those who help themselves." While we were still *helpless,* Jesus died for *un*righteous people, *im*moral people, *un*godly people. These two verses from Romans are the very heart of the Bible: *Christ died for the ungodly.* For you see, in the Lord's sight *all* of us are ungodly Samaritans, but *while we were still sinners Christ died for us.* We don't even have to wash our hands first. Draw near today with renewed faith as our living Lord speaks to us all in the words he spoke to that outcast Samaritan woman: "Whoever drinks of the water that I shall give him will never thirst; the water that I shall give him will become in him a spring of water welling up to eternal life."

AMEN.

L I
J. Temptation

The Old, Old Story

CHRIST CHURCH CATHEDRAL, HOUSTON, TEXAS
TEXT: ROMANS 5:12-21

A great many people my age have had the somewhat unnerving experience of learning that our grandchildren are at home in a world of electronic technology that we will never really master. There are a few septuagenarian techies, but not many. Most of us will learn to use the Internet up to a point, and we can make a call on a cell phone, but easy familiarity with all the intricate capacities of these devices will never be ours.

At the height of the youthquake that occurred in the late 1960s, the famous anthropologist Margaret Mead gave some lectures addressing the new generation gap.[1] She intended these lectures to be revolutionary, and when I read them at that time — they were collected into a book — they certainly seemed revolutionary to me. My copy of them is full of underlinings and exclamation points and "how true"s. Mead speaks of prefigurative and postfigurative cultures.[2] A postfigurative culture is one in which children learn from their elders. A prefigurative culture, which she heralds as something entirely new in the world, is one in which the elders must learn from the children. In a postfigurative setting, she writes, the elders cannot conceive of change, so they can only con-

1. Margaret Mead, *Culture and Commitment* (Garden City, NY: Natural History Press, 1970).

2. She uses the term "cofigurative" to denote learning from peers.

vey to their descendants a sense of changeless continuity.[3] Well, I can assure you, when I read this as a thirty-something parent, I made up my mind then and there that *I* wasn't going to be one of these geriatric elders who couldn't conceive of change; no sir, I was going to join the new generation. My husband and I both committed ourselves to supporting the young. We found Mead's views, and those of others like her, to be tremendously exciting. We too wanted to be part of writing a new story.

Mead wrote, "I believe a new cultural form is emerging. . . . The elders used to be able to say to the young, 'I know, because I used to be young [like you].'[4] But now the young can say, 'Yes, but you were not young in the world I am young in, and you never will be.'"[5] If the elders accept this new arrangement, Mead wrote, then the children will be "free to grow, straight and tall, into a future that must be left open and free."[6]

Today, Margaret Mead's view seems oddly naïve. To be sure, the "deep, new, unprecedented, worldwide generation gap" that she describes does exist and has caused much pain and bafflement to us elders.[7] But her optimism about the new possibilities have not been borne out by events. Incredibly, she thought that the new global perspective would eliminate distinctions between friendly groups and enemy groups, insiders and outsiders.[8]

Her certainty about the capacities of the young seems starry-eyed today. She wrote that there were no adults anywhere in the world who could teach the young of the late sixties what the next steps should be. Therefore, she thought, the role of the elders would be to foster a dialogue with the young who would then "lead the elders in the direction of the unknown." Mead's book is full of opti-

---

3. *Culture and Commitment,* p. 2.

4. She expands on this: "Children today face a future that is so deeply unknown that it cannot be handled within . . . a stable, elder-controlled and parentally modeled culture."

5. *Culture and Commitment,* pp. 62-63.

6. *Culture and Commitment,* p. 96.

7. *Culture and Commitment,* p. 80.

8. *Culture and Commitment,* pp. 75-76.

mism and faith — it is, in a sense, deeply religious — but views such as hers played a part in creating new generations of parents who have no confidence, who think they have nothing to teach, who decide it is best simply to turn their teenagers loose. "We trust them," parents will say, not recognizing that young people not only need but crave adult guidance when it is given in a noncoercive way. Every day when I go downtown I see young people adrift, standing aimlessly in groups, sharing information about who has drugs and who wants hookups. If you were to ask their parents, they would shrug and say either, "What are you gonna do?" or "We trust them."

In this book, Mead speaks of a wide-open future, a new and better story of humankind. At the time of the turn of the third millennium, many banalities were uttered about the wide-open future. That was in the year 2000 — long, long ago.[9] If you believe that we are really able to move out from under the shadow of the past, then perhaps you can believe the banalities. Prince Harry of England has forgotten about the Holocaust, if indeed he ever knew.[10] Which of our young people are aware that the twentieth century was the most murderous in human history? What makes us think that the twenty-first will be better? Such ideas arise out of the boundless human capacity for wishful thinking.

Where is that wide-open future in which children will grow up straight and tall and unfettered? When I was a child, my friends and I would go out on Saturday morning with our bag lunches and play outdoors all over town all day long. No one called us up on cell phones to find out where we were. No one had to make play dates for us. Games of Capture the Flag and Kick the Can went on all over the neighborhood until it was too dark to see. Is today's world more open and free than that? To come here on the plane, I had to take off my shoes, belt, jewelry, sweater, jacket, hat — and after all that I still had to be patted down. Is that an open and free world? What

9. By this I meant to indicate that September 11, 2001, was a watershed in American life.

10. A storm of protest occurred in Great Britain when the young Prince went to a costume party dressed as a Nazi with a swastika armband.

lies ahead? Who knows if it will be dirty bombs, bioterror, pandemics, earthquakes, more genocides?

On this first Sunday in Lent, we do not come together for worship in order to exhort one another to construct a new world of freedom and openness. Instead, we are recalled to an old, old story. Not a trendy new story about a "paradigm shift," but an old story that tells how we entered this ever-recurring cycle of folly, cruelty, destruction, disease, and death. Today's story begins in the book of Genesis, in the Garden of Eden, and it tells us why we have not been able to create a brave new world.

The lesson from Genesis and the reading from Romans go together. The apostle Paul assumes that the Christians in Rome are going to know the Genesis story, so he doesn't bother to introduce it. He just launches in:

> Sin came into the world through one man [Adam], and death came through sin, and so death spread to all human beings because all human beings have sinned, [and the consequence is that] sin won dominion through death.[11]

Now it is very important to recognize that this is not the usual way of thinking about sin. The usual way is to think of a sin here and a sin there, a little sin and a big sin, a venial sin and a mortal sin, but always in terms of individual discrete acts of omission and commission. "We have left undone those things which we ought to have done, and we have done those things which we ought not to have done."[12] That's one of the best definitions of sin ever written, and I wish we had not given up saying it, but even that great prayer doesn't quite get at the heart of Paul's conception. This passage from Romans depicts Sin as a reigning monarch, in league with its fellow tyrant Death, advancing through the world like an annihilating army.

11. Translation from Ernst Käsemann's German in his *Commentary on Romans* (Grand Rapids: Eerdmans, 1980), p. 140.

12. Thomas Cranmer's General Confession, rarely in use today in the Episcopal Church, from *The Book of Common Prayer,* Order of Morning Prayer.

This picture of Sin in Paul's letters is related to the exorcisms of Jesus depicted in the Gospels. When the Son of God was born into this human sphere, he did not arrive unchallenged. The territory was already occupied. Sin and Death had gained dominion. That's why it's important to notice the exorcisms that our Lord performed. He was driving the demons out of the territory where the Enemy held sway. In the Gospel reading today, Christ is confronted by Satan in head-to-head combat. The Temptation story is not just a story about Jesus being tempted just as we are. It is that, of course, but it is much more than that. It is meant to show us that God has a very real personal Enemy who is bent on victory, who is permitted to rampage around the world. The "axis of evil" is not over in the Middle East somewhere. The axis of evil has gained dominion everywhere, in every human heart.

Paul assumes something that no one in our world ever assumes unless they are trained in Scripture. Adam was placed in the Garden of Eden with a choice. Adam could choose to live in perfect harmony with God and God's creation, with Eve and with himself, free from sin. Adam made a different choice, and the result is that from that time forward there has been *no choice.* You can choose what kind of car to buy — if you have the money, that is — but *no one* has been able to choose to step outside the iron rule of Sin and Death. Whether you believe that there was really a man named Adam or not makes no difference; the point is that we are all born into a condition of rebellion and sickness-unto-death, and "Adam" is the name that is given to this fact about our situation. Old-timers used to say, when someone behaved badly, "That's the old Adam in him." Paul hammers away at this:

> Many died through one man's [Adam's] trespass. . . . The judgment following [Adam's] trespass brought condemnation. . . . Because of one man's trespass, death reigned through that one man.

Paul really, really wants us to understand this. If you look at the passage you will see that he says this no fewer than five times:

"One man's trespass led to condemnation for all men." We are trapped in Sin and Death. The human being does not have the capacity to create a wide-open future. On the contrary: terrorism and the technology to spread hatred worldwide have dragged us willy-nilly into a pinched, constricted, fear-ridden world in which Americans are seriously considering the betrayal of our own highest values by suspending civil liberties by torturing prisoners. This is what the reign of Sin and Death has brought us to.

Now listen to the way that Paul has taken those statements about Adam and opposed them with announcements of what God has done to deliver us from a future of our own making.

> As many died through one man's trespass, much more [has] the free gift in the grace of that one man Jesus Christ abounded for many. . . . The judgment following one trespass brought condemnation, but the free gift following many trespasses brings justification ["rectification" is a better translation]. . . . Because of one man's trespass, death reigned through that one man . . . how much more will those who receive the abundance of [God's] grace . . . reign in life through the one man Jesus Christ. And again, as one man's trespass led to condemnation for all men, so one man's act of righteousness leads to acquittal and life for all men.

Paul repeats this two more times after that, a total of seven times in this one passage: one man's sin meant the death of all human beings; another man's rectification of that sin means life for all human beings.

I hope with all my heart that you can see what this repeated proclamation adds up to. I am only here with you for this one day. I have only this one passage to leave with you, only this one sermon to give to you, only this old story which is ever new, this promise of a completely remade future that is the gift of God. There is no new son of Adam or daughter of Eve who can lead the elders into the future. The supposedly new young person is the same old Adam, world without end. There is only one new human being, and he is Jesus Christ. He is the new man who is able to create a new humanity. It is in his story that all our stories are remade. This is the story that the children must hear from the elders. This is our responsibility and our calling, to tell them this old story as if their very lives depend upon it. As Psalm 145 says, "One generation shall praise thy works to another, and shall declare thy mighty acts."

But we must remember, there is only one way that we can participate in Christ's victory over the demonic Powers. We can only do it by doing it his way. If we try to do it our way we will be back into the rule of Sin and Death. The only way of victory is through the Cross. That is why the true mark of a Christian is not indignation about evil. The distinguishing mark of Christians is the way we behave when other people are in our power. That's what makes Christianity different; that is the sign of the one who prayed from the Cross for the ones who were torturing him to death. That is the distinguishing sign of the Crucified One. When that is mocked, the Christian story is mocked and there is nothing to differentiate Christians from anyone else.

Young people today are faced with so many pressures to assume so many "lifestyles." The messages are all essentially the same: get the job, make the money, have the hookups, buy the car, flatten the abs, invest in the stocks, acquire the real estate and you will be free and your lifestyle will be limitless.

It's a lie. All of it is a lie. None of these things can give life. The sign of Sin and Death lies across them all. But there is news today. I am among you as a fellow prisoner who brings news of impending release. The first man, Adam, is strong; but the second man, Christ, is stronger still.

Where sin increased, grace abounded all the more, so that, as sin reigned in death, grace also might reign through [God's] righteousness to eternal life through Jesus Christ our Lord.

AMEN.

My Enemy, Myself

TRINITY CHURCH, PRINCETON, NEW JERSEY
TEXTS: ROMANS 5:6-9; ROMANS 8:1; 1 CORINTHIANS 6:19

NOTE TO THE READER: This sermon was preached as a contribution to a conference on torture as a compelling issue for America in the post-9/11 era.

Even people who do not know much about Jesus know that he said we should love our enemies. Here is a passage from the Sermon on the Mount:

> "You have heard that it was said, 'You shall love your neighbor and hate your enemy.' But I say to you, Love your enemies and pray for those who persecute you." (Matthew 5:43-45)

My work takes me to churches all over America, small churches and large churches of all denominations. They all seem to have one thing in common: they aren't praying for our enemies. Our troops, yes; our enemies, no.[1]

Nor do I hear the churches discussing issues like the use of state-sponsored torture. University towns like Princeton may be exceptions, but as a former member of a university church (at the University of Virginia) I can testify that such congregations have their

---

1. There is a fine prayer for enemies in our Episcopal Prayer Book, but I have never heard it used except when I requested it myself. (I have since been told that the National Cathedral uses it.)

own problems and tend to be smug about their liberal commitments. Speaking of the American churches generally, the issue of torture barely registers. The newsmagazines have been running cover stories on American-sponsored torture of suspected terrorists ever since the Abu Ghraib pictures first came out, but only a minuscule number of our citizens seem interested.[2] In fact, in my lifetime I do not remember any major public question being so studiously ignored as this one. We need to ask ourselves why this is so.

Last year in my home state of Virginia, a black man named Julius Earl Ruffin was released from prison after twenty-one years of incarceration for a crime he did not commit. In 1982, an all-white jury convicted him of assaulting a white woman solely on the basis of her doggedly insistent visual identification of him as her assailant. He was released after being exonerated through DNA testing. The white woman, whose name was Ann Meng, did a rare thing. She wrote to him expressing her profound remorse for misidentifying him. She sat next to him at a state government hearing designed to discuss reparations for him, and she testified on his behalf. She stated that she, like members of Mr. Ruffin's family, believed that the all-white jury identified more with her, the victim, than with the accused black man. And she said this to the government panel:

> I feel a personal responsibility for Mr. Ruffin's incarceration. However, our system of criminal justice also must bear some responsibility. There was no one on this jury who saw themselves, or their son, or their brother, when they looked at Mr. Ruffin.[3]

That, it seems to me, is the heart of the matter. We do not care about torture in Iraq or Afghanistan because we do not see ourselves, or anyone in our families, as members of the same species as a

2. Mark Danner, who spoke at the conference on Friday, has for many years been a burr under the American government saddle, but he has been a very lonely voice. He gets published, but he says that it seems no one is listening.

3. Tim McGlone, "State Urged to Pay for 21 Lost Years," *Norfolk Virginian-Pilot,* February 4, 2004.

prisoner being tortured. I read a newspaper column the other day by a politically conservative woman who said she could not get worked up about the fact that American citizens were being spied upon. The reason for her indifference, I thought, was that she had never had her own phone tapped, or a family member's phone tapped, and in her passionate loyalty to the present Administration she could not imagine such a thing ever happening to her. She thinks of herself as invulnerable to such intrusions. Those of us of a certain age, however, can remember only too well the FBI surveillance of Martin Luther King and our own friends who had done nothing more sinister than protest against the Vietnam war.

To be able to see an accused human being as potentially our own son, or brother, or indeed as our own selves — that is the significance of the well-known saying "There but for the grace of God go I." These words were first said by a sixteenth-century Englishman, John Bradford, who, when watching a group of prisoners being led off to the gallows, did not say, "They are getting what they deserve." Rather, he said, "There but for the grace of God goes John Bradford."[4] This simple saying has been preserved against the odds for more than four hundred years because it expresses the deepest, most fundamental truth about God and the human race.

Have you noticed how often, these days, advertising speaks of what we deserve? Just two examples from my recent listening: "You deserve an Audi!" and "Come to Mt. Sinai Hospital for the health care you deserve." Where did this idea of "deserving" come from? Who decides who deserves what? We now know that after 9/11 there was a secret White House rewrite of military law. Vice-president Cheney described it this way: "We think [this plan] guarantees that we'll have [available and ready] the kind of treatment of *these individuals* that *we believe they deserve*." I am not making a partisan political comment but giving a simple human gut reaction when I say that I would not want to find myself on the wrong side of this Vice-President. Yet he too is a human being like myself, equally undeserving of the grace of God and equally sought after by God.

4. John Bradford (1510-1555). Cited in *Bartlett's Familiar Quotations.*

Dietrich Bonhoeffer wrote that torture was inflicting pain "while taking advantage of a relative superiority of strength."[5] The Christian, by definition, does not take advantage of superior strength.[6] Columnist Andy Crouch writes, "If Christians are sometimes called to acquire power [and we often are], we should probably begin by watching our Lord abandon it."[7] Children need to be taught from an early age that they should never bully another person, that is, take easy advantage of a "relative superiority of strength." The term used by the U.S. military forces to denote Iraqi prisoners is PUC (pronounced "puck") meaning "person under control." The emphasis here is on the superior strength of the captor and the impotence of the captive.

We would not have to teach this if there were not a component in human nature that delights in the suffering of others. There have been numerous reports that abuse of Iraqi prisoners was American troops "blowing off steam." This was said offhandedly, as though it was no big deal, as if it was well understood that causing pain or humiliation to another person was a handy stress-reliever. One of the soldiers who testified for a Human Rights Watch report last fall said, "In a way it was sport."[8] People typically will deny these tendencies in themselves, but they have not understood the dark undercurrents in the human psyche. In the Christian tradition these dark undercurrents are called by the name of Sin. When Lent comes, as it soon will, we in the churches will go through the traditional motions of confessing our sin. It would be a good thing if we

5. *Ethics* (New York: Macmillan, 1965), p. 185. Bonhoeffer's point about taking advantage is conspicuously missing from the Justice Department's definition of torture, but it is crucial. (This infamous August 1, 2002, memo on interrogation was written largely by John Yoo of the University of California–Berkeley law faculty. To be considered torture, says the memo, techniques [what a word] must produce suffering "equivalent to the pain accompanying serious physical injury such as organ failure, impairment of bodily function, or even death." This has been widely and repeatedly quoted, as for instance in *The Washington Post,* December 26, 2005).

6. That is the whole point of C. S. Lewis using a lion, traditionally the most lordly and powerful animal, as a symbol of Christ.

7. "Always in Parables" column, *Christianity Today,* February 2004.

8. "Torture in Iraq," *The New York Review of Books,* November 3, 2005.

as a nation genuinely came together to identify and repent of our sins. Our greatest presidents, Washington and Lincoln, called for repentance on a national scale; it is hard to imagine any president doing that today.

In a recent book, *Washington's Crossing,* the historian David Hackett Fischer describes how George Washington personally set the American policy toward "persons under control."

> After the battles in New York, thousands of American prisoners of war were treated with extreme cruelty by British captors. . . . Some [Americans] escaped, and their reports had the same impact as those of American prisoners of the Japanese in the second World War II.
>
> [But] an American policy on prisoners emerged after the battle of Trenton. George Washington ordered that Hessian captives would be treated as human beings with the same rights of humanity for which Americans were striving. The Hessians . . . were amazed to be treated with decency and even kindness. . . . The same policy was extended to British prisoners after the battle of Princeton. Washington ordered one of his most trusted officers . . . to look after them: "You are to take charge of [211] privates of the British Army. . . . Treat them with humanity and let them have no reason to complain of our copying the brutal example of the British army in their treatment of our unfortunate brethren." [Note the use of the term *unfortunate brethren.*]

Hackett concludes,

> Congress and the Continental army generally adopted [this] "policy of humanity." Their moral choices in the War of Independence enlarged the meaning of the American Revolution.[9]

The argument of those who support torture as a means of extracting information is that since 9/11 we are dealing with a differ-

9. David Hackett Fischer, *Washington's Crossing* (Oxford, 2004), pp. 378-79.

ent type of enemy, an enemy that does not deserve to be treated as George Washington treated the Hessians. But this is not a new argument. This idea that the human race can be divided up into the deserving and the undeserving is a universal notion. Making distinctions on this basis is something we all do from birth, and the distinction between the righteous and the unrighteous is built into religion. That's why St. Paul's declaration in Romans 3 is so irreligious and radical: "For there is no distinction; since all have sinned and fall short of the glory of God, they are justified by his grace as a gift, through the redemption which is in Christ Jesus."

So now it is time to make the transition from American values to the universal Christian gospel. From the standpoint of Christ Jesus, any talk of "deserving" is treacherous territory. Everybody seems to love the hymn "Amazing Grace," but not everybody understands what it means. The very meaning of the word "grace" is "*undeserved* favor." If it is deserved, then it is not grace and it is certainly not amazing.

Amazing grace can be fully understood only from the standpoint of the Christian gospel. The teaching of Jesus about love for the enemy makes no sense at all if it is detached from his death and Resurrection. If it were not for Good Friday and Easter, we would be justified in putting his teachings in a nice gilded box that we could bring out for admiration on ceremonial occasions and keep respectfully on a shelf the rest of the time. We cannot make Jesus into a nice religious teacher. Without the Cross, we could not take his teaching seriously. The Christian faith rests on a unique, unrepeatable event which has fundamentally altered the way we understand reality. The Cross shows us that in Jesus Christ we see God exchanging his divine life for the life of his enemies.

Who were these enemies? Trinity Church and guests, a few minutes ago I was a stranger to you and you to me. But now in the power of the gospel we are one. Listen to Romans 5:

While we were still helpless, at the right time Christ died for the ungodly. Why, one will hardly die even for a righteous man [let alone an unrighteous one!]. But God shows his love for us in that

> while we were yet sinners [unrighteous and undeserving], *Christ died for us. . . . While we were {God's} enemies we were reconciled to God by the death of his Son. . . .* (Romans 5:6-9)

And in 1 Peter we read,

> Christ died for sins, once for all, the righteous for the unrighteous, that he might bring us to God, being put to death in the flesh [on the Cross] but made alive in the Spirit [in the Resurrection]. . . . (1 Peter 3:18)

Do you see how this is inclusive of everyone? Peter and Paul show how we are all recipients of the undeserved grace of God. This is what makes us brothers and sisters beyond any distinction that we can dream up.

What would you want done with the body of your brother, or your father, or your sister? It is remarkable that we have this Epistle lesson appointed for today. "Do you not know that your body is a temple of the Holy Spirit within you, which you have from God? . . . So glorify God in your body" (1 Corinthians 6:19). Paul is teaching the Corinthians about bodily life. The Corinthian congregation was very "spiritual." They thought that bodily life wasn't important to God; it was the "spirit" that counted. Paul's letter to them is a reprimand and a corrective. God is not to be glorified in vague, mystical, amorphous ways but in the actual, bodily life of Christian disciples.[10] The body is the person, a very Hebrew idea.

But there is more. Here is the complete text:

> Do you not know that your body is a temple of the Holy Spirit within you, which you have from God? You are not your own; you were bought with a price. So glorify God in your body.

You were bought with a price. What price was that?

---

10. The Corinthians passage is specifically about sexual morality, but there can be no doubt that it applies to all bodily life.

The price was the life of the Son of God, who exchanged his perfectly righteous life for the *universally un*righteous lives of sinful human beings. When I look at another human being, even if he is my enemy — especially if he is my enemy — I am looking at a human being for whom Christ died and for whom he was raised from the dead. That is the only way in which the teaching of love for the enemy can be understood.

Anyone can do good things for their *friends.* All good soldiers will die for their comrades in arms. That has always been the rule of the battlefield. There is nothing specifically Christian about it. The way that we embody Christ is by refusing to do bodily harm to our *enemies* when they are disarmed and in our power.[11] That is the Christian gospel in action.

AMEN.

11. The phrase "disarmed and in our power" is important. I am not necessarily recommending a thoroughgoing pacifism. There may be times when an armed and threatening enemy must be stopped by physical means.

That One Man

GRACE CHURCH IN NEW YORK

If, because of one man's trespass, death reigned through that one man, much more will those who receive the abundance of grace and the free gift of righteousness reign in life through the one man Jesus Christ.

ROMANS 5:17

Last weekend I picked up one of those airplane magazines that describe all the wonderful things you can do and places you can see if you buy a lot of airplane tickets. This particular issue had an article about roller coasters. It described the current boom in roller coasters and it rated the different rides all around the country, with a lot of hair-raising photographs to illustrate. I was particularly impressed by the statistics about how safe the rides were and how few accidents there have been. Well, as you know, this very week a young woman was thrown out of a roller coaster at the Great Adventure amusement park and was killed. She hadn't been strapped in properly.

It puts a whole new light on roller coasters, doesn't it? How easily we are lulled into thinking that all is well, that we are not in any danger, that in fact danger is just a pleasurable "high" on which we will spend money, that things are going to turn out just fine.

I have another illustration, quite a different one. Two weeks ago we had an experience in our family that I can only describe as terrifying. Our daughter Elizabeth was due to leave for Europe on Monday, June 8. This was a trip that had been deferred for a year owing to the brain tumor that she had and the massive complications that weren't cleared up until 9 months after her surgery. Words cannot express the emotional investment that all of us had in this European trip. Elizabeth spent weeks packing and organizing. By Thursday she was all ready.

On Thursday evening, June 4, Elizabeth reported to me that she was having trouble with her eyes. At 7:00 in the morning on Friday, she went to see the neuro-opthalmologist for an emergency eye checkup. At 9:30 she came back. Dick and I could tell from her footsteps as soon as she walked in the house that the news was bad. The examination had shown abnormal pressure on the optic nerve. It isn't possible to describe the waves of fear, nausea, panic, and horror that swept over us. We could not imagine that there could be any cause for this except the one great terror that we had tried to put out of our minds — the regrowth of the tumor.

A CAT scan was ordered at 11:30. We were told that we could expect a result at 1:30. We went to the neurologist's office to wait. We had seen him in the hospital corridor and we were not reassured by the look of alarm on his face that he could not control. Those were the longest four hours of my life — from 9:30 to 1:30. During that time I ran into a well-meaning suburban friend who tried to comfort me by saying brightly, "Maybe her symptoms are just from stress." I had a hard time controlling my anger; it reminded me of that parody that goes, "If you can keep your head when all about you are losing theirs, you don't understand the situation." I'm afraid I was very abrupt as I said, "The symptoms of papilledema are quantifiable — they're printed out on a computer."

At 1:30 we were called into the neurologist's office. Every aspect of his facial expression and bodily posture indicated to me right away that the news was good. He wasted no time in saying, "Elizabeth, you're going to be fine. The CAT scan is clear." After four hours of anguish, in a half-second Elizabeth's life and future was restored to us. There was no tumor. I collapsed in tears and had to be escorted out for Kleenex.[1]

Very few people knew about any of this. It all happened so fast that we didn't have time to tell anyone; besides, it didn't seem necessary to draw other family members into the agony and suspense until we had more concrete news. I discovered that, all during the afternoon and weekend, I was grabbing people and telling the story of what we had escaped. I soon learned that people just couldn't grasp the magnitude of the experience; it was impossible to convey. No one who had not actually undergone the deliverance could fully share our emotion.

In chapter 5 of the Epistle to the Romans, St. Paul, with all the considerable passion of which he was capable, writes of the danger that the whole world is in and the mortal peril that Christian believers have narrowly escaped. He is attempting to send a message to the church — in order to see what the human race has gained in Christ, we must understand the terrible destiny that would have been ours. He is trying to show the church the computer printout with the quantifiable, measurable, objective symptoms: without Christ, you are dead in your sins; you are lost, condemned, without a future and without hope. The whole world is sick, cancerous, tumor-ridden, "terminal."

St. Paul is very clear about the ubiquitous force of Sin. He personifies Sin in his writings, as though it were a reigning monarch (as indeed it is): "Sin won dominion" over all men, he says.[2] He depicts Sin with its favorite and characteristic weapon, Death, forcefully advancing through the world like an annihilating army (and it is like that): "Sin came into the world and death through sin, and so

---

1. Our daughter Elizabeth did go off to Europe on the following Monday — her eyes were sore and she took several hundred pills with her, but she was able to make the trip. The pressure on the nerve was caused by a different, treatable condition.

2. Translation of 5:21 by Ernst Käsemann in his commentary on Romans (Grand Rapids: Eerdmans, 1980). He also uses "sin gained dominion" to translate 5:17. To be sure, it is a translation of a translation, but Geoffrey W. Bromiley has well caught the essential emphasis.

death spread to all men because all men sinned" (5:1) and the consequence is that "Sin gained domination through death." This means
that we actually live in a domain of sin, a realm of death, truly an
"Empire of Evil"[3] from which there is absolutely no escape whatsoever, either by emigration or defection or crossing rivers at night or
escaping in boats or balloons or anything else.[4] Sin and death (who
are partners, according to Scripture) rule over us totally, and there is
no one — no one at all — who can choose to be born and to live
outside the orbit of sin.

Paul assumes that all his readers know the story in Genesis:
Adam was created by God and placed in the Garden of Eden with a
choice — Adam could choose to live in perfect harmony with God,
with Eve, and with himself, free from sin. Adam chose instead to
disobey God, and from that time on, there has been no choice.[5] No
one has been able to choose to live outside the iron rule of Sin and
Death. God has "handed us over," as Paul writes in Romans 1. "Sin
entered the world through one man [Adam], and death through
sin, and so death spread to all men because all men sinned." The
contagion of Adam's disobedience has caused the disobedience of
the entire race of human beings. Whether you believe that there
was literally a man named Adam or not makes no difference; the
point is that we are all born into a condition of rebellion and sickness-unto-death, and "Adam" is the name given to this fact about
our situation.

> The result of one man's trespass [Adam's disobedience] was con-
> demnation for all men. . . . Through the disobedience of the one

3. A much-noted phrase used by Ronald Reagan at the time to denote the Soviet regime.

4. These are references to escapes from the Eastern Bloc that were in the news at
the time.

5. Augustine of Hippo explains it this way: In Eden, Adam and Eve could
choose: it was possible to sin *(posse peccare)* and possible not to sin *(posse non peccare)*. After the Fall, it became impossible to choose not to sin *(non posse non peccare)*. In the new
creation that God is making, it will no longer be possible to sin *(non posse peccare)*.
Only then will we have true freedom.

[Adam], the many were made sinners . . . [and so] sin won dominion in death. (5:18-21)[6]

Adam and Jesus Christ. Each man determines a world: Adam's world is the world of sin and death; Christ's world is the world of new life and true freedom given by God. Adam's world originates in rebellion against God the Creator; the new world in Jesus Christ originates in the grace of the heavenly Father, and it is made effective through the obedience of Jesus which swallows up our disobedience in victory.

Paul devotes much space in Romans to describing the terrible predicament of man in Adam:

Sin came into the world through one man [Adam], and death through sin, and so death spread to all men. By one man's disobedience many were made sinners.

Paul is trying to tell us that our life in Christ has been snatched out of the jaws of death. He is grabbing us, so to speak, and urgently telling us the story of our deliverance. And he knows that unless and until we make this story our own, it will never be for us anything more than a story told at second hand by someone whose experience we have not shared.

It is difficult, nowadays, to gain a hearing for Paul. All this talk about sin! Sophisticated people in the twentieth century long since gave up talking about sin — we talk about obsessive behavior, or neurotic patterns, or deviance, or pathology, or disorder, or whatever (I do this myself), but not of sin. "Sin" is a term that makes sense only in reference to belief in a God who is the ultimate judge of human conduct, and since our culture has lost confidence in such a God, we don't talk about sin. We talk instead about stress; we think that if we take a stress-management course we can get every-

6. I have used Käsemann's translation throughout. Käsemann's commentary on Romans is a uniquely powerful (if prickly) work; my copy has been used so much over the years that it is almost worn out.

thing under control. Whereas Paul is saying, it's not stress![7] Sin is an objective, demonstrable reality and here's the evidence for it. It is a result of the disobedience that Adam set in motion and its inevitable result is condemnation, ultimate separation from God. It is a condition that has spread through the human race like a contagion, ever since Adam; this is the biblical source for the Christian doctrine of original sin.[8] Paul says, if you don't understand what it means to be part of the race of Adam, you don't understand the situ-

---

7. It may not be precisely clear that the story about our daughter has nothing to do with sin (except that disease and other afflictions came into the creation as a result of the Fall of Adam and Eve). I do not mean to suggest that our daughter's illnesses are in any way related to sin. The purpose of the story in this context is to illustrate the difficulty of bringing good news of deliverance to those who have not felt any need of it.

8. It is not necessary to think of "Adam" as an actual person. Perhaps Paul himself did not take Genesis 1–3 "literally." The power of the Genesis story is that it tells us that human rebellion against God has spoiled the perfection of his original creation and has infected us all.

For those who are interested in pursuing the interpretation of the story of the Fall, there is no better interpreter than Paul Ricoeur. Explaining that it is to be understood symbolically, he writes, "The story of the fall has the greatness of myth. . . . We must keep the idea of *event* as a symbol of *the break between two ontological regimes* and abandon the idea of past fact. . . ." [This "break," surely, is what Paul has in mind in Romans 5 with his extended treatment of Adam and Christ.]

Ricoeur continues: "The serpent represents the following situation: in the historical experience of man, every individual finds evil already there; nobody begins it absolutely. If Adam is not the first man, in the naïvely temporal sense of the word, but the typical man, he can symbolize both the experience of the 'beginning' of humanity with each individual and the experience of the 'succession' of men . . . [which is definitively drawn by Paul in Romans 5].

"The serpent . . . represents the aspect of evil that could not be absorbed into the responsible freedom of man. . . . The Jews themselves, though they were well armed against demonology by their intransigent monotheism, were constrained by truth . . . to concede something . . . to the great dualisms which they were to discover after the Exile. . . . Of course, Satan will never be another god; the Jews will always remember that the serpent is a part of the creation; but at least the symbol of Satan allowed them to balance the movement toward the concentration of evil in man by a second movement which attributed its origin to a prehuman, demonic reality." (Paul Ricoeur, *The Symbolism of Evil*, pp. 233, 235, 243, 257-59. Italics added.)

ation. This roller-coaster ride ends in death. To say that we are not strapped in properly would be to put it mildly. As children of Adam, we are completely at the mercy of forces that we cannot control, forces that seize our lives and dislocate them violently.

But it is critically important to recognize that the effectiveness of Paul's argument is not dependent upon his ability to convince anyone of the bad situation they are in. You will remember that, in the story about Elizabeth, I shed no tears until we were clear on the other side of danger. I did not fall to pieces until I was overwhelmed by the impact of our deliverance. It was the deliverance itself that caused me to break down. This is the point I am trying, with Paul, to convey. It is God's grace that illuminates the terror of our previous case. We recognize the enormity of the threat that hung over us only when we recognize that we are safe. Then we collapse in gratitude. Paul wishes above all to enable us to be thus overcome by thanksgiving and joy. Then we want to tell the story to everyone and draw them into it too. Listen now again:

> Sin came into the world through one man, and death through sin, and so death spread to all men . . . but . . . if many have died through one man's trespass, much more have the grace of God and the free gift in the grace of that one man Jesus Christ abounded for many. . . . If, because of one man's trespass, death reigned through that one man, much more will those who receive the abundance of grace and the free gift of righteousness reign in life through the one man Jesus Christ.
>
> As one man's trespass led to condemnation for all men, so one man's act of righteousness leads to acquittal and life for all men. For as by one man's disobedience many were made sinners, so by one man's obedience many will be made righteous.

As you can see, Paul is building up an argument from the lesser to the greater. "How much more," he says, does Christ's action of grace save us. "How much more" powerful and victorious Christ is than Adam was. "That one man," Adam, drew the whole human race into rebellion along with him; "how much more" does "that one man," Jesus Christ, give "the abundance of grace and the free gift of righteousness."

I can't prove this to you, any more than Paul could. We know these things only by faith in Christ, "that one man." Narrow escape is an impossible experience to convey to those who are not aware that they, too, have been snatched back from the brink of the abyss.

With all the passion of which I am capable I urge you to consider the situation. The life of Adam is precarious in the extreme. We are threatened at every turn by disease, crime, loss, accident, intrusion, insanity, terror; what is even worse, we are threatened by condemnation — exposure of what we really are, rejection by those whose love we most need, ultimate abandonment by God himself. Humanly speaking, this is our inheritance.

Paul says, this is what we have narrowly escaped! Jesus Christ, the son of the God who is our Judge, has come to our rescue. He has quite literally appeared on the human scene with divine power to save. It is an unparalleled drama of desperate peril and miraculous deliverance — and it is not only my story, but your story:

> As one man's trespass led to condemnation for all men, so one man's act of righteousness leads to acquittal and life for all men. . . . If, because of one man's [Adam] trespass, death reigned through that one man, much more will those who receive the abundance of grace and the free gift of righteousness reign in life through the one man Jesus Christ.

Paul wants more than anything else in the world for us to recognize our Savior, "the one man Jesus Christ," the one in whom we are liberated once and for all, set on our way, incorporated into the resurrection life of God, transferred from the dominion of death into the dominion of the Messiah and his victory over every form of evil.

At the mid-point of my life I become more and more aware of all the competing claims by other so-called saviors. The airwaves and bookstores are jammed with the appeals of various gurus, spiritual guides, self-styled redeemers. At the mid-point of my life I am increasingly more aware: there is no life in any of them. Indeed, we can speak still more strongly: they too are part of the race of Adam, they too, however "spiritual" they may seem to be, are part of the dominion of Sin and Death — as the preacher would be herself, were it not for the news imparted to her by the Holy Spirit of God.

Paul brings incomparable good news. We *already* stand in God's grace. The CAT scan is clear; we are *already* in his sphere of power, safe on the other side. Will you grasp the great salvation that comes in Jesus Christ? This is the urgent concern of the apostle, that we should acknowledge him and entrust our lives to him, the one man who can strap us in properly for our journey.

Yielding to him, trusting in him, is the way. I pray that you will not entrust yourselves to any of the fraudulent saviors. There is only one Savior who was not born into the dominion of Adam.[9] Only one. That one man, Jesus Christ — he alone is able to redeem us for a life free from the dominion of Sin and Death. In him alone, in that one man alone, is joy, peace, deliverance, acquittal, and a safe homecoming. In him only. In him alone. *That one man.*

That one name.

Jesus Christ.

AMEN.

---

9. The theologian Paul L. Lehmann used to speak of Christ as the Archimedian point from which God turns the world.

The Final Exit of the Baptized

TEXT: ROMANS 6:4-13

On this day when we celebrate the baptism of the Lord Jesus, our text is a passage from the Letter to the Romans which is directly related to baptism. St. Paul writes:

> Do you not know that all of us who have been baptized into Christ Jesus were baptized into his death? We were buried therefore with him by baptism into death. . . .
>
> But if we have died with Christ, we believe that we shall also live with him. For we know that Christ being raised from the dead will never die again; death has no more dominion over him.
>
> Yield yourselves [therefore] to God as those who have been brought from death to life. . . .

Nothing *surprises* me anymore, especially not in New York, but I am still capable of feeling *shocked.* I was profoundly shocked just before Christmas by something I saw in the window of one of my favorite bookstores, Shakespeare & Co., just a few blocks south of here on lower Broadway.

The store had a window display of books wrapped as Christmas presents. The gift-wrap of each book was torn back in an artful way so as to display the title and a bit of the cover design — part of Madonna's anatomy, in one case. That isn't what bothered me. What shook me to my foundations is that, along with copies of history books and novels and celebrity biographies, wrapped in Christmas paper just like all the others, there was displayed Derek Humphrey's book about how to commit suicide, *Final Exit.* Death for a Christmas present. I hope that all of you are as shocked to hear this as I was to see it.

I'm sure every one here is aware that a dramatic change has come over our society with regard to the subject. In just a few years, there has been such a lessening of horror, indeed such a romanticizing of suicide, that we can no longer feel the particular shock of the scene in *Hamlet* where Hamlet and Horatio, returning from a journey and unaware of what has taken place, observe the "maimèd rites" being conducted for a suicide, only to realize with pity and terror that the person who has taken her own life is Ophelia.

Yes, this is a strange subject to bring up on the Lord's Day. Yet I believe that the Feast of the Baptism of our Lord in the Jordan River summons us to look deeply into matters of life and death *precisely so that* we can understand and embrace the meaning of our own baptisms.

One is aware that there are acutely sensitive pastoral issues here. Suicide has come close to a great many of us. Some of us may have considered it for ourselves, someone we care about may have considered it or tried it, someone in our own family or the family of a friend may have died by his or her own hand. Several people whom I deeply love have had close contact with suicide recently in one or more of these ways. I can't speak *pastorally* from the pulpit, not directly, because to do so would require the utmost attention to each individual circumstance. Rather, it is my purpose to speak *theologically* about life, death, and the current revisionist thinking about suicide, in the context of Christian baptism.

Not long ago, I had an opportunity to speak with a man whose qualities of mind and heart I deeply respect, and I mentioned the bookstore window display. He, too, was shocked. I knew that, though he is Jewish, he is not religious in any conventional sense, so I asked him if he thought he would ever consider committing suicide. He said no. I asked why. He said, "Because it would be too much like surrender." I admired that, but because I am a Christian I am accustomed to assigning a positive meaning to surrender — as in, for instance, *surrendering* to the will of God. I have been mulling this over for several weeks, attempting to come up with something equally impressive from a theological point of view. The words of Paul came to my mind: "All of us who have been baptized into Christ Jesus were baptized into his death. . . . But if we have died with Christ, we believe that we shall also live with him. . . . Yield yourselves to God as men and women who have been brought from death to life."

For about a decade I have been keeping files of articles, clippings, and quotations on the subject of suicide. In recent months, since the appearance of *Final Exit* on the bestseller list and in the windows of bookstores, there has been a quantum leap in the number of such articles; I've been very busy with my scissors. Particularly noticeable is the increase in testimonies from people who want to justify the suicide of someone, either a person dear to them who acted alone, or someone whom they actually assisted in dying. There is to be a television program this very night, called "Last Wish," based on the true story of Betty Rollin and her mother. According to the review in the *Times,* the TV drama dramatizes and fervently supports the daughter's active participation in her ill mother's death.

From my files I have chosen just one item. Last year, when the famous writer Jerzy Kosinski quite unexpectedly committed suicide, it seemed that the whole of literary New York reeled and staggered. There was an outpouring of various explanations, rationalizations, justifications. An article in *New York* magazine quoted his wife: "Jerzy did what he had to do. He felt all his exits were being closed off." The journalist continues, "In that respect, Kosinski's suicide can be seen as an existential decision, a heroic gesture by some one who loved life too much to live it any other way than under the conditions he set."

The most impressive theological writing I know on the subject of suicide is in Dietrich Bonhoeffer's *Ethics.* It is only a fragment; he never got to finish it because, after two years of imprisonment, he was hanged by the Nazis. He begins his discussion by paying tribute to the "existential decision," the "heroic gesture." "Suicide," he declares, "is a specifically human action, and it is not surprising if it has on this account repeatedly been applauded and justified by noble human minds. . . . Suicide is the ultimate and extreme self-justification of man as man. . . . This deed will usually take place in a state of despair, [yet it is] a man's freedom to perform his supreme act of self-justification even in the midst of this despair."

Bonhoeffer is here paying his respects to the aristocratic philosophy called Stoicism, which, though ancient, still commands adherents today from among the strongest and most exceptional members of the population. Stoicism has always been a worthy rival to Christian morality, based as it is on a lofty view of human dignity. Polonius's words, "To thine own self be true," are a distillation of the supremely individualistic Stoic creed. When Bonhoeffer goes on to speak of "the terrible loneliness and freedom in which this deed [of suicide] is performed," he is paying homage to the "noble human minds" that have embraced a Stoic view of suicide. There is no surrender here. Nor is there any *theo*logy here, for there is no *theos,* no God. And so Bonhoeffer, taking on his role as Christian theologian, shifts into a new key: "If suicide must nevertheless be declared wrongful, it is to be arraigned not before the forum of mortality or of men but solely before the forum of God. It is because there is a living God that suicide is wrongful as a sin of lack of faith. Lack of faith is not a moral fault . . . but [it] takes no account of the living God. . . . Lack of faith is disastrous in that it conceals from a man the fact that *even suicide cannot release him from the hand of God,* who has prepared his destiny for him. . . . The freedom to die . . . is abused if it is used otherwise than in faith in God. God has reserved to himself the right to determine the end of life, because he alone knows the goal to which it is his will to lead it."[1]

As everyone knows by now, in just a few decades our post-Christian culture is showing signs of having been severed from its roots. It is exceedingly difficult nowadays to regain a working knowledge of our Judeo-Christian heritage. I have heard many Christian people speaking like Stoics without even realizing what they were do-

1. Dietrich Bonhoeffer, *Ethics* (New York: Macmillan, 1965), p. 168; emphasis added.

ing. We Christians therefore need to become much more intentional about what we believe and why. It is no longer possible simply to absorb it from the surrounding atmosphere. For this reason, coming to the church for baptism is becoming far more an act of courage and faith than it used to be when baptism was, in many cases, regarded as a social obligation. The very fact, often remarked upon, that Mikhail Gorbachev was baptized as a child has raised the consciousness of many, for it is a hint that the rite might be, not a mere form, but strangely powerful and mysteriously effective in a way that for a long time has not been considered in some circles.

Let us hear again what St. Paul has to say:

> Do you not know that all of us who have been baptized into Christ Jesus were baptized into his death? We were buried therefore with him by baptism into death. . . .
>
> But if we have died with Christ, we believe that we shall also live with him. For we know that Christ being raised from the dead will never die again; death has no more dominion over him.
>
> Yield yourselves [therefore] to God as those who have been brought from death to life.

I wonder if this strikes any of you as it strikes me. The baptized Christian has, in an important sense, *already died.* The baptized Christian has already made her "final exit" and has come through on the other side. Does this mean that we won't die? Clearly that is not the case, but for the Christian, death cannot be the last word. "Death has no more dominion." "Death, be not proud," wrote John Donne; "Death, thou shalt die." The last word for us is not death, but life. Human life, in and of itself, is of infinite value because eternal life is what God intends for all his children. The honoring of life, therefore, is proper for all Christians at all times, and a surrender to God's will can sometimes mean supporting life even when society deems that life to be socially useless.[2]

---

2. I repeat that I am speaking here of theological foundations, not of individual cases, each of which must be assessed individually according to such distinctions as that between allowing to die, on the one hand, and actual killing, on the other.

As Dietrich Bonhoeffer comes to the center of his discussion of suicide, he writes in terms that will be recognizable to anyone who has ever tried to help a suicidal person: "A man who is desperate cannot be saved by a law that appeals to his own strength [as if one were to say 'Pull yourself together!']; such a law will only drive him to even more hopeless despair. One who despairs of life can only be helped *by the saving deed of another.* . . . A man who can no longer live is not helped by any command that he should live, but by *a new spirit.*"[3]

A new spirit. That is precisely the language of baptism. Baptism is the gift of a new spirit, the spirit of life and not of death, the spirit of grace and not of law. This new spirit — the Holy Spirit — bestows courage and faith to live life, not under the conditions we set, but under the conditions that God sets, the God who never closes off our exits, but on the contrary has opened the door to eternal life. Such a life may seem to be lacking in the drama, the self-assertiveness, even the seeming heroism of the Stoic suicide; but such an assessment, Christians believe, is as Bonhoeffer says, "disastrous, for it takes no account of the living God."

There were two people in my own life who, I believe, gave me my faith. One was my father's mother; the other was my father's sister, my aunt, whose name was Mary Virginia — Mary V. for short. This is the story of my aunt's life-in-death.

When I was a tiny little girl, my grandmother read to me from the Bible regularly. When I was eight, she died, and Mary V. took up where she had left off. My sister and I have often spoken of what we owe to those Bible stories told to us by Mary V. When she said that God called to the young boy Samuel, I believed it; I believe it still, not so much because of my fancy seminary education, but because Mary V. told me. When I was in my thirties, Mary V. had a stroke. I think she was about 78 when that happened. After that, she never regained her mind. She was in a nursing home for ten interminable years. What little she said during those years made little or no sense most of the time. Visiting her and worrying about her took a lot out of all of us, especially my mother and father. My fa-

3. Bonhoeffer, *Ethics,* p. 169; emphasis added.

ther suffered most of all; when he would come back after visiting, he would be visibly depleted.

On Christmas Day, 1979, my father and mother went to see Mary V. in the nursing home in Franklin, Virginia. This was about a year before she died. My father barely endured these visits; I never fully knew what they cost him physically and emotionally, though I could guess. At the time of this story Mary V. was about 88, and my father, who eventually lived to be 91, was, I think, 85.

After the visit to the nursing home on Christmas Day, my father went to his office and dictated everything that Mary V. had said that day. He was a lawyer, and the transcription bears all the marks of his methodical concern for accuracy. I'm going to give it to you in his and her exact words (somewhat abridged), which preserve the brother's and sister's slightly quaint way of talking very precisely. The only explanation I need to give you is that the story Mary V. told is populated with people from the past, including a distinguished art historian from Richmond named Dick Cossitt who had come frequently to Franklin to give lectures about art. Here is my father's account:

> "Alice [my mother] and I went to see Mary V. this morning. I read her the Christmas story and at the end of it said, 'That is the Christmas story from St. Luke.'"
>
> "She said 'Yes, now let me tell you something that is remarkable to me. Last week I was at Emilius and saw Jesus at the house of Martha, Mary, and Lazarus their brother.' I asked her if she meant Emmaus, and she said yes, but called it Emilius.
>
> "I said, 'How did it happen?' She said, 'I was standing there outside of church and a voice near me said "Mary, come walk with me." It was Dick Cossitt. I said "Where are you going, Dick?" and he said he was going to Emilius. I asked him why and he said he had heard the Master was going to be there having dinner with friends and that until he got further information he assumed it would be at the house of Martha, Mary, and Lazarus their brother. And that's where it was.'
>
> "I said 'Had Lazarus already been raised from the tomb?'

Mary V. said, 'No, he hadn't even been sick. Martha was a big strong woman and constantly moving about and I guess she was cooking dinner. And just think — *Jesus was at the table.*' She said there were a lot of people there [she named several people from our little home town]. She said that she had heard that Dick Cossitt saw a good deal of the Master. She said Peter's wife was sick of a fever and that Jesus touched her and the fever went away. 'He put his hand on her, that was all.' And she said, 'You remember there was a big storm. There was a lot of wind and the water was very rough. Jesus was sleeping in the front of the boat and they waked him. When he waked up he said, "Peace be still," and the winds died down and the water became calm and there was no more storm.'

"Alice said at the end, 'Mary V., I really am thrilled to hear all this,' and Mary V. said, '*I* was thrilled.'

"When she had told us all of this we were all[5] so impressed. We asked her to tell us again and she told it all again. The whole story with its retelling took probably 20 minutes. Mary V. talked slowly, haltingly, but she gave the impression that she was telling exactly what had happened and that it had happened recently."

Ten years of being in a semi-vegetative state most of the time (though obviously not quite all the time) is too long by any standards. I would not wish it on anyone and I would not wish for any family to have to endure it. But I believe today that the Master with whom my dear aunt walked all of her life is the Lord of life and not of death, and that in this little story we see the furnishings of a life lived so interchangeably with the Word of God that there was no seam between past, present, and future, no disjunction between Emmaus and Emilius, Bethany and Franklin, no separation between the Master and Dick Cossitt, who, together with Lazarus, would come to be in need of the resurrection of the dead.[6]

5. One of the nurses was also present. In those days, it would have been a sure bet that a nurse in Franklin, Virginia, would have been a devout Christian.

6. Not the least remarkable feature of the story is that Mr. Cossitt had been

My father and Mary V. are both now lying in the cemetery side by side. I walk there often when I am back in Franklin. For me it is a place of life and not of death. It is a reminder that "there are more things in heaven and earth, Horatio, than are dreamt of in your [Stoic] philosophy." Her faith, and my father's and mother's (and the nurse's) response of awe and wonder on Christmas Day, are their gifts to me and mine to you. The final exit of the baptized is today. "All of us who have been baptized into Christ Jesus were baptized into his death. . . . But if we have died with Christ, we believe that we shall also live with him. . . . Christ being raised from the dead dieth no more; death has no more dominion over him. Yield yourselves to God as men and women who have been brought from death to life."

AMEN.

---

killed the year before, in 1978, in an automobile crash. It is possible that Mary V. was able to register this fact.

Death Shall Have No Dominion

Text: Romans 6:1-14

In four sermons preached this week, beginning on Palm Sunday, we have been concentrating on St. Paul's Epistle to the Christians in Rome. We are meditating on the death of Jesus Christ and what it means for us. This is no small question. Indeed it is *the* question of life and death. Everybody knows that Jesus of Nazareth met death by crucifixion, but few, even in the churches, are able to give a coherent account of what that meant. Perhaps at the end of this week all of us together, including the preacher, will have a deeper understanding of why our Lord was crucified. That is my prayer.

I call your attention to a verse in chapter 6: "The wages of sin is death" (Romans 6:23). A good deal of the first half of Paul's letter is spent showing how Sin and Death go together. Paul wants us to understand that death is not simply a natural process, but a Power linked with Sin to deal destruction to the human race.

This is not a popular concept in optimistic, positive-thinking America, but the great writers have always understood it. When I was in New Orleans a few years ago I took a walking tour of the French Quarter. The guide was a local history teacher, Kenneth Holditch, who had known Tennessee Williams well.[1] I still think of

---

1. When I wrote this sermon, I did not know, or had forgotten, that Tennessee Williams was born in St. Louis, where this sermon was preached. Such is the blessed

it as the best walking tour I ever took. He showed us the house on St. Peter Street where Tennessee (as he called him) was living on the third floor when he was completing his most famous play. He had been tinkering with various titles for it. He made his decision when he realized that he was located between two streetcar lines. If you know anything about old New Orleans you will recognize this; one streetcar went in one direction to Desire, the other went the other way to Cemeteries. This, Tennessee Williams thought, was a perfect metaphor for the human condition. That's where we live, caught between Desire and Cemeteries. There it is: Sin (desire) and Death (cemeteries). "The devices and desires of our own hearts" imprison us in Sin, and "the wages of sin is death" (Romans 6:23).

When I write sermons about Sin and Death, I capitalize those two words. The purpose of doing this is to show that Sin and Death are not just components of human life, but Powers that rule over us. That is the way Paul understands the situation. In our text for today he uses words that indicate their sovereign sway. Sin *reigns,* he says; Death *has dominion;* we are *enslaved by* Sin. I hope you see the point here. Sin is not something we can choose to avoid, any more than we can choose not to die. We are trapped between Desire and Cemeteries.

The apostle Paul is poorly understood in many of our churches for reasons having to do with our failure to teach him properly. His letters are often difficult to understand and we need help to read him. I did not really "get" Paul at all until I was several years out of seminary, even though I had had some of the best teaching available. There is a sort of "aha moment" for people in understanding Paul and that is something only the Holy Spirit can control. All the preacher can do is to bear witness, to say "look in this direction!" Look tonight in the direction of what Paul says about Sin and Death. In chapter 6 he leaves behind the long descriptions of how we have fallen into the grip of Sin and he launches into a kind of rhapsody about what happens to Christians when we are baptized.

Providence of God who makes his Word applicable even when we don't know he's doing it.

What shall we say then? Are we to continue in sin that grace may abound? By no means! How can we who died to sin still live in it? Do you not know that all of us who have been baptized into Christ Jesus were baptized into his death? We were buried therefore with him by baptism into death, so that as Christ was raised from the dead by the glory of the Father, we too might walk in newness of life.

This is amazing. Paul's teaching is so audacious and original that I am swept away by it every time I preach from it. We wouldn't understand any of this if we had only the Gospels. The Epistles are essential for filling out the meaning of the stories about Jesus in the four Gospels. Paul says that those who are baptized into Christ are crucified with Christ, meaning that all the benefits of his death become ours. He says that our sinful selves are put to death on the Cross so that we are no longer slaves to Sin. Think about your own baptism, and the baptisms of your children and others whom you love. In baptism the Holy Spirit acts to unite the person to Christ in his death and therefore to the death of the sinful self. As I wrote this sermon, as I deliver this sermon, I am forcibly struck by the power of this message. All the things we find upsetting about ourselves, the habits we cannot seem to shake, the personality traits that get us in trouble, the secret obsessions and perversions that we struggle to hide even from ourselves — all of this has been put to death:

> Our old self has been crucified with him so that the sinful body might be destroyed, and we might no longer be enslaved to sin. . . .

Paul knew that there was a danger in this teaching, and that danger will continue to cause people to resist Paul's teaching of the gospel as long as it is preached. We are frightened to death of the message of God's grace. In order to understand this fright, we need to go back a bit in Romans. In the section just before this one, Paul explains that "Christ's act of righteousness [on the Cross] leads to acquittal and life for all human beings"; and then he says the even more dangerous thing: "Where sin increased, grace abounded all the more" (5:20). Paul knew that some people would misunderstand this and would say, "Wow! If grace abounds all the more when sin increases, bring it on! Let's sin all the more!"[2] But this is indeed to misunderstand totally, as Paul says in our text tonight: "Are we to continue in sin that grace may abound? By no means!" We need to give a lot of emphasis to that *By no means!* Paul's tone is more like this: "No, no, no! if you think that, you have gotten the whole thing wrong! You aren't even in the ball park! How can we who died to sin still live in it?"

I've been trying to think of a way to put this across. If you've been living in a prison and are set free, would you want to go back to it? If you conquer a bad habit, would you want to take it up again? But that doesn't really work, does it? It is well known; we *do* go back to bad habits, more often than not. People who lose weight gain it back. Recovering alcoholics fall off the wagon. People who have committed adultery once find it easier to do it the second time. We say "never again" to genocide, and just look at what is happening.[3] These things occur constantly. The fact that this is so is evidence of the power of Sin, which "reigns in death" (Romans 5:21). It is precisely this fact, that Sin has such a grip on us, that points to the Crucifixion of our Lord:

> Our old self was crucified with him so that the sinful body might be destroyed, and we might no longer be enslaved to sin.

But again: what are we to make of the fact that we slip back into Sin so frequently? Yes, Paul seems to be saying, but Sin no longer determines us. It no longer rules our lives in the same total way. In our baptisms something objective has happened, something that

2. This was the problem in the Corinthian church. They were so thrilled with the good news that they thought they had already become free from sin. The Galatian church had the opposite problem; fearing the license of churches like Corinth, they were becoming more legalistic.

3. The genocide in Darfur was being widely ignored by the world, just as the Cambodian and Rwandan genocides were.

comes to us from outside ourselves, and as we grow into the baptismal life we more and more recognize how we can appropriate this great truth:

> For if we have been united with him in a death like his, we shall certainly be united with him in a resurrection like his.

Union with Christ! United with him in his death, united with him in the resurrection of the dead. In other religious systems, in Gnostic systems, the religious elite are supposed to do this for themselves. We seek after union with the divine and if we get it right, we find enlightenment, or the higher consciousness, or some other sort of oneness with the divine. The Christian story is the opposite of this. We could do nothing for ourselves, religiously or otherwise, because the iron grip of Sin and Death separated us from God by such a chasm that there was no hope for us. God bridged that gap in his own person. It is in our new identity with him that we find our future. This news is so incomparable that Paul is seized by its joy. He says in several different ways, as if he can't ever tire of saying it:

> We have been united with Christ in a death like his,
> we shall be united with him in a resurrection like his. . . .
> We have died with Christ,
> we believe that we shall also live with him.

So this unity with our Lord Jesus is something that exists in real lives and cannot be defeated by Sin. Our union with him is something that God has done, and therefore there is nothing we can do to undo it, because he is stronger than Sin, stronger than Death. He has shown this in the Resurrection of Christ from the dead:

> Christ being raised from the dead will never die again; death no longer has dominion over him. The death he died he died to sin, once for all, but the life he lives he lives to God. So you also must consider yourselves dead to sin and alive to God in Christ Jesus.

This breathtaking declaration of deliverance for us makes all the difference in the world. Indeed it is a new world, not anything like the old one. We have a new power over Sin now. We can live as new people. That's what Paul means when he says, by no means! You aren't going to sin more so that grace may abound; "How can we who died to sin still live in it?" And he makes this passionate appeal:

> Do not yield your members to sin as instruments of wickedness, but yield yourselves to God as people who have been brought from death to life, and bring your members to God as instruments of righteousness. For sin will have no dominion over you, since you are not under law but under grace.

"Bring your members [all the constituent parts of your self] to God as instruments of righteousness." Perhaps you have heard that Paul's ethical teaching can be summarized in these words: "Become what you already are!" You already are an instrument of God's righteousness because he has made you that way, by uniting you with Christ in your baptism. Now you can actually be an instrument of God's righteousness! You can act like one! What liberation!

There is a paradox here, however, that nothing I can say will remove in this life. The paradox must remain until the Last Day. In this life we remain, as Martin Luther put it, saints and sinners simultaneously *(simul peccator et iustus)*. We are sinners, but everything has changed because we are now justified sinners. We are sinners not only declared righteous but actually on our way to being made righteous. We hinted at that in the sermon yesterday; it is God who does the making righteous. Only God can do this work. He has already done it, in the death and Resurrection of Christ. We are assimilated into his Cross, into his risen life.

Tennessee Williams died a very sad death. He died alone in the Chelsea Hotel in New York City. The autopsy disclosed that something had lodged in his throat; he had choked to death, with no one to assist him. Drugs may have been involved; alcohol may have been involved. He was certainly not a model citizen, nor was he a Christian in the conventional sense. But the guide on the walking tour told us something else. I was so struck by it that I wrote down what he said.

> The house Tennessee owned and lived in is on Toulouse Street, but his first choice of a house to buy had been the large one at the corner of Orleans and Dauphine. The reason he wanted it was that the upper windows afforded a view of the statue of Christ behind the St. Louis Cathedral. Christ is lifting his hands in blessing, and at night the spotlights cast a shadow much larger than the statue itself, making the statue's embrace seem universal. Tennessee said that it seemed to him as if Christ was comforting the suffering world and it gave him a sense of peace to look at it.[4]

Isaiah prophesied that the Messiah "would not break a bruised reed" (Isaiah 42:3). If we think Tennessee Williams died beyond the reach of Christ's embrace, we deny our Lord his ultimate victory. All of us will die as sinners, but in our text tonight Paul promises: "Sin will have no dominion over you, since you are not under law but under grace." Sin will have no dominion over you, and death shall have no dominion.

It is true that some of us bruised reeds are more bruised than others. Many times I have looked at the statue behind the Cathedral in New Orleans and I have thought of what a bruised reed I am. Drugs, drink, and debauchery may not be my particular temptations, but I too am caught between Desire and Cemeteries. I too will die as a sinner. But I will die as a baptized sinner, a justified sinner, a sinner united to Christ not by my "spirituality" but by his prior action on my behalf.

For everyone within reach of these words tonight, the gospel comes to you with all its original power. The death and Resurrection of Christ was not something that was over and done with long ago. It is present in all its majestic force this very night, for the

---

4. Professor Kenneth Holditch, March 24, 2000.

Word of God is living and active, creating new lives and new hope and new victories wherever it is heard.

> What shall we say then? Are we to continue in sin that grace may abound? By no means! How can we who died to sin still live in it? Do you not know that all of us who have been baptized into Christ Jesus were baptized into his death? We were buried therefore with him by baptism into death, so that as Christ was raised from the dead by the glory of the Father, we too might walk in newness of life.

AMEN.

Divine Love Meets the Strongest Animal

ST. FRANCIS EPISCOPAL CHURCH, POTOMAC, MARYLAND

The wages of sin is death.

ROMANS 6:23, RSV

Since therefore the children {of God} share in flesh and blood, {the Son of God} himself likewise shared the same nature, so that through death he might destroy him who has the power of death, that is, the devil, and deliver all those who all their lives were held in slavery by the fear of death.

HEBREWS 2:14-15, NRSV

Those of us who are over 60 will never forget how the whole country gathered around its black-and-white television sets for the funeral of John F. Kennedy. I can still see it as if it were yesterday — the caisson, the riderless horse, the Kennedy women in black veils. Most of all I can still hear that drum roll, over and over and over, with its unrelenting demand, *memento mori,* remember Death. We remember, too, that when Jacqueline Kennedy returned to Washington from Dallas, she asked for research materials about Abraham Lincoln's funeral. We owe her a great debt for that. Flannery O'Connor wrote a letter to a friend, at the time, in which she made a very important observation. She wrote, "Mrs. Kennedy has a sense of history and of what is owing to death."[1]

What does that mean, "what is owing to death"? Today, this Good Friday, we have gathered not around television sets or movie screens, not in theaters or entertainment centers, but together as a family in this place, with the flowers all gone and the church bare of comfort, to pay Death what is owing to it, to acknowledge the reality, the remorselessness, the implacable power of Death.[2] When our Lord drew near the tomb of Lazarus, the Evangelist John tells us, he groaned deeply in his spirit three times as he faced down the Power of Death. St. Paul writes that Death is *the last enemy* of man and God (1 Corinthians 15:26). If death is only a small thing, a passing thing, a negligible thing, then the victory won by our Lord is only a small, passing, negligible thing, a religious idea among other religious ideas, having no special distinction or significance.

The last enemy, Paul calls Death in I Corinthians. In Romans, he spells out another truth about the enormous, annihilating Power of Death. This second truth about Death is its diabolical partnership with the Power of Sin. Paul writes that we were "slaves of sin" (Romans 6:17, 20). This word *slave* carries a big freight. Slavery means servitude, bondage, imprisonment with no capacity to free ourselves. "The end (*telos,* goal) of sin," Paul continues, "is death." We can't understand this fully unless we understand Sin as a Power, a personal intelligence with an implacable purpose, and that's ex-

1. *The Habit of Being* (New York: Farrar, Straus and Giroux, 1979), p. 552.

2. As indicated in the Introduction, in this written version of my sermons I generally capitalize the words Sin, Death, and Power, to indicate their status as independent entities (as "principalities and powers"). These enemy forces are external to and independent of the human being, operating under their own source of power and arrayed against God in the cosmic arena. Sin is more than the sum of human misdeeds, and Death is more than individual deaths. All of this is personified in the symbolic figure of Satan. No one has written better about the Powers, especially Death, than William Stringfellow in his various books.

I also capitalize Love in this particular sermon in order to show that it, too, is a Power — a Power strong enough to conquer the Enemy because it is the power of God himself.

actly what Paul means to say.[3] The aim of Sin is Death for the human being. "Sin works death in me," Paul writes (Romans 7:13). And in case we did not get the point, he says it another way: "Sin pays a wage, and the wage is death" (J. B. Phillips translation) or, more familiarly, "The wages of sin is death" (Romans 6:23). So the truly terrible thing about Death is not simple mortality. The truly terrible thing is the bonding of Death with Sin in absolute, total enmity toward God and the human being.

There is another text that illustrates this further. It is from the Epistle to the Hebrews:

> Since therefore the children [of God] share in flesh and blood, [the Son of God] himself likewise shared the same nature, so that through death he might destroy him who has the power of death, that is, the devil, and deliver all those who all their lives were held in slavery by the fear of death.

The writer of Hebrews, whose identity is unknown to us, explains that Jesus the Son of God shared our flesh and blood, not on general principles because it was a nice companionable thing to do, but for a specific purpose. He shared our flesh and blood, our vulnerable material existence full of suffering and pain, so that *through death* the power of Death would be destroyed. The only way to conquer Death was to engage Death on its own territory, *mano a mano*. Listen again: the Son of God shared our flesh and blood "so that *through death* he might destroy him who has the power of death."

The Power of Death is given a name in this Hebrews text. Behind the power of death is the power of the devil himself, the great Antagonist of God, who has the unique capacity to overwhelm all our good intentions and set in motion a spiral of retribution that takes on a life of its own. This Antagonist, this Enemy must be resisted. The Church is called to this ministry of resistance. The

---

3. Flannery O'Connor says this too. "Our salvation is played out with the Devil, a Devil who is not simply generalized evil, but an evil intelligence determined on its own supremacy . . ." (letter to John Hawkes, November 20, 1959).

deadly temptation, however, is that because of Sin, Death's co-equal Power, even our resistance can get drawn into the orbit of death. This is true of every person and every group, whether it be in the church or in our country. A recent *New Yorker* magazine article tells the story of a Muslim man from Sarajevo, in Bosnia, who was abducted in his own country by mysterious masked figures, at least one of them an American, who shipped him off to Guantánamo where he has remained for three years, although his own government was unable to charge him with anything at all. His case was brought to the Pentagon's review tribunal in October and was rejected, no reasons given. The article quotes from his wife's letters, pleading for some sort of help. In response to this case, a former CIA lawyer, now a professor of law in St. Paul, Minnesota, had this to say: "As a society, we haven't figured out what the rough rules are yet. . . . It's the law of the jungle. And right now we happen to be the strongest animal."[4] That's an American speaking. This is a *professor of law* speaking. This is the way that people and governments become drunk with the power to deal out judgment upon others.

"The strongest animal." I have a grandson so I know that all little boys love dinosaurs. They love strength and power. Children always want to be the strongest animal. When they grow up to be law professors and CIA agents and politicians they still want to be the strongest animal. But no one, no one at all, can be trusted with absolute power. The stronger one becomes, the greater the temptation to abuse power. That, by the way, is the message of J. R. R. Tolkien's book *The Lord of the Rings.* The celebrated story is not about a simple struggle of "Good vs. Evil." Tolkien's theme is the capacity of the Enemy to overtake even the best among us.[5] No one among us is free of the grip of Sin and Death.

The gospel message in Paul and in Hebrews is that our Lord destroyed the Power of Death *through* (or *by*) Death. How are we to

---

4. Jane Mayer, "Outsourcing Torture," *The New Yorker,* February 14-21, 2005.

5. Tolkien makes it abundantly clear, not only in his book but also in his letters, that his principal "good" characters, Gandalf and Aragorn, are not immune to the demonic powers.

understand that? The ordinary way of thinking about destroying an enemy with his own weapons is to use his own weapons against him. Jesus Christ did something entirely different. Christ defeated Death by Death, but here is the key: he did not use the weapons of Death. He *suffered* Death in order to *conquer* Death, he *underwent* Death in order to *overcome* Death, he *submitted* to Death in order to *subdue* Death; but he fought Death *not by duplicating its methods,* but *by entering its realm,* entering it with no defenses whatever except trust in the ultimate purpose of God the Father.

And so the only Christian way to resist the Enemy is by the way of renunciation of the Enemy's weapons. If you go to Westminster Abbey in London, you will see above the main entrance ten statues, unveiled in 1998. They are twentieth-century Christian martyrs, male and female, from countries all over the world. They include Martin Luther King, Bishop Romero of El Salvador who was shot while celebrating Mass, and Anglican Archbishop of Uganda Janani Luwum who was murdered by Idi Amin.[6] The ten represent all the Christian martyrs of all the ages.[7] They are to be distinguished from terrorists who call themselves martyrs, because suicide bombers seek the deaths of others in their own deaths. They cannot defeat Death this way, for they are using Death's own weapons. Christian martyrs do not do this. They give themselves up to Death by bearing witness to God's purpose of peace. The twentieth-century martyrs of Westminster Abbey lit a flame for the rest of us that can never be extinguished. All over the world at this very mo-

---

6. Dietrich Bonhoeffer is also represented. It is occasionally said of Bonhoeffer that he is not a true martyr because, in order to resist Hitler, he took up Hitler's own weapons. In a narrow sense that is true. But it was not without the greatest soul-searching and most profound humility and hard-won submission to the will of God, with clear-eyed knowledge of the consequences and full acceptance of his fate. He believed that this was something that had to be done and therefore he would do it himself. He would not send someone else to do it. He would put himself in the place of utmost danger. He would seek only the death of Hitler and his closest colleagues, no one else — especially not innocent bystanders. Dietrich Bonhoeffer was truly a Christian hero: a witness, a martyr.

7. The Westminster Abbey website gives detailed information about all ten. Go to www.westminster-abbey.org and click on "West Front of Abbey."

ment there are Christians being held hostage for their faith. May our Lord grant them courage and strength to bear their witness to his victory over the machinery of Death.

Some of you may have read Thomas Friedman's column day before yesterday.[8] It has a witty title: "George W. to George W." It is a message from George Washington to George W. Bush. Friedman is very upset (as we should all be) that 26 prisoners have died in American military custody. He has been reading the new book about George Washington crossing the Delaware, and he has found an important lesson in it. When Washington's army had successfully crossed and had captured the Hessian garrison, the question arose about giving quarter to the large number of prisoners that had been taken. It seems that, in Europe, giving quarter was optional. You could give it, or you could not give it. General Washington ordered that in America, it would always be given. Americans would always treat prisoners with humanity. That would be the American way. On a higher level, we might say that it is *the mind of Christ.*

The whole world is watching America, because we are the "strongest animal." The whole world knows that we are a deeply religious people. American evangelical Christianity is now making headlines around the world in ways that would have been unimaginable a year or two ago. The question becomes, what sort of Christianity is this? Are we showing forth the mind of Christ? Is ours a religion that in the end becomes indistinguishable from nationalism? Will we conduct ourselves in a way that speaks of our Lord who entered the realm of Death with no weapons at all except trust in God?

Now, this Good Friday, the lens which has been focused on the geopolitical world narrows its focus to you, gathered today to hear the word of the Cross. What can you do, what can I do, what can we do here — just outside the Beltway — to gird ourselves for our own battles against Sin and Death? I am going to offer a suggestion which I pray the Holy Spirit to bless.

On Good Friday the Church stands first in line to admit its

8. Thomas Friedman, *The New York Times,* March 24, 2005.

own complicity. We admit that, had we been there, we would have joined our voices to those of the mob in the biblical story. We do this as an act of prayer and contrition, an act of solidarity with other Christians around the world who do not want to be let off the hook but desire this day to acknowledge a very deep truth: the Lord is being tortured to death, not only to take the part of the victims of the world, but also and most incredibly, to take also the place of the perpetrators. When Jesus prayed on the Cross, it was not for the victims that he interceded. When he prayed "Father, forgive them," he was interceding for the perpetrators.

In order to put ourselves into this story, we are going to sing a hymn, kneeling, as a prayer. This hymn was written in the seventeenth century by a Christian man who wanted to help others to be drawn into the meaning of our Lord's Passion and death, for themselves, personally — for *ourselves,* personally. "I crucified thee."

Singing this hymn will prepare us for the Reproaches which will follow. The Reproaches have a tragic history because, in the Middle Ages, they began to be interpreted as having to do specifically with the Jews. If you follow the words, you can see how that happened, since the story they tell is the story of the Jews, As we sing "Ah, holy Jesus," however, we will see what a tragic mistake it was to think that the Reproaches referred only to the Jews and not to Christians. We will sing of *our own* role in Christ's sufferings — not the role of the Romans, not the role of "the Jews," but your role and mine. *We* are the people who are being "reproached."

In a strange way, this is what binds us all together at this third hour. We are making our confession that we are all complicit in the rule of Sin and Death. This is the most important thing we can do today. "There is no distinction," Paul writes in Romans, for "all human beings . . . are under the power of sin" (Romans 3:9, 22). By recognizing our own involvement in Sin and Death, we thankfully and joyfully embrace the deliverance that has come to us *from a realm outside this reign of terror.* In recognizing the full extent of the Lord's mercy to those who tortured and killed him, we will find ourselves never wanting to abuse our power to wreak torture or vengeance on anyone. We will find our greatest strength, not in being the strongest animal in the jungle, but by binding ourselves today to the power of Jesus Christ's self-sacrificing love. It is this Love that has come to save us from ourselves. It is this Love that overcomes Death: "Love divine, all loves excelling, joy of heaven to earth come down."[9] It is this Love that looks upon you, this day, looks upon your heart and sees you as you really are within yourself, sees you with all your contradictions and flaws, your deceptions and your failures, your sorrows and your losses, and bids you abide in him and be remade with a freshly cleansed heart and a completely new spirit.

> Ah, holy Jesus, how hast thou offended,
> That man to judge thee hath in hate pretended?
> By foes derided, by thine own rejected,
> O most afflicted.
>
> Who was the guilty? Who brought this upon thee?
> Alas, my treason, Jesus, hath undone thee.
> 'Twas I, Lord Jesus, I it was denied thee,
> I crucified thee.
>
> Lo, the Good Shepherd for the sheep is offered;
> The slave hath sinnèd, and the Son hath suffered;
> For our atonement, while we nothing heeded,
> God interceded.
>
> For me, kind Jesus, was thy incarnation,
> Thy mortal sorrow, and thy life's oblation;
> Thy death of anguish and thy bitter passion,
> For my salvation.[10]

9. Hymn by Charles Wesley (1707-1788).

10. Hymn by Johann Heermann (1585-1647). Translated by Robert Seymour Bridges, 1899.

The Reproaches

Because I, the Lord thy God, brought thee forth from the land of Egypt: thou hast prepared a cross for thy Saviour.

Holy God, holy and mighty, Holy and immortal, have mercy upon us.

Because I, the Lord thy God, led thee throughout the desert forty years, and fed thee with manna, and brought thee into a land exceeding good: thou hast prepared a Cross for thy Saviour.

Holy God, holy and mighty, Holy and immortal, have mercy upon us.

What more could I have done for thee that I have not done, saith the Lord thy God? I indeed did plant thee, O my vineyard, exceeding fair, and thou art become very bitter unto me: for vinegar thou gavest me to quench my thirst, and thou hast pierced with a spear the side of thy Saviour.

Holy God, holy and mighty, Holy and immortal, have mercy upon us.

I, the Lord thy God, did scourge Egypt with her first-born for thy sake; and thou hast scourged me. I led thee forth out of Egypt, through the Red Sea: and thou hast delivered me unto the chief priests. I did open the sea before thee: and thou hast opened my side with a spear.

O my people, what have I done unto thee; or wherein have I wearied thee, saith the Lord? Testify against me.

I did go before thee in the pillar of cloud: and thou hast brought me unto the judgment hall of Pilate. I did feed thee with manna in the desert: and thou hast stricken me with blows and scourges. I did give thee to drink of the water of life from the rock: and thou hast given me to drink salt and vinegar.

O my people, what have I done unto thee; or wherein have I wearied thee, saith the Lord? Testify against me.

I did smite kings for thy sake: and thou hast smitten my head with a reed. I did give thee a royal scepter: and thou hast set upon my head a crown of thorns. I did raise thee on high with great power: and thou hast hanged me upon the gibbet of the Cross.

Holy God, Holy and mighty, Holy and immortal, have mercy upon us.

Who Will Feed the Wolf?

The Bethlehem Chapel in the National Cathedral, Washington, D.C.

I have been told that I have only eight minutes to speak to you this morning. Some of you I may never see again. I wish to speak to you as George Whitefield said of himself: "I preached as one never to preach again . . . , as a dying man to dying men." May the Holy Spirit give me something to say that you will not forget, that indeed will be received by you as the Word of Eternal Life.

My text is from St. Paul's letter to the Romans, chapter 7:

> I find it to be a law that when I want to do right, evil lies close at hand. For I delight in the law of God in my inmost self, but I see in my members another law at war with the law of my mind and making me captive to the law of sin which dwells in my members. Wretched man that I am! Who will deliver me from this body of death? Thanks be to God through Jesus Christ our Lord! (Romans 7:21-25)

The story I am going to tell is all over the Internet. It probably comes in several different versions. Here is the version that I heard a few days ago.

An old Cherokee is instructing his young son. "Son," he says, "everyone has two wolves inside of them. One wolf is violent, wild, and destructive. The other wolf is disciplined, wise, and benevolent. They are fighting inside of you. Which wolf will win?"

The boy, looking alarmed, says, "I don't know."

The old man says, "The wolf that will win is the wolf that is fed."

St. Paul describes this conflict that goes on in every soul: "I delight in the law of God, in my inmost self, but I see in myself *another law* at war with the [good] law of my mind, making me captive to the law of sin which dwells in me." Two wolves, the law of God and the law of sin. As it happens, the Oscar-winning movie *Crash* illustrates this in exquisite detail. None of the numerous major characters are pure evil or pure good; both forces are *at war* within the same person.

You want to do the right thing, don't you? You want to be honest in business, a good citizen, available to your spouse and children, attentive to your colleagues and friends. You want to be vigorous, fit, free of anxiety. You want to be kind, unselfish, generous. So why do you find yourself being stingy, slothful, duplicitous, self-centered, neglectful, and bad-tempered?

This works on the national level as well. America has two wolves fighting for dominance. The good America is open, generous, and free. The ugly America is arrogant, bullying, triumphalist.

And indeed, this predicament is universal. As Paul puts it, all human beings are "captive to the law of sin," and what's more, the whole creation is "in bondage to decay" (Romans 8:21), in bondage to the principalities and powers, in bondage to the same antagonisms, the same prejudices, the same wars, world without end. The more young men we arm and send overseas to be heroes, the more come back with post-traumatic stress disorder.

One of the most fatuous slogans ever dreamed up is "the triumph of the human spirit." Which human spirit is that? The good one or the ugly one? Which wolf will win?

The one that is fed.

Who is going to feed the good wolf? Are you? Then why are you so neglectful of your obligations? Why are you giving away so little of your substance? Why is the service of God only one thing among many things in your life? To quote one of our great Lenten hymns, why is "our prayer so languid and our faith so dim"? Why?

Because, as blessed Thomas Cranmer wrote in the Collect for the third Sunday in Lent, *we have no power of ourselves to help ourselves.* We are "captive to the law of sin."

And so Paul is speaking for the whole lot of us when he cries out, "Wretched human being that I am! Who will deliver me from this body of death?"

We cannot deliver ourselves from the demons of our worse nature. Left to ourselves, we will feed the carnivorous wolf every time. But we are not left to ourselves. The deepest meaning of the Christian story is that we have been delivered by the self-offering of the Good Shepherd, the one who, as he said himself, lays down his life to keep the wolves from destroying the sheep (John 10:11-15). And so Paul concludes: "The law of the Spirit of life in Christ Jesus has set me free from the law of sin and death" (Romans 8:2). Here is food indeed, here is drink indeed, the bread and wine and Word of eternal life. Thanks be to God through Jesus Christ our Lord!

AMEN.

Frodo and Free Will

NOTE TO READERS: This sermon was originally written
for a Presbyterian congregation. It was preached in two
Presbyterian contexts during 2002, the year following the release
of Peter Jackson's first, wildly popular *Lord of the Rings* movie.
This version was delivered at an evening service at the Episcopal
Church of the Ascension, Lafayette, Louisiana, April 13, 2002.
These insights are expanded in my book *The Battle for
Middle-earth: Tolkien's Divine Design in "The Lord of the Rings"*
(Grand Rapids: Eerdmans, 2004).

*I do not understand my own actions. For I do not do what I
want, but I do the very thing I hate. . . . I can will what is
right, but I cannot do it. For I do not do the good I want, but the
evil I do not want is what I do. Now if I do what I do not want,
it is no longer I that do it, but sin which dwells within me. . . .*

ROMANS 7:15-20

*The law of the Spirit of life in Christ Jesus has set me free from
the law of sin and death.*

ROMANS 8:2

Any Presbyterians here this evening? When I was young I was told
that Presbyterians were bad because they believed in predestination. Nobody had any freedom, everything was figured out for you

ahead of time and there wasn't anything you could do about it. But you can't fool all of the people all the time. As a young Episcopalian I discovered something in the back of the Prayer Book called the Thirty-Nine Articles. They are still there, although the people who designed our present Prayer Book put them into teeny-weeny print so nobody would read them. I used to sneak a look at the Thirty-Nine Articles when I got bored with the sermon. They were put together by the Church of England during the Reformation. Article XVII is entitled, "Of Predestination and Election." It's quite long so I will only read a bit of it.

> Predestination to life is the everlasting purpose of God, whereby before the foundations of the world were laid he hath constantly decreed . . . to deliver from curse and damnation those whom he hath chosen in Christ . . . and to bring them by Christ to everlasting salvation. . . .
>
> . . . the godly consideration of Predestination, and our Election in Christ, is full of sweet, pleasant and unspeakable comfort. . . .

When I read that as a teenager, it sounded pretty good to me. What I fastened on, without entirely realizing it, was the idea that somehow I, this young unformed person, was part of God's everlasting purpose before the foundation of the world. It did indeed seem like "sweet, pleasant and unspeakable comfort" to me — and it does still.

As I grew older and studied theology more seriously, I began to hear more about people's horror of "predestination." Anything suggesting predestination was completely unacceptable, I was told, because it was contradictory to the great American gospel of Free Will, which was even more sacred than the Bible itself. All during my ministry I have noticed that questioning the doctrine of Free Will, more than any other subject, will cause a discussion group to go completely off the rails. The Bible, God, Jesus, miracles, prophets, apostles, church — all that is well and good, but the center of it all is the human decision, the human choice. Right? But on the other hand there are those passages in Scripture that suggest otherwise — perhaps you will remember what Jesus says to the disciples in the Gospel of John: "You did not choose me, but I chose you and appointed you that you should go and bear fruit and that your fruit should abide" (John 15:14).

Well, goes the argument, OK, God chooses us, but then it's up to us to decide whether to accept his choice of us or not. So the emphasis is back on us again; the action moves away from God. God is no longer the subject of the sentence; we are. Our decision, our choice, becomes the center of attention.

But let's listen again to what St. Paul says about this. "I do not understand my own actions. For I do not do what I want, but I do the very thing I hate. . . . I can will what is right, but I cannot do it. For I do not do the good I want, but the evil I do not want is what I do. Now if I do what I do not want, it is no longer I that do it, but sin which dwells within me. . . ."

Paul is describing a war that goes on in the human being all the time. William Faulkner, in his Nobel Prize speech, said that the most important subject of literature was "the human heart in conflict with itself." After Paul, the person who best described this situation was St. Augustine of Hippo in North Africa. To this day, Augustine remains astonishingly fashionable. New material is being published about him all the time. He uses the example of the mind giving the body an order: for example, the order to the hand to move. The hand moves so rapidly that there is no distinction between the command and the execution of it. When the mind commands the will to do something, however, the will does not obey. Just think of it. Have you tried to stay on a diet? Have you tried to control your temper? Have you vowed not to go over your credit card limit? Have you resolved to do your exercises faithfully? Have you told yourself not to be resentful of others' success? Have people said to you, "Get over it!" when you know you can't? The list goes on. The theologian Karl Barth says it is like trying to pull ourselves out of a swamp by our own hair. When Bob Dole was running for president, his speech coach taped reminders to his refrigerator — finish your sentences, emphasize the most important words, don't call yourself "Bob Dole." At the same time, the coach later admitted, he knew that Dole would not be able to follow the advice.[1] The command does not translate itself into a change of will. The good that I would do is not what I do.[2] Augustine concludes, "The enemy held my will, and he made a chain of it and bound me by it — by my own iron will."

So Paul and Augustine both depict a conflict in which every individual is caught, unable to gain mastery over the forces at war within himself. The more supposed "choices" we have, the more we are deceived about this. Too much "choice" is bad for us. Years ago, I used to go to the store and buy either Dijon mustard or Heinz mustard . . . two choices. Now I go to the store to buy mustard and I am confronted by fifty different kinds of mustard. My anxiety level rises. Should I learn more about mustard? Somebody else out there knows more about mustard than I do. Choosing among mustards may make us feel free for a moment, but it is only an illusion of freedom. I can choose a mustard, but I can't seem to make myself stop procrastinating.

Whatever you may think of Sigmund Freud, there is no going back on his major discoveries about the power of the unconscious. People do things without having any idea why they are doing them. We pursue destructive courses for reasons deeply buried in our psyches from long years before. Someone will say of another person, "He is his own worst enemy," not realizing that we are all our own worst enemies. It's just that it's more obvious with some people than others. There are people who have no trouble keeping thin. They work out every day. (Don't you hate them?) They gave up smoking years ago. They have never been fired from their jobs. All their children are good looking and smart and successful. Those are the people who love to say, "God helps those who help themselves." We all know people like this, people who for one reason or another

1. *Newsweek,* November 18, 1996.

2. And what of choices made by society, by nations? A few days ago (March 10, 2002), another cultural critic, James Gorman, writing in *The New York Times,* wrote these devastatingly ironical words: "The year 2001 was designated 'The United Nations' Year of International Cooperation.' That went well."

have never been forced to confront their own failings. If only we could tell them!

Martin Luther, following Augustine and Paul, wrote about the bondage of the will. American Christians don't like this train of thought. If we grant that our wills are impotent, it seems as if we're giving away something absolutely fundamental. Isn't making the right choices the very basis of the moral life? If we have no capacity to choose the right thing, doesn't that make us robots, mere puppets?

Now we have arrived at Frodo and *The Lord of the Rings*.

As most people probably know by now, *The Lord of the Rings* is a thoroughly Christian story. You wouldn't know it from the movie; it's the book that counts. The free will debate is right in the middle of the whole thing. What is most important, human choice, or the overarching purpose of a Higher Power?

The movie ads quote Frodo talking to Gandalf.[3] He says, "I wish the Ring had never come to me. I wish none of this had ever happened." "So do I," said Gandalf, "and so do all who live to see such times. But that is not for [us] to decide. All we have to decide is what to do with the time that is given us."

Now that, surely, puts all the focus on the human decision, or the hobbit decision as the case may be. In this view, Frodo's choice becomes the main theme of the story. But if you look more closely at the book, something else emerges.

For those who might not know, let's just explain that the Ruling Ring in the story is not only all-powerful but also all-evil. No one can use the Ring for good, yet the temptation to try to do so is overwhelming for absolutely everyone. It is universally agreed that Tolkien's great theme is that no one can be trusted with absolute power, no one at all. Virtuous people are especially endangered because they think they can use the Ring for good. I was reminded of this so much last week when I read an article by the eminent British scholar Timothy Garton Ash. He loves America and lives here half

---

3. From 2001 to 2003, one of the three *Lord of the Rings* movies were released each December. This sermon refers to the first movie and its advertising.

the year, but he thinks America has too much power for her own good. He writes in *The New York Review of Books,* "Not even an archangel can be trusted with so much power."

All through *The Lord of the Rings,* we see the struggle within each person between the power of the Ring and the power of . . . well, what? Listen to what happens at the council of Elrond. Everyone has turned to Frodo to see if he will accept the assignment to destroy the Ring.

> A great dread fell on [Frodo] as if he was awaiting the pronouncement of some doom that he had long foreseen and vainly hoped might after all never be spoken. An overwhelming longing to rest and remain at peace . . . in Rivendell filled all his heart. At last *with an effort he spoke,* and wondered to hear his own words, *as if some other will was using his small voice.* "I will take the Ring," he said, "although I do not know the way."[4]

The book is full of hints like this, hints of "some other will," a higher will, at work. Early in the story, Gandalf says to a very reluctant Frodo, "'There was *something else* at work, beyond any desire of the Ring maker. . . . Bilbo *was meant* to have the Ring, and not by its maker. In which case you also *were meant* to have it."[5] When Frodo looks into the mirror of Galadriel, he sees "many swift scenes [that he] in some way knew to be parts of a great history in which he had become involved." This comforts and strengthens him — it encourages him.

The climax of Frodo's struggle (in the first volume) comes near the end. Finding himself alone and in extreme danger, he is seized by an irresistible temptation to do what he knows he must never do. He puts the Ring on his finger. It is a parallel to Adam and Eve, who took the forbidden fruit. Frodo's calamitous action yields him up to the Dark Lord. He is carried off into the Black Land [Mordor] by the Ring.

4. J. R. R. Tolkien, *The Lord of the Rings: The Fellowship of the Ring* (Boston: Houghton Mifflin, 1965), p. 284; emphasis added.

5. Emphasis added.

All hope left him. And suddenly he felt the Eye. There was an eye in the Dark Tower that did not sleep. He knew that it had become aware of his gaze. A *fierce eager will* was there. It leaped towards him . . .[6]

Frodo heard himself saying two opposite things at once.

He heard himself crying out, Never, never! Or was it, Verily I come, I come to you? He could not tell. Then as *a flash from some other point of power* there came to his mind another thought: Take it off! Fool, take it off! Take off the Ring!
   The two powers strove in him. . . . he writhed, tormented. Suddenly he was aware of himself again. . . . Frodo rose to his feet. A great weariness was on him, but his will was firm and his heart lighter. He spoke aloud to himself. *"I will do what I must,"* he said.[7]

Here in this climactic scene we see before us the struggle that St. Paul depicts. There is a "fierce eager will" leaping toward us. This is called by Paul the Power of Sin and Death. This Power does not rest in its determination to enslave us all. It is not passive; it actively reaches out for us, and without aid from another source, we are powerless in its grip. "The enemy held my will, and he made a chain of it and bound me by it — by my own iron will." But we are not powerless. Aid has come to us from "some other point of power." That is how we find ourselves free, *free to follow with an unburdened heart what has already been determined for us:* as Frodo puts it, "I will do what I must."
   The very best description that I know of this strange but ultimate paradox is given by Tolkien's friend C. S. Lewis in his second volume of his space fantasy, *Perelandra.* The main character, Ransom, has to make a decision. Is he going to engage Satan in hand-to-hand combat, or not? The freedom of the unfallen planet Venus de-

6. *Lord of the Rings: The Fellowship of the Ring,* p. 418; emphasis added.
7. Emphasis added.

pends on it, but he may fall into Hell as a result. He struggles with his decision. Suddenly

> . . . there had arisen before him, with perfect certitude, the knowl-edge [that] "about this time tomorrow you will have done the im-possible." . . . The future act stood there, fixed and unaltered as if he had already performed it. . . . *You might say, if you liked, that the power of choice had been simply set aside* and an inflexible destiny sub-stituted for it. *On the other hand,* you might say that he had been delivered from the rhetoric of his passions and *had emerged into un-assailable freedom.* Ransom could not, for the life of him, see any difference between these two statements. *Predestination and freedom were apparently identical.* He could no longer see any meaning in the many arguments he had heard on this subject.[8]

Predestination and freedom were apparently identical. That is the Christian gospel.

It is amazing how strongly we resist this glorious message. Here is a verse from Philippians which expresses it exactly. You have heard the first half of this verse many times, because we prefer it; rarely do we hear the all-important second half. Listen closely to the way the second half of the verse gives the meaning for the first half:

> Work out your own salvation with fear and trembling; for God is at work in you, both to will and to work for his good pleasure. (Philippians 2:12-13)

Whose will would you rather have, your will or God's will? Your choice, or God's choice? What do we say in the Lord's prayer — thy kingdom come, thy will be done? Do we mean that? No, we don't, not left to ourselves we don't. To quote our Prayer Book again, "We have followed too much the devices and desires of our

---

8. C. S. Lewis, *Perelandra* (New York: Macmillan, paperback edition, 1965), p. 149.

own hearts." But we are not left to our own devices. Romans 7 is followed by Romans 8:

> The law of the Spirit of life in Christ Jesus has set me free from the law of sin and death. (Romans 8:2)

Now we come back to *The Lord of the Rings* one more time. I pray this evening that many of you, right now, will see yourselves in the midst of this story. Think now about the character called Gollum. He was once a normal person {or hobbit-like person}, but he has become completely corrupted by the evil forces of the Ring. Crazed by lust for it, he murdered his best friend. Gollum has become a slimy, hideous, disgusting creature who skulks about in the dark. When Gandalf tells this story to Frodo, Frodo says the story is "loathsome," but Gandalf says, *"I think it is a sad story, and it could have happened to others."*

Frodo says, "If he [came to] hate the Ring, why didn't he get rid of it . . . ?" Gandalf replies,

> "He hated it and he loved it. . . . He could not get rid of it. *He had no will left in the matter . . .* it was not Gollum, Frodo, but the Ring itself that decided things."

This is pure Christian doctrine right out of Romans 7 and 8. The sad story has happened to everybody. Sin and Death decide things for us. We have no will left in the matter. But "the law of the Spirit of life in Christ Jesus has set me free from the law of sin and death." And what this means is that in Christ there is a new will for those whose will is in bondage. This is the heart of the new story that is written in the Cross of Christ.

Now if my past experience is any guide, some of you here today will continue to cling to the doctrine of Free Will. Some of you will even feel angry. You will say that any talk of God's will overriding our own will violates your personhood and robs us of the capacity to act. But there are others here among you who by the grace of God recognize that you, too, not just other people, are unable to change yourself by yourself. You know you need help, you know you need aid, you know you need to be reshaped and you are not ashamed to say so. That is not weakness, it is power — because it is the power of God. You will see that when your own "power of choice has been set aside," you are then aligned with that "other point of power." You will find that your security lies in the great history of God's purpose, and it is a source of "sweet, pleasant and unspeakable comfort."

But being comforted is only the half of it. You can now say with Frodo (and with C. S. Lewis's Ransom), "I will do what I must." In the knowledge of the "other point of power," you can go forward with confidence to do those good works that God has prepared for you to walk in. Then truly, you can do great things that you thought you could never do. You can visit a prison, mentor a child, forgive your spouse, fight against prejudice, change an attitude, reach out to an enemy, oppose a wrong — not in order to gain credit or shore up your self-esteem, but because God is working his purpose out in your very own life. *For the law of the Spirit of life in Christ Jesus has set me free from the law of sin and death.*

God helps those who help themselves? This is the gospel that many like to inflict on others. But is it a gospel? Is it good news? Which do you prefer? What about "help of the helpless, O abide with me"?

You choose.

* * *

As St. Augustine discovered, predestination and freedom are the same thing. Together, let us pray his great prayer:

> O thou who art the light of the minds that know thee, the life of the souls that love thee, and the strength of the wills that serve thee: help us so to know thee that we may truly love thee, so to love thee that we may fully serve thee, whom to serve is perfect freedom.

AMEN.

The Condemned Man

GRACE CHURCH IN NEW YORK
TEXT: ROMANS 7:21–8:6

One of the most familiar images that I remember from almost a half-century of going to the movies is that of the courtroom as the verdict is handed down. The person on trial sits and waits, and all the onlookers sit and wait, to hear the decision of the jury. One by one, the members of the jury are polled. The camera focuses on each as he or she stands in turn and, in crushing repetition, one after another pronounce the word — "Guilty!" "Guilty!" "Guilty!"

I believe this image has a power to engage our emotions far beyond the significance of a handful of mediocre films and television dramas. The fear of being pronounced guilty by some terrifying power haunts us all our lives, and few civilized people are free of this fear, no matter how much in control of our lives we may appear to be. I was struck, a few months ago, by the reactions of several powerful men whom I know to an article in the *New York Times* Sunday magazine section. It was one of the columns called "About Men," and the title of this particular one was "Making the Cut." The author, John Tarkov, wrote:

Making the cut — the phrase comes from the vocabulary of sport, but the experience extends beyond the realms of gyms and practice fields. Getting a job, starting out alone in a new city, stretching a paycheck, holding a marriage together, scavenging for status and power . . . if things work out poorly, the message a man so easily hears remains the same: You aren't good enough. That is the message of the cut. There is a gear in a man's inner workings that grinds against those words . . . they can hound him into a rage or into a fixed posture of defeat.[1]

It was interesting to me to note the deep emotional response of several men to this description, because these were men who, to my eye, had "made the cut"; yet, those words, "you aren't good enough," seemed to have as much resonance for them as though they had been obvious failures.

A member of our congregation, Willy Welch, has written a song that many of you have heard called "Playing Right Field." It's all about the misery of the boy who has been chosen last and is now standing way out in the grass praying that the ball will never be hit in his direction. This song never fails to invoke a sense of recognition in its audience, which always causes me to wonder how it can be that *everybody* reacts to such a memory. Surely not everybody was hopelessly un-athletic and always chosen last, the way I was? When I was at my college reunion a few weeks ago, about twenty-five of us were sitting around reminiscing, and somehow this ubiquitous memory of being chosen last came up, and *every single* woman there was laughing and groaning in unison at the recollection of the anguish of it. I looked around in amazement — I knew for a fact that some of those women had always been chosen *first* for the teams, so how could *they* understand that fear of not being good enough? But this is a universal perception, apparently; either one is not athletic enough or not popular enough or not smart enough or not pretty enough or, somehow *not good enough.*

During the Falkland Island crisis, a good deal was written about Sir Anthony Parsons, the distinguished British diplomat who presided over the negotiations. A man of formidable attainments and remarkable personal qualities, he sounded to me like an ideal man. At the end of an article describing him, a journalist noted that

1. John Tarkov, "About Men" column, *New York Times Magazine,* September 25, 1983.

he was an avid reader and that one of his favorite novels was Joseph Conrad's *Lord Jim.* "Why *Lord Jim?*" asked the interviewer. "Because," said the ambassador, "it is about the fact that every human being has a perfect conception of what kind of character he should have, and about the consequences of his failure to attain it."

In Albert Camus' short, highly compressed novel, *The Fall,* we read the confession of a man of the world, Jean-Baptiste. "I was altogether in harmony with life," he says; "my company was in demand. . . . To tell the truth . . . I looked upon myself as something of a superman." One night, however, as he walks home through the streets of Paris, Jean-Baptiste sees a young woman standing on a bridge. He passes, and moments later he hears her throw herself into the water. He does not stop, though he hears her cry out several times; he goes home and does not report the incident to anyone. Thereafter, he says, "I couldn't deceive myself as to the truth of my nature. . . . It was not love or generosity that awakened me [towards others], but merely the desire to be loved and to receive what in my opinion was due me." After this discovery, his life takes on a fugitive shape as, he says, "Above all, the question is to elude judgment."

The process of "eluding judgment" teaches Jean-Baptiste that:

> People hasten to judge in order not to be judged themselves. What do you expect? The idea that comes most naturally to man, as if from his very nature, is the idea of his innocence. From this point of view, we are all like that little Frenchman at Buchenwald, who insisted on registering a complaint with the clerk, himself a prisoner. . . . The clerk . . . laughed: "Useless, old man. You don't lodge a complaint here." "But you see, sir," said the little Frenchman, "My case is exceptional. I am innocent!"
>
> We are all exceptional cases. We all want to appeal against something! Each of us insists on being innocent at all cost, even if he has to accuse the whole human race and heaven itself. . . . The essential thing is that [we] should be innocent. . . . As I told you, it's a matter of dodging judgment.
>
> . . . Believe me, religions are on the wrong track the moment they moralize and fulminate commandments. God is not needed

to create guilt or to punish. Our fellow men suffice, aided by ourselves. . . . God's sole usefulness would be to guarantee innocence.

. . . I'll tell you a big secret, *mon cher.* Don't wait for the Last Judgment. It takes place every day.

Not innocent! Not good enough! "Guilty!" "Guilty!" "Guilty!" In the New Testament, St. Paul calls it "the law of sin and death." The word "law" has many meanings here, but one of them is that of an inexorable activity that has been set in motion, a continually operating process, like the law of gravity, or the laws of thermodynamics. As we are all subject to these "laws," we are all subject to the Law of Sin and Death, which is the ultimate form of condemnation. This is the condition which, in Romans 5, Paul calls "Adam"; "the result of one trespass [Adam's] was condemnation for all men."

In my experience, the fear that we all have of condemnation, of being judged not good enough, is almost pathetically mundane and embarrassing in its origins. It comes to us in the form of parental displeasure. There was a cartoon in *The New Yorker* a few weeks ago. It depicts an enormous statue, towering over the small human figures at its base. The statue represents a man in resplendent nineteenth-century garb, with an expression and pose of grandeur and mastery. The inscription on the base of the statue reads:

SOLDIER

STATESMAN

AUTHOR

PATRIOT

BUT STILL

A

DISAPPOINTMENT

TO HIS MOTHER

The reason that the world's fairy tales are full of wicked witches and fearsome giants is that there is this primitive terror in all of us, the terror of being undone by our parents. We live with this all our lives. The chairman of the board is reduced to inarticulate helplessness in the presence of his five-foot, silver-haired mother. The woman who is president of her own company is still trying to gain the love and admiration of a father who has been dead ten years. I have seen it over, and over, and over — a hundred times. This is what gives humiliating immediacy to "the message of the cut," the thundering verdict that "you are not good enough!" which "can hound [a man] into a rage or into a fixed posture of defeat." It is no accident that Darth Vader turns out to be Luke Skywalker's *father.* We can no more free ourselves from the Law of Sin and Death, which brings condemnation, than we can choose new mothers and fathers. The inexorability of it, the inevitability of it, the hopelessness of it caused St. Paul to cry out, "Wretched man that I am! Who will deliver me from this body of death [this cycle of condemnation, this knowledge that we are "not good enough," this fear of judgment]?" (Romans 7:24).

And then Paul gives the answer, the answer that has been revealed to him by the true Father of us all:

There is now no condemnation for those who are in Christ Jesus.

Before I even came to Grace Church, and then after I did come to work here three years ago, people kept telling me — and I believe it — that this verse was the power behind the renewal that began to take place here in 1975. "There is now no condemnation for those who are in Christ Jesus." This is the gospel; this is the good news. Just as "one man's [Adam's] trespass led to condemnation for all men, so one man's [Christ's] act of righteousness leads to acquittal and life for all men" (Romans 5:18). Acquitted! "Not guilty!" "Not guilty!" "Not guilty!" In Jesus Christ we are set free! No wonder people started pouring in these doors. This is the message we want so much to hear. The verdict has been dramatically reversed by the only one who has the power to reverse it — by the One who will come to be our Judge. There is now no condemnation for those who are in Christ Jesus, for when Jesus gave himself up to death, he himself became "The Judge Judged in Our Place."[2] When Jesus submitted to crucifixion, he, the only innocent one, took upon himself the judgment that we spend our lives trying to "evade," and in so doing he "set us free from the law of sin and death."

It gives me the greatest imaginable joy to preach today on this text which has been at the center of so many renewals, so many reformations, so many transformed lives. "There is now no condemnation for those who are in Christ Jesus!"

I believe, however, that we do St. Paul and, ultimately, ourselves an injustice if we do not hear this great verse in its full context.

"There is now no condemnation for those who are in Christ Jesus, because through Christ Jesus the law of the Spirit of life has set me free from the law of sin and death."

You see, if we don't read *both* these verses, we might end up believing, with Jean-Baptiste, that "God's sole usefulness would be to guarantee [our] innocence." This would indeed be a poor rendering of the Bible's meaning. God has not pronounced the verdict of acquittal over us solely in order to let us go back to our same old ways. When God "condemned sin in the flesh" (Romans 8:3), as Paul says he did when Jesus died as an offering for sin, our entire situation was completely changed. We had been living "under the law of sin and death, but through Christ Jesus the law of the Spirit of life has set us free." When Jesus entered the world of sin and death leading to condemnation, he brought with him a "gift of power"[3] which creates an entirely new sphere, the sphere of the Spirit, where the Law of Sin and Death no longer has dominion. Therefore, Paul speaks not only of "Christ for us," but also of "Christ in us," or rather, of our being "in Christ." He has brought us into the new sphere, not only of his *protection from condemnation,* but also of *his power for transformation.* Because of what Jesus has accomplished and will accomplish in us, we are set free

2. The title of Karl Barth's chapter on the Cross in the *Church Dogmatics,* IV/1 (Edinburgh: T. & T. Clark, 1956).
3. A phrase borrowed from Alexander McLaren.

to live "not according to our sinful nature, but according to the Spirit" (Romans 8:4).

On Friday, two days ago, when I was laid up with foot surgery, I received a visit from a lovely woman who became a Christian only a few months ago. Let's call her Dorothy. She came with her Bible and sandwiches, and we had a wonderful lunch discussing the things of God and "the law of the Spirit of life in Christ Jesus." I was profoundly moved and humbled by the open sincerity and trustfulness of Dorothy's new life in Christ. She told me how she had read in her Bible that the way of anger was not the Christian way, and that she was now praying to the Lord to help her be more patient and less irritated with the other people in her office. A friend of hers, a woman who has been a Christian much longer, had pooh-poohed this, in a modern style of "letting it all hang out"; anger just shows that you're human, she said. But Dorothy, in only a few short months, has been granted a wonderfully clear-eyed view of her new situation, of the new sphere of power, of "the law of the Spirit of life in Christ Jesus." She said, *"Shouldn't* I expect Jesus to be working in me to help me change my anger?"

"Yes," I said, "Yes!" "Through Jesus the law of the Spirit of life has set us free from the law of sin and death."

There are at least three kinds of people here today:

1. There are people here who are living their lives in a kind of uneasy balance between thinking about condemnation and not thinking about it. The fear of not being good enough lurches to the surface every so often in various ways, but as long as life remains on a fairly even keel without too many unpleasant surprises, the fear can be kept submerged a lot of the time.

2. There are people here who, like Jean-Baptiste before his experience on the bridge, have succeeded in convincing themselves and others that they are supermen or superwomen. These brothers and sisters don't get ulcers; they give them. They judge others instead of worrying about being judged.

3. And there are people here who are living in an absolute panic because they know only too well, with St. Paul, that "nothing

good dwells within me. . . . I can will the good, but I cannot do it." For you, the verdict of "Guilty!" is sounding in your ears all the time, and it is making your life very difficult.

Only you can decide which of these three groups you belong in — but whichever it is, in the last analysis, every single one of us is in the same group. As Paul writes in Romans 3, "All human beings . . . are under the power of sin . . . there is no one righteous, not even one . . . there is no distinction, for all have sinned" (3:9-10, 22-23). As Joseph Conrad's narrator, Marlow, says to the woman who loves "Lord Jim" in the novel, "Nobody, nobody is good enough."

And so to every single one of us this morning, for those who have ears to hear and hearts to believe, the great word comes, the gospel which pronounces a new verdict and creates a new world, a new world where rage and defeat have no place:

There is now no condemnation for those who are in Christ Jesus, because through Christ Jesus the law of the Spirit of life has set me free from the law of sin and death.

"Not guilty!"

AMEN.

Sunday, July 14, 1996

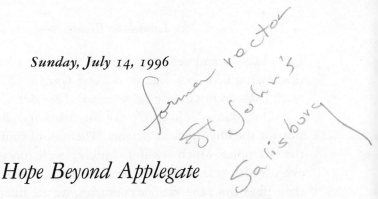

Hope Beyond Applegate

NOTE TO READERS: This sermon had a particular context and should be understood in that light. Serious misconduct by a person highly placed in the congregation had been brought to light, and that person had been publicly disgraced. The congregation was struggling with this at the time of the sermon.

> *For the creation waits with eager longing for the revealing of the sons of God; for the creation was subjected to futility, not of its own will but by the will of him who subjected it in hope. . . .*
>
> *For in this hope we were saved. Now hope that is seen is not hope. For who hopes for what he sees? But if we hope for what we do not see, we wait for it with patience.*

ROMANS 8:19-25

What is the purpose of church? Why come at all? Many people think they can get closer to God by being out in nature than they can in church. It is no wonder that people think this, in view of the amount of sin that there is to be found in the church. When we say this, we are not talking about *some other* church people's sins, because as we said in the sermon last week, the General Confession that we say together teaches us to recognize that every single one of us is a sinner in need of God's mercy. We don't learn that on the golf course or by the ocean or hiking in the mountains. I love nature deeply, and in fact I am a card-carrying charter member of the environmental movement — I am proud to say I marched on the first

{ 229 }

Earth Day — and yet as a reader of the Bible I know that whereas the environment may lead us *to thank God for his creation,* it cannot teach us *to praise God for his remission of our sins.*

Our country is in a frenzy of anticipation right now in preparation for the Olympics in Atlanta. There is, of course, a mystique of the Olympics. Much wishful thinking wells up in us at this time every fourth year. When we see the groups of massed athletes with their flags from the various countries, we are likely to think pleasant thoughts about peace and harmony among the peoples of the earth. I read in the paper that the largest peacetime security operation in American history is taking place in Atlanta right now. "Intelligence agents are preparing an 'antipathy matrix' of who in the world is angry at whom." What a perfect example of how the whole world is in the grip of sin![1]

Last week we heard St. Paul in the Epistle to the Romans talking about the problem of sin:

> I can will what is right, but I cannot do it. For I do not do the good I want, but the evil I do not want is what I do. . . . Now since I do what I do not want, it is no longer I that do it, but sin which dwells within me. So I find it to be a law that when I want to do right, evil lies close at hand.

This classic description of sin is generally understood to refer to the individual. Each of us struggles in our own personal lives with the pattern of repeated undesirable behavior. In today's passage from Romans, though, Paul broadens the picture. Not only the individual, he says, but *the whole creation* is suffering from the effects of sin. The environment itself is, as C. S. Lewis described it, "bent," distorted, out of kilter. I am always amused by those who think that Annie Dillard is a nice nature writer. I love this line from her book, "Fish gotta swim, birds gotta fly, insects, it seems, gotta do one horrible thing after another," and she goes on to illustrate. The behav-

---

1. *The New York Times,* July 12, 1996. This was soon to be illustrated by the bombing of the Olympic Games. See also the sermon, "From Denial to Victory."

ior of insects, she says, "is an assault on all human value, all hope of a reasonable god."[2]

Did God create insects to devour each other slowly and horribly? I don't know, but the prophet Isaiah gives us a hint of what's gone wrong with the creation in his famous picture of the kingdom of God:

> The wolf shall dwell with the lamb, and the leopard shall lie down with the kid, and the calf and the lion and the fatling together, and a little child shall lead them. . . . The sucking child shall play over the hole of the asp, and the weaned child shall put his hand on the adder's den. They shall not hurt or destroy in all my holy mountain. (11:6-9)

This imagery is replicated every year on a thousand Christmas cards with pictures of lions and lambs lying down together. What's not so obvious in this popular image is its implication that nature is not all right as it is. Something is wrong with it, something that needs to be fixed. And when it is fixed, it will not be by an act of man, but by an act of God. And so Paul writes, "The whole creation has been groaning in travail together until now; and not only the creation, but we ourselves . . . groan inwardly as we wait for . . . redemption."

The biblical view is that we are all in this together. We are all implicated in the huge primeval dislocation that took place as a result of what Milton calls "man's first disobedience."[3] Russell Baker got it exactly right in his column yesterday. Writing about all the "gates," such as Watergate, Irangate, Whitewatergate, *etc.,* he says, "It is flattering to American ego to think that -gate history begins on our shores, but the truth is far more interesting. The -gates go back to the dawn of recorded history, and perhaps beyond. The line's founder is generally said to have been Applegate, a nasty situ-

2. Annie Dillard, *Pilgrim at Tinker Creek,* Perennial Library (New York: Harper & Row, 1985), p. 63.
3. John Milton, *Paradise Lost.*

ation that developed in the Garden of Eden."[4] This is precisely what the Bible, from the book of Genesis through the prophet Isaiah and on to the Epistle to the Romans, tells us. Something ancient and dreadful happened to us because of our rebellion against God's good plan, and we have been living with the consequences ever since.

When I am up here in this part of the world I like to pretend that there is nothing wrong with it. Up where we have our house in Berkshire County, one of my favorite walks ends with a gorgeous view of hills and a pasture full of sheep. I always think of one of my favorite choruses, from Handel's *Judas Maccabeus:* "O lovely, lovely peace. . . . Let fleecy flocks the hills adorn, and valleys smile with wavy corn." But then on the way to the supermarket I pass the counseling center, or the hospital, or the fire house, and I know that the image of peace we see in nature is fleeting and imperfect. Or I think of the article I just read about the terrible conditions that migrant farm workers live in, just a few counties away from us here, as they pick the onions and strawberries that we so unthinkingly enjoy, and I know that sin is alive in the rolling hills.

So we can't get the whole picture about God out in nature. Nature does not do for us what coming together on the Lord's Day does. Sunday morning worship is communal, not individual. It is the *sharing,* all together, of the confession of sin and the prayers of the church for the whole suffering creation that makes the act of worship what it is supposed to be. Only as we hear the Word of God read and interpreted in the context of coming together do we come to understand the depth of our human predicament and the breadth of God's divine plan.

All of us here in town drive every day past the sign for Hope Hill Farm. I don't know who owns this farm, but for some years I have taken delight in that name, "Hope Hill." "They shall not hurt or destroy in all my holy mountain," says the Lord. It will always remind me of the passage today from Romans: "For in this hope we were saved. Now hope that is seen is not hope. For who hopes for what he sees? But if we hope for what we do not see, we wait for it

4. *The New York Times,* July 13, 1996.

with patience." Romans tells us how the whole creation has fallen and is to be redeemed "by the will of him who subjected it," yes, subjected it to its own sin, but "subjected it *in hope.*"

I read in the paper that our neighbor to the east, Sam Waterston, has gone to Cambodia on a mission of hope.[5] There is no safe place to step in the rural Cambodian landscape; there are a million land mines buried in the killing fields, one for every man, woman, and child — talk about the perversion of nature! The presence of a famous actor there might be dismissed as grandstanding, but it might also be interpreted as a sign of solidarity, a sign that the suffering of the Cambodian people is not forgotten by the world.

But we don't have to go to Cambodia to do something hopeful. Last Wednesday was a wonderful day in the parish hall because people were just pouring in and out, volunteering to work for the Fall Festival.[6] Now some may say that this is trivial. But little things really can mean a lot. They can be signs of life. They can be occasions for fellowship. Above all they can be strategies of hope. Any thing that we can do to show that we are not going to be part of the "antipathy matrix" is a blow struck for the kingdom of God. The church is the community of believers who are learning how to crank down the level of antipathy.

Last summer I attended a performance of Mozart's *Don Giovanni* at the Glimmerglass Opera. Perhaps some of you saw this wildly controversial production; people either loved it or hated it. One of the many odd things that the director dreamed up was to have a little child in a powdered wig and satin knee breeches, obviously intended to be Mozart himself, wandering through the production from beginning to end, making things happen. One of my friends hated this intrusion so much that he kept referring to the child actor as "the brat." He had a point, but I had a different reac-

---

5. The famous television actor Sam Waterston starred in the movie *The Killing Fields,* about the genocide in Cambodia.

6. This seems frivolous in the extreme following a mention of the Cambodian genocide. But this parish had been through a calamitous period of betrayal and decline, so these signs of renewal were not as trivial as it might seem.

tion. Let me tell you what happened at the end of the opera. You know the story, how the archetypal seducer, exploiter, and deceiver Don Giovanni is exposed in his colossal wickedness and is dragged, unrepentant, into hell. I listened to this scene on tape yesterday in the car driving up here, and I can tell you, it made my hair stand on end. Well, in this particular production, at the very end, after the damnation scene, while all the other characters are standing around singing about how the Don got what he deserved, the child Mozart figure is leading the Don by the hand safely through the flames while on his (the Don's) face there is an expression of stricken awe, as though he has glimpsed the impossible possibility of redemption.

Was this director's conceit distracting? Yes. Did it do violence to Mozart's intention? Probably. Did the director intend anything theological by this? Almost certainly not; he most likely just meant to suggest that art confers immortality. But in the context of this passage from Romans 8, I will tell you what it suggested to me. It suggested that the creator loved his creation so much that, however wicked, however unrepentant, however bent on his own destruction Don Giovanni might have been, his creator would not, finally, let him go. And I think this is a good image of what Paul is proclaiming to us today, that our Creator loves his creation and his creatures too much to let us go.

> The flame shall not hurt thee; I only design
> Thy dross to consume and thy gold to refine.[7]

"Getting close to God" is not really the purpose of coming to church. That would be too individualistic a way of understanding it. We come together on the Lord's Day to be the people of God, to enact strategies of hope, to bear witness together that "the creation itself will be set free from its bondage to decay and obtain the glorious liberty of the children of God." The church is you and me, not as isolated individuals, but part of an organic whole, all of us together, representing God's suffering creation with all its disap-

---

7. Hymn, "How Firm a Foundation," K. in John Rippon's selection, 1787.

pointment and cruelty and pain, but, at the same time, bearing a message of hope.

The church is one organic whole. As the people of God, Paul writes, "If one member suffers, all suffer together; if one member is honored, all rejoice together" (1 Corinthians 12:26). If one church is burned, all churches are burned, and all Christians are there to remind us that when the church building is burned, the church, that is, the people of God, remain. To be the church means to be a community of solidarity with the whole creation, waiting with hope for the glorious redemption that God brings. We don't see it yet; it is out in front of us. That is why we have hope, Paul writes, for "who hopes for what he sees? But if we hope for what we do not see, we wait for it with patience." Patience (*hupomonē*) in the New Testament has much more active force than our word *patience*. It means fortitude, endurance, perseverance. It is grounded in hope and carries more than a hint of joyfulness with it because it looks forward to "the revealing of the sons of God." Do you know what that amazing phrase means? It means that we, yes, even such as we are, we are being remade, by faith and patience, in the image of God's own Son, Jesus Christ. The whole creation, Paul says in this astonishing passage, is waiting for this promise to come true. "The creation itself will be set free from its bondage to decay and obtain the glorious liberty of the children of God." This is the sure and certain hope in which we trust. And so we sing in our closing hymn,

How firm a foundation, ye saints of the Lord,
Is laid for your faith in his excellent word. . . .

"The soul that to Jesus hath fled for repose,
I will not, I will not desert to his foes;
That soul, though all hell shall endeavor to shake,
I'll never, no never, no never forsake."

AMEN.

The Remaking of the World

ROMANS 8:3-4, 35-39

The best-known passage in Paul's letter to the Romans is almost certainly chapter 8. The last part of it is often read at funerals.

> Who shall separate us from the love of Christ? Shall tribulation, or distress, or persecution, or famine, or nakedness, or peril, or sword? . . . No, in all these things we are more than conquerors through him who loved us. For I am sure that neither death, nor life, nor angels, nor principalities, nor things present, nor things to come, nor powers, nor height, nor depth, nor anything else in all creation, will be able to separate us from the love of God in Christ Jesus our Lord.

Because of the context in which this passage is so often heard, American Christians generally think of it as a promise made to individuals at the time of death, or in time of personal trouble. That is certainly not wrong, and I will probably have it at my own funeral. But hearing it exclusively in this way prevents us from understanding the full gospel that Paul proclaims.

In order to hear this gospel in its fullness, we have to go back to the early chapters of this letter to the Christians in Rome. Paul writes extended passages about a threat to humanity far greater than the death of individual persons. Indeed, he is writing on a cosmic scale. In the first chapters he writes about the wrath of God against the universal disobedience of the entire human race. When he gets to chapter 8, he enlarges this; he writes of the whole creation having been "subjected to futility." He says the entire cosmos is "in bondage to decay." He has the whole of human history and all of the created universe in view. He could not have imagined the dangers presently threatening our planet and its ecology, but it is no stretch to think of the "decay" now taking place in our rain forests, lakes, wetlands, and glaciers because of untrammeled exploitation. When he speaks of angels, principalities, and powers, he is thinking of forces, beings, systems, and structures that were created by God for his good purposes but are now fallen from their place and actively opposed to God. Think for instance of business interests and their power to prevent us from doing anything about global warming; that's the principalities and powers at work.[1] Think of the Internet, how much good it has brought, but how much evil as well — sites where anorexic girls are encouraged to keep on starving them-selves,[2] sexual predators making contact with children, instructions for making terrorist bombs — and the genie cannot be put back in the bottle. Think of the machinery of war, how once it gets into mo-tion how close to impossible it is to stop. Humanity is enslaved by these principalities and powers, but Paul declares that none of them can separate us from the love of God in Christ Jesus our Lord.

What we have trouble understanding in our culture today is that the only thing we had any right to expect was rejection by God. We don't grasp this because we live in a religious atmosphere that speaks exclusively of God's love, never of God's judgment. The message is a hundred variations of the message that God includes everybody, embraces everybody, accepts everybody just as they are. The idea that there is *something seriously wrong with all human beings* is not part of the church's message these days in America. Yet a funda-mental presupposition of Paul's gospel message is the fact that, as

1. In his book and movie *An Inconvenient Truth,* Al Gore quotes Upton Sinclair: "It's difficult to get man to understand something when his salary depends on his not understanding it." That's a perfect illustration of the way that the principalities and powers take hold of the human will.

2. These sites are called "pro-ana."

he writes in chapter 3, "There is no one righteous, no, not one. . . . For there is no distinction; since all have sinned and fall short of the glory of God. . . ." Nothing Paul says in Romans can be understood apart from that diagnosis of the human condition.

Let's think a minute about those words, "There is no distinction." Paul specifically means that before God there is no distinction between Jew and Gentile, godly and ungodly, believer and pagan, "good guys" and "bad guys." All are in bondage to the Powers of Sin and Death, and being "religious" does not do any good. Being religious is just one more way that we seek to justify ourselves. "Religion" and "spirituality" won't do the trick. Being religious is just one more thing that human beings do, and Paul is clear: there is nothing we can do about our bondage. We cannot free ourselves from the imprisoning grip of the principalities and powers.[3] We are locked in by them.

Let's consider a couple of illustrations:

An op-ed article in last week's paper tells a story from the Iraq war. The author is a veteran of the first Gulf War, fifteen years ago, who is now teaching English at a college in Arkansas. The subject of one of his courses is the literature of American wars. Among other things the students read is an account of the massacre at My Lai during the Vietnam War. A young man who was in Iraq last fall as a second lieutenant in the National Guard came to see the teacher to confess a war crime. He told how his platoon was searching an Iraqi home where an Iraqi man, a civilian, had just been killed. The dead man's brother was sobbing uncontrollably for his loss. The young American lieutenant yelled, "Would somebody shut him the f—— up?"

The English professor continues, "That was his crime. The young man wept as he told the story. I think he realized that he had crossed a line. I think he realized how easily such an outburst can become a shove or a slap, a poke with a rifle muzzle or a kick in the ribs, a gun butt to the head. This [young lieutenant] was no weak-

---

3. Romans 7 is carefully constructed to spell this out. It concludes, "Who will deliver me from this body of death?"

ling; he had risked his life for his men. I respect him immensely for owning up to his remorse and, in the process, in his own small way, raising the standard for wartime behavior."[4]

A few days later, a letter to the editor responded to this with another story. The letter-writer's father, a World War II veteran, had told her of an incident in his company during that war. A fellow soldier snapped and shot a 12-year-old German girl because she was giggling.[5]

The letter does not say, however, if the World War II soldier was remorseful afterwards. Returning to the young lieutenant who yelled at the distraught Iraqi man whose brother had just been killed, we can say that his tears of repentance are the sign of the Spirit at work in him. This is what Paul means when he says earlier in the chapter:

> For God has done what the law, weakened by the flesh, could not do: sending his own Son in the likeness of sinful flesh and for sin, he condemned sin in the flesh, in order that the just requirement of the law might be fulfilled in us, who walk not according to the flesh but according to the Spirit. (Romans 8:3-4)

That sounds complicated, so let's try to simplify it:

1. All human beings are under the power of Sin.[6]
2. The Law (the commandments and teachings of God) cannot save us from our worst instincts — like mistreating civilians in wartime.
3. Since the Law was impotent, God performed a uniquely potent deed to accomplish what the impotent Law could not; he sent his Son to enter into combat with Sin.
4. Because of what God has done in Jesus Christ, the good com-

---

4. Alex Vernon, "The Road from My Lai," *The New York Times,* June 23, 2006.
5. Letter to *The New York Times* editor, June 28, 2006.
6. I capitalize "Sin" in this written manuscript so as to emphasize its status as an independent Power.

mandments of God are grafted into our hears by the Holy Spirit. That's what was happening to the young lieutenant as he confessed his sin.

But now what of the heartbroken Iraqi? What man would sob uncontrollably like that? He must have loved his brother very much. Perhaps he was a beloved younger brother, or a revered older one. But were they insurgents? Suppose they were, does that mean they have no right to mourn for their dead? These are big questions.

When we send young men off to war we expect them to do terrible things in our name and keep quiet about it later. Stories about World War II veterans who never talked about what they saw or what they did continue to crop up sixty years later. "He never talks about it," a wife will say. Why is this? Deeds in wartime, it is believed, are just too horrible to talk about. This is true of many other aspects of life as well. Active alcoholism is not discussed by the family; everyone plays an elaborate role to cover it up. Children grow up never knowing that their parents or grandparents were embezzlers or drug dealers or worse. At their funerals people get up and talk about what great guys they were; I have seen this personally many times. This sort of whitewashing is a fatal psychological mistake; but worse, it is also a theological mistake. When deeds are not hidden but brought out into the light, then the Spirit of Christ can do his redeeming work.

We are accustomed to thinking almost exclusively about good guys and bad guys. The men in Guantánamo must be bad guys or they wouldn't have been put there. American soldiers are good guys; it's assumed. We were in the airport the other day and a number of Army men in their desert camouflage uniforms came through. They were greeted with prolonged applause. I heard one mother say to her young children, "They're heroes." But once you really know a person from the inside, you know that these lines are not so easily drawn. When we read about prisoner abuse in Guantánamo or Iraq, surely we must think about who it is that is doing the abusing. In a significant sense these American soldiers are victims too. The young men and women in Iraq who have committed atrocities have lost their bearings, or perhaps never had any bearings to speak of, and they suffer from a lack of strong, principled leadership.[7] Anyone in a combat zone is vulnerable to the dark powers; sometimes the participants in war crimes are the victims and sometimes they are the perpetrators, and sometimes we can't entirely tell which is which.

Paul says in Romans that there is no human way to sort all this out. We are all of us truly lost creatures, powerless over the Law of Sin and Death, which grabs us at any moment when we least expect it. Who is more to be pitied, the man who lost his brother or the man who lost his cool? Who can say? Only God can sort it out. That is what he has done in Jesus Christ.

> For God has done what the law, weakened by the flesh [human nature], could not do: sending his own Son in the likeness of sinful flesh [human nature] and for sin, he condemned sin in the flesh [human nature of Jesus], in order that the just requirement of the law might be fulfilled in us, who walk not according to the flesh [sinful human nature] but according to the Spirit.[8]

This is the context for Paul's extraordinary promise at the end of Romans 8. When he asks, "Who will separate us from the love of Christ?" he isn't just thinking of death with a small "d." He is thinking of Death as an annihilating Power that rules over us even now, in life, with Sin as its sinister cohort. He means the whole complex of forces that throw humanity off course, that pervert our

---

7. At the time of this sermon, five major criminal cases were pending in American military courts, each involving suspected murder and rape by American soldiers and marines in Iraq. Four of these occurred in the first months of 2006. Even so, according to *The New York Times* (July 9, 2006), this is a low figure compared to the Vietnam War when a total of 125 soldiers and marines were not only charged but convicted of murdering civilians. It is certain that this represents only a small number of the actual total of officers and enlisted men who committed serious crimes in Vietnam (Elizabeth Kolbert, "The Fall: Bob Kerrey's Vietnam," *The New Yorker*, June 3, 2002).

8. The term "flesh" *(sarx)* as Paul uses it is confusing. He does not mean material flesh. The New International Version helpfully translates it "sinful [human] nature."

best instincts and distort our best efforts. He means the consequences of disobedience, the result of rebellion against the purposes of God — in other words, the judgment of God. And as he has already made clear, that judgment was due to every human being *without distinction.*

So now listen again to the climactic verses:

> If God is for us, who is against us? He who did not spare his own Son but gave him up for us all, will he not also give us all things with him? Who shall bring any charge against God's elect? It is God who justifies; who is to condemn? It is Christ Jesus, who died, yes, who was raised from the dead, who is at the right hand of God, who indeed intercedes for us. . . .

It is God who justifies. We don't need to justify ourselves and indeed we cannot, so we can just stop trying. It is God who justifies; it is Christ Jesus who died, who was raised, who sits at the right hand of God where he intercedes for us. Can we get our minds around this picture? Our Lord himself who died for us is the one who pleads our case against the accusing Powers.

"Who shall bring any charge against God's elect?" Who are God's elect? It might seem obvious. But it is not so obvious. The last line of the Psalm we read earlier in our service was, "The desires of the wicked will perish" (Psalm 112). Who are "the wicked"? Who is this who has wicked desires? Who is a hero? Who is a villain? Who is a victim? Who is a perpetrator? The lines shift. Who determines the worth and the destiny of each person? Each of us here in the church this morning can probably think of someone by whom we would not want to be judged.

Only one Judge counts. "Who is to condemn? It is Christ Jesus who . . . intercedes for us." Only one Spirit counts. Only one Spirit can do the work of righteousness in us, and that is not the generic New Age spirit but the Holy Spirit, the third person of the blessed Trinity, who is at work in us who wait upon the Lord.

And what of the cosmos? What of the creation? How will it be freed from its bondage to futility and decay? Here is the great promise: Only one Victor will remain on the field when Sin and Death are overcome for ever. He is the Lord of all, the one through whom God made all things, the one whose "word of power" preserves the universe against self-destruction (John 1:3; Hebrews 1:2). "If God be for us, who shall be against us?" Can these things be against us: tribulation, distress, persecution, famine, nakedness, peril, sword? Can we be conquered by these things? Paul gives the signal of triumph: "No! In all these things we are *more than conquerors* through him who loved us."[9] No, this is not about individual deaths. This is about a whole world of Death which has been undone in Christ. Our Lord did not just offer himself as a sacrifice. He fought and won a battle against everything that would destroy us. That is why Paul is able to say that he is certain that neither death, nor life, nor angels, nor principalities, nor things present, nor things to come, nor powers, nor war, nor pandemics, nor terrorism, nor global warming, nor anything else in all creation, will be able to separate us from the love of God in Jesus Christ our Lord.

Nothing in all creation can defeat the redemptive purpose of God for all his creatures. The Iraqi man and his dead brother and the young German girl and the soldier who killed her, none of these, none of you, none of us is beyond the reach of the One who has conquered. Each Christian plays a part in bearing witness to Christ's triumph. The repentance of the young lieutenant as he made his confession is a small sign, very small but very significant, that God will be victorious over all that is wrong, and in the meantime he has done his part to raise the standards of wartime conduct. Make no mistake, all of us are in a war against the principalities and powers, but those who take arms against them fight on the winning side.

There is no vision in all "religion" as vast as this. This is not about one person here and one person there dying and going to heaven. This is about the conquest of all that is out of joint in the world, and about the Spirit working through each of us to give out

9. The NEB and J. B. Phillips translations render this as, "Through Christ we win an overwhelming victory through him who loved us."

our own small signals that the future belongs to God. This gospel of Jesus Christ is about the remaking of the entire creation according to the purpose of the One who called it into being in the beginning and will bring it to fulfillment in the End.

And so now unto him who reigns upon the throne be all glory, might, majesty, dominion, and power now and for ever.

AMEN.

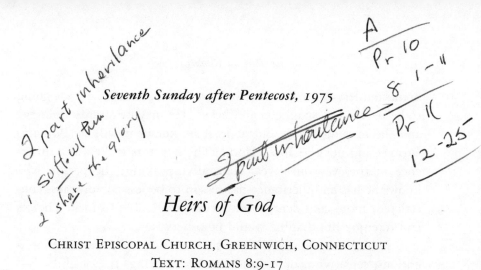

Seventh Sunday after Pentecost, 1975

Heirs of God

CHRIST EPISCOPAL CHURCH, GREENWICH, CONNECTICUT
TEXT: ROMANS 8:9-17

Newspapers of all kinds, especially the tabloids that are sold at the grocery check-out counter, are addicted to describing people as "heirs" and "heiresses," as though that were enough to guarantee the interest of potential readers. "Heiress elopes with chauffeur!" "Heir to plastics empire injured in crash!" "Starlet sharing love nest with oil heir!" Even the staid *New York Times* acknowledges this fascination with vast inheritances; Christina Onassis is regularly identified as an "heiress," and, indeed, this essentially unremarkable young woman would be of little interest to us otherwise. The marriages and suicides and kidnappings of "heirs" and "heiresses" attract wide attention, even though the individuals in question may have no other distinguishing features whatever.

Now, I am not an heiress. There is no fortune, vast or otherwise, in my future. But, like most of you, I have had at least some experience of financial security, even in this shaky economy, and I think I can imagine something of what it must be like to have a large inheritance. An inheritance allows a person a degree of security, a degree of freedom, a degree of hope that he would not otherwise have. He knows he can send his children to Princeton if they are smart enough to get in. If he gets sick, he knows he will have a private room and the best doctor. In a bad year, he may go to Nantucket instead of Mallorca, but he will not have to go without a vacation altogether. These days, he may be eating more often at

[245]

home and less often at La Crémallière, but he knows he's not going to be reduced to spaghetti and beans. He may be afraid of old age and the nursing home, but at least he knows it will be Putnam-Weaver and not the Town Home. These factors make a big difference in the way one lives. Generally speaking, the person who knows he has an inheritance has reason to be less anxious, less constricted, more confident, more secure, more able to make choices and to enjoy life than he would be otherwise.

I think we could also agree that, at least in the case of conscientious, sensitive people, inheritance also brings responsibility — the responsibility of stewardship. The creation of charitable foundations, the gift given towards a matching grant, the creative loan, the gamble taken on a struggling new program, the donation made without self-serving strings attached, the generous distribution of funds in one's will — when inheritances are put to this type of use, all of society benefits from what would otherwise be one person's private privilege.

There are other types of inheritances that give meaning, security, and purpose to our lives. For instance, a stable family heritage is a very precious thing. Children whose parents and grandparents remain married to each other, are scrupulously honest in all their dealings, are active in the community, and derive pleasure from nature and the arts, are much less susceptible to divorce, cheating, apathy and boredom. As for the *American* heritage, this is its year. In the Bicentennial celebration, especially this Fourth of July, we commemorate the fact that we are heirs of the Declaration of Independence, of the Bill of Rights, of Thomas Jefferson and Patrick Henry, of a New World outlook, a noble conception of liberty and equality under law, a degree of religious freedom previously unknown to civilization. We are heirs also of some rather less noble episodes in our history: the disinheriting of the American Indian by force and by deception, and the subsequent isolation and humiliation of this proud people; the importation of a vast population of black slaves, whose descendants suffer still from a pervasive system of discrimination; the presently continuing exploitation of Third World countries in order to maintain our American way of life. We are heirs not only of the glorious American Revolution but of the very inglorious Vietnam war.

Inheritance, then, is a complex matter. We inherit the bad along with the good, the responsibility along with the privilege, the shame along with the pride.

Our text is from the Epistle for today. St. Paul, writing to the Christians in Rome:

> We are God's children, and if children, then heirs. We are God's heirs, and Christ's fellow-heirs, since we share his sufferings now and will share in his glory hereafter.

Martin Luther said of this text, "It were good that this text were written in letters of gold, so admirable is it, and so full of comfort." Karl Barth calls the passage the "song of the redeemed." Children and heirs of God! That, incredibly, is what we are. There never was and never will be another legacy like this one. Moths and rust do not corrupt it, thieves do not break through and steal. It cannot be lost in the stock market or burned in the night, or confiscated in a *coup d'état,* or cancelled out by inflation. This legacy gives us hope when all else fails. It guarantees us a future when we cannot imagine how there can be anything left in life for us. St. Paul says the Holy Spirit himself is the guarantor of our inheritance. When a Christian cries out "Father!" to God, however inarticulate the prayer, however sinful the petitioner, however desperate the cry, it is the Spirit speaking for him, guaranteeing that his hope is not in vain, that God hears him, that God has adopted him as his heir, that he has prepared an inheritance for him that nothing can destroy. Jesus Christ himself is the fore-runner, the first-fruits; we are fellow-heirs with him in his resurrection and will share his glory. Martin Luther is right — it is a text written in letters of gold, so full of comfort is it.

And yet — and yet — there is something more that has to be said. Like every other statement about the Christian gospel, it is both comforting and disturbing at the same time. Martin Luther's understanding of St. Paul's message was won only through the greatest emotional, physical, and spiritual turmoil, when he had risked security, reputation, position, friends, home, life, everything, for the sake of Christ. If you think the American Revolution was a revolution, just compare it to the gospel of Jesus Christ. If there's one thing I hope to do before I die, it is to pass on, at least to a few people, the fact that the Christian faith is revolutionary. Heirs of God, and fellow heirs with Christ! "Blessed are the meek, for they shall inherit the earth" (Matthew 5:5). Did you ever hear anything more audacious than that? Do you believe *that?* Jesus said, "Everyone who has left houses or family or lands for my name's sake will inherit eternal life" (Matthew 19:29). Strange, disquieting, revolutionary statement, since acquiring a house and a family and land is the American dream.

Heirs of *God!* Here is what St. James says: "Has not God chosen those who are poor in the eyes of the world to be rich in faith and to inherit the kingdom he has promised?" (James 2:5). Poor in the eyes of the world! Not the heirs and heiresses, then, not the rich and influential, not the prominent and successful, not the presidents of companies and the members of country clubs and the citizens of the most powerful and best-armed nation, but the "*poor* in the eyes of the world." "The last shall be first and the first last" (Matthew 20:16). Revolutionary! By no stretch of the imagination can this message be construed as comforting to you and me.

How then does St. Paul intend us to respond? "We are God's heirs, and fellow-heirs with Christ, since we share his sufferings now and will share his glory hereafter." We have a two-part inheritance. One part is glory. The other part is suffering. Fellow-heirs with Christ, we will be raised with him in glory. But we will also suffer and die with him on the cross. There is nothing more certain in the Christian life. If we think we can receive the inheritance without pain, without struggle, without sacrifice, we have misunderstood the whole gospel. This Christian legacy of ours is a revolutionary one. For the sake of this inheritance, Francis of Assisi gave away all his riches; William Bradford left England's green and pleasant land for a barbarous foreign shore where half his little company died in the first winter; the Rev. Beyers Naudé of the Dutch

Reformed church in South Africa spoke out against apartheid and lost his pulpit and his social position; Korean Christians are in prison at this very hour — *for the sake of this inheritance.* Heirs of God! That is the essential fact about Christians everywhere. My financial status, my family, my English ancestors, my American heritage are so much sand that will wash away when the tide comes in. There is only one rock to build on and that is Jesus Christ. "He has scattered the proud in the imagination of their hearts, he has put down the mighty from their thrones, . . . the rich he has sent empty away" (Luke 1:51-53). Whereas a common criminal, executed by the government, "has been appointed the heir of all things" (Hebrews 1:2). Revolution!

Here in Greenwich we do not feel very revolutionary. Our inheritances of green lawns and good schools and a low crime rate are very dear to us. Here in Greenwich it seems that we are not called to leave our families, to go to prison, to risk our lives. Do not let that fact lull you into thinking that it is only *other* Christians at *other* times and in *other* places who are called to behave like heirs of the kingdom of Christ. You too are heirs. I am an heir. *It makes a difference* to know that. People who have an inheritance can be more free, more confident, more secure. I want to behave like a fellow-heir of Christ, not like a fearful, temporizing, guilt-ridden weakling, afraid of what may happen tomorrow, hedged in by "buts" and "ifs," never leaving my own neighborhood, unable to open my home or business to strangers, poor of spirit and poor of soul. I don't have to be like that; I am an heir of God!

People who have an inheritance guaranteed to them can take all kinds of risks. People who have a legacy coming can afford to be reckless. I can't help thinking of my grandmother. Everybody in the family used to tell her not to take alcoholics into her home, not to give money to people she knew nothing about, not to risk life and limb going out in all sorts of weather at age 90 to visit sick friends. She would fix us with a look of mixed reproach and determination and say, "How can you suggest that I not help someone in trouble?" And she went right on taking in the alcoholics. She was swindled out of a thousand dollars by a flim-flam man when she was 92, and she was far from rich, but it never fazed her. She went right on handing out money and taking risks to the end of her days.

I think of three couples I know, all impecunious by Greenwich standards. Each of them gives 10 percent of their income to their church. They make their pledge first, before they budget the rest of what they need for themselves and their children. What's more, they do it cheerfully, gratefully, and as a matter of course. I think of a man, Mr. Victorius, who had a picture-framing shop in Charlottesville, Virginia. His policy was to hire people that no one else would hire. There is no telling how much money he lost over the years to theft and embezzlement, no telling how many man-hours were wasted because of laziness, goldbricking, and incompetence. His picture-framing shop was not his principal investment, you see; he laid up his treasure somewhere else, where the return on his investment was guaranteed by the Holy Spirit. His inheritance was incorruptible. Let us be reckless in the name of Christ! If we suffer for our recklessness, that is part of our inheritance as it was part of Christ's. The pain of the world must lie — *must* lie — very close to a Christian's heart. It is half the story of the gospel, the story of a crucified Lord. The other half of the story is the glory and the reward.

> Then the king will say to those at his right hand, "Come, O blessed of my father, inherit the kingdom prepared for you from the foundation of the world." (Matthew 25:34)

AMEN.

July 22, 1990

Creation on Tiptoe ⟍

GRACE CHURCH IN NEW YORK
TEXT: ROMANS 8:18-25

On a day like this, full of joy and thankfulness, our deepest instinct is to want to protect these precious soon-to-be baptized baby girls, Emily and Catherine, from any kind of hurt whatsoever. We would shield them, if we could, from all the pain, disappointment, and sadness that inevitably accompany growing up in this world. Today we have a lesson from St. Paul's Epistle to the Romans that seems to take account of this wish of ours. Anticipating our wish, and the impossibility of it, the apostle challenges us with these words: "I judge that the sufferings of this present time are not worthy to be compared with the glory that is to be revealed in us" (8:18).

The passage of Scripture that is before us today is most unusual. Some commentators refer to it as "unique." In this section of his letter to the Roman Christians, Paul mounts a frontal attack on the problem of suffering, and he does it in the context of faith and baptism. It is unique because it is the only place in Paul's letters where he explicitly links the destiny of human beings to the rest of the creation. In this age of anxiety about what we are doing to our environment, Paul's words have a new relevance for us.

Everything Paul says in chapters 5–8 of Romans has to do with baptism into Christ, and the baptismal gift of the Holy Spirit. It is the Spirit that makes the Christian life happen; and, as Paul makes clear in various ways, the Christian life is a process of being molded into the shape of Christ's life. What are the climactic events of that life? As we know, there can be no question that those climactic events are his Crucifixion and his Resurrection. And so, the life of the Christian community is also a kind of crucifixion and resurrection — as Paul writes in chapter 6, "We were buried . . . with him by baptism into death, so that as Christ was raised from the dead by the glory of the Father, we too might walk in newness of life."

For this reason, Paul is telling us, being joined to Christ in baptism means not only receiving all the benefits of his divine life, but also sharing with him in his sufferings. It means adoption into God's family, lasting fellowship with him and the other brothers and sisters, the forgiveness of sins, empowerment for a life of joyful service, and the promise of eternal life — but it also means, inevitably, entering into a life of identification with the world just as the Son of God did. For Jesus did not, as Paul says in Philippians, "hold on to" his divine privileges, but emptied himself, and, becoming human, entered into our life and was obedient even to death on the cross (Philippians 2:5-8). The Christian life follows this pattern on its way to the resurrection of the dead. As Paul writes in verse 17 of chapter 8, "We suffer with him in order that we may also be glorified with him."

Now let us turn our attention to Romans 8:18-25. Paul in this passage is beginning to enter into a state of exaltation that will come to a climax at the end of chapter 8 where he tells us that nothing, absolutely nothing, can separate us from the love of God in Christ Jesus our Lord. Verse 18 is the utterance of a man who has, by revelation from God, been authorized to make the solemn declaration that no amount of suffering in this world is even remotely comparable to "the glory that is to be revealed in us." Paul's powerful argument is that any afflictions suffered in the world as it presently is will someday be seen to be utterly transfigured by God's plan for redeeming and transforming the world.

Paul assumes, you see, that Christians will not be able to escape suffering. But we need to put this much more strongly. Paul does not refer to a mere passive acceptance of whatever is bound to come. Rather, he speaks of baptized Christians entering into a lifetime of engagement with the forces of sin, evil, and death, in the name of the Lord who entered this battle before us, for our sakes, and emerged victorious on the other side of suffering and death.

Paul's realism is notable. Never does he call the Christian community to look away from this troubled world to a blissful future. The opposite is true. In this passage — uniquely — Paul summons us to a new style of living *on behalf of the suffering cosmos* which does not know that its Savior is at hand.

Or does it? Let us read further:

> The creation waits with eager longing for the revealing of the sons of God; for the creation was subjected to futility, not of its own will, but by the will of him who subjected it in hope; because the creation itself will be set free from its bondage to decay and obtain the glorious liberty of the children of God. . . . (8:19)

In this age when the Christian Church is regarded with scorn or indifference in many parts of the world and our society, it is amazing to read Paul's bold words. The entire creation, he says — the whole created order, all of nature and the universe — is "standing on tiptoe" (J. B. Phillips translation) to see what God will do as he fulfills his promise to remake his children in the image of Christ. When this happens, it will mean that the effects of sin and death have been reversed forever, the image of God has been restored to humanity, and this whole "universal frame"[1] will enter into a new and permanent state of blessedness greater even than the original Paradise that God created. That original Eden was ruined by the sin of Adam, Paul has told us in chapter 5; to use his words in today's lesson, it was "subjected to futility." From this futility God has rescued us, not only the human race, but also the creation itself, and set us "free from bondage to decay," free for "the glorious liberty of the children of God."

It may seem somewhat absurd to think of nature standing on

---

1. John Dryden uses this phrase in his glorious poem (set to music by G. F. Handel) about the remaking of the universe, "A Song for St. Cecilia's Day" (1687). The final stanza is reminiscent not only of Romans 8:19 but also of 1 Corinthians 15:52.

tiptoe ("waiting with eager longing") for the final revelation of God's baptized children. After all, we Christians — and sometimes especially we clergy — are a pretty sorry lot, and the news media won't let us forget it. The creation seems to be largely indifferent, indeed sometimes actively hostile, to the Church. Yet Paul means exactly what he says. God's purpose, which cannot fail, is to restore the creation *through the agency of his church as it suffers on behalf of that creation.* This is the true Christian motivation for involvement in the environmental movement. Paul suggests that wounded nature senses something that human beings do not; one commentator gives the wonderful illustration of the station-master's dog who runs out to greet the approaching train long before the waiting passengers hear it or see it. The Lord of nature will return to restore his creation, and he is at hand.

To be a baptized Christian, then, means to be actively involved in the world as Christ was — not standing apart from it while it goes to hell, but taking its wounds, scars, and afflictions upon ourselves. This is what is meant by "the revealing of the sons of God"; when that day comes, the creation will recognize its crucified Savior and Lord in the self-giving acts that were done in his name by his disciples. Nowhere in Scripture is it more clear that being a Christian does not mean a flight from reality.

But what gives us the strength to march into this battle? Look at these two infants — how are they going to meet all the challenges of the world, let alone the call to be Christ's faithful soldiers and servants? That's what we used to say in the baptismal service — I wish we still did:

> We receive this child into the congregation of Christ's flock, and do sign her with the sign of the cross, in token that hereafter she may not be ashamed to confess the faith of Christ crucified, and manfully to fight under his banner against sin, the world, and the devil; and to continue Christ's faithful soldier and servant unto her life's end.

Isn't that thrilling? But when we think of what's involved, it might turn out to be more heartbreaking than thrilling.

Many of you know by now about Fran Holmes, who was a seminarian here, her husband Doug, and their fatally ill daughter Carin Grace.[2] For two years and more they have suffered not only the anguish of trying to care for this beloved child, but also the even greater suffering of knowing that there is no earthly hope and that all the signs point to an end. The affliction itself is dreadful enough. The Christian is confronted with the additional challenge of trying to remain faithful when there is no evidence of any meaning or sense in what is happening. Doug writes, "We are not sure why we are having to go through all this or what the future holds." Fran writes, "I do not sense deliverance is near at hand nor do I see in the present much purpose, yet we continue to hold on and be held on to and mutter 'Thy will be done' trusting that God has not abandoned us." It is this extremity of doubt that Paul understands and addresses in his eighth chapter. It is in the context of seeming God-forsakenness that Paul speaks of *hope.*

> In this hope [the hope of the redemption of all creation and the glorious liberty of the children of God] we were saved. Now hope that is seen is not hope — for who hopes for what he sees? But if we hope for what we do not see, we wait for it with endurance. (8:24-25)

It is the nature of Christian hope that it goes on hoping when there seems to be no basis for hope. Paul writes that the whole creation is waiting in this kind of hope — "waiting with eager longing" for the day when the wolf will lie down with the lamb (Isaiah 11:6-9), and swords will be beaten into ploughshares (Isaiah 2:4), and the barren woman will be a joyous mother (Psalm 113:9), and the eyes of the blind will be opened (Isaiah 35:5), and water will break forth in the wilderness (Isaiah 35:6), and the trees of the field will clap their hands (Isaiah 55:12). But why should we believe this?

2. Carin did not die. Her life was saved by a famous New York surgeon. She is a radiant young woman now, but severely handicapped and bound to a wheelchair. The challenges and obstacles for the family have continued to be tremendous over the years.

Little Catherine's father, Charles, wrote me a letter recently in which he expressed the frustration we all feel sometimes. Why do I believe? he asked. What reason is there besides "I believe because I believe?" What evidence is there for Christian hope?

In many respects there really is no evidence at all, not the kind that would ever convince a skeptic. And yet there do seem to me to be reasons for holding on to faith in God's future, in the glorious liberty of the children of God." These are some of the reasons I believe:

- I believe because the Holy Scriptures, the Old and New Testaments, have been for me an unfailing and inexhaustible source of life and renewal for fifty-two years of daily testing;
- I believe because the extraordinary lives of Christians like Dietrich Bonhoeffer and Martin Luther King and Desmond Tutu and Fran and Doug Holmes convince me of the truth they are ready to suffer for and even to die for;
- I believe because Jesus of Nazareth remains the single most compelling and commanding figure in human history and I simply cannot dismiss the claim that this crucified person was raised from the dead.

I am very interested in the baptism of infant girls right now because my own first grandchild, a girl, was baptized at St. Michael's Church uptown just one month ago. She was only two months old at the time. As you may know, St. Michael's has as its chief feature a drop-dead Tiffany window that wraps around the apse of the church, over the altar. This window depicts the moment in God's future when St. Michael the Archangel will have defeated the powers of sin, death, and the devil. St. Michael is not mentioned in any of St. Paul's writings; he appears in other parts of the Bible which are more pictorial and figurative. St. Paul, in Romans, speaks to us of God's apocalyptic war vividly, but usually in concepts; some of the other biblical writers dramatize it for us in images like that of St. Michael, who is the Lord's field-commander on the Last Day.

The priest at St. Michael's held our tiny grandchild under the window of the triumph of the heavenly host over every form of evil and he prayed the old prayer, that she would remain Christ's faithful soldier and servant until her life's end. The juxtaposition of the infant girl and the battle imagery would have been either preposterous or monstrous were it not for the source of our baptismal strength, the Christian hope to which the window bore witness — the coming triumph of God, prefigured in the Resurrection of Jesus Christ from the jaws of death.

The window over the Grace Church altar is not as staggering as the St. Michael's window, but it tells the same truth. It depicts Christ in majesty. Jesus is Lord. We are baptized into his death and into his victory. This is the source of courage. This is the source of hope. This is the source of faith. Doug Holmes recently wrote, quoting from Romans 8:28 — "In everything God is working for good for those . . . who are called according to his purpose." He said that Carin had a picture of Jesus which she calls "my Jesus." Is he her Jesus? Is he powerful beyond the grave? Will her brief life have a meaning? Will your life, and my life, and Emily's and Catherine's lives, have meaning?

The whole creation, straining on tiptoe with eager anticipation like the stationmaster's dog, joyfully answers Yes. Yes. "Amen, come, Lord Jesus."

AMEN, AMEN.

From Denial to Victory

Who shall separate us from the love of Christ? Shall tribulation, or distress, or persecution, or famine, or nakedness, or peril, or sword? As it is written, "For thy sake we are being killed all the day long; we are regarded as sheep to be slaughtered." No, in all these things we are more than conquerors through him who loved us.

ROMANS 8:35-36

As far as I can tell, the word "denial" was never used in a psychological sense until very recently. The definition in Webster's Second Unabridged Dictionary doesn't even come close. The Shorter Oxford English Dictionary of 1993 does better, with this entry: "refusal to acknowledge the existence or reality of a thing."

This is an important subject for a congregation of Christian worshippers, not because we need to master the latest therapeutic lingo, but because it is a central issue in Christian life. Denial, interpreted theologically, means "unwillingness to suffer."

It is well known that you don't know who your real friends are until you get in trouble. Not long ago I was talking to a woman who said that she was in the supermarket when she saw another woman coming along whose husband had just died. The first woman, who had the grace to be ashamed of herself, told me that she turned and went down the other aisle rather than try to think of something to say to the bereaved widow. I myself remember the people who, when our daughter had a brain tumor, neither wrote nor called, and never said anything about it afterwards, as though it had never happened. I don't dwell on it, but I can't say I think as highly of them as I did before. A hallmark of Christian existence is a capacity for suffering alongside others.

Denial does have its uses, up to a point. There are times when we must draw a curtain over some of our disappointments simply in order to function. There are times when we do not want to talk about or think about our sorrows, not because we deny that they exist, but because we need to be productive in other areas of our lives. The problem comes when, because of our persistence in living in an unreal world, we either fail to meet the needs of others, or fail to get the help we need for ourselves.

I think of families I have known through my ministry. I remember one family that would not admit that one of its members was dying. The sick man felt that he had to keep up a happy face and was never enabled to have the proper pain medication or talk about his impending death. It is very difficult to plan funerals when family members will not discuss their wishes. Idealization of a family member is another form of denial. Some years ago, trying to plan a funeral of a man I had not known well, I spent an afternoon with his two daughters. "Talk to me about your father," I said. I was unable to elicit anything that sounded real. One daughter actually said, "He was a perfect father." This was an exaggerated case of denial. That daughter has been divorced three times, looking for a perfect man.

A fundamental part of marriage is willingness to suffer. We have to suffer the loss of the person we thought we married and adjust to the person that actually exists. That is what love does. I don't know if you men know this or not, but there really are few things more predictably funny than long-married women talking about their husbands. There are universal complaints, rolling of eyeballs at the ceiling, and groans of mutual recognition, but underneath it all is an unconquerable affection and — yes — love. Real marriage is based on a long-term willingness to *suffer* the loss of illusion and build a lasting relationship based on reality.

Suffering lies at the very heart of Christian faith. No one argues this more forcefully than St. Paul, whose letter to the Romans we are reading all this summer. He writes:

> Who shall separate us from the love of Christ? Shall tribulation, or distress, or persecution, or famine, or nakedness, or peril, or sword? As it is written, "For thy sake we are being killed all the day long; we are regarded as sheep to be slaughtered." No, in all these things we are more than conquerors through him who loved us.

In this well-loved passage from chapter 8, Paul makes an important assumption. The Christian life involves suffering. The Christian way is not at all like some of these popular "spiritualities" that we hear so much about nowadays. The Christian path is not a self-indulgent flight into a world of angels and spirits and religious fantasy. It is grounded in the real struggles of flesh-and-blood people, our brothers and sisters who sometimes irritate us no end but are nevertheless given us by God to be our neighbors. When St. Paul writes about the love of Christ, he doesn't mean hearts and Valentines. He means the daily struggle to act with love toward one another even when we feel we can't stand each other, because that is the only way we can truly embody the life of the Savior who gave himself up to his enemies and a terrible death for our salvation.

A member of this congregation (let's call her Frances) told me of being in the hospital for weeks, very ill, sharing a room with a complete stranger of another race who was not only less ill, but was also extraordinarily disagreeable. "She said awful things about me," said Frances. Being seriously ill in the hospital with a roommate like that sounded like real suffering to me. After a week of this, Frances finally said, "Louise, may I ask you a question?" The hostile roommate grudgingly said yes. "Louise, can't we be friends?" A miracle occurred. Louise's attitude turned around completely and she actually began to do nice things for her fellow sufferer. Frances' exact words were, "After that, she couldn't do enough for me." I mention this because it shows how real breakthroughs occur as we are willing to take risks. Risks for Christ's sake always involve possible rejection. "For thy sake we are being killed all the day long," Paul writes; we are like "sheep about to be slaughtered." Paul knew that Christians would be called to face these kinds of challenges, but it is precisely in the midst of such challenges that God acts redemptively.

One of the most significant events of this past week was the reopening of Centennial Park in Atlanta after the bombing.[1] The spirit of the event was caught in a story by Pulitzer Prize–winner Rick Bragg, who told of two grandmothers from Georgia, one white, one black, neither of whom had intended to come to the Olympics at all, but met at 6:30 A.M. in the line of people waiting to reopen the park. They warmed to each other at once and became inseparable during the day. We came, said one, because we wanted to assert "victory over fear and a twisted mind." That little episode seems to me more remarkable than a dozen gold medals. The park was reopened by 50,000 people, many of whom seemed to come in a spirit, not of denial that anything had happened, but of resistance against violence and hatred. "We need this," said Cremia McGee, African-American of Atlanta, "for the freedom of knowing that no maniac can keep us from gathering together." Evelyn Winborne, fifth-generation white Atlantan, said, "It's saying to the buffoon with the bomb that we are not going to succumb, that we are bigger than you are."[2] And so, as Paul writes in Romans, "in everything God works for good with those who love him" (8:28).

Even cynical journalists acknowledged that Andrew Young was the man of destiny in Atlanta at the reopening of the park. Virtually all recognized that on this defining occasion he had resumed his original role of Christian preacher. One reporter said that Young recalled "Martin Luther King Jr.'s oft-repeated evocation of the re-

1. America was in shock over a seemingly senseless bombing at the Olympic Games in Atlanta.

2. Story by Bob Hohler, *Boston Globe,* July 31, 1996.

demptive power of unearned suffering." Andrew Young knows something about suffering. Over the years he has been hated, simply for being black and successful. I remember being at the beach in North Carolina and listening to a group of my white friends saying terrible things about Andrew Young for no reason that I could understand. Yet God used Mr. Young powerfully this week to reclaim Atlanta from nameless wickedness. The former Mayor was at the center of his city's triumph over adversity. On Tuesday, the reporter continued, Mr. Young's lament for what had happened "became a kind of invocation. 'We want everyone to know that there is no need to be alienated. . . . There's nothing that keeps you out but the unwillingness to open your heart, open your mind, to the love and fellowship that this planet offers to all its citizens. . . . So we say to those who suffered here, we assure your suffering was not in vain. . . . We will define the future not with bitterness, not with alienation, but with joy.' And when he was through, a crowd of 50,000 people — people who saw coming to this park as an act of defiance, as a chance to show the bomber that he had accomplished little beyond the murder of innocent people — cheered in a dozen languages."[3]

It could be objected that the family of the woman who was killed, and her daughter who is still in the hospital, can scarcely be expected to share in the celebration. Was it all a gigantic exercise in denial? To some extent, human nature being what it is, perhaps so. But for the most part, I think not. Certainly not those two grandmothers. Even the flowers that were put on the spot where the bomb exploded could be interpreted, not so much as a wish to prettify the event as an attempt, however feeble, to acknowledge and share the pain. I believe we can understand the reopening of the park as a movement of God to restore the human spirit in the midst of a situation that at first seemed so awful that many of us could not even speak when we heard the news. The verse from Romans is often mistranslated as "All things work together for good." That's not what Paul meant. That's denial. It's not true. Things don't necessar-

---

3. Combined from two *New York Times* articles by Rick Bragg and Ronald Smothers, July 31, 1996.

ily work out for the best. What Paul says is quite different: "In everything *God works* for good with those who love him."

I used to have a rather grandiose idea of suffering. I thought suffering for Christ's sake meant that you had to become a missionary to Africa and be crucified on an anthill, like Celia Coplestone in T. S. Eliot's *The Cocktail Party.* I thought that Christian suffering meant you had to defy tyrants or march in the streets or stand before firing squads. Now I realize that for most of us it means something much less glamorous and more mundane. Being mindful of the needs of others, giving of ourselves in a Christlike, sacrificial way, does not necessarily mean lying down in front of a tank. It might mean making a call on a bereaved person. It might mean reaching out to a person of a different background or race. It might mean asking your children or your spouse to forgive you for your defects. It might mean confronting a friend about a self-destructive habit, or it might mean asking for help with one's own self-destructive habits. In everyday situations such as these, we are among those who *for Christ's sake are being killed all the day long,* and yet *in all these things we are more than conquerors through him who loved us.*

A case can be made that the very best type of humor is black humor. I heard something this week that won my heart. Many of you know that there is a covered, elevated walkway at our local retirement village, so that wheelchairs can go back and forth between the buildings. Now the administration of a retirement community would typically call this the Rainbow Bridge, or the Yellow Brick Road, or some other jolly, upbeat name. But the residents of the community call it after the famous Venetian landmark — the Bridge of Sighs. This is wonderful. It is both funny and sad. It is both rueful and defiant. It refuses to deny but it equally refuses to be vanquished. Yes, suffering for the sake of the love of Christ is a hallmark of Christian life; "For thy sake we are being killed all the day long; we are regarded as sheep to be slaughtered." But we may be confident that

in all these things we are more than conquerors through him who loved us. For I am sure that neither death, nor life, nor angels, nor principalities, nor things present, nor things to come, nor powers, nor height, nor depth, nor anything else in all creation, will be able to separate us from the love of God in Christ Jesus our Lord.

AMEN.

Who Is to Condemn?

It is God who justifies; who is to condemn?

ROMANS 8:33-34

Many of my clergy friends and I look forward to the time, every three years, when St. Paul's Epistle to the Romans is read all through the summer. It affords an unparalleled opportunity to preach straight through this great letter. I am always thrilled when the third year comes around again. One of Paul's most important themes could be stated as "There but for the grace of God go I."[1] If we can learn to say this in any and all circumstances, we will have come a long way toward appropriating the gospel message. There is liberation in the Christian confession of sin and unworthiness before God. The knowledge that each one of us is a sinner in need of God's mercy is strangely and wonderfully freeing. I do not need to set myself up against others as though I were more deserving than you. We are granted a measure of compassion in our dealings with one another because we know we cannot accurately evaluate the hand that

---

1. The original saying is attributed to a sixteenth-century Englishman, John Bradford (1510-1555), who, when watching malefactors in London being taken off for execution, did not say, "They are getting what they deserve," but rather, "There but for the grace of God goes John Bradford."

[265]

another person has been dealt. Mercy shown to that other person is a sign that we trust God to make that evaluation and to be at work in that person's life as he is in ours.

And yet the Christian way of mercy and forgiveness is often perplexing, not only to those outside the faith, but sometimes especially to those inside. We are often genuinely confused as to how we should react to grave injustices. Dietrich Bonhoeffer, the famous German theologian who resisted Hitler and was hanged by the Nazis a mere three days before the Allies overran the German lines, makes a useful distinction: He wrote that the grace of God is free, but it is not cheap.[2] When Bonhoeffer wrote this, long before his own ordeal, he was thinking of the sacrifice of Jesus, who as the eternal Son on the right hand of God emptied himself of deity, privilege, power, riches, and reputation in order to give himself up to disgrace and death on the Cross in place of us sinners (Philippians 2:6-8; 2 Corinthians 8:9). God's grace is *free,* but it is *not cheap,* for it cost the Lord a price so great that even the biblical writers must grope for words to convey it. Paul refers to it in today's passage, saying that God "did not spare his own Son but gave him up for us all."

Forgiveness and mercy, therefore, are costly. They do not come easily. We should learn to beware of forgiveness that comes too quickly, too glibly, with insufficient cost to the forgiver. Last week, Father Lawrence Jenco died of cancer. Perhaps some of you will remember that he was one of those who was held hostage in Beirut for eighteen months by Islamic radicals in the 1980s, along with Terry Anderson and Terry Waite and others. Among other brutalities, he was kept in solitary confinement for six months and was told three times that he was about to be released, only to learn hours later that it was a joke. He wrote a book about his experiences called, *Bound to Forgive: The Pilgrimage to Reconciliation of a Beirut Hostage.* This is a striking title. In the first part, *Bound to Forgive,* he indicates that as a Christian he is under orders to forgive; forgiveness is not an option in this service. But the second half of the title, *Pilgrimage to Reconcil-*

---

2. Dietrich Bonhoeffer, *The Cost of Discipleship* (New York: Macmillan, 1959), the chapter on "Costly Grace."

iation, shows that forgiveness is not necessarily instantaneous. It involves struggle and sacrifice, patience and endurance — like a pilgrimage. Father Jenco writes, "I don't believe that forgetting is one of the signs of forgiveness. I do not forget the pain, the loneliness, the ache, the terrible injustice. But I do not remember [these things] in order to inflict some future retribution."[3]

In South Africa an extraordinary process is going on. Anglican Archbishop Desmond Tutu is head of a special commission that is conducting hearings about atrocities committed by the government and police during the apartheid era. Nelson Mandela's administration has no interest in inflicting retribution. Mandela has set a personal example by reaching out to whites and pursuing future-oriented policies of reconciliation and healing. The decision has been made, however, that there will be no amnesty for torturers and murderers without full disclosure. That is the purpose of Bishop Tutu's hearings. I recently read that the details given by the witnesses of the brutalities they endured caused the normally effervescent Archbishop to put his head down on the table in the courtroom and weep.[4]

No, forgiveness will not come easily in South Africa. The great thing, though, is that the leadership has determined that, in God's time, it will come. The nation is being taught by word and example that it is on a "pilgrimage to reconciliation" and that black South Africans should be watchful to receive the gift of forgiveness when it comes; "the readiness is all," as Hamlet said. This is part of what we mean in the Lord's Prayer when we say, "Forgive us our trespasses as we forgive those who trespass against us." Our forgiveness of others is derivative from God's forgiveness of us. It is not something we produce in ourselves by force of human will. We receive it as a gift from God, whose perfect will is at work in us: *Thy* will be done, on earth as it is in heaven. Our part is to expect the gift of forgiveness and to welcome it when it arrives.

3. Obituary in *The New York Times,* July 22, 1996.

4. As this book is prepared for publication ten years later, the Truth and Reconciliation Commission of South Africa is held up as an example around the world. Bishop Tutu's book about it is called *No Future without Forgiveness* (New York: Doubleday, 1999).

And yet — and yet. When we attempt to express the totality of what God does in us, forgiveness is too weak a word. Some of you may have seen a powerful column in the paper Wednesday about Susan Cohen, a woman who lost her only child, Theodora, age 20, seven years ago on Pan Am Flight 103 over Lockerbie. Seven years later, her grief and rage have scarcely abated. "The pain will not go away," she said. "It will never go away. Theo's murderers are still out there. No one has been punished."[5] What we notice here is the overpowering sense of injustice and wrong. It isn't just a sense of grief and loss that she feels, though that is bad enough; she must struggle against her utter impotence in the face of unnamed and presumably unrepentant terrorists who go free. The Christian message of forgiveness is pallid and insufficient if it does not take account of the agony of those who suffer injustice.

And so Paul does not use the word "forgiveness." He uses another word. It is a huge challenge to interpret this word; sometimes one wishes that Paul had chosen an easier one. Preachers and Bible teachers have been struggling for years to find the best way of making this word live. Here it is in our passage from Romans for today: "It is God who justifies; who is to condemn?" (8:33).

This is such an important message that I wish I could put neon lights around it. *It is God who justifies; who is to condemn?* The reason that Christians are free from the need to be vindictive from here to eternity is that God is going to take care of injustice. God is going to take care of wickedness. God is going to take care of treachery and terrorism and every kind of evildoing. That is what *justification* means: God is going to justify, God is going to rectify, God is going to make the figures come out right. God isn't just going to pat humanity on the head and say, "That's all right, it's all forgiven and forgotten, let's just indulge in a little erasure here and a little rearrangement there and put it all behind us and go forward." In the lingo of today, that is called denial and it is bad for everybody. That's not what God does.

What then is God going to do? How is he going to accomplish

5. "Our Towns" column by Evelyn Nieves, *The New York Times*, July 24, 1996.

this rectifying? How is he going to make everything come out right? That's a bit of a mystery for which our present language is only partly adequate. The Bible describes it in metaphorical language, the language of new creation. "I consider," says Paul, "that the sufferings of this present time are not worth comparing with the glory that is to be revealed in us." Paul stretches for imagery, and it is noteworthy that many communities that have suffered greatly have found great comfort in the book of Revelation with its picture of the decisive defeat of evil and the establishment of a new heaven and a new earth in which all pain and sorrow will be done away with forever.

Imagine something that we have all seen from time to time, a phenomenon that is often written about in feature articles as it was this past week in a *New York Times* story about a group of hobo craftsmen who had reclaimed their lives from drunkenness. Imagine, if you will, a man who through his own weakness and culpability has lost everything — position, home, wife, children, community, reputation, human future. Like Cain, he becomes a pariah on the face of the earth, marked for life. Can there be anyone present for Christian worship today who would not wish for that man to be restored by God to health and blessing? Yet we recognize that it cannot be without cost. We cannot just go to a cocktail party with a person who has committed great wrongs and be jolly as though nothing had happened, any more than the people of South Africa can pretend that no evil was ever done. Part of God's *rectification* consists of our acknowledgement that there has been great wrong.

Nowhere in the Bible is it suggested that wrongdoing will simply be overlooked by God. No Christian can expect to escape judgment for sin. There are many places in the New Testament that make this clear, including the description of the Last Judgment in Matthew 25. Paul himself says in Romans 14:10 that "We shall all stand before the judgment seat of God," and he specifically includes himself (in 1 Corinthians 4:4). Our sins will be brought to light; the Lord "will bring to light the things now hidden in darkness and will disclose the purposes of the heart" (1 Corinthians 4:5). He will indeed come to judge the quick and the dead. But! and this is the big *But!* As we heard two weeks ago from Romans 8:1, "There is therefore now no condemnation for those who are in Christ Jesus." There is judgment before God; but Christ's death on the Cross — the ultimate price — has removed the everlasting condemnation from us, once and for all. Forgiveness is not cheap because it cost God everything.

James F. Kay, a friend who teaches preaching at Princeton, is writing an article analyzing a proposed new Presbyterian baptismal service in which the participants are asked to renounce "the ways of sin that separate us from Jesus Christ." This proposed text, as Dr. Kay points out, is precisely the opposite of what the Epistle to the Romans promises us. *Nothing* can separate us from Jesus Christ. Sin cannot separate us from Christ. If it can, we are indeed doomed. Paul's message is that our renunciation, such as it is, of sin in this life will always be inadequate, given our frail human nature, so we cannot have confidence in it. We have confidence rather in the love of God, and Paul says that *nothing* can separate us from the love of God, "neither death, nor life, nor angels, nor principalities, nor things present, nor things to come, nor powers, nor height, nor depth, nor anything else in all creation," not even our own worst selves, "will be able to separate us from the love of God in Christ Jesus our Lord" in whom we can rest all our cases, knowing that in his future there will finally come not only the forgiveness of sins but also the rectification of all things, so that by a power beyond human imagining, the lost daughter will be returned to her father, and the lost son will be returned to his mother, and the lost parents will be returned to their children.

> If God is for us, who is against us? He who did not spare his own Son but gave him up for us all, will he not also give us all things with him? Who shall bring any charge against God's elect? It is God who justifies; who is to condemn? . . . Christ Jesus, who died, yes, who was raised from the dead, who is at the right hand of God, indeed intercedes for us.

AMEN.

The Israelite Connection:
Three Sermons on Romans 9–11

relationship betw.

Jew & Xn

The Clue on the Beach

NOTE TO THE READER: This sermon and the two
following are a three-part series on Romans 9–11 and
therefore are printed together in a section of their own.
Other sermons on 9–11 follow in the next section.

*I am speaking the truth in Christ, I am not lying; my conscience
bears me witness in the Holy Spirit, that I have great sorrow
and unceasing anguish in my heart. For I could wish that I myself were accursed and cut off from Christ for the sake of my
brethren, my kinsmen by race. They are Israelites, and to them
belong the sonship, the glory, the covenants, the giving of the
law, the worship, and the promises; to them belong the patriarchs, and of their race, according to the flesh, is the Christ.
God who is over all be blessed for ever. Amen.*

ROMANS 9:1-5

Last summer I read a book that made a powerful impression on me.
It was written by a young Baptist minister, David Gushee, who
adapted it from his doctoral dissertation at Union Theological Seminary.[1] The name of it is *The Righteous Gentiles of the Holocaust,* and it
is stunning. It has one of the best, clearest short surveys of what

---

1. David Gushee has gone on (since 1996) to do much fine work. His cover
story about torture in *Christianity Today* (February 2006) broke new ground for that
publication.

happened to the Jews under the Nazis that I have read, making it worth the price for that reason alone. What affected me most, however, was the note of lament struck throughout by the author, a believing Christian who is profoundly, almost inconsolably grieved that the six million met their fate in the very heart of Christian Europe as most of the members of the churches turned away their faces. Christians must live with this terrible fact till the close of the Age.[2]

These three chapters, Romans 9–11, have had an interesting history. They more or less dropped out of sight in many circles for many years. For example, the famous nineteenth-century preacher Alexander McLaren, during his lifetime, preached through the whole Bible. His sermons have been published in seventeen volumes. When McLaren arrives at Romans 9–11, however, there is a big blank. He simply skips the section. He goes straight from Romans 8 to Romans 12 as though there were nothing in between. This has been typical of much biblical interpretation over the centuries.[3] No more. Now we *must* reckon with Romans 9–11, because we must reckon with the failure of Christians to protect Jews during World War II. I believe we can all discover together, if you will stay with me, that Romans 9–11 is the very heart of the gospel message and is therefore astonishing good news for everyone.

In the passage read today, at the beginning of chapter 9, Paul tries to come to terms with the well established fact that first-century Jews, for the most part, did not convert to Christianity. Paul the apostle grieved deeply over this. Jesus was a Jew, Paul was a Jew, the Holy Scriptures were Hebrew, the prophecies about the Messiah were from the Hebrew prophets, the teachings of Jesus

2. The one serious criticism that I have brought against Gushee's book is that it does not take account of Romans 9–11, a very strange omission. Still, it is a splendid piece of work.

3. For example: a popular book of the 40s and 50s, *The Bible and the Common Reader* by Smith College professor Mary Ellen Chase, states that "the argument [of Romans] rises to its culmination in the magnificent 8th chapter." It is as though 9–11 with its concluding doxology did not exist.

were given in synagogues and in the Temple; how could it be that Jews were refusing to come to faith in Christ? Here is what Paul says:

> I am speaking the truth in Christ, I am not lying; my conscience bears me witness in the Holy Spirit, that I have great sorrow and unceasing anguish in my heart. For I could wish that I myself were accursed and cut off from Christ for the sake of my brethren, my kinsmen by race.

This sounds overwrought, perhaps, but this motif is deeply woven into the Scriptures. Just as mothers and fathers would gladly, willingly, without even stopping to think, give up their lives for their children, so the apostle says he would give up his own salvation for the sake of the Jews, his *brethren,* his *kinsmen by race.* This is the same prayer made by no less a figure than Moses, who said to God, "If thou wilt not forgive the sin of thy people, blot me, I pray, out of thy book which thou hast written" (Exodus 32:32).

I have often heard Presbyterians reviled for the question that used to be asked of those being ordained: "Would you be willing to be damned for the glory of God?" Yes, they really did ask that in the old days. If we today understood biblical theology better, we would not be so horrified. This vow is in the great tradition from Moses to Paul. It is above all a window into the mind of Christ himself, who gave himself up to condemnation on the Cross in our place.

Many Christians must feel as Paul does in these verses that we have today. I myself find it very hard, even heartbreaking, to see our own American Christian tradition becoming so attenuated. It grieves me deeply to see that worship on the Lord's day has become merely an option among many options, that many families do not even own (let alone read) a Bible, that evening prayers and grace before meals are not said in Christian homes, that many young people with Christian backgrounds are turning away from Christ to the latest "spiritualities" by the self-styled gurus of the month. I hope you will not think me overly melodramatic if I say that I truly can understand Moses and Paul saying, in effect, that they would be willing to be damned for the glory of Christ if only the people would come to know him.

In these multicultural times, we hear a good many appeals to the "Judeo-Christian tradition," but I'm not sure that very many people know what it is. I myself was very blessed, because I had an aunt named Mary Virginia. I talk about her all the time because she and my grandmother opened the Bible to me. She used to refer to Jews as "Israelites." I don't think she knew a single Jew, having spent her life in Franklin, Virginia, but her love of the Old Testament and her use of the term "Israelites" has stayed with me in a powerful way. One of the hopeful things that David Gushee points out in his book is that it was characteristic of some devout European Christians to have a deep reverence for the Jews. This is the "Israelite" connection. "They are Israelites," writes Paul here in the Romans passage. He calls up the ancient name of the Jews in the Hebrew Bible in order to evoke the incomparable heritage of the Jews: "They are Israelites, and to them belong the sonship, the glory, the covenants, the giving of the law, the worship, and the promises; to them belong the patriarchs, and of their race, according to the flesh, is the Christ. God who is over all be blessed for ever. Amen" (9:4-6). We Christians would be nowhere without the Jews. They were and they remain the Chosen People.

Or do they? Paul asked himself that question. "I ask, then, has God rejected his people?" (11:1). I will never forget a class I was teaching at Grace Church in New York on this very subject of Christians and Jews. We always had a certain number of newcomers in our classes who had been formed in various ways different from us in the mainstream churches. Many times we would have to bring the class to a screeching halt in order to describe yet again the foundations on which our teaching stood. This was not an easy task on any occasion, but the day I am about to describe took the prize. A man I had never seen before raised his hand and, in a tone of authority, said, "The Jews died in the war because God had rejected them for their unbelief." An audible gasp of horror rose from the audience. Everyone looked at me to see what I would say. What would you have said? I think all Christians need to ponder this matter.

In our response, we need to know the Bible. Most clergy, most of the time, will preach not on the Old Testament lesson or the Epistle, but the Gospel for the day. This is a great mistake. One of many key reasons for focusing on the Bible *as a whole* is the question of the Jews. There is nothing in any of the four Gospels like Romans 9–11. Reading only the Gospels — especially John's — and the book of Acts has given many people the idea that Jews are bad and bound for hell. It is the apostle Paul who puts the "Israelites" in the most sweeping perspective.

What do we say to the man who declares that God has rejected the Jewish people? We point to these words of Paul:

> I ask, then, has God rejected his people? By no means! I myself am an Israelite, a descendant of Abraham, a member of the tribe of Benjamin. God has not rejected his people whom he foreknew. (11:1-2)

Part of Paul's meaning here is that the fact that there are a few Jewish Christians, not many, but a few, is a sign of God's ultimate plan for us all, and he cites his own election as a prime example.

Paul's line of thought in what follows is very challenging. He is saying that there is a purpose, not only for belief, but also for unbelief. He continues, "So I ask, have they stumbled so as to fall?" In other words, are the Jews cut off from God's promises because they did not come to Christ?

> By no means! . . . through their trespass [their unbelief] salvation has come to the Gentiles, so as to make Israel jealous. Now if their *trespass* means riches for the world, and if their failure means riches for the Gentiles, how much more will their *full inclusion* mean! . . . For if their *rejection* means the reconciliation of the world, what will their *acceptance* mean but life from the dead? (11:11-12, 15; emphasis added)

This is intricate, but let's give it a try. Paul puts some words in one column and others in a second column:

Trespass	Full inclusion
Failure	Acceptance
Rejection	Life from the dead

Paul is saying that the continuing unbelief of most Jews (their trespass, their failure, their rejection of the gospel) is part of God's plan to enfold and enrich the Gentiles, who had previously been excluded and impoverished. This, he says, will in God's time make Israel "jealous," and will lead to their full inclusion and acceptance. Indeed, the last will outdo the first, Paul says in one of his typical "how much more" passages. If the exclusion of the Jews means spiritual riches for the Gentiles, how much more will it mean when eventually they are brought back in again!

In Walker Percy's famous novel, *The Moviegoer,* the main character, Binx Bolling, a classic good-for-not-very-much Southern WASP, plays around with the possibility of a "search" for meaning — indeed, a search for God. "To become aware of the possibility of the search is to be onto something. Not to be onto something is to be in despair." Then he confides, "I have become acutely aware of Jews. . . . Jews are my first real clue. . . . When a man awakes to the possibility of a search and when such a man passes a Jew in the street for the first time, he is like Robinson Crusoe seeing the footprint on the beach."[4]

The continuing presence of the Jews in the world is the sign that God is faithful, that God is true, that God is actively at work to redeem the world. It means that God has reached out to grasp the whole human race. It means that the story of ancient Israel, "the adoption as sons, the glory, the covenants, the giving of the law, the worship, and the promises," all these great and wonderful things, belong to the Jews still, "for the gifts and the call of God are irrevocable" (11:29). The miracle is that they have been given also to us, the Gentiles, the heathen, the ungodly.

Brothers and sisters in Christ: this is not the story of some peo-

---

4. Walker Percy, *The Moviegoer* (1962; New York: Alfred A. Knopf, 1977), pp. 13, 88-89.

ple way back in Bible days. This is *our* story. The Jews are the clue on the beach, the footprint of God. The good news today is that we stand fast, not by superiority to anyone else, Jew or Gentile, black or white, high or low, godly or ungodly, but by grace alone *(sola gratia)*. We are held, not by our own efforts, but by God's own mercy. We are not "onto something"; *some One is onto us.*[5] That's the gospel. For the apostle Paul announces, quoting from the Old Testament, that the story of the Jewish people means this for all of us:

> [God has] revealed [him]self to those who did not ask for [him]. (10:20)

> Those who were not my people I will call "my people" [says the Lord]. (9:25)

> In the very place where it was said to them, "You are not my people," they will be called "children of the living God." (9:26)

> And so there is no distinction between Jew and Greek; the same Lord is Lord of all and bestows his riches upon all who call upon him. For "every one who calls upon the name of the Lord will be saved." (10:12-13)

AMEN.

---

5. At the end of *The Moviegoer,* Binx Bolling learns maturity, not through "spiritual enlightenment" or a clear conclusion to his "search," but by making a commitment to a troubled young woman and to his own family. That is a good example of the Judeo-Christian tradition at work.

The Better Bet

Text: Romans 9–11

In memory of Rabbi Arthur Hertzberg (1921-2006)

The Republican convention this week has been fascinating. There was a general consensus that the tone set by the party in 1992 and 1994 was too harsh. This week there has been a concerted effort to show that Republicans are compassionate and inclusive. Whether these attempts are sincere or not remains a matter of debate, but certainly there was a good deal said about it. "The Republican Party must always be the party of inclusion," declared General Powell in his speech to the Republican convention on Monday. He continued, "We have to make sure that reduced government spending doesn't single out the poor and the middle class. Corporate welfare and welfare for the wealthy must be first in line for elimination. All of us — all of us, my friends — *all of us* must be willing to do with less from government."

This emphasis on the responsibility of the fortunate for the unfortunate is the Judeo-Christian tradition at work, even though we may not recognize it. All through the Old and New Testaments, beginning with the story of Israel and culminating with the story of Jesus Christ, there is a powerful theme of God's special concern for the poor, the weak, the defenseless, and, most radically, his mercy toward the undeserving. We are talking about these things right now because we are in the middle of Romans 9–11, the section of St. Paul's letter that deals with the relationship between Christians and Jews. I have been preaching from the Scripture lessons appointed for the given Sunday for twenty-one years now, but much as I admire the work of those who put our lectionary together, I have come to see that there are many problems with it. Take for instance the selection from Romans today. Look at your printed insert. You can't tell that fourteen verses have been omitted. They haven't even put in any of those little dots. You would think that the passage went directly from verse 15 to verse 29.[1] This is one of many reasons that every Christian should have and read his or her own Bible. In the omitted section, Paul declares that unbelief has a purpose, and the purpose is the revelation of God's salvation to the Gentiles, who were previously considered to be without hope.[2]

Here is the omitted portion:

> Have [the Jews] stumbled so as to fall? By no means! But through their trespass [their unbelief] salvation has come to the Gentiles, so as to make Israel jealous. Now if their trespass means riches for the world, and if their failure means riches for the Gentiles, how much more will their *full inclusion* mean!
>
> Now I am speaking to you Gentiles . . . if [the Jews'] rejection means the reconciliation of the world, what will their acceptance mean but life from the dead? . . . Lest you be wise in your own conceits, I want you to understand this mystery, brethren: a hardening has come upon part of Israel, until the full number of the Gentiles come in, and so all Israel will be saved. . . . For the gifts and the call of God are irrevocable. Just as you were once disobedient to God but now have received mercy because of their disobedience, so they have now been disobedient in order that by the mercy shown to you they also may receive mercy. For God has consigned all men to disobedience, that he may have mercy upon all.

1. Admittedly, Paul's letters occasionally contain parenthetical sections. However, this is not the case with Romans 9–11. The thought pattern is drawn in a continuous line throughout.

2. Ephesians 2:12.

This astonishing passage should take our breath away. The apostle Paul and the prophet Isaiah have the most "inclusive" visions in all the Bible, yet the Bible story books don't know what to do with them. The sum total of most people's knowledge of Isaiah and Paul is that Paul saw something on the road to Damascus and Isaiah wrote Handel's *Messiah*.[3] We are for the most part entirely ignorant of the radical visions of these two towering servants of God. I'm not even convinced that the learned designers of the lectionary quite get it, because they unaccountably omit the phrase that Paul uses to describe God's plan for the Jews: *full inclusion*.

In order to understand this fully, we need to start thinking about who is an insider and who is an outsider, who is "included" and who is not. In the Bible, it is generally the Israelites, or Jews, who are the insiders and the Gentiles who are the outsiders. In today's Gospel reading, Jesus has a sort of verbal sparring match with a Syro-Phoenician woman. She is not a Jew; she is a foreigner, one of the "ungodly." This is one of the most misinterpreted stories in the Gospels. Many people have seized upon this story to try to show that when Jesus said, "It is not right to take the children's [the Jews'] bread and give it to the dogs [Gentiles],"[4] it proves that Jesus was susceptible to prejudice like all the rest of us. If that were the case, it would be against the grain of every other story about Jesus in the New Testament. What is actually going on is that Jesus, who sees into the woman's heart as he always does, and immediately senses that she is one who can hold her own in debate, proceeds to conduct a demonstration for the disciples who wanted to get rid of her. His purpose is not only to heal the Syro-Phoenician woman's daughter, but also to use her gutsy response to teach a lesson. She replies to him with more gumption and cleverness than we today can easily grasp: "Yes, Lord, but even the dogs eat the crumbs that fall from their master's table." It is as though Jesus allows her to win her own case, to participate in raising her own stature. She par-

3. Just kidding . . . but he did write some of it. "Comfort ye, comfort ye, my people, saith your God . . ."
4. Matthew 15:26.

ticipates with him in demonstrating that faith in the Messiah knows no national, racial, or religious boundaries and that he responds to an "ungodly" person as readily as to a godly one. St. Paul's term for this in Romans is *the justification of the ungodly* (4:5). Thus God breaks out beyond the usual boundaries to include those who were thought to be completely beyond the pale.

The Republicans at the convention were talking about inclusion. The Episcopal Church is also talking about inclusion, some would say *ad nauseam;* in fact, it has become the key word for the 90s. The question for the church, however, is this: *what is a concern for inclusion based on?* What belief stands behind it? Take for instance Anne Frank's famous sentence, "In spite of everything I still believe that people are good at heart."[5] The play and movie about her life end with these words. The playwright has been much criticized for this sentimental conclusion; many have doubted that Anne's optimism would have survived the camps.[6] Do we construct an inclusive vision on our hope that there is something good inside every person? Paul certainly did not. In Romans 3 he states definitively: "All human beings, both Jews and Gentiles, are under the power of sin, as it is written: 'None is righteous, no, not one; no one understands, no one seeks for God. All have turned aside, together they have gone wrong; no one does good, not even one'" (Romans 3:10-12).

If we cannot hope in our fellow human beings, then what? Eighteen months ago I read an article by David Rieff (Susan Sontag's son) called "God and Man in Rwanda." As we now know, the church in Rwanda did little to stop the massacres there, and in some cases actually collaborated with the killers. "The story goes," wrote Mr. Rieff, "that a French priest in Rwanda who had survived the massacres of the spring of 1994 was asked if he had lost his faith in God. 'Absolutely not,' he replied. 'But,' he added matter-of-

---

5. Written on July 15, 1944. The Frank family was being betrayed as she wrote: the Gestapo came on August 4.

6. In any case, the context of her sentence in the actual diary makes it much less starry-eyed than it sounds when isolated.

factly, 'what happened in this country has destroyed my faith in mankind forever.' In Rwanda these days," Rieff continues, "even an atheist has a hard time pushing away the thought that God is a better bet than man."[7]

Again, this is the Judeo-Christian tradition defined by the Bible. As the Hebrew prophet Jeremiah wrote, "My people are skilled in doing evil [says the Lord], but how to do good they know not. . . . The heart is deceitful above all things, and desperately corrupt, who can understand it?" (4:22, 17:9) The biblical view of humanity is bluntly realistic. A true and lasting commitment to "inclusivity" can't be based on sentimentality about human nature. It can't be based on blinkered views of an America that can do no wrong. It can't be based on ideologies that have room for every kind of deviation except for those who hold other beliefs. It can only be based on something much bigger than any construct of mere human imagination. In the Judeo-Christian tradition, that base, that foundation, that rock is the mercy and also the justice of the Lord God, the Holy One of Israel.[8] "God is a better bet than man."

There is a verse in the Romans passage appointed for today that I have heard described as assuredly the most inclusive sentence in the whole Bible, yet most people do not even know of its existence. "God has consigned all men to disobedience [in order] that he may have mercy upon all."

Paul is saying that we are all in the same situation before God and no one has any advantage over anyone else. God has consigned *all* to disobedience [in order] that he may have mercy upon *all*. Second, it says that God is going to make our disobedience, our sinfulness, work not *against* us but *for* us. We need to let this sink in and understand how wrenchingly impossible it would be if we were talking about anything less than the God who is really God. Only God is larger than human wickedness. Truly, "God is a better bet

---

7. *Vanity Fair,* December 1994. There is a striking parallel here to a passage in the biblical history of King David: "David said to Gad [his prophet], 'I am in great distress; let us fall into the hand of the Lord, for his mercy is great; but let me not fall into the hand of man'" (2 Samuel 24:14).

8. *The Holy One of Israel* is Isaiah's special designation for God.

than man." This is not just another way of saying "Everything works out for the best." The Bible never says that. What it does say, in Romans 8:28, is that "in everything *God* works for good with those who love him." It is not "things" that work out for the best, it is God who is working for the best in spite of "things," in spite of sin, in spite of disobedience, in spite of the things we human beings do to one another.

A few weeks ago I had a long lunch with Arthur Hertzberg, in my opinion the most impressive writer on Jewish subjects in the English-speaking world today. He told me of a high-powered interfaith meeting he had attended recently in Europe. The participants attempted to come up with one bedrock commitment that all religions could agree on. Hertzberg proposed something that was eventually accepted. "What was it?" I asked. He replied, "The defense of the defenseless."[9] I was deeply moved. But I was also thunderstruck. Surely, I thought, this was bedrock for Christians and Jews. But what about Hindus, with their untouchable classes? I asked. He hesitated. Yes, well, he admitted, that was a problem, but they were making progress. I confess to you that my personal bias is showing here. I believe that the defense of the defenseless is such a strong Jewish-Christian thing that it has influenced everybody else without their even realizing it.

As Rabbi Hertzberg and I parted on 67th Street, I suggested, "You know, the reason this is so important is that ultimately it includes everybody. The tables can turn at any time. Even a rich and powerful person can become defenseless and weak at any moment." Yes, he agreed, and he spoke with deep feeling of his brother who was helplessly enduring a terrible illness at that very hour.

But why is the defense of the defenseless at the heart of the Judeo-Christian tradition? Is it just one of mankind's better religious ideas? The answer is no. It is at the heart of the tradition because it is the very nature of God. It is central to Jews because God

---

9. On this very day, August 18, 1996, Arthur Hertzberg was quoted on the front page of *The New York Times* about the special concern of God for the little people of society.

commands it out of his own care for the needy. We still see the strength of this tradition even among secular Jews, with their emphasis on philanthropy and service. But now listen to this: the defense of the defenseless is central to Christians because in the central event of all human history, the Son of God *made himself defenseless* for the salvation of the world, even for those who are the ungodly.

In order to make the majesty, the terror, and the ineffable joy of his message as clear as possible, Paul arraigns the whole human race before the bar of judgment, including himself: "We shall all stand before the judgment seat of God" (Romans 14:10). God must exclude before he includes. He must judge even as he redeems. There will be no place in the new creation for anything that obstructs the loving purpose of God. He will exclude those things. Therefore God has consigned all human beings to the consequences of our own disobedience. This is precisely the message of Romans 1:18–3:20, with its three-times-repeated "God gave them over. . . ." In the day of judgment we will all be defenseless. We will not be able to bring any fancy defense attorneys with us on that day, because they will all be under indictment too. There will be only one defense attorney in that day. God is a better bet than man, for on the last day, the Defense Attorney and the Judge will be one and the same.

> Who shall bring any charge against God's elect? It is God who justifies, who is to condemn? [It is] Christ Jesus, who died, yes, who was raised from the dead, who is at the right hand of God who indeed intercedes for us [who pleads our case for us]. (Romans 8:33-34)

> There is therefore now no condemnation for those who are in Christ Jesus. (8:1)

> God has consigned all men to disobedience [in order] that he may have mercy upon all — *all of us*. (11:32)

AMEN.

[286]

Sunday, August 24, 1996

God's Cosmic Inclusion Plan

Now if {the Jews' unbelief} means riches for the world, and if
their failure means riches for the Gentiles, how much more will
their full inclusion mean!

ROMANS 11:12

Imagine my surprise, and possibly yours too, when I picked up *The
New York Times* on Thursday and discovered on the front page, no
less, an article about a controversy raging in the Reformed Church
of America about whether salvation is available apart from Jesus
Christ.[1] This is precisely the subject of the series of sermons being
preached here at St. John's this month. We are reading the Epistle
to the Romans, which has at its heart (Romans 9–11) a breathtaking discussion of unbelief, specifically related to the anguish felt by
St. Paul as most first-century Jews refused to come to faith in Jesus
as the Messiah of Israel.

Many people in America today are mystified by such controver-
sies. Christianity has become so diluted and so peripheral to most
people's lives that the unique claims of Jesus Christ are of little interest to them. Many churchgoers even feel this sort of detachment. I

---

1. "Christian Split: Can Nonbelievers Be Saved?" by Gustav Niebuhr, *The New
York Times*, August 22, 1996.

admit that it is hard for me to understand this. When you come to know the Lord Jesus, his death on the Cross for our salvation and his resurrection for our eternal life, there is nothing else comparable. There is no other creed that says, "crucified under Pontius Pilate," there is no other empty tomb. St. Paul wrote that there were all kinds of religious quests: "Jews demand signs and Greeks [Gentiles] seek wisdom, *but we preach Christ crucified*" (1 Corinthians 1:22-23).

"We preach Christ crucified." As one clergyman said to the *Times* reporter, Mohammed, Buddha, and Joseph Smith are not preached in the same way as Jesus at all. There is a qualitative distinction between Christianity and the various religions of the world. There is only one person of whom it is said that "in him *all the fullness of God* was pleased to dwell" (Colossians 1:19). Despite the current spate of Jesus-bashing that is going on among disgruntled scholars and publicity-seekers, his uniqueness remains. The New Testament proclamation of his cosmic significance will stand forever. The revelation of God in his only begotten Son is for all people in all times in all places. Only one death in all the history of the human race has saving power for the whole world.

St. Paul's discussion of Christians and Jews in Romans 9–11 is partly related to this question of other religions and partly not. In the sense that it is concerned with those who do not believe in Jesus as Messiah and Son of God, it is directly related. But in another sense it is specifically concerned with the Jews as the Chosen People of God. For Christians, Jews will always have a special significance. Jewish faith and identity is not rightly identified simply as "one of the world's great religions" alongside others. Paul uses the image of the olive tree in chapter 11. The Jews, he says, are the cultivated root or trunk, onto which we Gentiles, as wild branches, have been grafted by the sheer mercy of God.

> For if you have been cut from what is by nature a wild olive tree, and grafted, contrary to nature, into a cultivated olive tree, how much more will these natural branches [the Jews] be grafted back into their own olive tree (11:24). So do not become proud, but stand in awe. (11:20)

Paul's argument here is that the ungodly Gentiles have been brought in by God from outside the religious boundaries. Only God can do that. Only God can say, "I have been found by *those who did not seek me; I* have shown myself *to those who did not ask for me*" (10:20). In other words, only God can create faith where there is no faith. This is Paul's theme throughout Romans.

The *Times* article states that a key verse in the controversy about salvation is the saying of Jesus in the Gospel of John, "I am the way, and the truth, and the life; no one comes to the Father, but by me" (14:6). This verse is part of a text that is read at funerals. I have often heard it omitted for fear of offending. There have always been those who take offense at Jesus. In the Bible, he is called the "stumbling-stone." Paul combines two passages from Isaiah (8:14-15; 28:16), as follows:

> Behold, [says the Lord], I am laying in Zion a stone that will make men stumble, a rock that will make them fall. (Romans 9:33)

Many will take offense at the point of faith in Christ. As Paul says: "They have stumbled over the stumbling stone" (9:32). But with regard to the Jews, Paul continues,

> So I ask, have they stumbled so as to fall? By no means! But through their trespass salvation has come to the Gentiles, so as to make Israel jealous. Now if [the Jews' unbelief] means riches for the world, and if their failure means riches for the Gentiles, how much more will their *full inclusion* mean! (Romans 11:11-12)

It's that phrase, *full inclusion,* that is so suggestive in the context of the debate about salvation. What does Paul mean by *full inclusion?* What does he mean when he says: "All Israel will be saved" (11:26)? What does he mean when he writes (our verse from last week): "God has bound over *all* men to disobedience so that he may have mercy upon *all*" (11:32)?

One thing we can be sure of. Paul is not saying that it doesn't matter whether we believe in Jesus or not since we're all going to be saved anyway. Paul did not travel around the Mediterranean world for years suffering shipwrecks, beatings, imprisonment, threats of death, and ultimately execution by the Emperor Nero in order to say it doesn't matter. On the contrary, Paul writes (to the Philippians):

> God has . . . bestowed on him the name which is above every name, that at the name of Jesus every knee shall bow and every tongue confess that Jesus Christ is Lord. (Philippians 2:9-11)

There will come a time, envisioned in Matthew 25 with its image of the Last Judgment, when every human being who has ever lived will acknowledge Jesus as Lord. Whether this means salvation for every single individual human being is impossible for us to say. Many passages in the four Gospels would lead us to think not. The full meaning of Paul's word ALL must remain known to God alone. In particular we cannot know his full plan for the Jews. But we can know and must continually affirm that, as Paul says so clearly in Romans 9:4-5,

> To them belong the sonship, the glory, the covenants, the giving of the law, the worship, and the promises; to them belong the patriarchs, and of their race, according to the flesh, is the Christ. God who is over all be blessed for ever. Amen.

The riches and depths of the vast vision of Romans 9–11 can only be hinted at in a sermon-teaching like this. If we seek to enter into the passages honestly, though, we can acknowledge at least this much:

- Paul's vision of cosmic salvation "includes exclusion." That is to say, it involves judgment. It involves a final, definitive negation of all that is opposed to the will and reign of God. In that sense the whole world and the whole human race will be judged by God.

- Paul's vision of the cosmic triumph of God at the end of Romans 11, however, is a vision not of triumphant judgment and condemnation, but of triumphant mercy. It is a vision not of ultimate disobedience and disbelief, but of ultimate grace and faith — and the Jews are a prior and indispensable part of that ultimate purpose.
- Paul's vision of the final triumph of God's purpose emphasizes, as Jesus himself does, that "many that are first will be last, and the last first" (Mark 10:31).
- Paul's vision of the triumph of God's purpose makes it plain that nothing and no one can resist his ultimate will (Romans 9:19-24). Therefore it is clear that God is also able, if he wishes, to be victorious over the human will not to believe.[2]
- Paul's vision is that no one will be saved without Christ. Exactly how they will be brought to him is part of God's plan now hidden from us, but *all* will come to acknowledge him as Lord. Every knee will bow to him, every tongue will confess him.

Paul does not say any of these things arrogantly, or coercively, or imperialistically. As we shall see in the end, he says it humbly, with amazement and awe, and with full knowledge of the price that was paid by the One who was "put to death for our transgressions and raised for our justification" (Romans 4:25).

I have been with you in this parish for less than two months. You and I do not yet know each other very well, though we have made a lot of progress toward that goal. There are many things

---

2. Nicholas R. Ayo, C.S.C., editor of *The Sermon-Conferences of St. Thomas Aquinas on the Apostles' Creed* (Eugene, OR: Wipf & Stock, 1988; previously published by University of Notre Dame Press), discusses Thomas's difficulties concerning the destiny of unbaptized children and unbelieving adults. Figuratively throwing up his hands, he writes, "The Middle Ages simply did not know what to do with the unbeliever." Here we may say that the Epistle to the Romans proclaims that God knows what neither the Middle Ages nor our own age knows, and furthermore that God holds unbelievers in his purpose. As Ayo further admits, Thomas's logic did not take sufficient account of "the infinite resourcefulness of the God who wishes to save everyone."

about each other that we have yet to discover. There is something about me that I want you to know now. My faith in the Lord Jesus Christ has survived almost fifty-nine years of sometimes severe testing. I am not ordained to preach the gospel because I believe that all religions teach the same truth. I do not give up my weekends in order to stand here and tell you that all roads lead to the same place. I have not come out of private life to return to the demands of ministry to preach that Jesus Christ is one religious option among many, one slice out of the pie among many other slices.[3] It is not possible to give more than a hint of the greatness of our God and the uniqueness of the gospel of Christ in one sermon or even in many sermons, but I pray and hope that I may be permitted to make a beginning.

Only the Christian gospel speaks of "the justification of the ungodly" (Romans 4:5). Our God is able to save people that nobody thought could be saved. Suppose all the godly Jews had immediately come to faith in Christ? It would have been so obvious! It would have been so predictable! Instead, God called forth a great multitude of *the ungodly* (that's you and me, the Gentiles) in order to demonstrate his freedom and to remove every possibility that faith and salvation might be thought to rest on human moral or religious or spiritual achievement. God is able to make believers out of unbelievers, otherwise you and I would not be here. It is all God's work from beginning to end. "So do not be proud," Paul says, "but stand in awe" (Romans 11:20). Your faith and my faith is a gift from God, not an achievement of our own that we can use to make ourselves feel superior to others — and especially not the Jews.

Yesterday was the first funeral since I came to this community. There is no greater test of Christian ministry. What do we offer a congregation when we are standing on the brink of the grave? Do we back away from the news about the Lord Jesus Christ? Do we of-

---

3. This image of the pie and the slices was used by one of the clergy quoted in the Gustav Niebuhr article. How can that be right in view of the consistent claim of the New Testament and the Church Fathers that God's revelation is complete in Christ?

fer vague religious consolation based on wishful thinking about life after death? Do we detach the apostle Paul from his own Christ-centered message so that he says "nothing can separate us from the love of God" (Romans 8:38-39) only in a generic sense, meaning you have your God and I have mine? If we are going to back away from the unique claims of the Lord Jesus Christ, let us be sure we understand what we are giving up. Most people do not realize that here in the Epistle to the Romans we have the distillation of the most truly radical message that the world has ever known, beside which the calls we hear to "be more religious" or "be more spiritual" pale into insignificance. There is nothing else, anywhere in the world's religious traditions, like the Incarnation, the Cross, and the Resurrection. How anyone can turn away from Christ is truly beyond me, as it was beyond Paul. In Romans 9–11 he ponders this conundrum of unbelief. He closes the section in a kind of ecstasy. The passage is appointed to be read this Sunday morning. It is a summary of all the apostle's reflections. Paul sees God calling the whole world to behold the final working out of God's plan for salvation, when Jews and Gentiles alike will take their places before the Lord as recipients of his conclusive and final act of mercy. Paul is so overwhelmed by the picture God has revealed to him that he bursts out of the letter-writing form altogether, ending the section with a doxology, a hymn of praise.

The news articles always use the wrong word. They always say, "proselytize." That's all wrong. It isn't "proselytizing." It's *evangelizing. Evangel* in Greek means *good news.* If you have good news, it's selfish and, indeed, impossible to keep it to yourself. It is in the character of Christianity to bear witness. Whether other people come to faith in Christ or not is up to God. But that driving force to go out with the news, to share it, to bear witness to it is so deeply embedded in the character of Christianity that it cannot be excised without destroying the faith itself. This is the only begotten Son of God we are talking about. This is the action of God to bring his entire lost world back to himself. May we never be quiet about it. Paul could not keep quiet. At the end of his great passage about the Jews he simply passes into the mode of praise, which is the best form of witness. Will you join me in the reading of this passage as our own act of praise as we end the sermon?

> O the depth of the riches and wisdom and knowledge of God! How unsearchable are his judgments and how inscrutable his ways! "For who has known the mind of the Lord, or who has been his counselor?" "Or who has given a gift to him that he might be repaid?" For from him and through him and to him are all things. To him be glory for ever. Amen. (Romans 11:33-36)

AMEN.

Sermons on Romans 9–16

Year ——

Quoting the Good News Right

ROMANS 9:30-33; 10:3-4

People don't quote from the Bible the way they used to. Years ago, the King James Version was part of everyone's language, from the most educated to the least. Nowadays, when people quote Scripture, they are often quoting it wrong. This has had unfortunate results. Let's take a look at some examples. Here is a true story about a verse from St. Paul's letter to the Philippian church.

Last year while out of town on a preaching trip, I attended weekday Evening Prayer in a large Episcopal parish. The service was led by lay people. One evening there was a very interesting mistake. An older woman came forward to read the lesson. She looked like an archetypal WASP, born and bred for propriety and rectitude. The evening lesson was a section of chapter 2 of Philippians. She came to verse 13 and with great solemnity began to read it: "Work out your own salvation with fear and trembling . . ." and then she stopped. She didn't just drift off, as if she had lost her place or forgotten something. She came to a full stop deliberately, emphatically, at the comma instead of the period. If she had shaken her finger at us, it couldn't have been more clear; it was an order from her to us. It was as if she were saying, "I've worked out *my* salvation, now you work out *yours,* and it had better be with plenty of fear and trembling!" It would have been funny if it hadn't also been so serious.

After the service was over I sneaked up to the front and took a peek at the big lectern Bible. I thought perhaps it had been marked wrong. Not so; there was one of those little yellow sticky notes on the page, saying, "Begin at verse 3 and end at verse 13." Not only that, but as God is my witness, it was stuck on precisely at the *end* of the sentence, *below* the words that the reader had so thunderously omitted. Here's the whole sentence as Paul wrote it:

> Work out your own salvation with fear and trembling; for God is at work in you, both to will and to do [or, to work] for his good pleasure. (Philippians 2:12-13)

So that lady had turned one of the best verses in Paul's letters into one of the worst. She had the good news right in front of her and she took it and turned it into bad news. Instead of bringing us the wonderful message of the Christian gospel ("good news"), she was saying to us, "Behave yourselves!"

Now there is no doubt in my mind that if I had met that lady at a social event we would have become friends. She and I are the same age, dress the same way, love the church, love to read the Bible in worship, and probably share a lot of the same ideas about the way things ought to be. Indeed, one of the great struggles of my life has been to set aside that aspect of my personality that says, "Behave yourself!" "Behave yourself!" has its place, but it is not the gospel. It is not the Good News.

So now we have looked at one well-known misquotation from the Bible. Here is a second one. It goes like this: "God helps those who help themselves." What book of the Bible is that from?

Various polls have shown over and over again that huge numbers of church-going people think that saying is in the Bible. I hear people quote it constantly. The point is almost always to make a subtle or not-so-subtle distinction between the person who is quoting and another person who is thought to be not trying hard enough. For example, I was talking recently with a layman who is active in a much smaller, struggling Episcopal congregation. He was wondering whether they would ever be able to recover from their doldrums. The wrong kinds of people were running the church, he said. They were no doubt well-meaning, but (he implied) they were incompetent. The people who ought to be running the church, he said, were his own group, the ones who had built up the church endowment. The others, according to him, were clearly less able, since they weren't as prosperous as himself and his friends. As it happens, the saying about those who help themselves is found in Benjamin Franklin's *Poor Richard's Almanac.* I guess you could call it the great American gospel. The Christian gospel is opposite to it. In Paul's letter to the Romans, the apostle writes, "While we were still *helpless,* Christ died for the *ungodly*" (Romans 5:6).

Misunderstanding the gospel in this way is a very American thing, but it is not anything really new. Paul had the same problem in his congregations. In Romans 9 and 10, Paul writes about the people in the church who persist in focusing on self-help.

> Gentiles who did not pursue righteousness have attained it, that is, righteousness through faith; but Israel, who pursued the righteousness which is based on law, did not succeed in fulfilling that law. Why? Because they did not pursue it through faith, but as if it were based on works. They have stumbled over the stumbling stone. . . . (Romans 9:30-32)

Here is Paul at his most radical, but first we have to make a couple of substitutions. We don't make the same kind of distinction today that Paul does between "Gentiles" and "Israel." To understand, we need to substitute something like "heathen" or "pagan" or "godless" instead of "Gentiles." Gentiles, to the Jews, were the outsiders, the unrighteous, the unclean. Today we could substitute those whose behavior and beliefs are strange, or distasteful, or repellent to us. "Israel," on the other hand, means something very deep and significant in Paul's writing — it means God's chosen people. *Israel:* these are the righteous ones. This is the godly community. There is no irony intended. "Israel" means something very close to "us," the inheritors, those who take our privileged status for granted. We Episcopalians, we dedicated church members, we upstanding citizens, we God-fearing people — we are "Israel." The "Gentiles" are the aliens, the ones who simply do not measure up to any of our standards of righteousness. We can think of "Gentiles" either as powerful enemies who threaten us, or as weak, marginal groups whom we scorn, but either way, they do not meet any of our religious criteria. Yet Paul says that *Gentiles who did not pursue righteousness have attained it.* It's hard for us today fully to appreciate how shocking that statement is. It undercuts everything that we believe about the importance of godliness.

How did this state of affairs come about? How did these outsiders, these persons with no spiritual qualifications, attain righteousness? They attained it, Paul declares, *through faith.*

What? Through faith? Is that all? How can that be? Paul, are you saying that the struggle of religious people to live holy and righteous lives is to no avail? Are you saying that the tax cheats and harlots are going to get into heaven ahead of the good and the godly? Yes, Paul *is* saying that, but who said it first? Jesus said it first (Matthew 21:31). Who did he say it to? He said it to the chief priests and the elders, that's who; he said it to the most prominent, most accomplished, and most respected members of the religious community. This is the archbishop, the dean and the chapter of the cathedral. These men are at the very top of the spiritual ladder.

In the writings of Paul, the sayings and actions of Jesus are given theological shape. This happened decades before the Gospels were written down as we have them today. Don't fall for the popular misconception that Paul messed up the simple teachings of Jesus. On the contrary, Paul illuminates them, focuses them, draws out the implications that we might otherwise miss.

> Israel, who pursued the righteousness based on law, did not succeed in fulfilling that law. Why? Because they did not pursue it through faith, but as if it were based on works. They have stumbled over the stumbling stone. . . .

This is an almost exact description of the response of the chief priests and elders to the words of Jesus about the tax collectors and harlots. Once again we need to remember that this is us. We are "Israel"; we are the community of the upstanding, the association of the godly. We are no different from the chief priests and elders. "Work out your own salvation," we say to others; "God helps those who help themselves." The members of the religious community spent their whole lives in pursuit of the righteousness based on good ethics and morals, but when the incarnate fulfillment of those ethics and morals was standing right in front of them, they stumbled over the stumbling stone. To quote Paul again,

> Being ignorant of the righteousness that comes from God, and seeking to establish their own, they did not submit to God's righteousness.

It takes some time and effort to understand the way Paul thinks. Here's an example. When Paul says, "They did not submit to God's righteousness," he doesn't mean some yardstick that God holds out, or a test that he administers. When Paul says, "the righteousness of God" in verses like this, he means our Lord himself. Jesus Christ *is* the righteousness of God. At the beginning of his letter Paul says, "the righteousness of God is revealed" (Romans 1:17). What he means is, *the Son of God is revealed.* Christ is the true righteousness of God come to dwell among us in person, yet we did not submit to him; we stumbled over the stumbling stone because we were, and we are still, *seeking to establish our own righteousness.* That's why we continue to miss the point of so many Scriptures.

Paul continues:

> For Christ is the end of the law, that every one who has faith may be justified.

This word "end" *(telos)* means several different things. It means conclusion or termination, but it also means goal or consummation. Jesus Christ brings the religious law to an end because he completes it in himself. Because he himself has "fulfilled all righteousness" (Matthew 3:15), the law no longer serves the same function that we thought it did. It no longer exists as an external moral standard to strive for; it is now written on our hearts,[1] indwelling us by the power of the Holy Spirit given to us by God in Jesus Christ. We receive this righteousness of God, Paul declares, not by works but by faith in what God has done.

Even unconsciously, however, we are still busily at work undoing this good news. Here's one more story about a misquotation. This one was accidental, but in an amusing way it illustrates exactly what we're getting at this morning. A few years ago I attended a large conference of Episcopalians. There was an opening service of major dimensions on which no end of attention had been lavished. Everyone received a handsomely designed and expensively printed service bulletin. However, there was a typographical error in the booklet, the kind that the spelling checker would never catch. Only the human eye could have caught it, and the human eye missed it — just as the woman reading from Philippians missed that yellow sticky note. The typo was in the familiar prayer in the Eucharist where we ask God to "bring us with all your saints into the joy of your eternal kingdom." But it didn't say that. Instead, it said, "bring us with all your saints into the job of your eternal kingdom."

Isn't that just like us — always wanting to turn the *joy* into a *job!* Why do we do this? Why do we always want to turn everything into a morality lesson? Why do we take the *joy* and make it into a *job?* "Work out your *own* salvation!" Why do we take the blessed news of the grace of God and twist it into a new form of law?

I think we do it from ignorance, and we do it from insecurity. Paul says it: *Being ignorant of the righteousness that comes from God, we seek to establish our own righteousness.* We don't trust God to do it, for a number of reasons. We are afraid that if we let the standards down, all kinds of people might get through the door and then maybe things wouldn't be the way we like them anymore. We are afraid that if we don't make people toe the line they might step out of their place and get in our way. And most tellingly, way down deep, we are afraid of our own dark side that needs to be kept under close control. If we can keep *other* people in fear and trembling, maybe they won't notice our

---

1. 2 Corinthians 3:3-6; see also Deuteronomy 30:14; Jeremiah 24:7; Ezekiel 36:26.

own. I think of a man who terrorizes his employees because he has not come to terms with himself. I think of a woman who goes into tailspins if the flowers on the altar are not exactly right, because she herself lives by the law of rightly-arranged everything. I think of some people in church headquarters who constantly wax eloquent about tolerance and inclusiveness but will not allow one single deviation from the great god of bureaucratic process. All these people know how to carry out a *job,* but they surely have lost sight of the *joy.*

What I want more than anything to communicate this morning is that if St. Paul had not been able to communicate the joy of the gospel, the good news, there would be no Christian Church.

We cannot and do not earn the grace of God. It is already given to us in our baptism. There will always be plenty of people who will want you to think you have to earn it. Don't ever believe them. You couldn't earn it even if you tried. It is free. I wonder if you noticed how the *Private Ryan* movie took a turn for the worse in the last scene when the young soldier is told that he has to "earn" the sacrifice of the man who has saved him. "Earn this," says the dying Tom Hanks to Private Ryan, who then has to spend the rest of his life wondering if he has been good enough to earn it. There couldn't possibly be anything more different from what Jesus says to us. He doesn't say "earn this." He says "Come to me and I will give you rest." He didn't say "God helps those who help themselves." He said "I have come not to save the righteous, but sinners." When Jesus was dying on the Cross, he didn't say, "Earn your salvation with fear and trembling." He said, "Father, forgive them for they know not what they do." So you see, taking St. Paul's wonderful words and turning them into a version of "Earn this!" is a travesty of the gospel.

Think for a minute about that man who was so dismissive about the working-class members of his parish. When we hear a story like that, we are shocked. We think, "How awful! How unChristian!" What we hardly ever do is to stop and think, do I do that sort of thing myself? What would motivate us to reflect on our own unkind words and thoughts? What would move us to stop being critical of others and, instead, yield to a transformation of ourselves?

If the motivation is "Behave yourself!" or "Earn this!" you will be able to act only out of compulsion, guilt, or insecurity. That's the difference between the bad news and the good.

Paul sometimes uses the image of the racecourse, but once again we tend to get it wrong. Imagine Jesus standing at the finish line, waiting until we stagger across. Is that the way it is? No! It is not like that at all. Christ, through the Holy Spirit, has already implanted himself within our hearts. His power is with us *in* the running, *in* the pressing on, *in* the laying hold of the prize. He is never simply standing by, watching to see how we perform; he is actually *present in* the actions we take on behalf of the poor, *present in* the reconciliation of sinners, *present in* the recovery from addiction, *present in* the congregation gathered to praise him and receive his mercies anew at each Eucharist. He is powerfully working in us to guarantee the future of his beloved children.

Because he himself *is* the righteousness of God, and because he is raised from the dead and his living powerful presence is with us, the saying "Work out your own salvation with fear and trembling" has a completely different meaning — "for God is at work in you, both to will and to work for his good pleasure."

Let's think one more time about that snobbish churchman who was so ready to say, "God helps those who help themselves." What is his only hope in life and in death? Is it his own capacity for change? or is it our Lord's capacity to change him? What is your hope? What is my hope? Is it your own righteousness? Is it my own superior virtue? The day will come for that man, the day will come for me, the day will come for us all when the universe will yawn at our passing. At that time and in that extremity, the only right words for us will be the words of the well-known hymn so often sung at funerals:

Help of the helpless, O abide with me.[2]

AMEN.

2. Hymn by Henry Francis Lyte (1793-1847).

Preaching without Distinction

GRACE CHURCH IN NEW YORK
TEXT: ROMANS 10:5-13

I have two texts today. One is from the pages of *People* magazine. A few weeks ago the magazine conducted a poll on sin. Here is a letter to the editor in response:

> I was astonished to see what is essentially an archaic religious concern (i.e., "sin"), appropriate and consequential only to the Pilgrims or the Bible, on the pages of *People.* Did you write this issue in church? To me, the phrase "It's a sin" became strictly a slang expression years ago. . . .
>
> Let's have more hard news or I'll burn your magazine at the stake!
>
> Judy D. Mann
> Yardley, Pennsylvania

My second text is taken from Paul's letter to the Christian Church in Rome.

Those of us who have been hanging around Grace Church for the past ten years could very well slip into an attitude of taking the Epistle to the Romans for granted. After all, haven't we taught it year in and year out? Haven't we preached from it in season and out of season? Isn't it well known that the renewal at Grace Church grew out of Romans? Don't we throw around the term "radical grace" with the ease of long familiarity? Don't many of us holler out

"Romans 8!" or "Romans 11:32!" or "Romans 5:8!" like football coaches sending in plays?

On the other hand, those of you who may be new, or visiting, or back in church for the first time after a long absence, will already be thinking to yourselves that if Grace Church really does revolve around an obscure old writing like the Epistle to the Romans, then it must be a very strange and uncomfortable place for most people, and you will think twice before coming back. Nothing, after all, is more unwelcoming than "in-group" talk that makes most people feel like outsiders.

So the preacher who has chosen the Romans text for the first Sunday in Lent is faced with a double problem. First is the problem (for some of us) of seeming over-familiarity — don't we already know Romans? On the other hand, there is the problem of insiders and outsiders, which is as old as religion itself.

The very act of preaching, in fact, sets up questions and problems. Most people no longer understand the difference between preaching and other types of public speaking; I certainly didn't until a wise professor in seminary demonstrated it to us in class. Many people think of a sermon as an occasion for being entertained, instructed, or inspired in matters of religion — hence the customary comment at the church door, "I enjoyed the sermon." Nowadays, it is only congregations who have been engaged in a new way of thinking for a long time who are going to sit expectantly waiting for the Word of God to be spoken — for preaching, properly understood, is *the good news that God preaches* through human beings. Astonishingly enough, this is the method of communicating that God has chosen. This is an offensive idea; there are a hundred complaints to be brought against it. Most common is the objection, "How can anyone presume to speak the Word of God?" Or to put it another way, "How can any human being be so arrogant as to think he is a mouthpiece for God?" How indeed? It is a very good question. The validity or invalidity of preaching rests on such issues as these. If the preachers are not preaching "hard news," we ought to be burned at Judy Mann's stake.

Well, assuming that some of us cut our teeth on Romans, and

some of us have never heard of Romans, and many of us are somewhere in between, let's listen again to a portion of the text that was
read to us.

> Moses writes that the man who practices the righteousness which
> is based on the law shall live by it [Leviticus 18:5]. But the righ-
> teousness based on faith says, "Do not say in your heart, 'Who
> will ascend into heaven?'" (that is, to bring Christ down) "or
> 'Who will descend into the abyss?'" (that is, to bring Christ up
> from the dead). But what does it [the righteousness based on
> faith] say? "The word is near you [Deuteronomy 30:11-14], on
> your lips and in your heart" (that is, the word of faith which we
> preach); because, if you confess with your lips that Jesus is Lord
> and believe in your heart that God raised him from the dead, you
> will be saved. . . .
>
> For there is no distinction between Jew and Greek; the same
> Lord is Lord of all and bestows his riches upon all who call upon
> him. For "everyone who calls upon the name of the Lord will be
> saved" [Joel 2:23]. (Romans 10:5-8, 12-13)

Now in some ways this is a very "in-groupy" sort of text. For
one thing, chapter 10 is so dense with quotations from the Old Testament that you have to have a concordance to figure it out. For another thing, the primary distinction that Paul is making is very familiar to some, but completely unknown to most others. He speaks
of "the righteousness based on the law" and he contrasts it with "the
righteousness based on faith." Frankly, most people nowadays don't
think of "righteousness" at all, so it hardly seems worth making the
effort to understand Paul's language. Why bother to decipher these
"archaic religious concerns"? Isn't this "appropriate and consequential only to the Pilgrims or to the Bible"?

But look at it this way. Even the Judy Manns of the world have
a sense of "righteousness," though it is never called that anymore.
There is no one alive who does not make explicit or implicit judgments on other people's "righteousness." The overwhelming grief
and distress that swept the nation after the explosion of the Chal-

lenger shuttle was based to a great extent on our perception of the seven astronauts as good people. Most of us, I think, would be willing to say, these days, that President Marcos and "Baby Doc" Duvalier are not "good people."[1] There would likely be a wide agreement across the ideological spectrum that Anatoly Shcharansky is a heroic, noble, "righteous" man.[2] So in spite of our wholesale abandonment of biblical language, we still have a sense, however vaguely articulated, of a standard of goodness or righteousness out there somewhere.

If we don't believe in God, or if we believe in a vague, fuzzy sort of God, we can alter these standards to suit ourselves, thus guaranteeing that we will always be on the right side of the law. The variations are infinite. We can measure our worth and other people's by fashion, educational level, weight and fitness, taste in music, degree of hipness, ability to get past the rope at clubs, and a thousand other things. If you have an Actor's Equity card you are already way ahead of 90 percent of our aspiring-actor parishioners, but as one of you said to me the other day, the Actor's Equity card is worth everything until you have it, and then it isn't worth anything, because you may still not be able to find work. That's a perfect example of how striving never ends when you are trying to measure up.

Similarly, we can assign personal qualities to people, labeling them in the process. We can perceive people as beautiful, mature, open, caring, loving, loyal, and courageous, thereby declaring them worthy. Or, we can identify them as flaky, weird, uptight, devious, controlling, rigid, judgmental, and so forth — and we can rate them accordingly, always making sure that we compare ourselves favorably with the rating we give to them. This is a religious exercise, because it is a way of assigning determinative value.

Well, suppose there really is a God — not a god of our own

1. The reputations of the former president of the Philippines and the dictator of Haiti still don't look so good twenty years later.

2. Natan Sharansky, as he now spells his name, has turned out to be a more complicated figure in 2006 than he seemed in 1986, but he certainly retains some of the heroic character that he had when he was a prisoner of conscience.

mental devising, but God who is independent of what we think about him. And suppose that God is a holy and righteous God, as the Bible says he is. This would then mean that he would apply *his* standards, not ours. In that case, our chances of measuring up — our chances of achieving worth, our chances of being accounted "righteous" — are not so good.

Last night, I prepared bay scallops for dinner. As they say in the pretentious restaurants, we had them "served with a reduced cream sauce with shallots and wine vinegar and a touch of Dijon mustard." After dinner, Dick, who loves to tease me, said, "On a five-point scale, that was about a 2.4." After a split-second pause, I laughed, because I knew it had been more like a 4.8; but what was interesting and startling to me was what went on in the pit of my stomach during the pause. For just that fleeting microsecond, I had this tiny little flash of fear. And there was nothing at stake at all but a Saturday night dinner! Suppose it had been something really serious! How would I have felt then? We labor, all of us, under the fear of not measuring up. How will we be rated? How will we be rated by bosses, by spouses, by children, by lovers, by professors, by interviewers, by colleagues? What if we only get a 2.4? Maybe even a 4.8 is not good enough! Maybe God will require a 5.0!! This is the first Sunday in Lent, a time to be thinking about those "archaic religious concerns" called sins. Ash Wednesday was a tough day for me. As we went through the Litany of Penitence, I could see that I rated about a minus-point-one on every item. How can I survive the scrutiny of a righteous, holy God? How can I ever be free from anxiety about not being good enough?

Every attempt that we make to raise our rating by our own efforts Paul calls "the righteousness based on law." In particular, it is *religious* effort that Paul is talking about here. He is talking about pious achievements that can be measured: deeds of charity, hours of service, frequency of prayers, numbers of religious experiences, amount of tithes, intensity of emotion, quantity of tears shed, fidelity to spiritual discipline — all of it "righteousness according to the law," all of it useless for establishing our merit in the sight of God. Paul refers to religious effort as attempting to "ascend into heaven to bring Christ down," as trying to "descend into the abyss to bring Christ up." There is nothing we can do to force God's hand in our favor. When all our works are added up, we are still in the most dire predicament before God. When we measure ourselves according to legal righteousness, we are left with a dread of being outsiders forever.

One of the people who is, perhaps, being overly revered in our day as a "good person" is Thomas Merton. Walker Percy, in a recently published interview, tells how he made a pilgrimage to meet Merton at Gethsemani Abbey. Percy's most vivid memory of their conversation was that of Merton saying that even the Trappist monks at the abbey, with all their pious devotion to nonviolence, nevertheless exploited and violated each other in various ways. So what rating do we give them? And how would you and I compare? Would we give ourselves a better or worse rating than the Trappist monks? And how will God evaluate us?

All this kind of thinking belongs to "the righteousness according to the law." This kind of righteousness, says Paul, has been brought to an end. In the new order brought by Christ, the only kind of righteousness that counts is "the righteousness based on faith."

> The righteousness based on faith says, "Do not say in your heart . . . ascend into heaven . . . or . . . descend into the abyss. . . ." The word is near you, on your lips and in your heart (that is, the word of faith which we preach); because, if you confess with your lips that Jesus is Lord and believe in your heart that God raised him from the dead, you will be saved.

In these words Paul shows us the futility of our flailings, our strivings, our desperate journeys. We do not need to go to the Andes like Shirley MacLaine. We do not need to go to Burma like Thomas Merton. We do not even have to go (forgive me) to a Cursillo.[3] You do not go to find Jesus; he comes to find you.

---

3. The Cursillo program, when in its heyday, meant a great deal to some people, but those who did not go, or did not have the same response, were sometimes made to feel "spiritually inferior" in subtle ways.

The word is near you, on your lips and in your heart, the word of
faith which we preach. . . .

"The word of faith which we preach." What of us preachers?
Who are we and what is our preaching? I will tell you. We are no-
bodies, but we have got "hard news." As Paul says, "It pleased God
through the foolishness of what we preach to save those who believe"
(1 Corinthians 1:21). It pleased *God*. Everything depends on this. Do
you see? Judy Mann is right; let us have hard news or no news at all.
Religious rumors come and go like boutiques on Lower Broadway —
the Pilgrims yesterday, *People* magazine today, the planet Pluto tomorrow. But this is no rumor, this "word of faith which we preach"
— this is the gospel of God. Paul says it is "the power of God for salvation to everyone who has faith" (Romans 1:1, 16). "The word of
faith" for salvation draws near to you at this very moment, not because of anything you have done, not because of anything the
preacher has done, but *because it pleases God to draw near through this
word*. The preaching is of the good news — the good, hard news that
by the merits of Jesus Christ you are receiving a five-point rating on
a five-point scale, and you are receiving it for all eternity because it is
God's gift to you, not your gift to him. And this gift is given without distinction. "There is no distinction," Paul writes; "the same
Lord is Lord of all and bestows his riches upon all who call upon
him" (10:12-13). This means that I don't have to be Julia Child as
well as Karl Barth, and Ken Swanson doesn't have to be Thomas
Merton, and Carol Stein doesn't have to be Mother Teresa, and Mark
Berner doesn't have to be William Buckley, and Kendyl Monroe
doesn't have to be Millard Fuller, and emerging young clergy women
don't (God forbid) have to be Fleming Rutledge.[4] We can all rejoice
to be ourselves, each with his or her own particular configuration of
gifts from the Lord, and none of us feeling inferior or superior to the
others, for "there is no distinction; the same Lord is Lord of all and
bestows his riches upon all who call upon him." No insiders, no outsiders, just needy people redeemed by the Father of all goodness.

4. These are real names from the clergy and congregation.

This is radical grace. This is hard news. This is the gospel. This is "the word of faith which we preach." "The word is near you, on your lips and in your heart." God makes it happen. The preacher and the congregation are taken up into the powerful message, as Paul says: "Faith comes from the message, and the message comes from the preaching of Christ" (10:17). For some of you, perhaps for many of you, this is happening at this very moment — faith is being awakened or strengthened in you, because "the word of faith" has drawn near. And when this happens, we confess with our lips, *Jesus is Lord,* and we believe in our hearts that *God raised him from the dead,* and we hear with new assurance the promise of the Almighty Father, "You will be saved."

There is nothing you can do to add to this. It is God himself who is calling forth this response from us. Two confessions of faith: *Jesus is Lord,* and *God raised him from the dead.* "Everyone who calls upon the name of the Lord will be saved." This is "the righteousness that comes from faith," and it is the only righteousness that we can trust before God, because it is his own gift. Believe him in your heart right now, and confess him with your lips as we sing the next hymn, and be assured for today and forever that you are the very one of whom Jesus said, "This man, this woman went home justified" (Luke 18:14).

AMEN.

November 10, 2003

The Order of the Sentence

ROMANS 10:14-20

NOTE TO THE READER: Please bear in mind that this sermon
was preached to a congregation of seminarians and faculty
at Luther Seminary in St. Paul, Minnesota.

Last week, a friend of mine who teaches theology was in a gathering
of what you might call the New York intellectual elite (which
means, pretty much by definition, people who are aggressively disdainful of Christian faith). The conversation turned to the subject of
books about extreme adventures and natural disasters and why people like to read them. It was suggested that we like to read about
heroic survival. This led to a mention of Noah's flood, possibly because some one in the group was trying to be considerate of the clergyman present, and a woman commented enthusiastically that the
story celebrated Noah's capacity to overcome in a great test of
strength and endurance. My friend looked at her incredulously and
said, "The story isn't about Noah! It's about God!" The group received this revelation with stunned silence. After a few moments
the conversation resumed with references to the geographical location of Mt. Ararat and the flood motif in ancient literature, as
though the name of God had never been spoken.

   I found this story amusing, because it duplicated my own experience exactly. I will never forget a day about eight years ago
when I was having lunch in New York City with a person well
enough known and sufficiently sophisticated to be a bit intimidat-
ing. He cocked his head to one side and said in a confidential tone,

"Do you believe in God?" I was not as shocked by this as you might think; after all, I had been around in the church long enough to know that members of the clergy believed pretty much anything and everything these days. What saddened me was that my luncheon companion *knew this,* indeed took it for granted, and seemed to assume that if I did believe in God I was the exception.

You may think this is extreme. Yet from my perspective it is not. I need to explain that I bring one thing to my task as a preacher that is almost unique. I have probably heard more sermons by more clergy in more churches in more denominations than any other preacher I have ever met. I have been in parish ministry for twenty-two years, but the great majority of the Sundays and holy days of my sixty-five years have been spent listening to other people preach. For instance, last year I preached on fifteen Sundays. The rest of the year I was in a pew somewhere in the United States. Therefore I speak with a certain amount of authority when I say that there are a lot of clergy out there who give every impression of not believing in God.

What then are the sermons about? Let me come at that indirectly by telling another experience I had. I have been keenly interested in Tibet all my life and I continue to follow events there, so two weeks ago I went to hear a lecture and slide show on that subject. The woman who was lecturing is also a friend from my days in New York City. She has been to Tibet about ten times and has walked all the way round the sacred Mount Kailash three times, an amazing feat for a woman my age at that altitude. It takes about four days to do it. Now you understand that this circumambulation is supposed to free you from impurity and pile up spiritual capital for you. So, during the Q and A after the lecture, someone asked the speaker if she was a Buddhist. No, she said quite firmly, she had been raised Roman Catholic and, as she put it, "when you've been raised by the nuns, all of that Catholicism is fixed in you for life." But, she went on, "the thing that is so attractive about Tibetan Buddhism is that the emphasis is on *what you can do,* without reference to God."

That's what sermons today tend to be about. They are about

our doings, *our* spiritual journeys, *our* religious activities. Now to be sure, there has been a quite dramatic change in this regard since I was an M. Div. student at Union in New York. Back in the early 1970s, sermons were about boycotts and protest marches and assaults on the barricades of the oppressors. Today they are less likely to be about our doings in the socioeconomic arena and more likely to be about our "spiritual" activities — our journals, our pilgrimages, our prayer lives, our labyrinth-walking, our inner dispositions, our spiritual disciplines — but only marginally about God. When God's name appears today in the typical sermon that I hear, God is the object to be sought, not the acting subject. I originally began to notice this when a friend of mine who teaches homiletics complained about a sermon he had just heard by a student who was a self-identified evangelical. The student was shocked when his exasperated teacher said, "Do you realize you have just preached a sermon in which God is not the subject of a single sentence?"

Richard Hays, professor of New Testament theology at Duke, posts a sign at the beginning of his introductory course. The sign says, "It's about God, stupid!" Apparently he has learned that this is not clear to the entering students of divinity. They have been accustomed to prayers and hymns and sermons that concentrate on human religious activities and feelings instead of God.

I wonder about your reactions to the two incidents I mentioned — the one about Noah's flood and the one about the Tibetan program. I found the first incident amusing, even uplifting, and the second one just plain depressing. Why is that? By way of an answer, let me direct your attention to our Scripture reading from Romans 10. This passage seems to be about preaching. Well, preaching is a human activity, is it not? We could even call it a "spiritual" activity, I suppose, though most of the "spiritual" activity I hear about is more solitary, more interior than preaching is. But still, it is surely a human activity with God as the object. "How are they to believe [in God] . . . without a preacher?" The preacher, then, directs the attention of the hearer toward the sermon's object, which is God. Isn't that right?

It all depends on how the passage from Romans is read. If we read it without Luther and Calvin breathing down our necks, we will keep on thinking of God as the object. But the tradition of the Reformation has taught us to look again. Verse 17 is the key.

ara hē pistis ex akoēs, hē de akoē dia rhēmatos Christou.

So faith comes from *what is heard,* and what is heard comes by the preaching [or word] of Christ. (RSV and NRSV)

Everything depends on the crucial phrase "what is heard" *(ex akoēs),* how it is understood and how it is translated. I am a great lover of the King James Version, but here's an example of how it needed to be improved. The KJV says "Faith cometh *by hearing."* The NIV also has "faith comes by hearing." Ninety-nine out of a hundred will understand this to mean that *hearing* is a human response to the preaching of the gospel. That's not what the KJV translators meant to convey, since they go on clearly to translate that *hearing comes by the Word of God;* however, most people hearing the sentence today will understand it to say that *our receptive listening* results in faith. This in turn will lead to preacherly exhortations to have more faith, or to work harder at having faith, and consequently too much worry about not having a sufficient amount of faith, or an acceptable quality of faith, and this is the process that drove Martin Luther to distraction.

If we translate the word *akoē* as "hearing," with the human being as the acting subject doing the hearing, we'll never get this right. Paul's Greek word *akoē* is *semu'a* in Isaiah's Hebrew. Paul is explicitly quoting Isaiah when he writes this line: "As Isaiah says, 'Lord, who has believed our *akoē* [Isaiah's *semu'a*]?" So there really is no way to translate *akoē* as "hearing." It makes no sense to say, "Lord, who has believed our hearing?" For once, the New English Bible, of all things, has it right: "Isaiah says, 'Lord, who has believed *our message?*'" and Paul goes on, "We conclude that *faith is awakened by the message,* and the message that awakens it [faith] comes through the word of Christ." (The RSV and NRSV are also not too bad, rendering *akoē* as "what is heard," but "message" is clearer.)

So Paul is relying on the LXX translation of Isaiah's *semu'a* as *akoē,* which clearly means *the message itself.* Therefore if *akoē* is wrongly translated as "hearing" (NIV), the emphasis is on the human choice. But if it is translated "message," meaning *God's revelatory and performative word,* then all the emphasis is transferred to God's action, not ours. This is the message, the *evangel,* understood as victorious power, the power that removes human "spiritual" capacity to the margins altogether, so that God says (again from Isaiah),

"I have been found by those who did not seek me;
I have shown myself to those who did not ask for me."

So why was that first story energizing and the second one dispiriting? There is a single reason. In the story about the Tibetan program, the speaker's words — "It's about what we do, not about God" — fell like a dull thud and called forth no countervailing response. But in the first illustration, the message — the *akoē,* the *evangel* — was spoken. My friend bore witness. "It's not about Noah! It's about God!"

Did those who were standing around receive that witness? That is not the preacher's concern. Isaiah categorically states that his message was not heard. The apostle Paul, also, met a violent death at the hands of those who did not hear. But in the meantime the message itself, unleashed, was racing around the Mediterranean on its own power, and out of that message arose the faith which could not be stopped by mere disbelief or by any other human obstacle, because it is the faith of the *Kurios* himself, the Lord Jesus Christ.

It is that news, beloved in Christ, which is now being entrusted to you.

I ask, have they not heard?
Indeed they have.
Their voice has gone out to all the earth,
and their words to the ends of the world.

AMEN.

[317]

Gold Medals for Everybody

GRACE CHURCH IN NEW YORK
TEXT: ROMANS 11:5-6

NOTE TO READERS: This sermon was preached at an
evening service during the Summer Olympics of 1984.

How did you get here tonight? Did you come by subway, by bus, by
taxi, or on foot?

But how did you *really* get here tonight? I don't mean, what
method of transportation did you use? — rather, I mean, what was
going on in your head, what was going on in your heart, what was
going on in your life that brought you here on this dazzlingly beautiful evening to hear a sermon and to receive the body and blood of
our Lord Jesus Christ?

There are a lot of ways to answer that question. Some of you
might say that you didn't really want to come but you felt responsible to your prayer group. A few of you might say that you're
new in the city and wanted to see what this beautiful church was
like on the inside. Some of you might have come because you
want to see someone else who is here, or you are making up for
missing church on the weekend, or you have a thought of being
forgiven for something. Some might speak of a longing for security, or a search for truth, or a need to feel involved with something outside oneself, or a religious quest of some sort, or a spiritual journey.

But there is another way to answer this question, a simpler
one. How did you get here? To which the answer might be,

Gold Medals for Everybody

God brought me.

Now of course there are a lot of questions that we could raise about that statement, such as, how do you know that God brought you? and, why did he bring you and not somebody else? and so forth. But for the present let's keep it simple:

God brought me.

There is no question whatsoever about the way St. Paul would answer the question. *God had brought him,* Paul, out of bondage into freedom, out of judgment into mercy, "out of sin into righteousness, out of death into life."[1] Nor is there any question for Paul as to what had happened to the Christian believers in the early church; *God had brought them* out of disobedience and unbelief into faith and salvation.

Nowhere is this more clear than in Romans 9–11. All the sermons through September 5 are based on these chapters. It can be argued that these three chapters are the mother lode of all Scripture, the central core of God's revelation, yet they are little known, formidably difficult, and seldom preached! In these next three weeks, we are going to do our part to rectify this situation.

This evening, considering the fact that we are in the depths of August, we have a pretty good turnout of people. But in the vast swarming crowds of New York City, all those people coming home from work and shopping, we are a ludicrous number. Even in terms of our own congregation we are only a small minority. We are what is called in Scripture a "remnant." We are only a "remnant" of those who might be here, who we think should be here.

Paul, in the eleventh chapter of his letter to the Roman Christians, says that this is part of God's purpose.

At the present time, there is a remnant, chosen by grace.

---

1. Book of Common Prayer, Eucharistic Prayer B.

How did you, how did we, the remnant of the faithful, get here to-night? God brought us here. We have been "chosen by grace." What a thought!

Now at this point let us re-examine ourselves. *Why* have we been chosen by grace? Think about yourself. Have you been chosen because of your religious nature? Perhaps you have felt a kind of closeness to God ever since you can remember, even when you weren't coming to church. Is that why you were made part of the remnant tonight?

Have you been chosen because you have accepted Jesus Christ as your Lord and Savior, because you made a commitment to him a few months or a few years ago, because you made a "decision for Christ"? Is that why you came here tonight?

Have you been chosen because you are a spiritual person, because amazing things keep happening to you, because God speaks to you and you have experiences of healing and visions of life after death? Is that why you were "chosen by grace"?

Here is what Paul says — chapter 11, verses 5 and 6:

At the present time there is a remnant chosen by grace.
And if by grace, then it is no longer by works:
If it were, grace would no longer be grace.

If God chose us according to our spiritual capacities or religious enthusiasm or the quality of our faith in Jesus, then he would be choosing us on the basis of our works, and if that were so, then "grace would no longer be grace." This is a little hard for us to understand. We here at Grace Church are used to hearing that we are not justified on the basis of good works like being chaste and paying all of our taxes and staying in the shelter for the homeless, but we are always surprised to hear that we are not justified for our good works of belief and commitment and "religious experience" either. Faith is not a work. Faith is not the *cause* of our being chosen, it is a *result;* otherwise, "grace would no longer be grace."

Did you notice that, in this text, Paul uses the word "grace" as though it were a synonym for God, as though it were one of God's names? Chosen by grace, chosen by God. Grace is not a *quality;* it is an *active agent.* Paul uses words this way often, turning nouns into verbs. In Galatians he talks about "faith" as though it were a synonym for Jesus Christ's active power — he says "when faith came" as though he were saying "when Jesus came." And again, in 1 Corinthians, he uses the word "love" in the same way, a synonym for the active work of love which "endures all things." This is not an accident. St. Paul deeply understood, as the Old Testament writers did, that God's attributes — God's qualities — don't just stay within God but go powerfully out from God, creating a new situation. Those whom God chooses, those whom God *elects* (to use another good strong biblical word) partake of his *grace* and are given *faith* and are enabled to *love.* We need to remember this, because many Christians are prideful about their faith, their "decisions for Christ." Later on in this chapter, Paul warns, "Do not boast over those [who do not believe]." How can we boast about what is freely given to us?

Is anyone here who does not know what *grace* is? It means *unmerited favor,* just as mercy, according to an excellent dictionary definition, means "compassion or forgiveness where severity is expected or deserved." The phrase "unmerited grace" is a redundancy, like the "free gift" that the bank wants to give you. If it weren't free, it wouldn't be a gift; if it weren't unmerited, it wouldn't be grace. But how extraordinarily difficult it is for us to accept God's grace! We must have done something, somewhere, sometime, to deserve it. When something good happens, we say, "I must have been living right." We don't want unmerited, undeserved favor; we want *merited, deserved approval* like the winners of all those Olympic gold medals, that's what we want.

Listen: Telling the human being that he is capable of choosing God is like telling me to go out and become Mary Lou Retton. Would you agree that it is *impossible* for me to win a gold medal in gymnastics? And yet we persist in thinking that we can win a gold medal in religious development, so that *we* can choose God. What is the difference between me and Mary Lou Retton? I don't have her gifts. Precisely. Where did her gifts come from? From God. Ah, but you say, where did her grit and determination, her hard work and her moral fiber come from? To which the church's answer is, *All things come of thee, O Lord.*

Chosen by grace. And "if by grace, then it is no longer by works: if it were, grace would no longer be grace." We do not choose God; God chooses us, as Jesus himself said (John 15:16). If we chose him, then "grace would no longer be grace."

There is no such thing as merited, deserved approval from God. Why not? Because of sin. Not sin*s*, but Sin, Sin understood as a power, a slavemaster, a tyrant with absolute sway over poor fallen Adam, who is all of us. The human race, as far as God is concerned, is lost, doomed, gone. Except for one thing — *except for the decision of God* to make it come out differently because of his grace — the decision of God to give gold medals to all of us, this little band whom he has "chosen by grace," not by works.

Aha. There's the problem, isn't it? If everybody gets a gold medal, then there's no point, is there? If all the competitors win, there's no glory! If everybody is number one, then there's no feeling of achievement!

Exactly. This is why we don't want God's grace. Way down deep, in spite of our piety and our professed love of all God's people, we want to be better than somebody else by *achieving* his favor.

Again, it all comes down to very simple questions. Whose merits do you prefer, your own or Jesus Christ's? Whom do you trust to make ultimate decisions about the world, yourself or God? Whose choices do we ultimately want to prevail, ours or God's? Humanly speaking, of course, we want *ours*. But because of God's great plan, his plan to elect us, a "remnant, chosen by grace," we are being freed, at this very hour, here, tonight, every one of us, even if you have never been here before, to say Yes to God, Yes to his Son Jesus Christ, Yes to *his* merits and *his* purpose. God brought you here, "chosen by grace, no longer by works." If it were by works, grace would no longer be grace, and I for one would be left in the hopeless situation of knowing that I can never, never, never win a gold medal, no matter what I do.

But of course, the true destiny of us all will be a miracle. It will be the miracle, the impossibility, not only of winning the gold medal (the "prize," St. Paul calls it — Philippians 3:14) for oneself, but also the miracle, the impossibility, of rejoicing that everybody else has got one too, and that no one's gift, no one's glory is in the least diminished by anyone else's, but rather, that each one is perfected in the whole. And then we will stand, each of us and all of us, in our heavenly garments of righteousness and our golden crowns, and we will hear the chorus of angels and archangels and all the company of heaven in an anthem that will make "The Star Spangled Banner" sound like "Three Blind Mice," and we will not mind that no one is looking at us, far from it, we will not even be thinking of ourselves at all but only of him, the Lamb upon the throne, the Savior in his victorious majesty, the King of kings and Lord of lords, the Father of all creation who in his unfathomable mercy has extended his mercy to us all, even to you and me, "chosen by grace." Worthy is the Lamb that was slain.

AMEN.

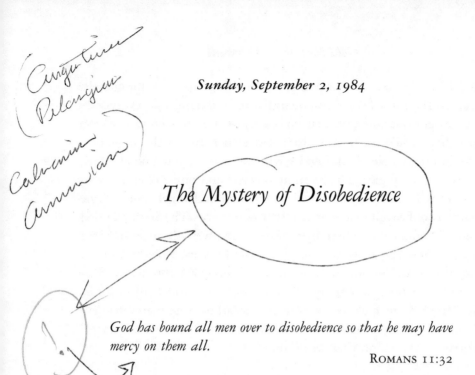

The Mystery of Disobedience

God has bound all men over to disobedience so that he may have mercy on them all.

ROMANS 11:32

Let's think for a moment about disobedience. Your attitude to it will depend a lot on whether you think of it from the parent's point of view or the child's. A lot of you are too young to know, but believe me, if you are a parent, what you want is a child who obeys. Don't touch the stove, don't go in the street, don't hit your sister, stay away from strangers, ride your bicycle on the right, don't smoke marijuana, study your lessons. On the other hand, if you are a child, disobedience has a certain glamour about it — which explains the ubiquity of the stories about cigarettes behind the barn. No child has to be taught to be disobedient. The fancy theological name for this fact is Original Sin.

Now God, who is our Father in heaven, wants us to be obedient to him just as parents do. The resemblance cannot be pressed too far, though, because whereas earthly parents make all kinds of mistakes and sometimes demand the wrong kind of obedience, God the Father really does know what is best for all his children, what will truly make us happy, and he never makes mistakes.

The rules that God has given his children to obey are called the Ten Commandments. We don't talk or think about the Ten Commandments very much today in the American churches. That's a mistake, I think. How are we doing on the Ten Commandments? Let's just take two of them this morning for purposes of the discussion.

Commandment Number One: "You shall have no other gods but me."
Commandment Number Four: "Remember the Sabbath Day by keeping it holy."

How are we doing? How are we doing as individuals, how are we doing as a community, as a society? Obedient or disobedient?

There is a theory in psychoanalysis for a stage in human development called "the myth of infantile omnipotence." A layman's definition of this term means that the baby thinks of itself as the center of the world and as having total control of the world. In my strictly amateur fashion I'd like to extend this into early childhood. Imagine the child — perhaps it is three or four — doing something that the parent doesn't like. The parent therefore says, "You are a bad child."

My experience is that the child will, first of all, believe this, since it is a parent talking, and second, the child will believe it to be a catastrophe of world-shaking proportions. No child is able to say to itself, "Oh well, it all depends on what you mean by bad, and after all I'm not so bad compared to all the other children in town, and Mom is just irritable today, she'll get over it, so I think I'll just go out and play." No child thinks that way. Rather, the child takes into itself the certainty that it is the one truly bad child on earth and that some colossal, nameless punishment is lurking just around the corner. The child is convinced, though it could not say so in words, that its own badness is the center of the world and that nothing can overcome such badness.

Two contradictory consequences result, and we all suffer from both these consequences. We grow up to do two things, neither of which work; in fact, they actually cancel each other out. First, we hate ourselves for being so bad (the current term for this is "loss of self-esteem"); second and contrarily, we try to transfer the blame on others. These types of behavior are two sides of the same coin. When we think that everything is our fault, that is just as much a delusion of the omnipotent self as its opposite number, the fallacy that we alone are blameless and all the rest of the world is wrong. Either way, we cling to our own righteousness; we attach ultimate importance to our own fault, or we attach ultimate importance to our illusion of being free from fault. In either case, the omnipotent self has become God.

Most of all, the child (and ultimately the adult), having become convinced of its badness, is equally convinced that God either can't or won't do anything about it. The unspoken message is always the same: You must be a good girl, you must be a good boy, it is up to you, you must be a success, God helps those who help themselves, and if you fail it will be your own problem, because God isn't going to overcome your badness by himself. He's going to be watching to see how you do (he's making a list and checking it twice . . .).

Badness, biblically speaking, has the specific form of disobedience. Disobedience was the first sin, the primal sin, the "original" sin, the sin of Adam — and Adam's first reaction was to cover himself, because all of a sudden he thought the whole world was looking at him. He became self-conscious for the first time, he lost all perspective on his place in God's creation. Shivering in his new self-importance, Adam hid himself from God, and when God discovered him, he blamed his wife — who in turn blamed the serpent. To Adam and Eve in their disobedience, God sorrowfully said, "You have both been *bad*."

But what Adam could not have foreseen or expected, and what we still to this day can scarcely believe, is that God did not abandon Adam and Eve when he drove them out of the garden for their disobedience. He could have; he should have; but he did not. In the very midst of his judgment upon them, God showed them mercy — compassion and forgiveness where severity and condemnation was expected and deserved.

So St. Paul says this very strange thing: "God has bound all human beings [all descendants of Adam and Eve] over to disobedience in order that he may have mercy upon them all" (11:32). It's as though Paul were actually suggesting that our badness has become part of God's ultimate plan to be good to everybody. Can we follow that train of thought for a few minutes?

Imagine a child who has just been told by some figure in authority, "You are *bad*." (Parents in the know are careful to make a verbal distinction between "You are bad," and "You have *done* something bad," but I'm not sure that the child doesn't hear it as condemnation in either case.) Imagine now the child saying back to the parent, "Yes, I am bad, but the Lord in his mercy is making me good and so I have nothing to fear." Children actually used to be taught to say such things in Jacobean prose; of course they didn't understand what they were saying, but it came back to them later. There was a lot that was valuable in the old catechisms.

> QUESTION: Do you not think that you are bound [to obey God]?
> ANSWER: Yes, verily; and by God's help so I will. And I heartily thank our heavenly Father, that he hath called me to this state of salvation, through Jesus Christ our Saviour. And I pray unto God to give me his grace, that I may continue in the same unto my life's end.

I want to be sure that I am making myself clear here. We are brought up from infancy believing that if we are "bad," we will be stuck with our badness forever and God will not only not help us but will condemn us. This is wrong on at least three counts:

1. It is a form of *idolatry* because it imagines an all-powerful self.
2. It is a form of *works-righteousness* because it supposes that God will assess us according to our merit or lack of it.
3. It is a form of *disobedience* because it refuses to trust in the Lord who has "bound all men over to disobedience so that he may have mercy upon all."

In this amazing text St. Paul shows us that God is infinitely, unimaginably bigger and stronger than our "badness", and that, in fact, he is ultimately going to make our "badness," our disobedience, work in our favor, because of *his* favor, his *unmerited* favor which is his grace.[1]

In this passage, Paul is talking about Jews and Gentiles. The Jews are the "godly" people, the chosen community. The Gentiles are the "ungodly," the pagans, the barbarians. As Paul writes, though, a surprising kind of shift is going on in the Roman church — or, perhaps, given human nature, it's not so surprising. Anyway, what's happening is that the Gentile Christians, who so recently were outcasts, have suddenly begun to be "conceited" (11:25) about their own faith, "boasting over" (11:18) the Jewish people, most of whom mysteriously have not become Christians. There's a reversal, you see — as soon as the "ungodly" people became Christians, they began to forget all about their recent condition and to congratulate themselves on having the good sense to become believers. This is what the human being always does. We cannot and will not believe that God actually overrides our badness, our ungodliness, our disobedience to create faith in us and begin making us good. God wouldn't deliberately choose the so-called "ungodly," we reason; God must have seen that we have some hidden "godliness" down underneath somewhere. The Gentile Christians in the Roman church were reasoning this way; they were beginning to believe that they had turned to God on their own with a little help from him.[2] Paul therefore warns them in 11:20, "you stand fast only through

1. I am on risky theological territory here. It is important to avoid the idea that sin, or evil, can serve any useful purpose whatsoever. I am not saying that. There is a crucial distinction between saying that God turns sin to his own purposes, and saying that sin has a proper place in the creation. The old idea of *felix culpa* (happy fault) is mistaken, though church choirs sing about it every Christmastide ("blessed be the time that apple taken was").

2. This hypothesis about the Roman church, admittedly, cannot be proved. Paul had not yet been to Rome. However, we know from chapter 16 that he knew many people there. He may have been receiving reports from the congregation. At any rate, the tendencies we are discussing are universal.

faith," so "do not become proud, but stand in awe." When we understand that faith is a pure gift of God, not a work of merit for which the human being can take credit, then we see that Paul is saying to the Gentile Christians, in effect, "In spite of your disobedience, your ungodliness, God in his mercy has chosen to save you by his grace." Quoting him verbatim now,

> Just as you [Gentiles] were once disobedient to God but now have received mercy because of their [that is, the Jews'] disobedience, so they now have become disobedient in order that they too may receive mercy as a result of God's mercy to you. For God has bound all men over to disobedience so that he may have mercy on them all.

This is the "mystery" (11:25): the "disobedience" of those who have not received God's Messiah is *temporary*. It is part of God's plan. *Mystery* in the New Testament does not mean just "a secret." It means "a secret revealed." The *mystery of disobedience,* Paul says, is this: God has chosen some for faith and some for temporary "hardening" (11:25) — "a hardening has come upon part of Israel until the full number of Gentiles come in, and so all Israel will be saved, as it is written — 'he will banish ungodliness from Jacob [Israel].'"

"He will banish ungodliness"! He will turn badness into goodness, disobedience into obedience, doubt into faith, death into life, yes, "life from the dead" as Paul proclaims (11:15). We will not do it; he will do it in us in spite of ourselves, in spite of the fact that we are "sold under sin" (7:14). He has chosen some for temporary unbelief, transient disobedience, in order to demonstrate his freedom and in order to teach those of us who have now received mercy that we live according to his power and his grace only. As Gentiles think of Jews, as the "godly" think of the "ungodly," as the obedient think of the disobedient, as the church thinks of the unchurched, we are meant humbly to think, "There but for the grace of God go I." We are meant to understand that *their* unbelief teaches *us* to trust in God only, and never in our own merit. For in the last analysis who of us keeps the Ten Commandments? Which of us is a good girl?

Which of us has loved the Lord our God with all our heart and soul and mind? "There is no distinction — all have sinned. . . . There is no one righteous, no, not one" (3:22-23); "All men, both Jews and Gentiles, are under the power of sin" (3:9-10). We are all in this together; "God has consigned all men to disobedience that he may have mercy upon all."[3]

Only recently in the history of interpretation has Romans 9–11 gotten the attention it deserves. I hope you will read it for yourself. Our own time is ripe for a new look at the passage. Most Christians over the ages have missed what is implied here. C. S. Lewis, for example, backed off from Paul's radical gospel at this point. He seems to have believed that, in the end, those who "choose" disobedience will be left to live with it.[4] He argues the case persuasively in *The Great Divorce,* but if it is true that we can lock ourselves into

3. The question inevitably arises: Does this mean that everyone will be saved (universal salvation)? We cannot say. There are many passages in the Gospels that imply condemnation for those who refuse the grace of God. It is in Paul's letters (together with Isaiah 40–55) that we find suggestions of universal salvation, but it is (deliberately) not worked out in terms of individuals. As George Hunsinger, the Presbyterian theologian, says, "We are permitted to hope for universal salvation." We cannot say for sure what God will do, but we know it will be his gracious decision, not ours. Therein lies our freedom — a paradox that admittedly is difficult to understand. The central figure here is Augustine, Bishop of Hippo (354-430). He expressed the paradox of freedom in many ways, holding together (as Paul does) the seemingly contradictory ideas of service and freedom. Augustine's definition of freedom was this: in the redeemed creation, *non posse peccare:* it will no longer be possible to sin. He refers to this as *beata necessitas non peccandi,* "the blessed necessity of not sinning" (*The City of God,* XXII, xxx). Again, the critical point here is that this will be entirely the work of God.

4. The issue here, again, is not "Will everyone be saved?" The issue is, "Will we be saved as a result of our own choice?" This is the classic issue at stake between Augustine and Pelagius in the fifth century, and between Calvinists and Arminians after the Reformation. Martin Luther's classic text, "The Bondage of the Will," sets out the argument against Erasmus' "The Freedom of the Will." Anglicanism has often tilted toward Pelagius, in spite of the best efforts of some of its earliest divines (see FitzSimons Allison, *The Rise of Moralism* [London: SPCK, 1966]). Indeed, Pelagius, who believed in freedom of the will, is the default setting for most Americans. At Grace Church in New York in the 1980s and 1990s, we had an April Fool bulletin for the non-existent "Feast of St. Pelagius."

hell by our own choice, then the ultimate decision is not God's but our own — in which case "we are of all people most to be pitied" (as Paul writes in another context — 1 Corinthians 15:19). I think J. Christiaan Beker has a better conclusion:

> The final apocalyptic triumph of God does not permit a permanent pocket of evil or resistance to God in his creation. The solution to the "dark side" of the created world lies in God's imminent eschatological triumph, in which evil, tragedy, and everything in creation that opposes God will be overcome or taken up in God's glory.[5]

Somewhere along the way most of us have been told, directly or indirectly, by some person in authority, that we were "bad," that we were failures, that we were undeserving. Well, it was true, but not in the sense that that person meant it, and not in the sense that we have felt it — as a lifelong burden. Yes, we are "bad," yes, in God's sight we are failures, yes, above all we are undeserving of his grace, but "it is no longer on the basis of works: otherwise grace would no longer be grace" (11:6). The *mystery of disobedience,* now revealed to us, is that those who deserve rejection have instead been chosen — chosen to wear the new garments of obedience in the kingdom of God where there will be no need for Ten Commandments anymore, for God's Law will be written on our hearts (Jeremiah 31:33), and there will no longer be any possibility of disobeying (God will not permit a permanent pocket of resistance in his creation), for we will belong to the one who *truly is omnipotent,* the Almighty God "in whose service is perfect freedom."[6]

AMEN.

5. J. Christiaan Beker, *Paul the Apostle* (Philadelphia: Fortress Press, 1980), p. 194.

6. There are two references here to Augustine. The first is his teaching that in the redeemed creation, it will no longer be possible to sin (*non posse peccare*). The second is related to the first and is a quotation from the Collect for Peace in the Episcopal Church's Book of Common Prayer: "whose service is perfect freedom" is a paraphrase of Augustine's "whom to serve is to reign as a king."

The Enemy Lines Are Hard to Find

Who can tell how often he offends?
Cleanse thou me from my secret faults.

PSALM 19:12

 Christ died for the ungodly.

ROMANS 5:6

 God has consigned all men to disobedience, that he may have
mercy upon all.

ROMANS 11:32

A friend of mine who is a child psychologist told me about something one of her young patients said. It is common practice to give toys to children in the treatment room so they work out their conflicts through play. This particular little boy was given toy soldiers, which he laid out and began to deploy. After he had done this for a while, he looked across his little battlefield with a puzzled expression and said, "The enemy lines are hard to find."

In late 1944, while the allies were rapidly advancing across Europe after the success of the Normandy invasion, J. R. R.

Tolkien, the author of *Lord of the Rings,* wrote a letter to his son Christopher who was serving in the R.A.F. (the British Royal Air Force). Tolkien himself, the father, had fought the Germans in World War I; he was in the infamous trenches of the Battle of the Somme. Obviously this father and son were not pacifists. It is therefore all the more notable that Tolkien wrote to his son that he was very disturbed by the way the British press was relentlessly depicting all Germans as irremediably evil. He quotes from one of the local English newspapers, whose editor was seriously advocating "systematic extermination" of the entire German nation because "they are rattlesnakes and don't know the difference between good and evil." Tolkien continues:

> *What of the writer?* The Germans have just as much right to declare . . . the Jews exterminable vermin, subhuman, as we have to select the Germans: in other words, no right, whatever they've done.[1]

Whenever a person takes to himself (or herself) the defining of another person or group as evil, he is in more danger than he knows. It is in the very nature of the human being to judge other people and groups as evil. We can then give ourselves permission to treat those others as less than fully human, to ostracize them or persecute them and eventually to destroy them. And once we have begun that game, it takes on a life of its own and it begins to dominate us without our even noticing.

Who decides who is evil and who is not? Two weeks ago, a *New York Times* article told of some Afghan boys who were displaced by the American bombing.[2] The boys are now living in Karachi, Pakistan — if you can call it living. The children in this particular news story live in the garbage dumps. They are paid pennies to pick

1. *The Letters of J. R. R. Tolkien,* ed. Humphrey Carpenter (Boston: Houghton Mifflin, 2000; first published in Great Britain by George Allen & Unwin, 1981), p. 93; emphasis added.

2. There was a TV documentary about this on the Discovery Channel on March 25, 2003.

through the rotting food, broken glass, and discarded syringes to salvage items to sell. They are indescribably filthy and smelly, and they are hungry much of the time. What is their hope? Their hope is the *madrasas* — the Muslim religious schools. We all know now, if we did not before, that many (not all) of these schools in Pakistan are run by hard-line extremists, and they were the breeding ground for the Taliban.[3] The *Times* reporter interviewed some of these Afghan refugee boys at the garbage dump. They are thrilled at the possibility of being taken as students by one of the *madrasas*. They said, "We'll get free food and clothing. It will make us very happy." The reporter asked them what they thought of Americans. "They are very cruel to us," said Muhammed, one of the boys. "They kill our people." Another boy named Shaheen said, "I want America to be finished. They destroyed Afghanistan. They bombed the whole country."[4]

It is an easy matter to teach children who is evil and who is not. I have another article in my files from a few years ago when the Albanians fleeing from Kosovo were in Macedonian camps by the hundreds of thousands. A father was catechizing his young son about the Serbs. "Who are our enemies?" asked the father. The child seemed confused, so the father answered for him. "The Serbs are our enemies! They killed our people!" he trumpeted. "And what will you do when you grow up?" This time the boy was ready. "I will kill the filthy Serbs!" he answered. The father was very pleased with his son.

One day it's the Germans, the next day it's the Serbs, today it seems to be the French.[5] The enemy lines are hard to find. We should remember that the *madrasas* were financed in part by the U.S. government during the 1980s when the Afghans were fighting the Soviets, and then we left Afghanistan to the tender mercies of

3. According to the article, about 40 percent of the 10,000 *madrasas* in Pakistan are moderate; 60 percent are run by the hard-line Deobandi sect.

4. David Rohde, "A Dead End for Afghan Children Adrift in Pakistan," *The New York Times,* March 7, 2003.

5. The Bush administration was infuriated because the French would not support the Iraq war. The French were caricatured in a New York City tabloid as weasels, and there was a brief vogue for "freedom fries."

the Taliban. We should remember also that during the Iran-Iraq war, we supported Saddam Hussein. The axis of evil lies here, there, and everywhere. Aleksandr Solzhenitsyn wrote these words from the Soviet gulag:

> Gradually it was disclosed to me that the line separating good and evil passes not through states, nor between classes, nor between political parties either — but right through every human heart. . . . This line shifts. Inside us, it oscillates with the years. And even within hearts overwhelmed by evil, one small bridgehead of good is retained. And even in the best of all hearts there remains . . . an uprooted small corner of evil.[6]

The season of Lent reminds the Christian community that the line runs through you and the line runs through me. It reminds us to beware of drawing lines between ourselves on the good side and others on the bad side. Those of you who were fortunate to be in church on Ash Wednesday will know what I mean when I say that reading Psalm 51 together on our knees, as we do on that day, is a very powerful act. We are acknowledging the truth about ourselves. In the words of that Psalm, "I know my transgressions, and my sin is ever before me." In the words of our Psalm for today, "Who can tell how often he offends? Cleanse thou me from my secret faults" (Psalm 19:12).

When we cannot hear such things about ourselves without bristling and becoming defensive, we are in trouble. When we are unable to utter a sincere apology and ask for forgiveness, our primary relationships are in trouble. When a nation treats dissent as unpatriotic, the whole world is in trouble. Repentance, the Lenten theme, is necessary for human well-being. Our leaders in former times seemed to know this. Our two greatest presidents, George Washington and Abraham Lincoln, both called the nation to repentance. It is hard to imagine any president of either political party doing that today.

6. Aleksandr Solzhenitsyn, *The Gulag Archipelago*, Part IV, Chapter 1.

I recently read an article about repentance by Frederica Mathewes-Green, a well-known writer on Christian themes. She grabbed my attention with a new definition. "Repentance is not blubbering and self-loathing. Repentance is insight."[7]

Repentance is insight. Repentance is not groveling. I'm sure you will recall that many people were turned off when Trent Lott seemed to be groveling.[8] Moreover, repentance is quite a different thing from saying "I'm sorry if anyone was offended" a dozen times. Repentance involves trying to understand *why* people were offended, *why* people were hurt, *why* people would like to hear a true and sincere apology, and why we ourselves have been offenders. "Who can tell how often he offends? Cleanse thou me from my secret faults."

Repentance means insight. That's what Tolkien meant in his letter to his son when he said, "What of the writer?" He meant that the newspaper editor lacked insight. He was so quick to label others as evil that he did not understand his own inclinations. That's the problem with the headlines that stir up readers to easy identification of Saddam Hussein as evil, and his sons as evil. That makes it so easy for us. We relish looking at the evil of *others* because it distracts us from the need to examine *ourselves,* a much more difficult task. I wonder if you have seen the movie, *The Pianist.* In my opinion it is the best movie ever made about the Holocaust. Among other things, it raises the question in the most acute way: What would I have done if I had been there? I have never seen a movie that illustrated so vividly the way that the line between good and evil becomes blurred under pressure. This movie offers insight.

Two weeks ago I was preaching in another church and I mentioned the book by former Senator Bob Kerrey in which he tells how when he was in Vietnam he got swept up into a massacre of women and children. Reflecting on this later, he wrote, "I did not recognize the person I had become." A man came up to me afterwards and said that he had had the same feeling about himself. He,

7. "Whatever Happened to Repentance?" *Christianity Today,* February 4, 2002.

8. The Senate majority leader had to relinquish his post because of an insensitive remark interpreted as racist.

too, was a Vietnam veteran. He had been a door gunner in a helicopter, a position which, I am told, is very dangerous. He told me that he was sure he had killed as many women and children as Kerry had, though from a bit of a distance. More important, he said he had felt an explosive rage within himself that he had not known was there. His exact words were, "It scared the hell out of me." He meant that he was more afraid of his own impulses than he was of being in the door of the helicopter.

The paradox of this is that when a Christian makes a confession of this kind in the context of the Christian community, though it is deeply sobering, it is also liberating. We make our confessions in the secure embrace of the gospel. What is the gospel? Listen to this verse from St. Paul's letter to the Romans: "God has consigned all human beings to disobedience, that he may have mercy upon all."

All of us share in the human condition; that is the secret of this season of Lent. All of us have dark impulses that could have become murderous had we been brought up in a garbage dump or been catechized by a vengeful father full of hate. Who knows if Saddam's sons are evil? Do you know? How do you know? Who told you? And if they are evil, who knows what influences made them evil? Let me be clear: action has to be taken against evil deeds. But the Christian will beware lest more evil deeds begin to erupt *from within* as well as from without.

It is God's plan to have mercy upon us. He "has consigned all human beings to disobedience, that he may have mercy upon all." The Epistle of Peter puts it another way: "Jesus Christ also died for sins once for all, the righteous for the unrighteous, that he might bring us to God" (1 Peter 3:18). The righteous died for the unrighteous: that is to say, he, the only truly righteous one, died for the unrighteous. And again Paul: "While we were still helpless, Christ died for the ungodly" (Romans 5:6).

The one great mistake we could make today is to think of ourselves in the wrong category. The Lord Jesus did not die for the righteous. He did not die for the godly. He did not die for the exceptional so that we, the saved, could delight in our own superiority and gloat over others. The Bible teaches us to see ourselves as God sees us. Suppose you and I were at the mercy of what our enemies think of us? Thanks be to God, the ultimate destiny of human beings is not to be determined by enemies. We live and die at the mercy of God, "to whom all hearts are open, all desires known, and from whom no secrets are hid." "Cleanse thou me from my secret faults, O God."

God sees you as you really are and he loves you. God sees those parts of you that you hide even from yourself and he loves you. God sees us all dividing up the world into good and evil but he, the only One entitled to divide the evil from the good, the One who could have remained enthroned above our struggles, out of his love came into the world to be "numbered among the transgressors" (Isaiah 53:12). Through his Son Jesus Christ he has entered into our condition, bowing his head under the onslaught of human vengefulness, indifference, cruelty, and hate in order to show mercy to us all, *especially to the perpetrators.*

He died the death of an outcast, he died the death of a condemned man, he died the death of one who had been declared an enemy of all the righteous of the state and of the church. With the last breath of his body and the last drop of his blood he has wrought the salvation of his enemies: that is to say, the salvation of each and every one of us.

AMEN.

August 26, 1990

Whose Way of Life?

GRACE CHURCH IN NEW YORK
TEXT: ROMANS 11:33-36

NOTE TO READERS: This sermon is included as an example
of the way news events in a specific year can be startlingly
relevant to news events sixteen years later.

We have been hearing a good deal in the last two weeks about "the American way of life." This is a phrase that we have heard all our lives, but in the context of the present frightening situation in the Middle East, it has become the focus of an urgent debate — for some, alas, it will doubtless be a matter of life and death.[1]

On the very same page of the Thursday paper, two different writers say two opposite things. One, the father of a young marine who has been called up, accuses President Bush of ordering troops to the Middle East to preserve the American "right" to buy cheap gas; the second writer, in the very next column, states that Bush is *not* ordering Americans to face death in the desert in order to save a few cents on the gallon. A couple of days before, Russell Baker wrote a funny but rather bitter column about how the real hostages in the situation are the American people and other Westerners who are enslaved by an insatiable need for oil and yet more oil, in order to maintain a style of life that is incomprehensible in most of the developing world.[2]

---

1. The context, which will become clear enough as the sermon develops, is the first Gulf War under the first President Bush.
2. *The New York Times,* August 22, 1990.

I am certainly not prepared at this time to make any conclusive judgments about these matters. What I am certain about is that there is nothing more important for Christians than wrestling with questions about our way of life. We need to wrestle with them as individual Christians making individual decisions, but, even more important, we need to wrestle with such question collectively, as the family of God. What is the *American* way of life? What is the *Christian* way of life? Are they compatible? If not, where do they differ? And what is our ultimate allegiance?

It seems to me that there are few issues in Christian faith more difficult for us than this one. American Christians, for the most part, see no real discrepancy between our country's interests and Christian commitment. For many, they are one and the same. When I was waiting for my train one morning last week, two men at the newsstand were delivering opinions on the subject in loud voices; they were both giving essentially the same speech in the same words, all about "the American way of life," Saddam Hussein as Hitler, and "God bless our American boys." It was a little startling to hear these phrases in that particular setting, where ordinarily one hears little more than the plunk of coins on the counter as the commuters pick up their copies of the *Wall Street Journal.* In times of international stress, it seems that even the sophisticated among us are apt to revert to the theme of "God bless America."

Please understand that this is not a sermon recommending some sort of new Munich. Being a Christian emphatically does not mean being naïve or weak — quite the opposite, in fact. What it does mean, though, is that we will be constantly reassessing the question about "ways of life." What way of life? Whose way of life? According to what standards? Under whose leadership? And *for whose benefit?*

One of the most basic instincts of the human race, right up there with the urge to eat and to reproduce, is that of allegiance to one's tribe or clan. In the beginning it must have had to do with survival itself. Nowadays we are more aware of the need to cooperate than we used to be, what with the threat of ecological disaster and nuclear extinction hanging over our globe. Still, we continue to cherish an almost atavistic loyalty to our own group, so much so that even the most thoughtful among us can lose our bearings when we think we are threatened.

These issues are related to the concerns of St. Paul in chapters 9–11 of the Epistle to the Romans. In these chapters, Paul is addressing himself to the vexed question of the relationship of the people of Israel to the newly emerging Christian church. Let us focus this morning on Paul's amazing outburst at the very end of the section. Some interpreters think that in this particular section of Romans, Paul went further than he had ever gone before, perhaps further than any other biblical writer had gone, with the exception perhaps of the second prophet Isaiah on whose shoulders Paul seems to stand as he looks into the future.[3]

Paul has been agonizing about the fact that so many of his own people have refused to recognize Jesus as the Messiah. He has given his whole life to preaching Christ, yet the people of Israel have turned away from him in droves. As he thinks out loud about his problem (dictating to a secretary), he seems to be seized by a kind of ecstatic vision, of the same sort that gripped the great Old Testament prophet of the Exile — a vision of God's purpose leading out from the narrow confines of one nation to many nations, from one people to many peoples. Like Second Isaiah before him, yet even more audaciously, Paul sees neither the Jews inheriting the kingdom of God, nor the Gentiles, but both together in God's own time. He sees God breaking out of the categories of religion and piety and morality to annex the irreligious, the impious, the immoral. This is what the Epistle to the Romans, in its entirety, proclaims — *the justification of the ungodly* (4:5).

There is no way to exaggerate the radical nature of this New Testament claim. There is nothing comparable to it in the world's

3. Most scholars today agree that Isaiah 40–55 comes from a prophet in the tradition of the first Isaiah but writing two hundred years later from the Babylonian Exile. Isaiah 40–55 is the longest sustained passage of prophetic poetry in the Bible, and without peer in the Old Testament for its exalted visionary promises of universal salvation. Romans 11 is the closest thing to it in the New Testament, with the arguable exception of the book of Revelation.

religions. This proclamation of the justification of the ungodly knocks all the props out from under "religion." We can no longer claim goodness or righteousness as our own, but only as God's, to bestow as he chooses. Paul rubs this in with the famous image of the potter and the clay, saying that the potter can make any kind of vessel he wants, no matter whether the clay likes it or not. It is a rather humorous illustration, in a way, calling upon us to imagine the absurdity of a pot saying to its maker, "I don't like the shape I'm in!" (Romans 9:19-21).

With this image, Paul defends God's right to shape different groups of people in different ways, and to have his own special purpose for each. No group can have any special claim on God — Paul emphasizes that by quoting from the Old Testament: Who has given a gift to God, that he might be repaid? (Job 35:7) God *does* pick groups of people for special purposes, and the most important of these is Israel; but surely we can argue that he has also given other groups special missions at special times — England in 1940, Southern blacks in the 1950s, the Polish Solidarity movement in the 1980s, Chinese students in 1989. I personally believe that it is demonstrably the case — demonstrable if you believe in God, that is — that God has given America a unique role to play in the world, vividly illustrated by the remarkable new museum at Ellis Island. All the more reason, therefore, for American Christians to be on guard against abuses of this sacred trust. There is a powerful illustration of this in a *Times* story this week about a Congressman from Boston, Joe Moakley, whose deeply felt Roman Catholic faith has led him to wage an effective personal crusade for an investigation of American complicity in the killings of the six Jesuits in El Salvador.

We can all agree, I imagine, that the parading of British families before Saddam Hussein's cameras was, to quote the British Foreign Secretary, "the most sickening thing seen in a long time." Exploitation of children is indefensible. But there is nothing remarkable about reacting in anger to the mistreatment of one's own. What would have been truly remarkable would have been a British or American protest last year or the year before, when Hussein was gassing Kurdish children within his own borders.[4] For several years now, the United States has turned a blind eye to Hussein's doings. Not until America's own interests were threatened did the Iraqi strongman suddenly become a Hitler. Does anyone think that American boys would be in the desert wearing moon suits if Kuwait were a country that had no oil?

What all this suggests is that it is easier to rant against the "goons" of other nations, as our columnists have been doing, than it is to look carefully at ourselves and take responsibility for our own "way of life." "My country right or wrong" has always been a powerful creed. Americans are not the only people who profess this creed. When Saddam Hussein says on videotape, "We Arabs will teach Bush how to be closer to God," we don't know whether to laugh or cry or throw something at the TV set. What the Christian way of life might require of us Americans, however, on this and on all other occasions is to take a good look at ourselves and the way that we so glibly claim God for America. We probably can't change Hussein's view of God; our special responsibility is to be vigilant about our own view.[5]

Paul's vision of God's purposes at the end of Romans 11 is comprehensive almost beyond human imagining. Paul breaks out into a kind of hymn, exclaiming:

> O the depth of the riches and wisdom and knowledge of God! how unsearchable are his judgments and how inscrutable are his ways! . . . For from him and through him and to him are all things. To him be glory for ever.

The *context* of this doxology is important.[6] This is Paul's invitation to us to join him in praising the Lord for including all kinds of ungodly people in his plan for salvation, even including you and

4. A dozen years later, Samantha Power analyzed Saddam Hussein's Anfal Campaign (now recognized as a genocide against the Kurds) and America's failure in her Pulitzer Prize–winning book *"A Problem from Hell": America in the Age of Genocide* (New York: Basic Books, 2002), pp. 171-246.

5. It hardly needs to be pointed out that this is true in 2007 to a degree that could not have been imagined in 1990.

6. A doxology is a hymn in praise of God's *doxa* — his glory.

me. It is not for nothing that we say the confession of sin every single time we meet together for worship. When Christian people gather for prayer, there is no time for calling other people goons; it is a time to repent of our own goonish behavior, and to admit that we have not always been the best representatives of the God whose name we so frequently invoke.

At the end of Romans 11, Paul envisions a time when God's purpose for salvation will encompass all the nations of the earth. The climax of this difficult but dazzling section of Scripture invites all who hear Paul's words to recommit themselves, not to Israel's way of life or America's way of life, but to *God's* way of life. Paul proposes a motto for the worst-favored-nation; it is "Do not be proud, but stand in awe" (1:20). Whenever a tribe or a country or a congregation or a group within a congregation begins to imagine itself closer to God than some other, it has already lost sight of what God really is up to. When Paul calls out, "Who has known the mind of the Lord? Who has been his counselor?" his rhetorical questions invite us to place our trust in the creating, redeeming, sustaining God whose plans for the Jews and the Iraqis and the British children and the Chinese students are so much bigger and better and more just and ultimately more truly human than anything you or I could possible devise from our limited, distorted, finite perspective. I myself believe this on a *global* scale because I have learned on an *individual* scale how the well-meaning among us can make a mess of what we care about most. You and I and this whole suffering world need a God who is great enough to rectify all this colossal and never-ending cycle of wrongdoing.

Let us turn away from the international stage and look at our own congregation. In the last few weeks these different people, relative newcomers to our midst, have described to me a certain discomfort they have felt about being here. One young man said, "I sometimes feel like a foreigner at this church." In each case, the specific problem was that they felt they were less devout, less "spiritual," less committed to a Christian way of life than the people they had met here. Now we sinners who know ourselves only too well are tempted to smile in disbelief at this; yet we do have some wonderful servants of God here, and the ones I'm talking about would be the last to think I had them in mind. It is true that God has bestowed qualities of holiness on some Christians among us that make the rest of us ashamed of ourselves, and we wonder if we can ever measure up.

The answer, of course, is that we can't. If newcomers will stick around long enough, they will see the cracks and holes and faults in *all* of us. If we as a congregation have learned anything at all, it is that each of us is a truly undeserving recipient of God's mercy. This knowledge is happy knowledge; it is joyful and liberating. We no longer need to be the judge of ourselves. There are no foreigners among us; none at all. Before God, no one has an advantage over anyone else, for as our Lord himself said, "God makes his sun rise on the evil and on the good, and sends rain on the just and the unjust alike." Indeed, it is well worth looking at the context of that pleasant sounding thought about the sun and the rain, for it is embedded in a very tough teaching from the Sermon on the Mount preceded by these words of Jesus: "You have heard that it was said, You shall love your neighbor and hate your enemy. But I say to you, Love your enemies and pray for those who persecute you . . . for [God] makes his sun shine and his rain fall on the evil and good, just and unjust alike" (Matthew 5:43-45). It is in exactly that radical context that Paul bursts out:

> O the depth of the riches and wisdom and knowledge of God! How unsearchable are his judgments and how inscrutable his ways!
>
> "For who has known the mind of the Lord,
>   Or who has been his counselor?" [Isaiah 40:13]
>
> "Or who has given a gift to him
>   That he might be repaid?" [Job 35:7]
>
> For from him and through him and to him are all things. To him be glory forever. (Romans 11:33-36)

With this great, climactic hymn of praise Paul invites us to join him in God's way of life — according to God's standards, under

God's leadership, for the benefit of all the *un*godly. Paul knows when he writes this that it will be deeply offensive to the self-righteous, but it will be water in the desert to those who confess their faults. In the company of the Lord's disobedient children, there are no foreigners. For from God and through God and to God are all things — the forgiveness of sins, the justification of the ungodly, the manna in the wilderness, the descent of the dove, the battle against Satan, the conquest of evil, and the resurrection of the dead.

So do not be proud, but stand in awe. And then we may truly and earnestly sing:

> America, America!
> God shed his grace on thee;
> And crown thy good with brotherhood
> From sea to shining sea.

AMEN.

August 22, 1993

Jesus saves =

God to the Rescue

Manhetten

ken verse 350

God has consigned all men to disobedience in order that he may have mercy upon all.

ROMANS 11:32

It is often said nowadays that the church has to give up using words like redemption, salvation, justification because people don't know what they mean. Our experience here at Grace Church would certainly suggest that that is not true. In any case, the Bible remains wise from age to age; those words are used repeatedly throughout the Scriptures, but in addition there are hundreds, if not thousands, of stories and illustrations from ordinary life. That, as every literary critic knows, is the secret of the Bible's hold on the imagination of humanity: the stories that illustrate the meaning of the words.

We had a story of salvation right here in New York this week, and the whole city is agog over it. When Harvey Cohen was pulled up out of his black, dank, filthy hole by the hand of Detective William Mondore, he said later, "I knew I was home, I knew I was safe, and God had smiled down on me."[1] Those could be the very words

1. The real name of the man who was rescued that week was Harvey Weinstein. I have substituted "Cohen" here because in the years since 1993 another Harvey Weinstein has become so well known that it would be confusing and distracting to

of the Prodigal Son. That is as good a description of redemption as I've heard in a long time: "I knew I was home, I knew I was safe, I knew God had smiled down on me." And, I suspect, there is hardly a person in New York City too blasé, too cool, too laid-back, to experience a lump in the throat, a catch in the breath, a quickening of the heartbeat when hearing the story of this remarkable rescue.

The name Jesus means "God saves." My favorite translation of the Hebrew name was suggested by Michael Green, a British evangelist and biblical scholar. He wrote that the name Jesus means, "God to the rescue!"

The entire Old Testament is the story of God coming to the rescue. The Psalmist cries out, "Save me, O God! For the waters have come up to my neck; I sink in deep mire" (Psalm 69:1). Jacob, standing terrified by the ford of the river Jabbok as his enemy approaches with a fighting force, prays as he has never prayed before, "O God of my father Abraham and my father Isaac . . . I am not worthy of the least of all thy mercies, but deliver me, I pray" (Genesis 32:9-11). Daniel, like Harvey Cohen, was put down into a pit, although in Daniel's case it had hungry lions in it, and when Daniel was released unharmed, even the pagan king gave glory to God, saying, "The God of Daniel . . . is the living God . . . he rescues and he delivers, he performs signs and wonders in the heavens and on the earth. He has rescued Daniel from the power of the lions" (Daniel 6:26-27).

The story of the Bible is the story of God coming to the rescue. God declares to Moses from the burning bush that he has seen the suffering of his people. "I have seen the oppression of my people who are in Egypt, and I have heard their cry because of their taskmasters, for I know their sorrows. So I have come down to deliver them out of the hand of the Egyptians" (Exodus 3:7-8). The Pass-

---

use the name here. The amazing story by noted reporter Francis X. Clines is well worth a search in the *New York Times* archives (August 19, 1993). Mr. Weinstein, an apparel company executive, had been buried alive by kidnappers in a 4 × 6 hole near the Henry Hudson Parkway for twelve days. He was upheld during this ordeal, in part, by recalling Arthur Koestler's writings on torture and isolation (which, as it happens, are highly relevant to today's debates about torture).

over and the Exodus are the shaping events of Hebrew history, and for Jews and Christians alike they are the central images of God's activity, so much so that the earliest Christians immediately understood the Crucifixion and Resurrection as the new Passover and Exodus, the climax of the drama of deliverance. The Christian story is a story of discovering that we are safe, that we are home, that God has smiled on us. The Good Shepherd has come down and has gathered his lost sheep into his fold; in the words of the hymn, "Perverse and foolish oft I strayed/but yet in love he sought me,/And on his shoulder gently laid,/and home, rejoicing, brought me."[2]

Not everybody knows that they are in need of rescue. A lot of people are unable or unwilling to admit that they are in trouble. There are two kinds of trouble: the kind that is imposed from the outside, and the kind that comes from within. In the past few weeks, through one set of circumstances or another, I have had some first-hand experiences of how awful it can be when a person cannot see that he or she has done something to cause trouble. Contrary to popular opinion in some circles, admission of fault is not a weakness; it is a strength. Real leaders must have the capacity for repentance. It has been very distressing in recent years to see so many public figures refusing to admit that they have erred: Gary Hart, Richard Nixon, Oliver North, Chuck Robb, Clark Clifford — I could go on and on.[3] There are many such people in churches; there are many in families. It is very destructive to human relations. It is very difficult to forgive a person who does not think she needs any forgiveness. It is very hard to go forward with any sort of relationship when there is no recognition of error and no repentance. Without repentance, we cannot understand the truth of our situation. Without a clear-sighted understanding of our need for God's redemption, we will be forever ignorant of the greatness of what the

2. "The King of love my Shepherd is," by Henry Williams Baker (1821-1877), paraphrase of Psalm 23.

3. This was 1993. At the time of preparing this book for publication, one might cite Lizzie Grubman, Martha Stewart, Kate Moss, Paris Hilton, Barry Bonds, Bernard B. Kerik, and various other shameless people who in many cases have not only been unrepentant but have gone on to greater triumphs.

living God has done for us. Part of the delight we all took in the Harvey Cohen story was watching him thanking his rescuers and rejoicing in his deliverance; how deflated and saddened we would have felt if he had just disappeared back into his former life as though nothing had happened.

The biblical story of salvation tells us that God has smiled down on us. It has already happened. It has already been accomplished. We are safe; we are home. Jesus has done it all for us already. Many of you have heard me refer to the Swiss legend beloved by Karl Barth about the man who, lost on horseback in the middle of the night, crossed the frozen Lake Constance without realizing what he was doing. When he reached safety on the other side and was told of the terrible fate he had just narrowly escaped, his knees buckled under him in terror and relief. This is the situation we are in. We have already arrived on the other side, because God has declared his favor and goodness toward us. If we do not recognize the seriousness of the predicament we were in, however, then we will never know the greatness of the rescue that has been accomplished for us by our Lord. It would be as if Harvey Cohen had never even noticed that he had been in a pit.

We are reading the Epistle to the Romans this summer in our Sunday lectionary. We have arrived at the end of the eleventh chapter, the theological and also the emotional center of the letter to the Romans. Some, and I am one of them, think it is the radical heart of the whole Bible. I call your attention to chapter 11, verse 32: "God has consigned all men to disobedience in order that he may have mercy upon all." When Joel Marcus was teaching here at Grace Church and getting a Ph.D. in New Testament, he used to nominate this verse as the key to the gospel. Just this past Friday I was reading the latest article by FitzSimons Allison, former rector of this parish, and was delighted to see that he, too, quoted this verse: "God has bound all men over to disobedience so that he may have mercy upon them all" (NIV).

This is the human story. We have all suffered the effects of sin and disobedience. Not only as individuals but also as communities, cities, groups, and nations, we are poisoned with greed, jealousy, violence, discord, strife, self-seeking of every kind. When we use the colloquial expression, "It's the pits," we are perhaps saying more than we know. Jeremiah the prophet found himself lowered into a pit with mire at the bottom, as we read in chapter 38, but his personal plight was not as dreadful to him as the impending judgment he saw hanging over Israel: "Since my people are crushed, I am crushed; I mourn, and horror grips me. Is there no balm in Gilead? Is there no physician there? Why then is there no healing for the wound of my people?" (Jeremiah 8:21-22).

When Jeremiah spoke those words, he had every reason to believe that the answer was *no, there was no balm* in Gilead. If we don't understand that there really might not have been any, we will never understand the magnitude of God's saving work. Two weeks ago while I was on vacation, Dick and I went to a church hymn-sing, led by a well-known church choirmaster. One of the hymns was the familiar "There is a balm in Gilead." One of the women present asked, "What does that mean?" No one knew. No one even knew that the words come from the Bible. The choirmaster did not know. I was staggered. How can we hope to grow in faith when we do not know what we are saying and singing? The words of the hymn are, "There *is* a balm in Gilead/to make the wounded whole;/There *is* a balm in Gilead/to heal the sin-sick soul." The words are cheap if we do not know that *there might not have been any* balm in Gilead. The Swiss horseman would never have known what he had escaped if no one had explained it to him.

"God has consigned all human beings to disobedience so that he might have mercy upon all." As surely as you and I are sunk in a pit of selfishness, idolatry, and godlessness, so surely has the Lord reached down to us "with a mighty hand and an outstretched arm," as the Old Testament says. As surely as we are deserving of God's wrath and condemnation, so surely has his own Son come to take our place in the pit, to rescue us. As Paul writes in Romans 5, "Since we have now been justified by [Christ's] blood, how much more shall we be saved from God's wrath by him! For if, when we were God's enemies, we were reconciled to him through the death of his Son, how much more, having been reconciled, shall we be saved through his life! Not only is this so, but we also *rejoice* in God through our Lord Jesus Christ" (Romans 5:9-11).

Here at Grace Church we are all sinners. We are a very long way from true righteousness. If you are a newcomer here tonight, I cannot promise you a perfect human response to all your needs. But I can say this: over the years, this congregation has been shaped by this gospel, and it has given us a kind of joy that comes with the knowledge of deliverance — deliverance from fear now, and the promise of deliverance from condemnation in God's final reckoning. It has given members of this congregation a deep inner gladness that has survived many earthly sorrows. There is an incomparable freedom and lightness in knowing that God knows the worst about us and has nevertheless found the way to rectify all that is wrong. We are, in all our sinfulness, a fellowship of people who know that we have received mercy. In this joyful knowledge, we welcome all newcomers and fellow travelers. Let us come now like children to the Father's table, where we are home, we are safe, and the Lord smiles down on us. "Rejoice! Again I say, rejoice!"

AMEN.

Presenting Ourselves

Last Monday, after four months of recuperation from major surgery, David Cone returned to the Yankees and pitched seven no-hit innings against the Oakland A's. The sensational comeback made front-page headlines in New York. Manager Joe Torre pulled Cone off the mound after 85 pitches (54 of them strikes) because not even a no-hitter would be worth having his best starter reinjured. Afterward, Dave Cone said something remarkable: "I've been humbled. When you go through what I've gone through, you realize your mortality. There's only so much tread left on the tire. I appreciate them taking me out. Getting to the World Series is more important."

Now I suspect that Dave Cone would be surprised to hear this, but those words are not far from the spirit of St. Paul's description of the church in Romans 12, which we are reading last week and this week.

> For by the grace given to me I bid every one among you not to think of himself more highly than he ought to think, but to think with sober judgment. . . . For as in one body we have many members, and all the members do not have the same function, so we, though many, are one body in Christ, and individually members one of another. Having gifts that differ according to the grace given to us, let us use them [for the building up of the body of Christ].

"I've been humbled," Dave Cone said; he does not think more highly of himself than he ought to think. "I realize my mortality," he said with what Paul identifies as "sober judgment." Cone knows himself to be an indispensable part of a larger team ("we, though many, are one body in Christ, and individually members one of another") and, in particular he understands that although we have "gifts that differ according to the grace given to us," and some of us have gifts that are more spectacular than others, nevertheless the use of our gifts is not for individual fame but for the good of the whole. To me, the most impressive part of Cone's statement is his saying, "I appreciate them taking me out. Getting to the World Series is more important." He was willing and even glad to sacrifice his own glory at the order of his captain who was thinking of the larger picture. That's what Christian soldiers do.

You will often hear me speak of the well-known dictum that sermons are written with the Bible in one hand and the newspaper in the other. All week I have been thinking about Dave Cone's remarks (the newspaper) in the context of these verses from Romans (the Bible), but the third partner in the process has been the body of Christ at St. John's Church. People have asked me when I am going to start recycling my old sermons. Well, I'm not likely to do that because, as I was taught long ago at Union Seminary by some extraordinary mentors in the Lord, Christian preaching should be very much in and of its context. You and I are the context, this morning, for a new hearing of the Epistle to the Romans as Paul moves into his direct appeal to the Christian congregation — that's you and me.

Last Sunday when I was celebrating the Rite I Eucharist with you I noticed as if for the first time how closely Thomas Cranmer based his eucharistic prayer on Romans 12.

> And here we offer and present unto thee, O Lord, our selves, our souls and bodies, to be a reasonable, holy, and living sacrifice unto thee; humbly beseeching thee that we, and all others who shall be partakers of this Holy Communion, may . . . be made one body with him, that he may dwell in us, and we in him.

This is directly patterned after St. Paul's words in chapter 12:

> I appeal to you therefore, brothers and sisters, by the mercies of
> God, to present your bodies [your selves] as a living sacrifice,
> holy and acceptable to God, which is your spiritual worship.[1] . . .
> We, though many, are one body in Christ, and individually mem-
> bers one of another.

This recognition of the direct link between Thomas Cranmer's
eucharistic prayer and Romans 12 caused me to begin thinking
more intentionally than ever about this congregation and its future.

So very much of the meaning of being a Christian is founded
on recognition. Many Christian educators worry that this will become impossible for us because we do not know our own tradition
well enough to recognize anything. The principal purpose of
Sunday school for very small children is to acclimate them to things
that they do not understand now but will recognize when they grow
up. It is thrilling to be able to connect pieces of hymns, biblical passages, prayers, paintings, and sculpture. Similarly, when we know
Romans 12 well enough to recognize it in the eucharistic prayer,
the impetus to be shaped by its message gains in power. "We offer
and present unto thee, O Lord, *our selves* . . . to be a reasonable, holy,
and *living sacrifice* unto thee. . . ." When we see that this Prayer
Book language is taken from the apostle's letter to the Christians in
Rome written only two or three decades after the Resurrection, we
realize that this is not just beautiful phraseology that the priest
mumbles week after week as though it were a mantra. When we
recognize the biblical connection, our hearts are lifted and we are
enabled to make changes in our lives. The thought of actually *offering ourselves* as *living sacrifices* becomes really operative for us, instead
of being mere words. On this very day as we hear Paul's invitation,
"I appeal to you therefore, brothers and sisters, by the mercies of

---

1. The Old Testament and New Testament writers do not make the distinction
between body and soul that later thinkers did, influenced as they were by Hellenistic
philosophy. Paul is talking about the person's whole self.

God, to present your bodies [your selves] as a living sacrifice," God is acting in your hearts to make this happen.

Throughout much of the Epistle to the Romans, Paul is preaching. It is traditional to say that in chapter 12, he moves from preaching to exhortation. That's only partly true. Chapter 12 is launched by the thrust of chapters 1–11. That's why chapter 12 begins with *therefore*.[2] ("I appeal to you therefore, brethren, by the mercies of God, to present your bodies as a living sacrifice . . .") When Paul says "by the mercies of God" he isn't uttering a stock phrase. He is speaking, or preaching, really, about something that he knows to be transforming in his own life and that he has seen at work in the Christian community. When he says such things as "Let love be genuine; hate what is evil, hold fast to what is good," he is not delivering mere maxims. He is not simply exhorting the congregation to do better. Rather, he is *describing the mind of Christ taking shape in the community by the power of the Spirit.* This is not something we do. This is something God does in us.

I must admit to being a bit dashed when, after one of my sermons, a parishioner said to me, "You certainly expect a lot of us." Ouch! If that's the way a sermon sounds, it isn't the gospel of liberation at all; it's some form of guilt trip. If Romans 12 doesn't sound liberating, then we need to go back and read the good news in the previous chapters all over again:

We rejoice in our hope of sharing the glory of God. (5:2)

God's love has been poured into our hearts. (5:5)

We are not under law but under grace. (6:15)

We serve not under the old written code but in the new life of the Spirit. (7:6)

2. A little phrase commonly heard in seminary training is, "What is the 'therefore' there for?" This is not as trivial as it may sound.

A famous paraphrase of Paul's ethical message is this: "Become what you already are!" How different that is from holding out a load of impossible expectations. Something has happened that changes everything. We are already serving in the new life of the Spirit. Paul describes what is already a reality because "God's love has been poured into our hearts." Chapter 12 is a description, not a prescription:

> Let love be genuine; hate what is evil, hold fast to what is good; love one another with brotherly affection; outdo one another in showing honor. Never flag in zeal, be aglow with the Spirit, serve the Lord. . . .

These are not nice religious thoughts such as we might find on greeting cards. These are descriptions of the mind of Christ, and the mind of Christ is alive and at work in the world because Jesus the Lord is alive and at work in the world.

My thoughts go back to Dave Cone saying that he appreciated being taken out of the game because the World Series is the most important thing. I think of church fights I have known. The altar guild member has her nose out of joint because someone else was asked to do the Easter flowers. The acolyte who had carried the cross on Christmas Eve for two years flung a fit because she wasn't asked for a third year. The vestryman who had been slated to become senior warden refused to serve because he was outvoted on an important issue. You may think these are caricatures. I assure you they are only a small sampling of real life that I have seen in my ministry. It is human nature to want its own way; Paul describes this in detail in Romans 1–3. But, Paul says, something new has happened in human life.

> We know that our old self was crucified with him so that . . . we might no longer be enslaved to sin. (6:6)

> The law of the Spirit of life in Christ Jesus has set me free from the law of sin and death. (8:2)

A new situation has come into being. That's why Paul says *therefore:* "I appeal to you *therefore,* brethren, by the mercies of God, to present your bodies as a living sacrifice, holy and acceptable to God."

What would St. John's look like if we were to do this in a new and fresh way this year? What would happen if each one of us this very day prayed seriously to God that we might offer ourselves to his service? What might we become, here in the Northwest Corner, if we made a fresh beginning together this season? We may look like a sleepy little community here, but when the Spirit of God is at work there is no such thing as a sleepy little community. A Christian community is a group of people who know themselves to be in a new situation — a situation of grace, a situation of mercy, a situation of promise, a situation of new life. How can that be? What is it that has made the difference?

Paul tells us. In words that lie at the very heart and soul of the Christian gospel, he writes,

> While we were still helpless, at the right time Christ died for the ungodly. . . . God shows his love for us in that while we were yet sinners Christ died for us. (Romans 5:6, 8)

That is what has made the whole situation new. You may not be fully aware of this yet, but as you come forward to receive our Lord's body and blood, you are being made new by the Holy Spirit. We are not doing this; God is doing this. We expect nothing of ourselves as we come forward to receive this gift; we expect everything from God. It is through this gospel of grace, it is in this new reality, it is by this power that we now are being enabled to become what we already are in Christ, so that we are presenting ourselves to him *"as a living sacrifice, holy and acceptable to God, which is our spiritual worship."* And when we do that, brothers and sisters, watch out, because God always finishes what he starts. He is making us holy and acceptable to himself.

And so today I place before us all a call. Will you, today, present yourselves to God as a living sacrifice? As we pray aloud together in a few minutes, will you think about what you are saying and, if you believe that God is calling you, will you use this brief moment to recognize, not only that you are invited to present yourself as a living sacrifice, holy and acceptable to God, but also that in Christ we present ourselves to one other, recognizing each brother and sister not according to their position on the social ladder, not according to their club membership, not according to who plays bridge with whom or who is a weekender or who has been here for five generations, but according to the mind of Christ taking shape in the community by the power of the Spirit.

If I am among you this year for any reason at all, this is the reason: to proclaim to you the most tremendous news in the world. "God shows his love for us in that while we were yet sinners Christ died for us." And along with this news comes the transforming result. The offering of God's Son for us meets with our corresponding offering of ourselves to him in service to one another. The kind of service God wants is the kind of service that Jesus gave to us: irrespective of persons, heedless of self, always seeking the good of the other, focused on showing God's unbounded love for all and for each. You have shown me far more love in these two months than I could ever deserve; now let the gospel message work in us to redouble our desire to serve one another, and, in doing so, to become day by day a *living sacrifice* for the sake of the whole created order. For verily, verily God says unto you, the ultimate "world series" belongs to Jesus Christ our Lord.

AMEN.

The Content of Our Character

TEXT: ROMANS 12:1-3

The Presidential campaign has focused on the question of character. Does Bill Clinton have a good character? Does Bob Dole?[1] *The Wall Street Journal* has been carrying on about this. A letter to the editor on Thursday quoted Horace Greeley: "Fame is vapor, popularity an accident, riches take wing. Only one thing endures and that is character." I remember hearing that Franklin Roosevelt had a second-rate intellect but a first-rate character. What is character? Martin Luther King Jr. said, "I have a dream that my four little children will one day live in a nation where they will be judged not by the color of their skin but by the content of their character." What does he mean by character?

Someone said that character is what you have at three in the morning when you are alone in the dark. I often think of prisoners, like Nelson Mandela, or prisoners of war who have endured unspeakable trials over a period of years and emerge without being embittered or broken. What sort of character do they have that enables them not only to withstand but also to conquer? Could you or I do that? Are rising generations being prepared to withstand deprivation? Surely character, whatever else it may be, is a capacity for perseverance through adversity. Dr. King said to the marchers on that great day, "you have been the veterans of creative suffering.

---

1. Clinton and Dole were running against each other for President at this time.

hypomone
endurance
character

Continue to work with the faith that unearned suffering is redemptive." The New Testament writers would certainly agree. A key term in the New Testament is *hupomone,* which is Greek for fortitude or endurance. It is often translated patience, which in English has a somewhat weaker sound but is actually a virtue of great power, because patience is a strong and mature characteristic that many of us must struggle for years to develop.

We could fill many pages with descriptions of good character from secular sources, from Marcus Aurelius to Colin Powell. There is a good deal of lament today about the loss of a sense of virtue in our culture. I hope we all share that concern. What is more important for us as members of the Christian community, however, is a mutual understanding of specifically *Christian* character. In the Gospel for today, our Lord speaks these words: "If any man would come after me, let him deny himself and take up his cross and follow me. For whoever would save his life will lose it, and whoever loses his life for my sake will find it" (Matthew 16:24-25). Christian character, in other words, is *cruciform* — it has the shape of the One who was crucified. It is self-sacrificing. It is willing to suffer. Christian character is distinctive because it is Christ-like. As St. Paul writes in Romans 8:29, we are "predestined to be conformed to the image of his Son." Everybody, no matter how anti-Christian or secular they may be, recognizes Christ-like character — and respects it.

The cover of the most recent *Newsweek* has a Presidential-looking picture of Clinton on it and a single word in large letters, "Makeover." My first thought when I saw it was: If you need a makeover, you don't have any character. My second thought was, on the other hand: We all need a makeover. St. Paul is saying something like this in the lesson from Romans appointed for today. "Do not be conformed to this world but be transformed. . . ." Anyone who has stayed with the reading of Romans that we have been doing all summer will understand that we *all* need to be transformed. If it is true, as Paul emphatically says, that "all human beings . . . are under the power of sin" (Romans 3:9), then assuredly we all need a big-time makeover. And that is precisely what God is up to in each one of us who comes to Christ in faith.

What's this makeover going to look like? Paul tells us.

I appeal to you therefore, brethren, by the mercies of God, to present your bodies as a living sacrifice, holy and acceptable to God, which is your spiritual worship. Do not be conformed to this world but be transformed by the renewal of your mind, that you may prove what is the will of God, what is good and acceptable and perfect.

In other words, we are going to be conformed, not to what the *world* thinks is "good and acceptable and perfect," but what *God* thinks. Christian lives are spent as *living sacrifices,* not on the altar of self, but on the altar of *the mercies of God.*

We live in a relentlessly self-centered culture nowadays. It is increasingly more difficult to gain a hearing for the Christian way of life, although, again, I've noticed that when someone actually does *live* in a Christlike manner it evokes admiration, however grudging. The challenge for us is to find the right balance between the talk and the walk. For Christians, living in a Christlike manner without acknowledging the *source* of Christlike life is a contradiction in terms and would have been incomprehensible in the New Testament church. On the other hand, Paul wants us to know that faithful *speaking* about the Lord issues forth in *doing* — in our offering ourselves as living sacrifices. Alas, the two rarely seem to come together. In a reserved culture like that of New England, speaking is difficult; it is much easier to criticize the born-again Christian who is misbehaving than it is to give open, unashamed testimony to the name of Christ as the author of any good that we may do.

In the interests of full disclosure, I am a Democrat (I promise not to mention that again from the pulpit until the election is over).[2] Like many Americans, however, I have misgivings about President Clinton. In spite of his much-vaunted capacity for feeling people's feelings, he seems remarkably small-minded sometimes. The latest example of this was not giving former President Carter

2. The congregation was about 80 percent Republican.

any role at the Democratic Convention. Largeness of spirit is certainly a Christian characteristic, as Paul strongly implies (a few verses later) in his description of Christian liberality. The proper response to the mercies of God is thanksgiving and a corresponding generosity.

So you will see that I am no great admirer of the President. No doubt we can all agree that anyone who hires a person of dubious character like Dick Morris probably deserves whatever is coming to him.[3] However, I recently read something about the President that struck me. He has taken to saying something when people ask him how he is doing. What he says is probably 10 percent sincere and 90 percent carefully crafted by the makeover people. Nevertheless, it is of great theological interest. People ask him how he's doing and he says, "Better than I deserve, thank you." For the purposes of our message this morning, set aside for just a moment the person saying this. No, on second thought, don't. If you are a Clinton-hater, it might have a special meaning for you, since you above all will agree that he is doing a whole lot better than he deserves.[4] But Paul's point throughout Romans is that *we are all* doing better than we deserve. That's why Paul says "by the grace given to me I bid every one among you not to think of himself more highly than he ought to think" (Romans 12:3). If we human beings got what we deserved, we would have destroyed ourselves by now. Did you ever reflect about that? Is it only the Rwandans and the Cambodians and the Bosnians who do terrible things to each other? Are Americans immune to such things? Ask the descendants of black slaves that question. Ask the villagers of My Lai. According to the apostle Paul, and indeed the entire Bible, there is no immunity anywhere. "God has consigned *all* men to disobedience in order that he may have *mercy upon all*" (Romans 11:32).

So the motive power behind Christian transformation is gratitude. I'm doing better than I deserve, *thank you*. This is why we

3. Clinton's close adviser Dick Morris had just been caught in an embarrassing sexual scandal.

4. It is remarkable that this is before the Monica Lewinsky affair.

"present our bodies (meaning, our whole selves) as a living sacrifice, holy and acceptable to God."

I've been reading an interesting book that one of our parishioners gave me, called *Encountering Darkness* by the Very Rev. Gonville ffrench-Beytagh,[5] a veteran of the anti-apartheid movement in South Africa. He was part of the English establishment, being the Dean of the Anglican Cathedral in Johannesburg. He was framed and arrested by the Afrikaner government, who wanted to get him off the scene. During his incarceration he was subjected to psychological torture and lived in terror of being physically tortured and killed. ffrench-Beytagh was not a conventionally brave or stoical man. He embarrassed himself by having several "weeping-fits" in the prison. But instead of comforting himself by a sense of superiority to his tormentors, he reflected upon how his fellow Englishmen had excluded the Afrikaners from the Country Club of Johannesburg and other aspects of upper-crust South African life. This encouraged a sense of inferiority among the Afrikaners which was in turn visited upon the black Africans. Through this reasoning, ffrench-Beytagh was able to think of his interrogators as human beings like himself, thereby emerging from his experience with his Christian character intact, and indeed as a hero of Christian faith.

Listen again to our text from Romans 12:

> I appeal to you therefore, brethren, by the mercies of God, to present your bodies as a living sacrifice. . . . Do not be conformed to this world but be transformed by the renewal of your mind, that you may prove what is the will of God, what is good and acceptable and perfect.

Don't be misled by that renewal-of-your-mind phrase. Paul doesn't mean self-improvement. He speaks of something quite different. He means *the mind of Christ* (1 Corinthians 2:16). When Paul says we have the mind of Christ, he is not talking about emulating Jesus, or even following the path of Jesus as though he were some

5. Apparently the first part of this Welsh name is lowercase.

sort of guru or spiritual master. He uses unique terminology to describe the relationship of the Christian community to its Lord; he says we are *in Christ.* We are not exhorted to have a better character as though it were up to us to create one; rather, it is declared to us as good news that the character of the living Lord Jesus is being formed in the Christian community. Of no other departed figure has this ever been said. But then, you see, Jesus is not departed, but is alive and present in the power of the Holy Spirit.

One of the most impressive Christians in America, Joseph Cardinal Bernadin of Chicago, is dying from pancreatic cancer. At 68 years of age he is without question one of the leading Roman Catholic moderates in the world. He was slated to be one of the key figures in building a bridge between this papacy and the next one. As the world understands such things, his life and work are being cut short. But he is not *conformed to this world.* Long experience of *the mind of Christ* has transformed his own mind. I read an article about him yesterday. He is a man who has suffered a great deal, most recently from a long siege of being under suspicion of sexual misconduct. The accusation was totally fraudulent, but it was a long time before that was proved. Throughout this ordeal Cardinal Bernadin showed himself to be a model of Christian character. Now, facing the ultimate test of a painful, debilitating death, he is a man at peace. In his final battle he is fortified with something very much more than general religious principles. He does not look forward to some sort of vague religious hope of life after death. Here is what he looks forward to, in his own words: "I know the Lord's promises — to be with him and to be happy with him. In faith I know the Lord will be waiting for me and his promises will be fulfilled."

All the scholarly squabbles about the biblical text and the "historical Jesus" pale beside this faith. This Jesus is a living Lord. It is his character that shapes that of his people. He gave himself for us in his death and he lives for us in his resurrection. He is on our side. Unearned suffering is not redemptive in and of itself. It is redemptive because Jesus was there first and we are assimilated to him in a way that no one and nothing can defeat. When we make the selfless choice instead of the selfish one, it is not a reflection of our own goodness. The motive power to live sacrificially derives from the Cross of the Savior who gave himself for us all. The capacity to bear suffering for others comes to us by grace through faith in the One who keeps his promises and is waiting for us at our end. For the Lord Jesus Christ himself, by the power of the Spirit, is the content of our character.

AMEN.

Transformation into Christ

NOTE TO READERS: this sermon was preached at
the institution of Anne Ryder as rector of Christ Church in
Sheffield, Massachusetts. This small church is noteworthy because
it has remained healthy when many parishes in the area have died.
Its preservation is a living witness to the power of God
working through strong leadership.

Be transformed by the renewing of your mind.

ROMANS 12:1-21

It is my great privilege and high calling tonight to bring the gospel message in the context of the celebration of Annie Ryder's new ministry. This congregation has loved the gospel message for a long time. I grant you that this love is a restrained Yankee sort of love, but it is no coincidence, I think, that since I first started coming here in 1982, you have had two and now three outstanding rectors who are deeply committed Christians. This is more unusual than you might think. It is a great gift from God, and this suggests that you have a distinctive calling. Our second text tonight is from chapter 12 of St. Paul's letter to the Romans. This passage will help us to reflect on what your calling might be — for this service is not really for Annie so much as it is for you, the members of this branch of the Lord's Church.

This is the week in which we commemorate All Saints and All Souls. On All Souls Day — which we are observing tonight — it is right to remember that of all the many writers in the Bible, it is the apostle Paul in Romans (with Second Isaiah close behind) who holds out in chapter 11 the largest vision of the redemption of those who are *outside* the visible Church. Paul gets so much bad press from people who do not understand him that it is important to acknowledge the truly radical nature of his message in chapters 9–11.

Our special reading from Romans, chapter 12, comes right after chapter 11. You may say "duh" to that, but what's important for us is not the sequence of *numbers* but the sequence of *thought.* Verse one of chapter 12, as you can see, begins with these words: "I appeal to you *therefore.* . . ." As some wag has said, "What is the 'therefore' there for?" The word *therefore* holds the clue to everything that follows. What Paul has already said reveals the meaning of what comes next. How then are we going to review the meaning of 11 chapters of the most densely packed, most demanding yet also — historically — the most revolutionary book of the Bible? And what difference will it make to us?

Today is All Souls Day, but what we have here is more an All Saints text, because this is a description of the saints. That is to say, it is a description of you. You are the saints. We are the saints. The Church is made up of the saints, not individual exceptional "saintly" people, but a collective body of flawed and sinful people *to whom something has happened.* When we read and remember this text, we remember together those things that have happened *to* us, and *for* us. That's the "therefore" that makes all the difference. That's what makes chapter 12 a reality. God's plan, outlined in chapters 1–11, is to expand the reach of his salvation through Jesus Christ beyond any conventionally religious boundaries that we can draw. Because this is so, we need always to be mindful of our special role in his plan, to be the image of Christ for those who do not yet know him. Chapter 12 is all about that special role.

With all due respect to a favorite hymn, there is a problem with "I sing a song of the saints of God." I go back a few decades in the Episcopal Church, and I well remember how, when I first started going to General Convention long ago, the big arguments in those days were about the Prayer Book and the Hymnal. That particular hymn was going to be removed from the new hymnal, but so many people protested that it was restored. What was the argument about?

A number of theologically astute people pointed out that there were some problems with the refrain. You remember how it goes. It lists various people who we meet in church, in school, in lanes, in shops, in trains or at tea (it's a very English hymn!) and then the refrain:

> They were all of them saints of God,
> And I mean, God helping, to be one too.

What's wrong with that? Well, all the emphasis is on the "I," as in "I mean to be one too." Now admittedly there is that phrase, "God helping," but it sounds decidedly secondary. The acting subject of the sentence is the "I." It sounds as if sainthood is a future condition that that *I, we, you* can attain some day if we just try hard enough. But this is not at all what our Scriptures tell us. It is the purpose of *God* that is primary, not what we have made up our minds to do. Saints are made in spite of themselves, by the action of the Holy Spirit. That is what has happened to us. Listen to what Paul says in chapter 6:

> We were buried therefore with him by baptism into death, so that as Christ was raised from the dead by the glory of the Father, we too might walk in newness of life. (Romans 6:4)

Who is doing all of that? God. We don't walk in newness of life because we "mean to," or intend to. We are not raised from the dead because we mean to be, or intend to be. We are not embraced by the Father's glory because we mean to be or intend to be. We are raised from death into the eternal life of God because *God* means it, *God* intends it, *God* does it. You might not have noticed it, but God is the subject of most of the sentences in the Bible. God is the chief actor, and what God begins, God brings to completion. That is one of the most important themes of Romans, and indeed of Scripture as a whole.

The letter to the Romans and all of Paul's other letters are about power. God is powerful to keep his promises and he gives power to the Church. The "therefore" is about power. You might think that Christianity is about the renunciation of power and that is true, but the renunciation of power for Christ's sake is an alternative mode of power. This is so important that I wish I could write it in flame. Paul describes this alternative power toward the end of chapter 12:

> If your enemy is hungry, feed him; if he is thirsty, give him drink; for by so doing you will heap burning coals upon his head.

The United States government is presently involved in a battle about the treatment of Iraqi and Afghan prisoners. "Detainee" is not the right word. A person completely in your power is a prisoner. The Senate voted 90 to 9 in favor of Senator McCain's resolution to place limits on the harsh treatment of prisoners, but Cheney and Rumsfeld say they don't want their "hands tied." A letter to the editor this week observed that the Geneva Conventions were supposed to refer to "normal enemies," but, the letter-writer went on, "Al Qaeda is not a normal enemy." When Jesus explicitly expressed his special concern for prisoners and said "Love your enemies," did he mean, "Love only your normal enemies"?

That is a serious question. How are we supposed to become lovers of our enemies? By "meaning to"?

In Romans 12, Paul is describing the saints. It is more like a description than an exhortation; the time-honored way of describing Paul's message is, "Become what you already are!" By the power of the Holy Spirit in the Church, *God creates* a different kind of person, a person who fits this description:

> Let love be genuine; hate what is evil, hold fast to what is good; love one another with mutual affection; outdo one another in showing honor. Do not lag in zeal, be ardent in spirit, serve the Lord. Rejoice in hope, be patient in suffering, persevere in prayer. Contribute to the needs of the saints [All Saints]; extend hospi-

tality to strangers [All Souls]. Bless those who persecute you; bless and do not curse them.

Bless those who persecute you; bless and do not curse them. Are you that kind of person? Am I? Is America behaving like a Christian nation according to this description? Are the Christian churches making themselves heard about this? Paul says, "Hate what is evil," yes, but further on in chapter 12 we find these words, "Vengeance is mine, saith the Lord, I will repay." And again, "Do not be overcome by evil, but overcome evil with good." Does that describe the typical Christian congregation? Again, a serious question.

People persist in talking about the "good guys" and the "bad guys," in movies and in life. The great virtue of J. R. R. Tolkien's book *The Lord of the Rings* is that it illustrates how the so-called "good guys" are susceptible to evil just like the so-called "bad guys."[1] This is the human predicament, as Paul describes it in Romans 7:

I do not understand my own actions. For I do not do what I want, but I do the very thing I hate. . . . So then it is no longer I that do it, but [the power of] sin which dwells within me.

Surely we can all recognize this. It is a description of the struggle of the godly person against his or her own worst impulses. But we are not left to our own resources in this predicament. Something has changed. The entire Christian message is grounded in the biblical announcement that God has done a new thing and will continue to do a new thing. The Church is continually being conformed to the mind of Christ. Listen again to our text:

I appeal to you therefore, brothers and sisters, by the mercies of God, to present your bodies as a living sacrifice, holy and acceptable to God, which is your spiritual worship. Do not be con-

1. I mentioned Tolkien because a program on the subject was being offered locally.

formed to this world, but be transformed by the renewing of your minds, so that you may discern what is the will of God.

Now, if you read this passage without the "therefore," you would think that the transformation Paul is speaking about is all up to us, that this is something that we manage by means of our own can-do attitude ("I mean to be one too"). On the contrary, there is a sense in which this transformation comes into being among us without our even realizing it. When you see this happen, you can't fail to recognize it, but often the transformed person does not know where the new power came from.

I am going to tell you a story about one of the saints, a very ordinary woman in many ways. I tell it in honor of Rosa Parks, an extraordinary witness to God's transformation, who died last week. The woman of whom I am speaking was a member of the tiny Episcopal church in Franklin, Virginia, where I grew up, almost exactly the size of this one. I always walk in the Franklin cemetery when I am there, to commune with my father and my grandparents and everybody I ever knew in town. One of the burial plots contains the grave of a young man. His father and mother are buried beside him. It is this mother of whom I speak. Her son's car was struck by another car, which happened to be full of intoxicated joyriding black youths. Now you have to understand the mood in rigidly segregated Southside, Virginia, fifty years ago. There was a real dread of the loss of what was called The Southern Way of Life, and there was a massive projection of that dread onto a vulnerable, downtrodden, formerly enslaved population. Northerners should not necessarily think of themselves as superior to this sort of thing; we are all susceptible to speaking and thinking disparagingly of minority groups and people whom we do not understand, or wish to keep at arm's length. In any case, I have never forgotten how the dead young man's grieving mother, some weeks after the accident, sat in my parents' living room having tea with my mother. This was a woman like most of the other white women in town — churchgoing, deeply devout, Bible-reading, brought up from infancy to be a segregationist and white-supremacist. She said this:

"I don't know why I don't hate those drunken colored people. I don't know why. I just don't."

It was clear to me, sitting there as a still-impressionable young adult, that she was hinting at the action of *another power* upon her mind:

> Do not be conformed to this world, but be transformed by the re-newing of your mind, so you may discern what is the will of God.

Again, unless you remember the *therefore,* it is not clear that this transformation and renewing is being done, not by us, but by God through the action of the Spirit.[2] This transformation into what Paul calls *the mind of Christ* (1 Corinthians 2:16) cannot be accomplished by an appeal to human will. It can only be done by the agency of God (to whom we pray, *"Thy* will be done"). Listen to this from Romans 8:

> God has done what the law, weakened by the flesh, could not do: sending his own Son in the likeness of sinful flesh and for sin, God condemned sin in the flesh, in order that the just require-ment of the law might be fulfilled in us, who walk not according to the flesh but according to the Spirit.[3]

If you listen carefully to that in the context of Paul's whole let-ter, you'll see that it's the work of God from beginning to end — as the older Prayer Book says, "all our works [are] begun, continued and ended in thee." It is the work of God that the just requirement of the law is to be fulfilled in us.

The story has a conclusion. The conclusion was one of the clos-est theological moments that my mother and I ever had. After the

2. Paul's use of the passive voice "be transformed" indicates the presence of God's action. The "renewing of your mind" refers to what is already being carried out by the activity of the Spirit. It is God who is doing the renewing. Our part is to recog-nize this and to cooperate with it.

3. We need to remember that when Paul uses the term "flesh" he doesn't mean material flesh; he means the whole sinful human condition. He contrasts "the flesh" with the redeemed condition, called "the Spirit."

visit with our bereaved guest ended, my mother and I cleared away the cups and plates in silence for a few moments. My mother is greatly beloved, but she is also a very brilliant woman with an academic background, and she had always been skeptical about the Baptist piety that prevailed in Franklin, Virginia. She burst out, "I don't see how she can forgive those people! I could never do that!" Another silence. I could almost hear my mother's mind working. Then she said, "Well, I guess I could if God made it happen."[4]

The message of Romans is about the power of God to bring his purposes to pass in spite of the obstacles we put in his way. God's purpose for the little congregations gathered in the name of Christ all over the Mediterranean is described in chapter 12 (as well as many other places in Paul's letters). God's purpose for his people: that is the connection between the story I just told and the celebration of a new ministry. We have all learned, this past year, how dedicated and tireless Annie is to lead *this* little congregation into the mind of Christ and to set an example of service in his Name.

None of us can possibly be satisfied with the world as it is. We want to have things set to rights and we want to be part of that movement. We would like to help. The promise of God is that this is exactly what God intends to do with us. Chapter 12 is a description of God's alternative mode of power. God's power is shown through people as simple and ordinary as Rosa Parks was before she became famous, when she was a loyal member of a very small AME church in Montgomery. It is shown through people like that bereaved mother whose testimony made such an impact on my mother and on me. It is shown through men like the one I read about in the paper a few days ago, the pastor of a little church in New Orleans who is trudging through the mud of the Lower Ninth Ward day after day, giving hope. Small churches can be very big. God is doing this. He can be trusted, not because we need something to believe

---

4. I have told this story once before, in a sermon called "The New Covenant" which is published in my book *The Bible and "The New York Times."* This version is more complete and, I think, closer to the conversation as I remember it, though both versions are essentially truthful.

in (though of course we do need that), *but because he is God.* God is the one who calls Christians of every age and station to walk in newness of life. That is not possible for us, but as our Lord himself said:

> With men it is impossible, but not with God; with God all things are possible. (Mark 10:27; Matthew 19:26)

It is even possible for sinners like you and me to be saints, not tomorrow, but today — because it is God's doing.

Were there to be any doubt about this I call to witness the words of our Lord himself from tonight's Gospel reading:

> You did not choose me, but I chose you and appointed you, that you should go and bear fruit and that your fruit should abide. (John 15:16)

AMEN.

The Twenty-fifth Sunday after Pentecost,
Commemoration of Benefactors and of the War Dead,
Sunday, November 12, 2000

Between the Two Thirteens

Harvard Memorial Chapel

Dedicated to the memory of Paul Louis Lehmann

Do this, understanding the present time.

ROMANS 13:11, NIV

The present crisis in the Electoral College has called forth many re-flections on what it means to be the United States of America.[1] No one last week, to my knowledge, approached the hubris of Mad-eleine Albright when she called America "the indispensable na-tion," but there have been many sober reminders that, in the words of one editorialist, "the world looks to the United States as a model of political stability."[2] And another wrote, "For everyone's sake, American democracy must be seen as being beyond manipulation. The stability of the world rests on that."[3]

Today we remember those whose names are engraved on the wall in the Memorial Room. These Harvard men and women who died for their country have, whether they knew it consciously or not, died for more than their country. Those of us who were young

1. It is hard to remember now, but for two weeks in November 2000 we were not sure who our new president would be.

2. *The New York Times,* November 10, 2000. In light of subsequent events, Ms. Albright now looks much less hubristic than she did in 2000.

3. Thomas L. Friedman, "Original Sin," *The New York Times,* November 10, 2000.

in the late 1960s remember what it was like to be bitterly disen-
chanted with America's role in the world, but nevertheless America,
through something much more like the grace of God than the superior virtue of her citizens, continues to embody the best hopes of the
whole world. Thomas L. Friedman wrote a few days ago about
"what makes America unique in the world"; the more he travels
abroad, he says, the more he appreciates the United States. Even
something as mundane as our Washington bureaucracy is cause for
thanksgiving, he reflected; people in countries like Indonesia and
Nigeria know what it means to be at the mercy of government that
is truly venal and corrupt and soul-killing.[4] Virtually every commentator on television has reminded us to be thankful that "the
tanks are not in the streets." A foreign-born friend said to me the
other day that although America has all sorts of faults, nevertheless
it continues to radiate "a sense of generosity and possibility." Today,
in this service of commemoration, we pause to reflect that this
priceless legacy and solemn responsibility has been bequeathed to
us by those who have gone before us.

A list of benefactors — those who have given particular service
to this University church — will be read today as part of our worship. The list touches me more deeply than I, being a non-Harvard
person, would have expected. On that list are both parents of a close
friend, and also a former rector of the Episcopal church that I served
for fourteen years in New York City — as well as Dr. Ferris of Trinity Church, Copley Square, who has meant so much to me as a
preacher. We give thanks today for such people, for as Dr. Gomes
said in his sermon on this commemoration day four years ago, we
are reminded that "we are not on our own, nor did we get here on
our own, nor is that which we have ours alone, or ours forever. To
give thanks, then, is [to acknowledge] that we are beholden to
someone else."[5]

It is not always so easy, however, to figure out who should be

4. Thomas L. Friedman, "I Love D.C." (Foreign Affairs column), *The New York Times,* November 8, 2000.

5. Peter J. Gomes, "What the Dead Have to Say," November 10, 1996.

honored in this way. The soldier who rescues a comrade from enemy gunfire may not be any more courageous than the paraplegic who is struggling to make a life for himself, or the medical missionary who knows she will be exposed over and over to tropical diseases, or the teacher in the inner-city school who fights for her students' minds and hearts day after day, year after year. There are many kinds of wars, and there are many kinds of war dead. There are many kinds of battles to be fought, and many decisions to be made about when and whether one should enlist. We've all heard the common expression that something is "to die for." This is generally said with regard to some consumer article — the latest in fusion cooking or personal electronics or Manolo Blahnik shoes — they're "to die for." But what *really* is to die for? This week's issue of *The New York Review of Books* has an article by Timothy Garton Ash about the Serbian revolution. He describes his visit to one Serbian town as the mayor and various local citizens were preparing for the trip to Belgrade. Garton Ash asked one of them what the object of his journey was. The "burly former paratrooper" replied that the object was to put Vojislav Kostunica on state television that very night. This day, said the mayor, "We will be free or die."[6]

Another journalist, Misha Glenny, was in Belgrade that day, October 5. As the demonstrators and protesters and freedom fighters poured into the city from the surrounding countryside, he went to Kostunica's headquarters. He was taking notes; realizing that he had forgotten the date, he asked one of the young receptionists what it was. *"Sudnji dan,"* she replied: Judgment Day.[7] The next morning the whole world saw the images of the smoke going up from the Parliament building. My mind went immediately to the nineteenth chapter of the book of Revelation where the wicked city is destroyed and the multitude in heaven exults, "Hallelujah! The smoke from her goes up for ever and ever" (19:3).

---

6. Timothy Garton Ash, "The Last Revolution," *The New York Review of Books,* November 16, 2000.

7. Misha Glenny, "The Redeemers," *The New Yorker,* October 30, 2000.

This morning we have before us two biblical texts, Romans 13 and Revelation 13. These two passages have quite a history of being brought together and allowed to speak to one another. I would be surprised if many of you didn't flinch when you heard the Romans passage read a few minutes ago. "Let every person be subject to the governing authorities. For there is no authority except from God, and those that exist have been instituted by God. Therefore he who resists the authorities resists what God has appointed, and those who resist will incur judgment." This text has been used over the centuries to justify every conceivable kind of oppression and tyranny. It has also been used to stifle criticism of "the powers that be" and to resist any effort at reform. This passage has been quoted at Sojourner Truth and Martin Luther King and the liberation theologians of Latin America. To most people who hang around places like Harvard, the passage sounds repressive. That was not always so, however. Until the Nazi era, most citizens were perfectly happy to acquiesce in this assessment. As Hitler rose to power, however, the German Lutheran pastor Dietrich Bonhoeffer found himself forced to rethink all that he had previously taken for granted. Sometimes it was necessary, he mused, "not just to bandage the victims under the wheel, but to put a spoke in the wheel itself. Such action would be direct political action."[8] Pastor Bonhoeffer himself became the spoke; he was hanged by the Nazis in April 1945. Exercising the spiritual gift called *discernment,* he had chosen direct political action against the Beast of Revelation 13.[9]

Discernment, wrote the Christian lay theologian William Stringfellow, "is basic to the genius of the Biblical life style."

> This gift enables the people of God to distinguish and recognize, identify and expose, report and rebuke the power of death in nations and institutions . . . while they also affirm the Word

8. *No Rusty Swords* (New York: Harper & Row, 1965).

9. *Aisthēsis* (Philippians 1:9, Hebrews 4:14) is "the power of moral discrimination and ethical judgment" (*Theological Dictionary of the New Testament,* vol. 1 [Grand Rapids: Eerdmans, 1964], p. 188).

of God incarnate in all of life, exemplified preeminently in Jesus Christ. . . . This [discernment] is the gift which exposes and rebukes idolatry. This is the gift which confounds and undoes blasphemy.[10]

The juxtaposition of Romans 13 and Revelation 13 calls for discernment. At this time of remembrance, at this time of suspense in our national life, at this season of the church calendar when one liturgical year comes to an end and the great season of Advent approaches, the community that gathers around the Word of God reflects on the next portion of Romans 13: "You know what hour it is, how it is full time now for you to wake from sleep" (Romans 13:11), or as the Revised English Bible translates, "Always remember that this is the hour of crisis." The word for "hour" in New Testament Greek is *kairos,* which is distinguished from *chronos,* ordinary time. To discern the *kairos* is to see through the events of the day to perceive the activity of God in and through those events.

But what is meant by the "hour of crisis," or *kairos?* There was a full-page advertisement in the Friday *New York Times,* paid for by media figures like Rosie O'Donnell and Robert de Niro, writers like Toni Morrison and E. L. Doctorow, academic stars like Peter Gay and Ronald Dworkin; it states that we are in an "election crisis" which threatens to become a "constitutional crisis." Leaving aside the question about whether the present situation really is a crisis or not, is this the kind of *kairos* that St. Paul has in mind?[11] What exactly does he mean by these words in Romans 13 (and by the way, this is the passage always associated with the first Sunday of Advent, now only three weeks away):

. . . you know what hour it is, how it is full time now for you to wake from sleep. For salvation is nearer to us now than when we

10. *An Ethic for Christians and Other Aliens in a Strange Land* (Waco, TX: Word Books, 1973), p. 139.

11. It is no accident that the New Testament Greek word *krisis* refers to a distinction, as between time and eternity or death and life, which calls for judgment and decision, and is thus related to *kairos.*

first believed; the night is far gone, the day is at hand. Let us then cast off the works of darkness and put on the armor of light . . . put on the Lord Jesus Christ. (Romans 13:11-13)

What does this mean, and what does it have to do with the earlier part of the chapter about honoring the government?

What Paul means is that the coming of Christ into the world, his crucifixion by the powers and principalities, his Resurrection from the dead, and his coming in the future have overturned all previous perspectives upon human life in this world.[12] The section in Romans 13 about the government sounds like ordinary conservative rhetoric about bowing down before the powers that be until you see it in its context. Our text is bracketed by, on the front end, Paul's radical world-displacing call, "Do not be conformed to this age" (New American Bible) and on the back end by "you know what hour it is . . . the night is far gone, the day is at hand." For most of the twentieth century, these dramatic texts have been the companions of Christians who have struggled against tyranny and oppression. Romans 13 in its context and Revelation 13 matched with it have created an extraordinary dialectic for reading the signs of the times.

William Stringfellow wrote a commentary on the book of Revelation. I once heard him say, "We have been sold a bill of goods on Revelation. I don't think it is such a difficult book." Elisabeth Schüssler Fiorenza of the Harvard Divinity School doesn't think so either. Much of her life's work has been focused on Revelation. Here is something she wrote:

> The present time [and by that she means any present time that we might find ourselves in] is of critical importance because a cosmic-political struggle has ensued with the death and exaltation of Christ. Revelation seeks to encourage Christians to participate actively in this struggle, the outcome of which is already

---

12. Paul Louis Lehmann, *The Transfiguration of Politics* (New York: Harper & Row, 1975), p. 37 and passim.

known . . . a qualitatively new earth will be the outcome of this struggle, a world that is free from all dehumanizing oppressive powers.[13]

In our own day and in my own denomination, the person whose life is most closely associated with this perspective from Revelation is Archbishop Desmond Tutu of South Africa, one of the heroes of the struggle against apartheid. In the dark days of that evil system, Bishop Tutu, with a large band of demonstrators and activists, was attempting to meet with government officials. This was not permitted, so they proceeded to the cathedral where they had a worship service. Standing ranks of police lined the walls, keeping a wary eye on the congregation. An eyewitness reported that, as his sermon gathered steam, Bishop Tutu suddenly looked out directly at the police. "You have already lost!" he cried. "We are inviting you to come and join the winning side!"[14] I don't need to tell you who was free and who was in chains that day. It was said also of Bob Moses, the charismatic leader of Freedom Summer in Mississippi, 1963, that he drove the white segregationists absolutely crazy because he persisted in behaving as though he were already free — even though he could have been shot at any time. Similarly, Adam Michnik, the intellectual leader of the Solidarity movement, wrote these words from prison during the struggle against Communism: "How has our nation been able to transcend the dilemma so typical of defeated societies, the hopeless choice between servility and despair? It seems that the Polish nation does not think it has been defeated."[15] This is the courage of those who have seen through the phenomena of the present age into the new world that the letters of Paul and the book of Revelation bring before us.

It is common to contrast Romans 13 with Revelation 13 as

13. Elisabeth Schüssler Fiorenza, *Revelation: Vision of a Just World,* Proclamation Commentaries (Minneapolis: Fortress Press, 1991).

14. Told by Jim Wallis in his new book *Faith Works* (New York: Random House, 2000).

15. Adam Michnik, "Letter from the Gdansk Prison," *The New York Review of Books,* July 18, 1985.

though they were total opposites. According to this understanding, if the governing authority is benign, then it is from God and Christians should obey it (Romans 13). If the governing authority turns oppressive, then it is Satanic and we should resist it (Revelation 13). This is the most familiar interpretation of the two texts. No better formulation of it exists than that of Bishop Oscar Romero of El Salvador, shot in the back at his own altar. In a sermon he said, "Let it be quite clear that if we are being asked to collaborate with a pseudo-peace, a false order, based on repression and fear, we must recall that the only order God wants is one based on truth and justice."[16]

As certain other commentators have pointed out, however, the relation between the two passages is even more subtle and more radical than the familiar interpretation allows.[17] *Both* of the passages call government into question because *both* of them make clear that government is only provisional. Neither Paul nor Revelation give ultimate legitimacy to any human institution. Once we know this, it keeps us from taking any present arrangement with anything more than temporary seriousness. So what Paul is saying is that we should take the government seriously, and we should not take it seriously. It's like that passage in 1 Corinthians 7 where Paul says *as though not* several times:

> I mean, brothers and sisters, the appointed time *(kairos)* has grown very short; from now on, let those . . . who mourn live as though they were not mourning, and those who rejoice as though they were not rejoicing, and those who buy as though they had no goods, and those who deal with the world as though they had no dealings with it. For the form of this age is passing away. (1 Corinthians 7:29-31)

16. Sermon, July 1, 1979.

17. E.g., John Howard Yoder *(The Politics of Jesus),* Vernard Eller *(Christian Anarchy: Christ's Victory Over the Powers),* Will D. Campbell and James Y. Holloway *(Up to Our Steeples in Politics),* William Stringfellow *(An Ethic for Christians and Other Aliens in a Strange Land),* Hendrikus Berkhof *(Christ and the Powers),* and Jacques Ellul *(The Ethics of Freedom* and various other works).

That may sound like the ultimate ethic of disengagement, but it isn't. It is the opposite. It means that we can enter into the challenges of the day with a kind of joyful confidence, knowing that the future belongs to the Lord. It is not our part to bring that future about. God is doing that. Our part is to discern the signs of what God is already doing and to take up our positions there, knowing that God's future of human liberty and human wholeness is, truly, to live for and, if necessary, "to die for." Wherever God is on the move, that is where we want to be.

As the whole world knows, Mr. Kostunica did appear on state television in Belgrade that night, and he called out, "Good evening, dear liberated Serbia!" It was a moment for the history books, as Garton Ash observed; the *kairos* had been seized. The beast from the sea had been overthrown. How shall America now respond? What we can do for the Balkans now, and for the Middle East, and for the developing nations, is to be the very best America that we can be — now more than ever. You and I most likely are not going to be called upon to die for what American democracy means for the world, but we may surely live for it. A few days ago, there was an obituary in the *Times* for a Harvard Law graduate, a man named Joseph F. Haas. He was a prominent leader of the Voter Education Project, which gave powerful support to the voter registration movement in Mississippi and made the Civil Rights Act of 1965 possible. Vernon Jordan was quoted in the obituary: "In the South in those days, you knew who the stand-up men and women were in the white community, and he was one of them."[18] Joseph Haas is one of a host of witnesses who discerned the *kairos* and went to take their positions on the front lines where God was — and is — at work to create a new reality for America. May the God of justice and mercy grant each of us the courage and faith to do the same in our own time.

AMEN.

18. Obituary, *The New York Times*, November 8, 2000.

September 11, 2005

Weak and Strong After Katrina

TEXTS: PSALM 6; ROMANS 14:7-13; MATTHEW 18:21-35

None of us could have imagined, a few days ago, that today's fourth anniversary of the attacks on September 11, 2001, would be overshadowed by another catastrophe very different in its causes but maybe not so different in the enormity of its effects. I am not going to dwell on anything personal this morning except to say that I have a deep emotional attachment to two particular cities in the United States, and those two are New York and New Orleans. I have more good friends in New Orleans than in any other city anywhere, and a good deal of my time this past week has been spent trying to communicate with them.

Some of the service this morning has been designed to reflect on the aftermath of Hurricane Katrina. The concluding hymn is a prayer to our Eternal Father who "bids the mighty ocean deep/its own appointed limits keep" — or not, as the case may be.[1] Psalm 6, which we just read, is not the one appointed for today. Let me explain why. There was an article in *The New York Times* about the scene in the Houston Astrodome as the evacuees poured in. The reporter observed a black woman, Cecile Conway, age 44, who swam

---

1. Anyone interested in pursuing this problem is urged to get hold of *The Doors of the Sea: Where Was God in the Tsunami?* (Grand Rapids: Eerdmans, 2005) by theologian David B. Hart. This brief but profound book is an expansion of a column in *The Wall Street Journal* that Dr. Hart, a young Eastern Orthodox theologian, wrote after the devastating tsunami in the Indian Ocean.

[385]

to safety but lost track of family members. Ms. Conway sat on her cot in the Astrodome reading the Bible, marking Psalm 6 with green pencil for emphasis (and using the King James Version as so many African-Americans still do):

> O Lord, rebuke me not in thine anger, neither chasten me in
>   thy hot displeasure.
> Have mercy upon me, O Lord; for I am weak:
>   O Lord, heal me; for my bones are vexed.
> My soul is also sore vexed: but thou, O Lord — how long?
> Return, O Lord, deliver my soul: oh save me for thy mercies'
>   sake.
>
> (Psalm 6:1-4)

The reporter notes this woman and her Bible reading and then passes on to something else.[2]

Studies have shown that journalists, as a group, are among the least religious of all Americans. When I read the article I wondered what this particular reporter thought about Psalm 6. Context means so much, doesn't it? Think for a moment about how we read this Psalm in our worship a few minutes ago. I don't know about you, but it is my impression that most Episcopalians go through the Psalms each Sunday as a matter of habit, without paying very much attention to the words. But imagine yourself as a person suddenly without a home, without family, having spent four days in the hellish Superdome and now, marooned, sitting on a cot with thousands of other people and no privacy in a strange city — and you are reading this Psalm. It has a different urgency in those circumstances, doesn't it? You search the words for a message that might mean the difference between *life with* or *life without* hope. In such an extreme situation, it would make a great deal of difference to you to know whether these words from Scripture are truly a message from the living God.

---

2. Ralph Blumenthal, "Astrodome an Orderly Host to Its Restless Guests," *The New York Times,* September 11, 2005.

The Bible is not just a religious book among other religious books. Unless it is lying to us, it is the Word of God. This is not the time to get into a discussion about exactly *how* it is the Word of God. The thing that counts is the claim of the Church, the claim of the Bible itself from first page to last, that the God who is *really God* has *really spoken* to us through this Word and that it can be trusted because he is trustworthy. The Christian faith stands or falls on that. The ministry of preaching stands or falls on that. If this Word is not in some real sense *from God,* then sermons preached on Sunday morning are nothing more than inspirational human thoughts, and you don't have to come to church to get those.

In our two New Testament lessons today, the Lord of heaven and earth tells us of his pity and mercy for those who are unfortunate and needy. He also delivers some strong words about those who are privileged and well-connected. It takes a little bit of effort to see this, however, particularly in the Romans text, so let's take another look. The reading for today comes in the context of Paul's discussion about "the strong" and "the weak." He is referring specifically to those who are weak in faith and strong in faith, but the meaning can be extended. He wants his congregations to understand that all their members, whether weak or strong, are in the same position before God "without distinction" (Romans 3:22). Furthermore, he wants us to know that each of us and all of us are knit together in the Lord in a way that cannot be humanly undone. "None of us lives to himself, and none of us dies to himself. If we live, we live to the Lord, and if we die, we die to the Lord" (Romans 14:7-8). More than any other biblical writer, Paul is explicit about the radical leveling of human distinctions that has occurred in Christ. He writes,

> Why do you pass judgment on your brother? Or you, why do you despise your brother? For we shall all stand before the judgment seat of God. . . . Then let us no more pass judgment on one another, but rather decide never to put a stumbling block or hindrance in the way of a brother. (Romans 14:10, 13)

If we think about it, all of us are under the judgment of this passage. How many times have I put a stumbling block in front of someone else, including quite probably some of you who are here today? More times than I can count. More times than I am even aware of. That's why it's so important to hold to the promise of God's Word. "As I live, says the Lord, every knee shall bow to me, and every tongue shall give praise to God." We will not be able to escape from the judgment and mercy of God even if we spend our whole lives trying.

The parable that Jesus tells in the Gospel lesson is quite shocking, and, like so many of his parables, it is meant to be shocking. We are meant to identify at first with the man whose debt (and it is a colossal debt) is forgiven. That's why the details are there about how he is to be sold into slavery "with his wife and his children and all that he had" (Matthew 18:25). We are meant to feel for him as he falls on his knees and begs. We are happy to hear that the master releases him and forgives the debt. The parable illustrates the mercy of God. Indeed, the words *mercy, pity,* and *forgiveness* are repeated several times throughout the parable. That should be the end of the story, shouldn't it? But no. Shockingly, the servant who was forgiven turns brutally against another man, a "fellow servant" as the text significantly identifies him, who owes him a much smaller sum, and refuses to show mercy to him. If we are listening to this story from the point of view of the self-righteous (which is the normal human point of view) we will be indignant and disgusted with the first servant. If we are listening to the story with a baptized mind, however, from the point of view of the Holy Spirit, we will recognize *ourselves. We* are the ones who owe our Lord everything, as a result of his utterly gratuitous mercy, yet we are also the ones who pick and choose among our fellows as to who we think is deserving and who is undeserving.

This picking and choosing, this assigning of persons to categories of worthy and unworthy of our compassion, is going on right now in the national debate about the human cataclysm in New Orleans. In an all-white, upper-middle-class congregation like this one,[3] many of us — even those who have worked hard at building

[388]

relationships with poor people — will admit that the sight of all those impoverished African-American people at the Superdome and the Convention Center caused all sorts of unChristian thoughts to pop into our heads. We didn't mean to have these thoughts; they just arrived, unbidden — thoughts like, "Maybe they brought this on themselves by being poor, indolent, overweight, illiterate. Maybe they're constitutionally disposed to go out and loot stores. Maybe this is the everlasting lot of black people." And then there are others who do not have these thoughts. They consider themselves to be "the strong." They are able to be smug about their liberalism because they have never had any significant contact with poor, badly educated black people and do not have any idea how much patience and hard work it takes to communicate across class and cultural, never mind racial, lines. Paul has his tongue halfway in his cheek when he writes about the strong and the weak, because before God we are *all* weak. Before God, we are *all* under judgment. In God's sight, we *all* fit the words of the Psalm: "I am languishing. . . . O Lord, heal me, for my bones are troubled. My soul also is sorely troubled. . . ." We are *all* afflicted with the sickness unto death and in need of the Lord's healing. When we realize that, it is the most liberating thing you can imagine. It means we can let go of our pretensions to be "the strong" and we can align ourselves with "the weak" who know their need of God.

Of the many affecting scenes on television from the first week of the Katrina aftermath, there were two in particular that haunt me. They were similar interviews with two different black women, one young and one older. Each of them were in their fourth or fifth day of living like animals in the streets. The younger one, crying uncontrollably, was offered one of those Meals Ready to Eat. She sobbed, "I want to go home. I want to eat my own food. This is not the way we live." (Note the word *we.*) The older woman was especially arresting in her dignity; she was filthy, she was disheveled, she spoke ungrammatically, but when she said through tears, "We don't live like this," it seemed that she was speaking for her whole

3. Or, for that matter, an upper-middle-class African-American congregation.

community of people who, though dirt-poor and sometimes barely literate, nevertheless worked hard to keep a semblance of decency and joy in their lives. She was speaking for thousands who kept their floors swept, their plants watered, their cooking pots clean, and their Mardi Gras decorations in boxes from year to year. These are not people who go to the bathroom in the street, who eat with hands unwashed for days, who live below the divide between the deserving and the undeserving.

As many of the best articles about New Orleans have observed, this is a city which is as much as 80 percent native. Perhaps more than in any other American city, the people of New Orleans have preserved their traditions and their history among themselves for generations. And there is something else. Among my many friends there is a woman who, though not a native, has lived for two decades in the Garden District and has grown to love the city deeply. I asked her to talk about its unique qualities. I particularly remember her saying, "The people here understand suffering."

All the more reason that they should not be asked to suffer one day more than we can help. May our Lord walk among the homeless of the Gulf Coast, but even more, may he open the hearts of all those who have known his mercy to help our fellow servants to arrive some day at a time when their traditions and histories will include these words from our Lord's lips: I was hungry, and you gave me food; I was thirsty, and you gave me a drink; homeless, and you brought me home again. That mercy lies at the heart of what our Savior Jesus Christ has already done for every one of us.[4]

AMEN.

---

4. At least two members of this congregation known to me, Dennis Sears and Grace Arnt, have adult children who have gone to aid the relief effort on the Gulf Coast. My own daughter has also gone.

Wednesday, June 19, 1985

Judgment and Grace

GRACE CHURCH IN NEW YORK

NOTE TO THE READER: This sermon comes from the specific context of the years 1975 to the late 1980s at Grace Church.

We shall all stand before the judgment seat of God.

ROMANS 14:10

We must all appear before the judgment seat of Christ.

2 CORINTHIANS 5:10

One of the wonderful things about working at Grace Church is that so many people in our congregation are young and fresh; I love that aspect of life here. A consequence of this, though, is that we don't have as much shared history as many congregations do. I remember when I first arrived here in 1981, only a year after Fitz Allison had left.[1] To me, Fitz was almost a legendary figure; the reason I wanted to work here was that I wanted to be part of the renewal that God began through him. One of the first things I did that September was to visit a prayer group. Imagine my amazement when one of the prayer group members said, "Who is this Fitz?" It turned out that fully half of the members of that group had come in after he had

1. The rector had left to become the Episcopal Bishop of South Carolina.

[391]

left. And, of course, this is a wonderful thing — the best legacy that any rector can bequeath.

So, many of you probably haven't been here long enough to remember what it was like at Grace Church five or six years ago. (I wasn't working here then, but I was around a lot.) It was as if the jailhouse doors had been thrown open. It was as if all the hostages in the world had been freed. It was as if the most ghastly burden had been lifted forever. People were pouring in the doors to hear for the first time that they were freely justified in Christ by the grace of God alone, that in Jesus Christ "there is now no condemnation" (Romans 8:1). People were hearing for the first time that "while we were still sinners, Christ died for us" (Romans 5:8). Every week from the pulpit, the great news was proclaimed: "A person is not justified by works of the law but through faith in Christ Jesus" (Galatians 2:16). It was like breathing pure oxygen every week: "God, who is rich in mercy . . . even when we were dead through out trespasses, made us alive together with Christ — by grace you have been saved" (Ephesians 2:4-5)! This is the pristine gospel, and whenever it is announced, people will hear it with joy, because it is the news of our deliverance from every form of condemnation or exclusion, from every judgment that others cast upon us, from every lurking suspicion of inferiority or unworthiness that we cast upon ourselves.

During the last two or three years, we have continued to preach and practice this gospel of grace, and it remains central for us. It would be fair to say, however, that we have also been wrestling with the working-out of this gospel in our community life, so that the message probably does not fall on our ears with quite so much regularity and purity as it once did. My guess is that many of you came into the congregation when that "first fine careless rapture" was beginning to wear off as we settled in to the daily business of being God's people in the midst of a sick world. Still, if you can imagine what that early intoxication was like, you can imagine this experience I had when I first arrived in the congregation.

I knew all about the atmosphere of grace and freedom here, because I had drunk deeply from that spring myself, and its truth remains "new every morning." Needless to say, though, I was eager to teach and preach on some of the biblical themes that excited me, and, as Advent was approaching, it was natural to speak about the apocalyptic framework of the New Testament, and in order to do *that,* it was necessary to mention the Last Judgment. I wonder if you can conceive of the wrath and indignation that came down on my head in November 1981 for having mentioned the subject of judgment! All the young people in our congregation were here because they had heard the incomparable message of *freedom* from judgment, *freedom* from condemnation, *freedom* from the fearful sentence of crushing guilt. I will never forget one young woman coming up to me after a class and setting me straight: "At Grace Church, we don't believe in judgment."

Well, now, seriously: if "there is now no condemnation for those who are in Christ Jesus," what are we to make of these frightening verses from 2 Corinthians and from Romans?

"We must all appear before the judgment seat of Christ."

"We shall all stand before the judgment seat of God."

It must have been very important to St. Paul or he would not have said it twice in almost the same words. It was important to Jesus, too; he speaks frequently of his own role as the one to whom God will give the power of final judgment in the last day. The most famous of these sayings of Jesus, of course, is in Matthew 25 where he says that the Son of man will come in his glory and "will sit on his glorious throne. . . . Before him will be gathered all the nations, and he will separate them one from another . . . the sheep on his right hand but the goats on the left." I doubt if there is anyone here who has not known the feeling of dread that this picture evokes, the fear of not "making the cut."

"Before him will be gathered *all* the nations." St. Paul says this too — "We will *all* appear before the judgment seat of Christ" — all who have ever lived, Christians and non-Christians alike. I don't care what sort of passionate believers we are, this has got to strike us with some sort of holy fear. Think of the words we heard a few moments ago — "Almighty God, to whom all hearts are open, all desires known, and from whom no secrets are hid . . ." — if that doesn't make us tremble, then we don't yet know God. To stand before God means to be laid open, to be stripped, to be openly revealed in the full and true reality of one's character; all our hypocrisies and concealments will be open to the scrutiny of Christ.[2]

St. Paul, in writing "We shall all stand before the judgment seat of Christ," wants us to understand with the greatest possible clarity that being a Christian does not mean escaping to a safe corner where we can clutch all our self-indulgence to our bosoms forever while only the bad people, the terrorists and murderers and people who don't believe in the grace of God, await a reckoning. There is a famous phrase of Martin Luther which was almost as important to the 1970s Grace Church renewal as the Epistle to the Romans: we are *simul peccator et justus* — saints and sinners simultaneously. Our sinful self (the old man, or the old nature, St. Paul calls it) will come under the final judgment of God and will be destroyed, and this will not be without pain to us, not without cost. It will be the purgation of which the prophet Malachi wrote: "The Lord whom you seek will suddenly come to his temple. . . . But who can abide the day of his coming? And who shall stand when he appears? For he is like a refiner's fire" (Malachi 3:1-2). Only if we are laid open to Jesus' refining fire are we enabled "to present right offerings to the Lord" (Malachi 3:3).

So Paul urges the Christians of Rome and Corinth to understand that "we must all appear before the judgment seat of Christ" for an intensely practical reason. It is in the daily, prayerful acknowledgment of our sinfulness, the continual willingness to be laid open by the divine Surgeon, that the Christian community is purified for its task. So it is not in *escaping* judgment that we are truly free, but in willingness to *come before* God's judgment, in solidarity with our brothers and sisters. As the German pastor Christoph Blumhardt writes,

2. Philip E. Hughes, *The Second Epistle to the Corinthians,* New International Commentary on the New Testament (Grand Rapids: Eerdmans, 1962), p. 180.

There are parties in Christendom who are already rejoicing that they will be transfigured and float up to heaven and then will laugh at the poor people left behind. But that is not the way it is. Now is the time to take upon ourselves a work in which *we* are the first to be given into judgment, not the first to have a sofa in heaven. For only those who are truly first, first to stand before the Savior in judgment, can become tools to further his work among the rest of mankind.[3]

But how can we stand before the fiery judgment? How can we come in our "filthy rags" as the prophet Isaiah writes?[4] How can we come before the pure righteousness of the one great judge?

Only this morning, as if dropped out of the blue — only, of course, not really — I received in the mail a picture from Mehrdad Abidari who used to work here as a seminarian. I think about two years ago he promised to send me this picture and I had forgotten all about it until it arrived in the mail this morning. It's a very small painting by Honoré Daumier, the French artist. The painting is called *Le Pardon (The Pardon)* — perhaps better translated by "acquittal." It shows a French courtroom. On the left are the three judges according to the Napoleonic law, sitting in their black robes; they do not really look like individuals, but rather like faceless figures of condemnation. (There is nothing I fear more than this image. In my worst dreams, there are men in black robes glaring at me, preparing to judge me.) Over here are the spectators and the jury. Here is the wretched defendant. And here, a little larger than life, is the defense attorney, also in a black robe with white tabs. He is pointing with an elongated finger to something over the head of the judges that the judges do not see. He is pointing to a large painting of the Crucifixion. That is all we see in the painting.

I haven't had time to bone up on the history of this painting,

3. This passage is based on 1 Peter 4:17: "The time has come for judgment to begin with the household of God."
4. "All our righteous deeds are as filthy rags" (Isaiah 64:6).

but I will tell you what I see. I am the defendant. You are the defendant. The Holy Spirit is the defense attorney, the advocate, the Paraclete — that is the real meaning of the term "Comforter." The Holy Spirit, as we have read so many times in the Gospel of John, is the defense attorney who testifies to the Blood of Christ. "Who is to condemn?" St. Paul writes. "Who shall bring any charge against God's elect? If God is for us, who shall be against us? It is God who justifies; who is to condemn? Is it Christ Jesus, who died, yes, who was raised from the dead, who is at the right hand of God, who indeed intercedes for us?" (8:33-34).

We cannot have a complete gospel without judgment. There must be judgment in order for God to make right all that is wrong. It is the *fairness* of God's judgment that Paul wants us to understand. No one escapes it, but the Church takes it on voluntarily for the sake of the whole world. The difference between the Church and the world in this matter is that the Church knows something the world does not know. We know that the judgment of God is completely enclosed in his mercy. This is the good news, the glad tidings that we have been entrusted to share. The words of the Te Deum express it perfectly:

> We believe that thou wilt come to be our Judge;
> We therefore pray thee, help thy servants whom thou hast redeemed with thy precious blood.

There is therefore now no condemnation for those who, like you and me, will surely come before the judgment, yet are safe already in the limitless mercy of Christ Jesus and the boundless purpose of Almighty God (Romans 8:1, 32-34).

AMEN.

Written Out, Written In

GRACE CHURCH IN NEW YORK
TEXT: ROMANS 14:5-12

NOTE TO THE READER: even in these post-9/11 days, New York City seems so vibrant and relatively free of violent crime that it takes some effort to recollect the context in 1990 when this sermon was preached. The theological message, however, remains as pertinent as ever.

In these times of urban chaos and international upheaval, Christianity is being tested in new ways. It has been borne in upon us lately that we no longer live in a Christian culture. We used to, but we don't now. This change has taken place within my lifetime; indeed, it is taking place all around us at this moment. Twenty-five years ago, no one objected to a painting of the Crucifixion hanging on the wall in an upstate school; last month, it was removed by court order. We can no longer assume that anyone in America is going to be a Christian or even that our fellow citizens will share our Judeo-Christian values. This presents a challenge to the Christian church of a sort that is unprecedented in American history.

Those of us who are Christians need to reflect upon our mission. Do we want other people to become Christians? Do we want to commend our faith and way of life to others? or do we just want to enjoy it all to ourselves, in a religious ghetto? Sometimes it seems as though the mainstream Protestant churches, once so powerful in American society, have lost any sense of having anything influential to say or do.

In a time of drastically waning church influence, there is one thing that Christians have left that is still of undeniable power, and that is the name and the person of our Lord Jesus Christ. He alone continues to compel attention. Here is a souvenir program, very lavish and expensive, celebrating "the first fifty years" of American Ballet Theatre. It has photos by Annie Leibovitz, earrings by Tiffany, fashions by Sant' Angelo, and so forth. In the main section, which seems to be imitating the Dewar's Scotch advertisements, the principal dancers answer various questions, one of which is, "Who would be your ideal, once-in-a-lifetime dinner companion?" There are eighteen principal dancers. The dinner companions mentioned once include Steve Martin, Mel Gibson, Bette Davis, Martha Graham, and William Shakespeare. The only person mentioned twice by the eighteen dancers is Diaghilev. No one is mentioned three times. The name that jumps off the page, out of the jewelry and leather and furs and arty photography and all the other names, not once, not twice, not three times, but *four* times is the name of Jesus Christ.

Now what we Christians need to remember is that there are thousands of people out there who would like to meet Jesus but who do not know that Jesus' dinner table is spread at the Eucharist and that Jesus speaks through God's Word preached, and that Jesus makes himself known through his followers. We know from everything our Lord said and did while he was on this earth that it *was* his will — *is* his will — to make himself known precisely through his people, through the Church. This has always been a bit of an embarrassment, but it is God's plan that we should overcome our embarrassment and say with St. Paul in the Epistle to the Romans, "I am not ashamed of the gospel" (1:16).

If people who consider themselves Christians want other people to be drawn to the Lord Jesus Christ, not just to have dinner with but to trust, follow, and obey, then there is one thing necessary, perhaps one thing only: Christians need to demonstrate that they are willing to take judgment upon themselves. We need to do this for a reason, perhaps one reason only: Jesus did it.

Jesus took judgment upon himself. What is more, he took judgment upon himself when he did not deserve it. He took upon himself the judgment that would otherwise have fallen on us, and in so doing he redeemed the world. This is the central proclamation of the Christian gospel. St. Paul writes in Galatians that "Christ became a curse for us" (3:13). The death of Jesus was not a clean, neat, peaceful death; it was a ghastly, humiliating, vile, and godforsaken death. We need to remember that. Crucifixion was specifically designed to show that the person pinned on that wooden apparatus was worth nothing but contempt, disgust, public mortification, and extermination. Crucifixion was not a means of killing, particularly; it was a means of passing judgment on a life. The placard over Jesus' head might as well have said, "Not fit to live." He had been judged by the human community, and, having bowed his head under that judgment, was delivered up by the political and religious authorities to be publicly exhibited as a condemned object. That was the fate to which the Son of God consciously, deliberately, voluntarily gave himself.

Why am I saying these things this morning? It is not even Lent, much less Good Friday. But I found myself led to it by two things: today's Scripture lesson from Romans, and the state of our society.

I don't need to tell you what the state of our society is. Three months ago I reported in a sermon about racism that we were being described as a city on the verge of a nervous breakdown.[1] Everyone I've spoken to agrees that the subway killing of Brian Watkins, who was trying to defend his father and mother, caused a feeling of having been finally pushed over the edge. My mother sent me a clipping from a newspaper in the hinterlands, with a column by somebody named Bob Greene who writes, "It's over for New York. Last week a crime occurred that is destined to become another signature event in the downfall of a once wonderful city. . . . It won't get better. . . . New York is doomed." In former days, such comments from the boonies could be knowingly laughed off. No more. For the first time, the "Metropolitan Diary" section of the *New York Times,* with its happy, encouraging little stories of uniquely New York

1. Article by Joe Klein in *New York* magazine.

street life, seems all but totally irrelevant, even desperate. The "Talk of the Town" this week is not in *The New Yorker,* but in *Time* magazine's cover story — "The Rotting of the Big Apple."[2]

What has struck me the most in the various commentaries is that the sense of being part of a shared civic enterprise has broken down. In the past, there was a perception that, even though we were made up of dozens of ethnic groups, we were nevertheless bound in the same direction with common goals. Now, as numerous observers are pointing out, it is group against group till death us do part and with little or no regard for the truth.

What role is the Christian community to play? St. Paul, in today's lesson from Romans 14, has in mind the tendency of his congregations to split into embattled factions. What he wants to prevent above all is "the fragmentation of society into mutually hostile groups."[3] In all his letters, this concern of Paul's plays a major role. In the section of Romans appointed for today, he moves into the very center of Christian community ethics when he writes,

> Why do you pass judgment on your brother? Why do you despise your brother? For we shall all stand before the judgment seat of God. . . . Let us no more pass judgment on one another, but rather decide never to put a stumbling block or hindrance in the way of a brother. Do not let what you eat [or do] cause the ruin of one for whom Christ died. (Romans 14:10, 13, 15b)

And in Galatians Paul writes similarly,

> Bear one another's burdens, and so fulfill the law of Christ. (Galatians 6:2)

2. New York City, as is well known, recovered spectacularly from this malaise in the 1990s, only to be hit on September 11, 2001.

3. Paul J. Achtemeier, *Romans* (Atlanta: John Knox Press, 1985), p. 216. Achtemeier expands: "He [Paul] is intent . . . on meeting the threat to Christian unity posed by the attempts of one of the groups to make its convictions about conduct the sole and exclusive measure of true and faithful response to God's gift of his Son."

The command, "Let us no more pass judgment on one another," is often misinterpreted to mean that we should simply engage in a broad, general, easy tolerance of everything and everybody and never attempt to discern wrong from right, evil from good, destructive from redemptive — a sort of Andy Warhol ethic where everything that's going down is cool. This is not what Paul has in mind.

What Paul has in mind first, last, and always is Jesus Christ. Everything he recommends to the Christian community is based upon "the Lord," as Paul never tires of calling him. But it is important to understand what Paul means by "the Lord." When Paul speaks of "the Lord Jesus Christ," he is not thinking primarily of the life and ministry of Jesus. He is thinking of his death — his condemned, accursed, godforsaken death. As Paul wrote to the Corinthians, "I decided to know nothing among you except Jesus Christ and him crucified" (1 Corinthians 2:2). He is thinking of the way that Jesus took judgment upon himself. He is thinking of the people in his churches, not as Jews and Greeks, males and females, slaves and free, but as people "for whom Christ died," in order that the just judgment of God would fall on him and not on us. So when Paul tells us not to judge one another, he does not mean that all kinds of behavior are to be permitted. He means something far more radical and more challenging. He means that Christians are to do what Jesus did; we are to bear one another's burdens, *especially* the burden of judgment.

Bearing judgment for one another means that one individual or group will never stand self-righteously at a distance from another. One faction will never cut itself off from another. Supreme Court nominee David Souter is a loyal Episcopalian and vestryman; let's hope he really meant it when he said in the Senate hearings this week that the most important thing for a judge was to *listen.* The act of listening to another person, entering into his concerns, understanding her plight, is a Christlike act. Just listening, however, is not enough by itself. Eventually a discernment must be made and action must be taken. In the Christian community, we practice listening and we practice discernment, so that, like the soldiers who are laboriously training for combat in the Arabian desert, we will be ready when the time comes to use them in the heat of battle, that is, in the streets of New York.

It's tricky to try to use a current ongoing event to illustrate, because the circumstances may be changing even as we are meeting together. Recognizing that risk, however, let's take a look at Friday's incident involving the young New Jersey woman who parked illegally and, upon discovering that her car was being towed away, burst hysterically into tears, attracting the attention and — would you believe it — the compassionate action of scores of passersby. Now, from the ethical as well as the human point of view, this was a complex happening. The young woman clearly violated the law, and the tow-truck operators were clearly doing the job they were supposed to do. Furthermore, they were doing it in compliance with the anti-bribery regulations, which in this corrupt society is no small thing. What apparently upset the onlookers, however, was the lack of sensitivity shown to the young, inexperienced out-of-towner. This sort of concern for a damsel in distress seemed so remarkable in this supposedly doomed city that it made the front page of the Metro section and, of course, the nightly news. As you know, the money for her fine was collected from sympathizers within minutes.

But there is more to the story. The first part of it could be written off as mere sentimentality, the sort that sends out the Coast Guard for days to save a stranded whale. The second part of the story has more guts in it. You will remember that when the police arrived on the scene, various bystanders attempted to persuade them to "give the girl a break." One of them was a young black man, a student. The police pushed him to the ground, handcuffed him, and carried him off in the paddy wagon. For twenty-four hours reporters could not even find out where he was. During the twenty-four hours, the young woman driver and various other witnesses testified repeatedly that this arrest was a clear case of racial discrimination. "There were plenty of people in business suits standing around," she said. "They picked a young black student to make an example of." She and others are now in the process of collecting money for *him.* In these days of Howard Beach and Bensonhurst and the Central Park jogger case, these are noteworthy actions.[4] The lines of ethical responsibility in the case are somewhat tangled, for surely a person who violates the parking law should expect to be towed. What is most impressive about the story is that the probably emotional and somewhat irrational willingness of the crowd to involve itself in the young, pretty white woman's predicament was translated into the rather more sober and rational decision of a significant number to stand up and be counted on the side of the young black man who had disappeared. Even if only for a moment, a blow for justice had been struck. People had shown themselves ready to take the burden of judgment upon themselves.

But let's push the story still further. There is yet another group of people involved and that is the police. From all accounts, they behaved badly. Does this mean they should be written off — as some segments of the city's minority population would like to do?[5] New Testament faith would say that *no one should be written off,* for the specific reason that, as Paul says, "Christ died for the ungodly" (Romans 5:6). Christ stepped out of the crowd and volunteered to be written off. "Written off" was exactly what he was. He was *written off* in order that all of us ungodly sinners might be *written in* — written in the book of life. So, writes the apostle, "Do not let anything you [do] be the ruin of one for whom Christ died." This means that Christians will be ready at any time and at all times, not only to listen and to empathize, but to act in a way that bears judgment for another person — because that, more than anything else, reveals Jesus Christ to those who are longing to see him.

American Christianity has not understood these things very well of late. There is a great deal of emphasis in our culture on gratification, and Christianity is all too often being interpreted as a

---

4. The references are to notorious race-related crimes.

5. The reader is asked to remember that in 1990 the police were not as widely revered as they have been post-9/11. In the 1980s there were a number of incidents provoking anger at the police, especially in the African-American community. And indeed, as this book is being prepared in 2006, another ugly incident involving the shooting of an unarmed black man is roiling New York City.

means of gaining gratification. There can be no denying that this type of "sell" has a certain appeal. As the apostle knew, though, and as Jesus himself taught, this kind of faith is shallow. Real Christian faith issues forth in a readiness to shoulder judgment on behalf of others.

There is a new book out called *The Arrogance of Faith,* written by a Cal State professor. All 517 pages of it are designed to demonstrate that Christianity has been specifically and particularly culpable in the promotion of racism, colonialism, and other evils. We are going to hear a lot more of this, not less, because we are now in a post-Christian society, make no mistake about it. This fact presents a great challenge and a great opportunity to American Christians. Perhaps the de-Christianizing of American culture is part of God's plan. Perhaps it will give us an opportunity as never before to demonstrate God's redemptive love for all human beings. We will demonstrate it best, not by talking about how God has answered our prayers about this or that, but by training ourselves, through the disciplines of prayer, worship, Bible study, and, especially, through meeting in small groups where burdens of difficulty, disagreement, conflict, and pain are borne in the spirit that Christ bore them. This kind of training prepares us to go out into the streets of New York bearing with us, as Paul writes, the cross of Jesus — "always carrying in our bodies the death of Jesus, so that the life of Jesus may also be manifested in our bodies" (2 Corinthians 4:10).

For, dear brothers and sisters, whoever you are and wherever you are in your lives, God has listened to you. He has heard you. He has understood you. But he has not only listened and understood. He has acted. He has radically changed the situation. We are not condemned. There is a completely new situation.

> If anyone is in Christ, there is a new creation; the old has passed away, behold, the new has come. All this is from God, who through Christ reconciled us to himself and gave us the ministry of reconciliation. So we are ambassadors for Christ, God making his appeal through us. We beseech you on behalf of Christ, be reconciled (*katallagete*) to God! For our sake God made him

[Christ] to be sin who knew no sin, so that in him we might become the righteousness of God. (2 Corinthians 5:17-21)

That, indeed, is a gospel not to be ashamed of. "There is therefore now no condemnation for those who are in Christ Jesus" (Romans 8:1). We are free therefore for service of the crying young woman *and* the falsely accused young man *and* the uptight police officers *and* all the other citizens of our beloved but beleaguered city, for Jesus Christ is Lord and Jesus Christ has died and Jesus Christ is risen and Jesus Christ is — yes — coming again.

AMEN.

Who Is Judged?

GRACE CHURCH IN NEW YORK
TEXTS: ROMANS 14:10-12; PSALM 130; MATTHEW 18:34-35

NOTE TO THE READER: The context is important here. In 1987, the homelessness in New York City was much more visible and omnipresent than it was ten or fifteen years later.

I read recently of a young woman who has the AIDS virus. She has three small children whom she has given to relatives because of her inability to mother them.

She contracted the virus from a man she still lives with, off and on. He is a junkie, and beats her, yet she has returned to him repeatedly because she is "afraid of being alone." He was in jail when she was diagnosed; when they told her what she had, she said she'd kill him, but when he got out, she went back to him because she "couldn't imagine life without a man."

To the *New York Times* reporter she said, "I just hope I don't suffer much, but I try not to think about it a lot. The way I ruined my life, I know one thing — I'm not going up there to God."

Recently my husband and I spent the weekend with friends — let's call them Sally and John. They brought up the subject of Christianity, for which they have little use. Late into the evening we discussed and argued. John was doing most of the talking, so I turned to Sally and asked her what she thought about Christian faith. With no hesitation whatever she looked me straight in the eye, and said, "Oh, I agree with John; I don't need it."

The next day, Sally told us with some intensity of a recent en-

[406]

counter she had with a deranged homeless woman. She was quite insistent about telling me all the details. If I had had my wits about me, I would have pressed her more closely about why it made such an impression on her. I wasn't sure if she was simply startled by the first homeless person she'd ever seen, or offended by the woman's behavior, or frightened by it, or what — but in some way, it was clear, the homeless woman had disturbed Sally's carefully ordered sense of the world.

I have been thinking about the words of St. Paul: "We will all stand before the judgment seat of God." The scene from Matthew 25 comes before me — all of humanity before the throne at the Last Judgment, and the Lord saying, "I was hungry, and you gave me nothing to eat," and the people on his left hand saying, "When did we see you hungry, Lord?" and the response, "Depart from me, you who are cursed."

How many homeless people have I helped this week? How many have you helped? In recent weeks we've been having more trouble than usual getting volunteers for our homeless shelter here at Grace Church. Who is more in need of Christianity, the woman with the junkie lover, Sally, the deranged homeless woman, you or me? Paul writes, "Each of us will give an account of himself to God."

"The way I ruined my life, I know one thing — I'm not going up there to God." How much does it take to ruin a life? What does it take for a non-needy peron to become a needy one? Which category are you in? What sorts of accounts are you and I going to give to God?

Psalm 103 is, by any standard, one of the greatest of all the Psalms:

> God will not always accuse us;
> He has not dealt with us according to our sins. . . .
> As far as the east is from the west,
> so far has he removed our sins from us.

Great words; thrilling words. But what sins? Whose sins? How many sins? I've been holding a grudge against somebody for something they did to me years ago; is this sin going to be removed from me, or am I going to be judged for it? If I give a sandwich to one street person, how many do I get to walk past before I give another one? I know a person who gives a coin and a kind word to every street person he passes — every single one. Watching him do that sure shook me out of my complacency, I can tell you. But is my guilty conscience going to make me better off, or worse off, in the Last Judgment? What about the person who doesn't have a guilty conscience? I have another friend, an enthusiastic Christian, who appears to be completely untroubled by the homeless; "I don't think I'm supposed to be Mother Teresa," she told me cheerfully. Will the good deeds she does for her affluent friends count as feeding the hungry and visiting those in prison?

By the time St. Paul got to the fourteenth chapter of his letter to the Romans, he was ready to make an assumption. He assumed that the Christians in Rome understood what he had written up to that point. He was counting on his readers to understand the difference between "the righteousness based on law" and "the righteousness based on faith" (Romans 10:5, 6). Here at Grace Church we can understand that because we have had so much wonderful preaching and teaching on Romans for quite a few years now. But I remember when I arrived here six years ago, the very mention of the word "judgment" would bring the wrath of dozens upon my head. In the same way Paul is aware that it is a constant temptation to make grace an idol, so to speak, to make justification by faith itself into a "work" of self-righteousness. Therefore he warns the Roman Christians not to look down on their less enlightened brothers and sisters in the church. "Why do you judge your brother? We will all stand before the judgment seat of God." There were those in Rome, Paul knew, who believed that they already stood clear of the judgment, that the judgment was for other, less sophisticated, less educated, less self-sufficient folk. Paul calls these two groups "the strong" and "the weak." He says that if the "stronger" teachers start feeling superior to the "weaker," then that means they have ceased to trust God, that they have begun instead to trust their own spiritual accomplishments — even their own superior understanding of justification by faith.

In a sense, I suppose I am preaching this sermon to Sally and

John, but they are not here. Yet every one of you who are here can recognize yourselves somewhere. Maybe you are a person who, like the woman with the junkie lover, continually engages in self-destructive behavior even though you know perfectly well how much you are harming yourself. Or maybe you are a person who feels superior to (who "judges") the self-destructive behavior of others. Some of you feel needy today; some of you don't. Some of you feel empathy with the woman who has the HIV virus; some of you just feel thankful that you are not in that situation. But every one of you somewhere, somehow knows what it feels like to be threatened by judgment. Everybody knows what it feels like to be labeled a failure, and everyone fears it.

In the baseball pennant races and at the U.S. Open, one person's success, or one team's success, is predicated on the failure of another. One can't win unless another loses. Perhaps for this reason we have difficulty grasping the nature of the kingdom of God where all such distinctions are done away. "Why do you look down on your brother?" asks Paul. *All* the teams are going to be in God's World Series. When the trophy is awarded at God's center court, there are going to be a lot of unseeded winners. That, I think, is what we really can't stand about God. "I tell you the truth," Jesus said, "prostitutes and tax collectors and people with AIDS and welfare mothers and homeless people are going into the kingdom of heaven ahead of you" (Matthew 21:31).

Who is "going up there to God"?

I suppose, though it is hard for me to imagine, that there are some people who, like Sally and John, know so little of God that they just don't care. But then God, in his sovereign freedom, is unlimited by our caring or not caring. His purposes embrace the whole created order, including people who do not believe they need him. Being part of the Church, though, means knowing something that those outside the Church do not know. Who is going up there to God?

I know this: I am not going up there, and you are not going up there, unless God is in charge. The gap between us and a perfectly righteous God is just too great, unless he makes the move. He has to do it. "As far as the east is from the west, so far has he put our sins from us." This means that our standing before God is purely dependent upon his grace, no more and no less true of us than of the woman who knows that she has ruined her life. The one advantage she does have is that she *knows* her only help is in God's grace. If only someone can be there to tell her, her help is in hearing and trusting the promise: "As far as the east is from the west, so far has he put our sins from us." *Ps 103*

No human distinctions are of any merit whatsoever when we come before the judgment. Christian regard for the poor and needy is not sentimental do-good-ism. It is based upon the radical obliteration of worldly criteria in Christ. It is the enactment of God's special regard for the least of Christ's brethren. When the Pope went to Little Haiti in Miami on Thursday, one of the Haitians said, "He is the Pope of the little people like us; you can see he cares." When it comes to trusting in God, the superstitious Haitian peasant with his little plastic statues is the equal of the proudest Reformed systematic theologian. This is precisely what Paul meant when he warned "the strong" not to look down on "the weak."

At the half-century mark of my life, I am convinced more than ever of two things. The first you will recognize, for it has been the Grace Church theme for some time: the destiny of the entire human race depends upon God alone, and the purpose of human life is to glorify him and give thanks for his amazing mercy and compassion.

The second conviction comes from our study of Matthew's Gospel this summer. God intends for his people to take holiness very seriously. Matthew is sometimes thought to be antithetical to Paul. Looking at the Epistle and the Gospel together, however, we can see that both apostles are in deadly earnest about the Christian life. It is not supposed to look like some other type of life with God tacked on as an extra. On the contrary. Our lives in the world *right now* are enactments of the coming future of the people of God, the future which depends exclusively on the overwhelming prodigality of God's mercy to all his creatures. The parable of Jesus about the unmerciful servant in Matthew 18 teaches us that there is something particularly terrible about hardheartedness, about unforgiv-

ingness, about holding grudges. If you want to talk about being antithetical, this is the real thing. Such attitudes as Matthew describes
are profoundly at cross-purposes with the purposes of God. In the
same vein Paul writes, "Why do you pass judgment on your
brother? Or you, why do you despise your brother? For we shall all
stand before the judgment seat of God." And it is Paul who reminds
us that in Christ we are justified before we can lift a finger: "While
we were *weak and helpless,* Christ died for the *ungodly*" (Romans
5:6-8).

And so everyone within earshot of the gospel message today
hears the news as if for the first time: whatever your failures, whatever your bondage, whatever your fears, whatever your sin, "the
Lord will not always accuse us, nor will he keep his anger for ever."
This amazing promise comes true in ways that we are not able to
force or predict. For example: that grudge I have held for years? One
morning I woke up and realized that it was no longer there. God
had done that in my sleep, so to speak, without my even knowing
it. "As far as the east is from the west, so far has he set our sins from
us." This unlooked-for, undeserved, unimaginable declaration of
mercy is the only hope we have and the only hope we will have
when the secrets of all hearts will be disclosed.

And in the Christian community, the mercy of God is enacted
each day in humorous patience with one another's faults, in forgiveness for the enemy, in restoration of the wanderers, in charity toward those who are in error, from now till kingdom come — to the
praise and glory of the One who has not dealt with us according to
our sins nor rewarded us for our wickedness, but instead has submitted to the Judgment in our place. To him be the glory for ever
and ever.

AMEN.